D1756396

THE POLITICAL ECONOMY OF SOUTH AFRICA

Edited by
Nicoli Nattrass and Elisabeth Ardington

1990
OXFORD UNIVERSITY PRESS
CAPE TOWN

Oxford University Press
Walton Street, Oxford OX2 6DP, United Kingdom

OXFORD NEW YORK TORONTO
DELHI BOMBAY MADFRAS KARACHI
PETALING JAYA SINGAPORE HONG KONG TOKYO
NAIROBI DAR ES SALAAM CAPE TOWN
MELBOURNE AUCKLAND

AND ASSOCIATED COMPANIES IN
BERLIN IBADAN

ISBN 0 19 570562 9

© Oxford University Press 1990

OXFORD is a trademark of Oxford University Press

Cover Design by Cliff Bestall

Published by Oxford University Press Southern Africa,
Harrington House, Barrack Street, Cape Town, 8001, South Africa

Layout and Typesetting by Desktop design, Cape Town

Printed and bound by Clyson Printers, Maitland, Cape

Contents

Contributors

Sean Archer is Associate Professor in the School of Economics at the University of Cape Town. His research interests are in the fields of industrial growth, alternative economic mechanisms, education and labour market issues.

Elisabeth Ardington is Researcher with the Centre for Social and Development Studies at the University of Natal, Durban. She worked with Jill Nattrass in the Development Studies Unit from its inception and has conducted research in rural Natal and KwaZulu relating to socio-economic, welfare and land issues.

Norman Bromberger is Senior Lecturer in Economics and Head of the Development Studies Research Group at the University of Natal, Pietermaritzburg. He has conducted survey research into socio-economic aspects of black settlements in Natal and KwaZulu.

Johann Graaff is Lecturer in the Department of Sociology at the University of Cape Town. He was previously Senior Research Officer at the Research Unit for the Sociology of Development at Stellenbosch University, and before that was Head of the Development Studies Department at the University of Bophuthatswana. His special interests relate to development theory and rural education.

Julian Hofmeyr is Senior Research Fellow in the Economic Research Unit at the University of Natal, Durban. He began his career as a chemical engineer but turned to economics after becoming interested in the socio-economic problems facing South Africa. His research interests include the development process and the labour market.

Merle Holden is Professor of Economics at the University of Natal, Durban. Her research interests lie in the fields of international trade and finance. Publications include studies of effective protection, employment effects of trade regimes, choice of exchange rate regimes and economic effects of sanctions.

Carolyn Jenkins is Lecturer in the Department of Economics at the University of Natal, Durban. Her major research interest is in the area of the likely economic implications of sanctions for South Africa, on which topic she has both published a variety of papers and acted as a consultant.

Meshak Khoza is a doctoral student in the School of Geography at Oxford University. He is completing his thesis on the black taxi industry in South Africa.

Pieter le Roux is Director of the Institute for Social Development, and Professor of Development Studies at the University of the Western Cape. His current research interests are alternative economic systems and post-apartheid economic policy. He was the South African co-ordinator of the Lausanne Colloquium on the future of the South African Economy.

Julian May is Honorary Fellow of the Rural Urban Studies Unit of the Centre for Social and Development Studies, University of Natal, Durban. His interests include rural/urban migration and social and economic differentiation.

Colin McCarthy is Professor and Chairman of the Department of Economics at Stellenbosch University. He has been actively involved in public and private sector initiated research on industrial development, regional growth and export promotion.

Mike McGrath is Professor and Head of the Economics Department at the University of Natal, Pietermaritzburg. His research interests include income distribution and macro-economic policy in South Africa. He is a graduate of Natal University where Jill Nattrass supervised his Ph.D thesis on personal income distribution in South Africa.

Charles Meth is Lecturer in Economics at the University of Natal, Durban. Prior to joining the university in 1978, he spent 17 years in industry, designing and commissioning special purpose machinery and process equipment. His research interests lie in the field of labour economics, especially productivity, skills and labour statistics.

Terence Moll is a doctoral student at St Johns College, Cambridge. He is currently completing a thesis on structural change and productivity in the South African economy. His research interests include macro-economic policy, redistribution and comparative economic growth. His Masters thesis on South African labour statistics was supervised by Jill Nattrass.

Mike Morris is Research Fellow at the Centre for Social and Development Studies, University of Natal, Durban. From 1982 to 1985 he worked as an organizer in the General Workers' Union. He graduated from the University of Cape Town and then read for his MA and Ph.D at the University of Sussex. He has published articles in local and international journals focusing on trade union issues, the agrarian question, political and economic development.

Nicoli Nattrass is Researcher in the Research Unit for the Sociology of Development at the University of Stellenbosch. She is also registered for a D.Phil. on the South African political economy at Magdalen College, Oxford. Her research interests include South African economic history, macro-economic profitability and the informal sector.

George Oldham is Senior Lecturer in the Department of Economics at the University of Natal, Pietermaritzburg. His current research is concerned with local government finance and policies for promoting local economic growth.

Charles Simkins is Associate Professor in the School of Economics at the University of Cape Town, at present on special leave and working as a consultant to the Urban Foundation in the fields of housing and urbanization policy. A Fellow at the Office of Population Research, Princeton University in 1985–86, he has published several papers on South African demography.

Sampie Terreblanche is Professor of Economics at the University of Stellenbosch. His research interests include political economy and social welfare in South Africa, the history of economic thought and development and restructuring towards social democracy. He has served on several government commissions and is currently economic advisor to the Democratic Party.

George Trotter is William Hudson Professor and Head of the Department of Economics at the University of Natal, Durban. He has a long-standing research interest in the economics of education and has recently completed a monograph entitled, 'The Social Costs of South African Education', for the Urban Foundation.

Francis Wilson is Professor in the School of Economics at the University of Cape Town. He is also Director of the South African Labour and Development Research Unit, UCT. During the 1980s he was Director of the Second Carnegie Inquiry into Poverty and Development. With Mampele Ramphele he co-authored the final report of the Inquiry — *Uprooting Poverty: The South African Challenge.*

Acknowledgements

We would like to thank Natal University, the South African Sugar Association, the 'Work for the Future Conference' and Professor Lee Nattrass for funding this project. We would also like to thank the Centre for Social and Development Studies at the University of Natal and Professor S.P. Cilliers of the Research Unit for Sociology of Development at the University of Stellenbosch for providing institutional backup during the editing stages of the book. Particular thanks are due to Lesley Anderson for help in word processing, to the referees who evaluated the contributions, and to Mandy Uys from Oxford University Press.

Nicoli Nattrass

Nicoli Nattrass
(Research Unit for Sociology of Development, University of Stellenbosch)

Elisabeth Ardington

Elisabeth Ardington
(Centre for Social and Development Studies, University of Natal, Durban).

Preface

We are pleased to be associated as sponsors with this collection of readings on the Political Economy of South Africa which is intended as a tribute to Jill Nattrass who contributed so much to the University and the wider community. In 1980 the South African Sugar Association and the University of Natal sponsored the 'Work for the Future Conference' which was inspired and chaired by Jill. It illustrated well her ability to bring together academics, labour, businessmen and the state in a way that encouraged constructive and informed thinking about the political economy of South Africa. We hope this volume will prove equally useful in the 1990s.

Peter Booysen
Vice-Chancellor
University of Natal

Glyn Taylor
South African Sugar Association

Dedicated to the memory of
Jill Nattrass

Introduction

Nicoli Nattrass and Elisabeth Ardington

As South Africa enters the 1990s with the prospect of fundamental change firmly on the agenda, it is important that the country's socio-economic patterns are widely considered and debated. In an effort to inform discussions on the economy, this volume explores key issues in a concise and accessible way. Contributions cover South Africa's historical development, possible future options, labour market and welfare issues and links with the world economy. It is hoped that these assessments will provide a basis for debate on economic options and strategies in a future non-racial South Africa.

Sampie Terreblanche and Nicoli Nattrass open the volume with a brief outline of the key political and ideological developments which have influenced South Africa's economic path from 1910. They conclude with a few speculative comments on the transition to a non-racial social democracy. Pieter le Roux takes up the discussion by arguing that a social democratic compromise is the only pragmatic and viable alternative facing South Africa. He believes it is only by allowing important roles for both the market and the state that key political-economic imperatives and demands can be accommodated.

Two chapters on the regional dimension of South Africa's political economy follow. Colin McCarthy, in his essay on development ideology, shows how certain aspects of South Africa's skewed development can be traced directly to regional policy informed by the ideology of apartheid and the view that South Africa is a combination of the first and third worlds. He argues that South Africa should be seen as a third world country itself and that regional policy should follow economic rather than political (homeland-centered) criteria. Johann Graaff's chapter on the bantustan state provides a radical perspective on homeland politics. He argues that viewing the bantustan states as Pretoria's puppets is inadequate and an underestimation of the extent to which they are capable of independent action.

The contributions by Terence Moll, Mike McGrath and Nicoli Nattrass focus on trends in the South African economy over the post-war period. All draw implications for the radical analysis of economic growth in South Africa. Terence Moll argues that South Africa's growth record is very average compared to similar economies and that in these terms, apartheid policy did not noticeably benefit South Africa's growth performance. He concludes that external conditions were by far the most important determinant of economic growth. Mike McGrath discusses income distribution in South Africa, and concludes that the radical analysis was consistent with the facts for the early part of the post-war period but that from the late 1960s racial income inequalities have lessened dramatically. Nicoli Nattrass arrives at a similar conclusion by examining profitability and the distribution of income between workers and capitalists in the manufacturing sector.

Julian Hofmeyr's chapter continues the discussion of black wages from a different perspective. He argues that market forces were fundamental to the rise in black wages from the early 1970s and to the fall in semi-skilled and unskilled wages in the 1980s. Institutional factors, in Hofmeyr's view, were important but conditioned by changes in the labour market. This contribution is followed by Mike Morris's essay on NUMSA's attitude to industrial councils. Drawing on Marxist concepts and his own experience as a trade unionist, Morris argues that organizational determinants are central to an understanding of trade union bargaining strategy. The focus on labour is completed by Archer, Bromberger, Nattrass and Oldham who review some aspects of the debate about unemployment in South Africa. They argue that the controversy over unemployment frequently stems from a lack of clarity as to what is being measured and what question is being addressed.

Julian May and Charles Simkins focus on questions relating to urbanization in South Africa. May analyses the changing dynamics of rural-urban migration and argues that urban pull forces have grown stronger while rural push forces have grown progressively weaker. He discusses the growth of squatter areas adjacent to cities and the growing phenomenon of commuting. Charles Simkins provides a more statistical analysis of past and projected urbanization trends in South Africa. On the basis of his results, he draws implications for housing strategy in the fields of subsidy policy and finance.

Meshack Khosa continues the urban focus with his essay on the phenomenal rise of the black taxi industry in South Africa. He provides a brief history of transport in the apartheid city and argues that the creation of SABTA was crucial to the rapid growth of capital accumulation in the black taxi industry. Nicoli Nattrass' chapter on small black business development places the taxi industry in a wider context. She notes that the potential for the development of small black enterprise as a means of helping solve the problems of poverty and unemployment is extremely limited.

The next two chapters focus on the welfare issues of poverty and education. Francis Wilson sketches a few key dimensions of poverty in South Africa and argues for political and economic restructuring as necessary conditions for its eradication. He counters the free marketeer critique of government intervention by arguing that the South African economy is far from overburdened by the public sector, and that relevant questions concern government policy alternatives rather than the existence of state policy itself.

George Trotter provides an overview of educational inequality in South Africa and argues that in the interests of fairness and rapid economic growth, the need for a restructured, non-discriminatory educational system is urgent.

The concluding chapters by Merle Holden, Carolyn Jenkins and Charles Meth shed light on key issues relating to South Africa's foreign trade sector. Merle Holden shows that South Africa's trade strategy has shifted from being strongly import substituting to providing limited incentives to exporters. She discusses the relationship between exports and development, and argues in favour of export-led growth. The chapter by Carolyn Jenkins outlines the history of the sanctions campaign against apartheid and discusses the effects of financial sanctions and disinvestment on the South African economy. She argues that the immediate results of disinvestment are less significant than the disruption caused by financial sanctions and the long-term effects of the decline in foreign investment on variables such as the rate of job creation. Charles Meth's radical analysis of the capital goods sector focuses on the closely related issue of South Africa's dependence on foreign technology. He argues that although the capital goods sector is weak, South Africa has a reasonably healthy machine tools industry. Given the structure of demand in South Africa, Meth concludes in favour of radical restructuring.

Each chapter was reviewed by at least one referee in order to ensure consistently high academic standards. However, great effort was taken to keep the contributions accessible to non-specialists, and economic technicalities have been kept to a minimum. The terms 'black', 'white', 'coloured' and 'Indian' are used whenever it is necessary to distinguish between people along official lines, or where apartheid legislation affects them differently. The use of these terms does not imply any acceptance of racial classification.

Jill Nattrass — a tribute

This collection of essays is dedicated to the memory of Jill Nattrass, the late Professor of Development Studies at the University of Natal. The contributions reflect Jill's interest in development and the political-economy of growth and change in South Africa.

The kind of economic analysis adopted in most chapters reflects Jill's accessible style of communication and unconventional approach to economics. She always harnessed economic tools and methods in the service of her vision of economic justice rather than in the construction of strictly consistent, supposedly 'value-free' models. Economics, in her perspective, was political-economy in both its ethical and theoretical senses. For Jill, the burning issues were poverty, inequality, unemployment, the provision of basic needs and appropriate and just welfare planning.

Her early academic projects included research into small businesses, a doctorate on migrant labour, participation in the Natal University Income Gap project and her textbook on the South African economy. With the launch of the Development Studies Unit at the University of Natal in 1982, Jill was able to initiate and co-ordinate research projects explicitly designed to make the university more relevant to the needs of the poor communities surrounding it. These included the dynamics of urban-rural linkages, labour migration and urbanization, the problems of poverty, employment creation, the informal sector, and black access to services; as well as investigations into income and expenditure patterns in KwaZulu. Jill saw the purpose of such research in terms of the potential it carried for generating awareness of development problems and in aiding the process of appropriate development planning.

Jill was admired and respected for her frankness, candour, complete lack of cant, and the intellectual insights she revealed about the troubled society in which we live. Her academic integrity was the hallmark of her character. Her concern was always with the robustness of the 'facts' and the quality of the argument. She believed in the inquiring mind and felt that the comfortable acceptance of existing theories was a sign of academic slothfulness. In the development of her own ideas she drew on both radical and liberal interpretations of South African development.

While accepting that there was an important role for market forces, she was critical of those who saw the unbridled free market as the answer to all economic ills. She dismissively labelled neo-classical economics with its simplifying assumptions as 'economics for the simple-minded' and argued that 'for the poor, economic freedom will largely mean the freedom to remain poor and even worse to get poorer still'. As one of South Africa's first social democrats, Jill believed in the provision of basic needs by way of a mixed economy.

Jill's distrust of neo-classical economics and faith in welfare-state alternatives can be traced to her sojourn in Cambridge during the late 1960s where she studied under political economists such as Robinson and Kalecki. Her brand of liberalism was thus more consistently in line with the Cambridge School than any other theoretical tradition.

Jill shared the assumption associated with liberal political economists in South Africa that expanding black access to economic power would serve as a major source of progressive political and social change. She believed that from the early 1960s the relationship between apartheid and capitalism had become increasingly contradictory and that political pressure from the growing black middle class, and economic pressure from business for skilled labour, would contribute substantially to the demise of apartheid.

At the same time, Jill's theoretical perspective was shaped in important ways by the radical critique of liberal South African historiography. Her approach to left-wing theory was simultaneously sympathetic and critical. While accepting certain radical tenets about South African political-economic development (such as the predominantly functional role the early South African state played in supplying the mines with cheap labour), she rejected others. To her, full-scale nationalization was likely to lead to socially unacceptable levels of inefficiency and would compound rather than solve the problem of concentration of capital and power. Rather, she believed that capitalism had to be transformed into social democracy. The energy she put into the 'Work for the Future Conference' in 1980 (which was attended by over 300 businessmen, public servants and academics) is an example of her determination to promote development and redistribution through compromise and negotiation.

Jill's theoretical position had very real implications for the nature of her political involvements. Her faith in reasoned argument as a political strategy, coupled with her acceptance of the potentially positive role government intervention could play, implied for her involvement in reformist politics. This drew her into the murky and treacherous political quagmire which most ivory tower academics avoid. In her effort to make a contribution to furthering economic justice in South Africa, she participated in a wide range of often controversial activities. These included serving on the State President's Economic Advisory Council (until she was excluded by exasperated state officials), acting as economic advisor to the Progressive Federal Party, participating in the KwaZulu Natal Indaba, serving on the Buthelezi Commission, advising the KwaZulu Finance Corporation on development policy and occasionally defending trade unions in industrial disputes. Her argument was always that it was better to get one's hands dirty and consider compromise than to remain politically pure and ineffective. If there was a chance that her intervention could encourage development and assist redistribution, she would participate in structures which her left-wing friends argued were simply bolstering and legitimating the system. Her work on the KwaZulu Government Committee of Inquiry into the implications for economic development of pension payments is a typical example of this. Jill believed that the appeal to reason should never be jettisoned in favour of boycott or violence, and that the importance of people always weighed more heavily than 'correct' political stances.

Despite her maverick positions on theory and politics in South Africa, she was widely recognized as a progressive academic. Her integrity and faith in research and reasoned argument as the only ways to further knowledge were very appealing. Students and colleagues found it easy to like and respect her while at the same time often fundamentally disagreeing with her. Jill always enjoyed a good argument but she never suffered fools gladly. Those who worked and lived with her were privileged to have experienced her intellectual standards, wit and warmth first-hand. It is with a great sense of pain and loss that this collection of essays is presented in her memory.

A periodization of the political economy from 1910

1

Sampie Terreblanche and Nicoli Nattrass[1]

Introduction

The relationship between economic growth in South Africa and the political power struggles which shaped it is a surprisingly undeveloped area of research in economic circles. Aside from Marxist scholarship (which is predominantly sociological in character and often errs by underplaying the role of unbridled ideology), economists have paid little attention to the politically structured nature of South African economic history. Notable exceptions include Horwitz (1967) who argued that 'the polity has always sought its ideal and ideology — the white man's supremacy. The network of economic development had to follow accordingly' (p. 12) and Lipton (1986) who concluded that the interests of capitalists were ambiguously and differentially served by apartheid. These kinds of research agendas are however conspicuous by their absence amongst South Africa's modern generation of economists.

The discipline of 'political-economy' needs rehabilitating. Theoretical space must be created for the role of politics in economic development, and this should go beyond the reduction of political phenomena to reflections on economic forces or the exclusion of political factors altogether via *ceteris paribus* assumptions. This essay presents a brief outline of some of the more important political power plays which structured South African economic development. The story is neither new nor comprehensive, but it is one which all students of the South African economy should constantly bear in mind. In the light of Jill Nattrass' recognition of political-economic factors in her own work, this essay is presented in her memory.

Periodizing South Africa's political-economic history since Union

It is almost 80 years since the Union of South Africa came into being in 1910. Political, economic, social, international and ideological developments over these years have contributed to a uniquely South African milieu of rapid growth and ongoing conflict. During this period, South Africa experienced several fundamental structural changes which altered the power framework within which the economic, political and social processes unfurled. An understanding of the more important power plays is vital for any political economic analysis of South African history.

We can divide the 80 years since Union into seven easily defined structural periods, each of about 12 years. The first, 1910–22, can be characterized by the economic and political dominance of the English establishment and the structuring of a racially segregated society. The second period, 1922–33, saw the birth of economic nationalism and the attempt of (mainly Afrikaner) farmers and white mineworkers to establish a welfare state. Between 1933 and 1948 the political power of the English establishment re-emerged and South Africa industrialized in a less economically and racially repressive mould. However the fourth period, 1948–60, saw the rise of Afrikaner upliftment and the further institutionalization of apartheid. The years 1960–73 can be characterized by the abortive attempt to institutionalize white (but mainly Afrikaner) dominance on the basis of Verwoerdian ideology in a period of rapid growth and industrialization, and the growing importance of black urbanization as a powerful social force. The sixth period, 1973–84, witnessed the growing realization that Verwoerdian (or any other manifestation of) apartheid was unsustainable, reproachment between the two white establishments, increasing power of black 'insiders' and a deceleration of economic growth. The current period can be characterized by the reluctant acceptance of the 'one nation' concept by the National Party government, rising tension between the co-optive dominance strategy of the bureaucratic state and the protest strategy of the extra-parliamentary forces, and a further decline in the economic growth rate.

An overview of the seven periods

1910–22

The Union of South Africa came into being in 1910 with blacks almost completely excluded from parliament.[2] White unity was considered the more important objective. By choosing General Louis Botha as the first Prime Minister, the British government enabled the English commercial and mining interests to build a successful coalition with important elements in the Afrikaner community. The long-lasting alliance between wealthier Afrikaner farmers (mainly in the Transvaal) and the capitalist mine-owners formed the backbone of the South African Party which guaranteed political control for the English establishment for almost 15 years. The English, with the Chamber of Mines as its financial and organizational core, controlled the economy — a control which still exists today, although to a lesser extent.

The alliance with the English did not go down well with the more nationalist-oriented Afrikaners, who broke away from the cabinet in 1912 under the leadership of General Hertzog. The 1914 'rebellion' against South Africa's entry into the war on Britain's side was further testament to the extent of Afrikaner dissatisfaction with political arrangements.

During this period, racially repressive legislation which undermined the economic position of blacks was introduced. The Mines and Works Act of 1911 laid the basis for the statutory colour bar in the workplace, and the 1911 Black Labour Regulations Act made it an offence for a black miner to break his employment contract or for anyone to attempt to persuade a worker, by offering higher wages, to break his contract. The 1913 Land Act not only restricted black access to land but also introduced strict measures against 'squatting' on white farms, in order to increase the supply of cheap black labour. This exacerbated the steady impoverishment of the black peasantry and gave rise to a growing black proletariat.

During the first 12 years after 1910, the Botha and Smuts governments attempted to create racially separated social and economic structures with the purpose of creating conditions conducive to a successful and profitable exploitation of South Africa's mineral wealth. Between 1910 and 1920, black miners' wages declined steadily (Van der Berg, 1989) as did the incomes of most groups except English speakers, wealthier farmers and foreign shareholders.[3] Between 1918 and 1919 black and white workers engaged in a wave of strike action in response to declining living standards. Whereas (predominantly skilled) white workers made some gains, black strikers were summarily and brutally repressed by government action.

1922–33

The white miners' strike and subsequent minor civil war on the Rand in 1922 was a great setback for the economic and political hegemony of the English establishment. The decline in the gold price in 1921 in the context of rising costs forced the Chamber of Mines to alter employment conditions in the mines and give more jobs and opportunities to the much lower-paid black mineworkers. The dictates of capitalist profitability thus acted to place mining capital in direct conflict with white workers.

The harsh repression of the strike (which left over 200 dead) lead to a class-based pact between the mainly English-speaking Labour Party lead by Creswell, and Hertzog's National Party. Mobilizing anti-capitalist and Afrikaner nationalist sentiments, this alliance took power in 1924. The socialist orientation of the Labour Party combined with the National Party's nationalist-inspired opposition to the economic and colonial power of the English to create the first serious challenge to colonial capitalism in South Africa.

With this electoral victory the economic philosophy of the government shifted from economic liberalism (in all affairs other than labour) to economic nationalism in the form of increased state intervention and protective external policies. Policies were implemented which were designed to further national economic self-sufficiency via a deliberate policy of import substitution. This operated through the reconstituted Board of Trade and Industries which selectively, but extensively, encouraged local industry via substantially increased import tariffs.[4] The establishment of ISCOR (Iron and Steel Corporation) in 1928 further boosted the manufacturing sector and increased the involvement of the public sector in the economy.

The other important arm of the Pact government's economic programme was its welfare state policy which was geared towards compensating poorer whites (of which over 80 per cent were Afrikaans) for the impoverishment and disruption they were suffering as a consequence of modernization and urbanization. Key aspects of this policy were the provision of financial support to farmers, the assurance of a supply of cheap[5] black labour to agriculture, mining and industry, and the protection of whites from black competition in the labour market. The central tenet of this latter policy (as laid down in the 1925 Wage Act) was that whites should get paid at a rate commensurate with a 'civilized' standard of living rather than in accordance with the dictates of the labour market. This, was given additional force by the Customs, Tariff and Excise Duty Amendment Act of 1925 which provided for industrial protection on the condition that a 'reasonable' proportion of 'civilized workers'were employed.

Whites were also given protected employment in certain sectors such as the South African Railways and Government Services.[6] As Johnstone points out, 'the pendulum had thus come full circle. The state which in 1922 had served as the instrument for the repression of white workers, was now in the hands of their representatives, and implementing protectionist policies for them' (1976, p. 167).

The mining industry was dealt a blow by the 1926 Mines and Works Act (familiarly known as the Colour Bar Act) which entrenched job reservation on the mines. This, according to Frankel & Horwitz, contributed to significant disinvestment in South African mining from 1924 to 1932 (cited in Lipton, 1986, p. 114). However, the interests of mining capital were ambiguously served by South African racial and segregationist policies. Despite the higher costs incurred as a result of protected white labour, horizontal controls on the movement of black labour (such as those laid down by the 1923 Urban Areas Act) worked in mining capital's favour. Black miners' real wages remained roughly constant between 1911 and 1972 (Wilson, 1975) whereas whites' real wages rose steadily from 1922. Black wages could be paid at a level designed to support a single migrant with access to rural resources rather than at a level needed to support an urban worker and his family (Wolpe, 1972; Johnstone, 1976).

As the Chamber of Mines itself explained:

> The ability of the mines to maintain their native labour force by means of tribal natives from the reserves at rates of pay which are adequate for this migratory class of native, but inadequate in practice for the detribalized urban native, is a fundamental factor of the economy of the gold mining industry (quoted in the Lansdowne Report, 1944, p. 8).

Whether the advantages of a repressed migratory black working class made up for the cost disadvantages of a protected white working class (as the neo-Marxist analysis implicitly maintains) is a moot point. However, if white workers had not managed to turn economic defeat in the labour market into political success at the polls, it is doubtful whether South Africa's white labour aristocracy would have remained as tenaciously entrenched. If mining capital could have had its way, the power of white labour would have been broken, job reservation scrapped, and the black migrant labour system maintained.

1933–48

With the advent of the great depression (between 1928 and 1932, when the GDP declined by 6 per cent per annum), Hertzog was forced into a coalition government with Smuts in 1933.[7] The task of economic rehabilitation was, however, made much easier by the economic upswing following the abandoning of the gold standard in 1932. The virtual doubling of the gold price and the devaluation of the South African pound saved the marginal gold mines and contributed to manufacturing expansion (which also benefited from the coming into production of the ISCOR plant in the early 1930s). Between 1930 and 1940, the South African economy grew at a rate of 5 per cent per annum.

Like 1924, 1933 was an important watershed in South African political economic history as it signalled significant reorientations in political and economic strategies. Although the fusion government was 'born out of a common desire to settle the constitutional relationship with the Empire and to pull South Africa out of economic crisis' (Davenport, 1987, p. 309), Hertzog and Smuts entered into the coalition with hidden agendas — both of which were successfully achieved. Hertzog's hidden agenda was to gain support for the removal of blacks from the common voter's role in the Cape and Natal. Smuts's hidden agenda was to stop Hertzog from increasing taxation on the now highly profitable gold mines.

The fusion government also enabled Smuts and the English establishment to regain political and economic hegemony. Particularly during the war years, the English were able to extend their economic influence from the mining and commercial sectors to the industrial sector. The outbreak of the Second World War had a decisive impact on South Africa both politically and economically. The fusion government collapsed after the parliamentary adoption of Smuts's motion that South Africa should sever its links with Germany and fulfil her obligations to the Commonwealth. Hertzog, who favoured neutrality, later joined the nationalists under Malan, who were totally opposed to fighting 'Britain's war'. Like the First World War, the Second shattered South Africa's fragile white national unity and lead to a nationalist breakaway which was to take power in the 1948 election and fundamentally alter the development path.

Despite a substantial degree of urbanization by the 1940s, the South African economy was increasingly facing skilled-labour bottlenecks (Lipton, 1986, p. 401). The colour bar, which had been circumvented more and more in the 1930s, was effectively made redundant with the outbreak of the war. The loss of skilled labour to the army, coupled with a more liberal (predominantly English) administration,[8] resulted in the government authorizing blacks to work in skilled positions. This development found its intellectual reflection in the Fagan Commission of 1948. The commission argued that permanent black urbanization should be unrestricted in order to meet the needs of industrial expansion and to provide a settled, stable, skilled workforce with improved education and wages so as to provide an expanding market for consumer goods. In a similar vein, the liberal-dominated Social and Economic Planning Council was set up and the Department of Native Affairs recommended the abolition of the pass laws. As a result, less protectionist and interventionist policies were adopted and the number of pass law related prosecutions declined dramatically. Black wages rose faster than white wages over the period (Lipton, 1986, p. 43) and in 1945 the National Education Finance Act freed black education from its constricting dependence on the level of black taxes.

The limit to these reforms, however, was aptly demonstrated by the brutal suppression of the black miners' strike of 1946 and the failure to reinstate the black voting rights removed by the 1936 Native Trust and Land Act. Black mine wages did not follow the upward path of those in manufacturing. Extensive recruiting of cheap migrant labour from neighbouring states served to undermine the bargaining power of black miners. For this reason, in the late 1930s the ANC requested that the government curtail the use of foreign labour. Unsurprisingly, the request was not granted.

Such liberalization as occurred in the field of socio-economic policy was regarded with horror by Malan's National Party. Riding high on nationalist mobilization (aided by events such as the 1938 celebrations of the Great Trek), anger over the war effort (which spawned fascist organizations such as the Ossewa Brandwag) and white fears of redundancy (especially amongst demobilized soldiers who returned to find blacks in skilled positions), the National Party was a formidable contender for power by 1948. The old Afrikaner/English rivalry emerged to polarize politics further when the government introduced an immigration scheme (which attracted 60 000 immigrants) to overcome manpower shortages. This was widely seen as an attempt to undermine the position of the

Afrikaner (Bradlow, 1978).

The indifferent attitude of the Victorian and *laissez-faire* oriented English towards the problems faced by the emerging Afrikaner proletariat,[9] further aggravated the deteriorating relations between the two groups (Terreblanche, 1988, p. 368). Afrikaner nationalism, by mobilizing against the political, economic and colonial 'powers' of the English speakers and their real and alleged exploitative effect on Afrikaner interests, grew into an aggressive force with a commanding political ideology.

Afrikaner nationalism had a clear economic interventionist thrust. Afrikaners, it was argued, had to take control of what they believed was rightfully theirs through 'volkskapitalisme' — that is, the mobilization of ethnic forces to foster Afrikaner accumulation (Marks & Trapido, 1987, p. 26). O'Meara goes so far as to argue that Afrikaner nationalism was the organized expression of specific class forces to secure a base for capital accumulation. He argues that in return for lucrative employment, Afrikaner workers formed an alliance with Afrikaner capitalists and the growing Afrikaner petite bourgeoisie (1983, p. 110ff).

1948–60

The election victory of the National Party on an apartheid ticket in 1948 heralded a profound change in the South African balance of power. The English establishment (which originally feared that the government might nationalize the gold mining industry and turn the country into a quasi-socialist Republic) was dealt a severe blow. Soon after taking power, the government put into operation a three-pronged programme designed to further the interests of Afrikaner nationalism. New discriminatory laws were added to the existing arsenal (and extended to coloureds and Indians), the bureaucracy and parastatal sector was enlarged[10] in order to generate Afrikaner employment opportunities, and a variety of welfare programmes were launched to redistribute wealth and uplift the poor (mainly Afrikaner) white population.

The government's policy of promoting Afrikaner interests was very successful. In 1946 the per capita income of Afrikaners was less than half that of English-speakers. By 1970, after many years of government pampering and patronage, it had increased to 70 per cent (Terreblanche, 1989, p. 13).

The limited reforms of the early 1940s were reversed in favour of the racially repressive and segregationist political and economic institutions which form the backbone of apartheid. The pass laws were tightened, particularly by the 1952 Black (Abolition of Passes and Co-ordination of Documents) Act which introduced the Reference Book; and convictions escalated dramatically. This conveniently provided a sizeable source of prison labour for white farms (Boyle, 1986). A plethora of segregationist legislation was passed, such as the 1950 Population Registration Act, the 1950 Group Areas Act, the 1953 Reservation of Separate

Amenities Act and the 1954 Black Resettlement Act. The 1953 Bantu Education Act pegged expenditure on black education back to the level of black taxes, and the 1957 Extension of University Education Act made provision for the creation of separate ethnic universities.

In the relentless battle for political supremacy during the 1950s, the coloured community became trapped in the cross-fire. Fearing that coloured voters might support the mainly English-speaking United Party against the National Party, the Malan government initiated a process which in 1956 removed coloureds from the common voters role.[11] In a similar vein, the 1951 Bantu Authorities Act and the 1959 Promotion of Bantu Self Government Act laid the basis for separate political representation for blacks.

Much of the overtly political legislation was, however, directed towards controlling black labour. The 1950 Suppression of Communism Act declared the Communist Party an unlawful organization and was used to smash the non-racial and black trade union movement (Lodge, 1983). The 1953 Natives Settlement of Disputes Act banned blacks from registered trade unions and provided them with a separate system of emasculated plant level 'works committees'. The 1956 Riotous Assemblies Act *inter alia* effectively banned picketing. With the 1956 Industrial Conciliation Act, provision was made for the extension of the job colour bar to industry.

The increase in the controls over most spheres of black life did not go unresisted. The African National Congress (ANC), which had maintained an essentially non-confrontationist position (apart from a brief spurt of worker militancy in the 1920s), became increasingly class conscious and radicalized in the late 1940s. The rapid increases in black urbanization and proletarianization since the war were major factors behind this shift.

Between 1939 and 1952 the black urban population almost doubled. The relaxation of the pass laws during the war facilitated the exodus of labour tenants from white farms and the townward drift of those responding to deteriorating conditions in the reserves. The revival of trade unionism and the development of community resistance as an anti-government weapon (such as the Alexandra bus boycotts against fare increases and the Johannesburg squatter movement) contributed to the radicalization of the ANC.[12] Two one-day protest strikes in 1950 and 1951 successfully withdrew labour in Port Elizabeth, Johannesburg and Durban. In 1952, after the government rejected an ANC ultimatum demanding the repeal of six 'unjust laws', the Defiance Campaign was launched. The 1953 Criminal Law Amendment Act, which imposed a three year sentence for violation of the law 'by way of protest against the law' put an end to the campaign. Extensive bans on leaders effectively immobilized further resistance.

In 1955 the ANC-initiated Kliptown Conference drew up the 'Freedom Charter' which comprised a list of basic rights and freedoms including welfare provision (such as housing, health and education), the ending of restrictions on labour, minimum wages, and the nationalization of mines, banks and industry (Carter, Gerhart & Karis, 1977, pp. 205–8). The state responded by banning 142 ANC leaders and charging 156 members of the Congress Alliance with treason.[13] It is not surprising that in the face of such state repression, the idea of civil disobedience gave way to the protest politics of the early 1960s.

1960–73

In March 1960, 69 people were shot dead in Sharpeville during the ANC-Pan African Congress (PAC) campaign against the pass laws. In response to the nationwide protest strike, the government cordoned off the townships, banned the ANC and the PAC and arrested thousands of people. Once underground, the ANC set up its guerrilla wing, Umkonto We Sizwe (The Spear of the Nation), which committed acts of sabotage until its leadership was rounded up at their headquarters Rivonia, and incarcerated for life in 1963. With this, black protest effectively disappeared for over a decade. In 1962 the powers of the police were extended with regard to interrogation procedures, and detention without charge for 12 days was permitted. This was extended to 90 days in 1963, to an indefinite period if authorized by a judge in 1965, and to an indefinite period without such authorization in 1976 (Davenport, 1987, p. 404).

The events of 1960 resulted in an economic as well as a political crisis. Capital poured out of the country and the value of the rand plummeted. This, along with the exclusion of South Africa from the Commonwealth (after becoming a Republic) and the United Nations voluntary arms embargo in 1963, forced some rethinking of government policy. The policy of apartheid was replaced by the allegedly less racist policy of 'separate development'. This package included independence for homelands and the stemming of urbanization via the creation of decentralized industries in border areas (see McCarthy's contribution to this volume).

Dr Verwoerd's policy of balkanizing South Africa into a multitude of ethnic states resulted in renewed tension between ideologically and religiously oriented Afrikaners on the one hand, and more pragmatic, liberal English-speakers on the other (Terreblanche, 1989, p. 14). However, from the mid-1960s, the power struggle between the two white establishments began to abate as the rapid economic growth of the 1960s brought benefits to all sectors. The Afrikaner's fear of black competition in the unskilled and semi-skilled labour market decreased in the context of ample job opportunities for all. Between 1960 and 1970, the economy grew at 5,6 per cent per annum and the average real per capita income increased at 3 per cent per annum. At the same time, a stronger Afrikaner business class emerged. In witnessing the way in which this class prospered under bureaucratic favours, the English-speaking business class softened its attitude toward the National Party government.

The long economic boom facilitated the process of social engineering by boosting government coffers. Forced resettlement continued apace and whole communities were destroyed (such as Sophiatown in 1956). At the same time, vast sums of money were poured into the homelands to create 'independent' political structures there. Controls on the movement of blacks tightened. The Labour Bureaux, provided for by the Native Labour Regulations Act, were activated by the 1964 Bantu Labour Act and the Bantu Labour Regulations of 1964, 1965 and 1968, in an effort to streamline and rationalize the flow of blacks to urban areas and between sectors.

Despite the construction of this costly draconian monolith, black urbanization increased, albeit at a slower pace. Cilliers & Groenewald (1982) estimated that the growth in the rate of black urbanization slowed from 6,4 per cent per annum between 1946 and 1950 to 3,9 per cent in the 1960s. However, by the end of the 1960s, an oversupply of unskilled 'illegal' labour existed side by side with a shortage of skilled labour in the cities (Lipton, 1986, p. 36). Black unemployment thus coexisted with rising real black wages and a narrowing white:black income gap.

1973–84

The political economic changes that took place between 1973 and 1976 were perhaps the most fundamental and dramatic in the 80 years since Union. Between 1971 and 1973 the price of essential commodities for black workers rose by 40 per cent (Hemson, 1978, p. 19). Workers responded with widespread strikes in 1973. These were very successful, largely because the strikers remained leaderless and committed to short sharp withdrawals of labour in order to elicit concessions rather than engage in negotiation — a strategy which protected them from co-optation and victimization (Lodge, 1983, p. 327). In the context of the overall shortage of skilled and semi-skilled labour especially, it is not surprising that militant black industrial action resulted in real economic gains (see Nattrass in this volume, Chapter 7). By the mid-1970s, both government and employer organizations were publicly committed to moving towards paying the rate for the job, thus ending the official 'civilized labour' policy on wages.

The process of liberalization in the labour sphere culminated in the acceptance of reforms laid out in the Wiehahn and Riekert Commissions (investigating industrial relations and labour requirements respectively), which reported in 1979. In addition to the scrapping of job reservation, Wiehahn recommended that the burgeoning independent black and non-racial trade union movement be legalized. The organizational power that this unleashed is amply illustrated by COSATU's current massive membership of 750 000 workers.

The Wiehahn and Riekert Commission proposals were geared at increasing the power of urban black 'insiders' (that is, those with legally sanctioned jobs and 'Section 10 rights')[14] relative to that of rural black 'outsiders'. Wiehahn proposed that migrants be excluded from trade union membership and Riekert proposed that lawful black urbanization be limited by the availability of employment and housing. However, after organized resistance from the trade union movement, trade union rights were extended to all workers. Likewise, the scrapping of influx control in 1987 represents the failure of Riekert's attempts to maintain distinctions between urban insiders and rural outsiders.

The coup in Lisbon in April 1974 precipitated the independence of Angola and Moçambique in 1975. This broke the *cordon sanitaire* of white minority regimes around South Africa. A completely different security situation developed — especially after the abortive invasion of Angola by South Africa in 1975. These regional developments played an important role in the transition from 'Verwoerdian separate development' to 'Vorster's pragmatic apartheid' and eventually to 'Botha's total strategy'. Under Botha, South African society was increasingly militarized in order to cope with the 'total onslaught' from 'communist-inspired insurgents'. On a regional level the major implication of this policy was the destabilization of neighbouring states sympathetic to anti-apartheid forces. According to Hanlon (1986), apart from any security function, destabilization benefited South Africa economically (as it forced dependence on South African imports and infrastructure)and ideologically insofar as it undermined any alternative black socialist models in the region.

The 1976 Soweto uprising, which left at least 575 dead and 2 389 wounded (Lodge, 1983, p. 330), is an important watershed in South Africa's political economic history. As in 1922 and 1961, South Africa reeled under both political and economic crises as widespread capital flight was induced. This, coupled with the world economic downswing following the OPEC oil price hikes, had a negative impact on South Africa's growth performance. Since 1974 the annual growth rate has averaged less than 2 per cent per annum and real per capita income has declined by 15 per cent (Van der Berg, 1989). Between 1976 and 1985 formal employment opportunities grew by less than 600 000 in contrast to a growth of almost three million in the labour force (ibid.).

The major factors responsible for these developments were the low growth rate and the sharp increase in capital intensity. The increase in capital intensity and the declining output:capital ratio largely followed from the excessive rate of investment stimulated in the 1960s and early 1970s by negative and low real rates of interest, an overvalued exchange rate and tax concessions on capital investment. Under the leadership of Vorster (1966–78) the government embarked on an economic policy designed to decrease South Africa's dependency on foreign suppliers of strategic goods. Large subsidies became available for import substitution, while strategic industries such as Armscor and SASOL were developed and expanded. Large subsidies were also available for industrial development in (homeland) border areas. For many English-dominated companies, these developments created lucrative investment opportunities.

The relationship between the bureaucratic state and the business community developed (or deteriorated) into an unholy marriage in the early 1980s. With the economy in the grip of stagflation and growing international isolation, the government and the business community appeared to be moving closer together in an attempt to consolidate and protect their own positions. Little attempt was made on the part of either Afrikaner or English business interests to break the stalemate on reform and end the tendency to 'short termism' (Terreblanche, 1988, p. 373). Social expenditure, perhaps the key indicator of apartheid, remained radically biased in favour of whites (see McGrath's contribution to this volume).

1984 onwards

1984 is another very important turning point in South Africa's history. In September of that year the tricameral parliament was introduced and the townships erupted in widespread rebellion.

Cumbersome and unacceptable though it may be, the tricameral constitution reflects the growing realization in government circles that apartheid is unsustainable and that the nettle of power sharing has to be grasped. It represents a first reluctant step away from separate development and white domination towards the idea of 'one nation' comprising whites, coloureds and Indians. At the same time, the constitution is untenable because it excludes blacks and continues to entrench white domination. It is ironic that the township unrest from 1984 (which can to a large extent be seen as a protest against the constitution) set the scene for the current political crisis and that the United Democratic Front (UDF), which was formed in 1983 to oppose the new constitution, played a major role during the mid-1980s in co-ordinating the mass democratic movement against apartheid.

If one compares the 'core' of the state in the 1980s with that of the 1960s, it is clear that dramatic changes have taken place. At the 'core' of the Verwoerdian State was the Afrikaner clan believing itself to be predestined to govern a 'pure' white South Africa. The 'core' of the bureaucratic state in the 1980s is a multiracial co-opted elite consisting of the upper echelon of the National Party, large sections of the Afrikaner and English speaking business community (with close patronage relations with the government), key securocrats in the State Security Council, and co-opted black, coloured and Asian leaders. This elite has a large vested interest in the maintenance of 'the system' and plays a crucial role in the government strategy of 'co-optive dominance' (Terreblanche, 1989, p. 26).

The most important aspect of the 1980s power play is the mounting tension between the co-optive dominance strategy of the bureaucratic state, and the growing power and influence of organizations in the mass democratic movement. When the history of South Africa is written in the 2020s, the 1980s will not be regarded as the decade in which apartheid was abolished. But they will in all probability be seen as a decade of rapid change and fundamental shifts in the balance of power. In the 1980s the main contenders for power have been a state comprising a co-opted elite, and the mass democratic movement. The struggle between the Afrikaner and English establishments has all but faded into insignificance.

In spite of the enormous power vested in the hands of the bureaucratic state, its effectiveness has been undermined by three things: firstly the legitimacy crisis of the 'system' as perceived from both the left and the right wings, secondly the ongoing deterioration of the economy, and thirdly the growing hostility of the international community. All three aspects are closely interwoven.

The poor performance of the economy since 1974 was aggravated by the Rubicon speech of President Botha in August 1985. In the past four years, South Africa has experienced an outflow of R27 000 million — half as the repayment of short-term debt and the rest as disinvestment and 'flight money'. Despite its much-publicized privatization and deregulation policies, the government has lost control over the economic and political destiny of South Africa. The country's economic future rests in foreign hands and we have only the National Party government with its policy of white dominance to thank for the situation.

On the 8th of May 1989, the Governor of the Reserve Bank, Dr de Kock, warned that:

> ... if adequate progress is not made in the field of political and constitutional reform, South Africa's relationships with the rest of the world are unlikely to improve to any significant extent. ... In that event, South Africa will probably remain a capital-exporting and debt-repaying country for years. ... In such circumstances, the average standard of living in South Africa will at best rise only slowly.

The real per capita income of South Africans will continue to decline until the South African government resolves its legitimacy crisis and normalizes its relations with the rest of the world.

Transition to a non-racial democracy

This exercise in periodizing South Africa's political economic history would be incomplete without some speculation about the transition to a non-racial democracy. We have isolated 1984 as the beginning of the final phase of apartheid. Once apartheid has finally expired, the country will no doubt experience a transitional period of nation-building which will hopefully culminate in a non-racial democracy. The interesting questions are how long apartheid will remain gasping on its death bed, and how long (and what form) the transition period will take.

As the average length of the phases presented above is 12 years, one could ask whether 1996 is a suitable guess for the end of apartheid. The chances of this happening are rather remote. Although the bureaucratic state cannot postpone the turning point indefinitely, the enormous power at its disposal, coupled with the strategy of co-optive dominance, is sufficient to retard the process for some years. It would be a mistake to underestimate the determination and organizational ability of the National Party to perpetuate its position of power and privilege, even if this necessitates a siege economy.

It is unrealistic to expect the crucial turning point to occur while the present government is in power. The National Party is constrained by its constituency and thus impotent to shed the last remnants of apartheid. The white electorate is still unprepared and unwilling to support fundamental reform.[15] Instead, they seem to believe that small gradual adaptations will suffice to perpetuate the social, economic and political structures in South Africa. This is reflected in the National Party's Five Year Action Plan (announced in June 1989). This contradictory document, which accepts the idea of a democratic future for all South Africans but maintains white power and supremacy, indicates that the Party is far from ready to play an instrumental role in the transition to a non-racial democracy.

Even the more liberal English-speaking business community seems unlikely to take the initiative for the final dismantling of apartheid. Their unwillingness to make a co-ordinated, open, firm stand against the government's policy of apartheid and to use their economic muscle against the bureaucratic state in order to break the stalemate on reform, raises interesting questions. Is it possible that the business community has become so dependent on state patronage that it cannot operate successfully without it? According to Terreblanche, it is:

> ... justifiable to conclude that large sections of the English-speaking business community have 'swapped' their traditional explicit hostility towards the National Party government for covert, but growing, economic co-operation because it has become far more convenient and more profitable to share in the 'spoils' of government (1988, p. 374).

The National Party will only fall from power once the cocoon of prejudice, ignorance and disinformation spun around the white electorate has been unravelled. Whites need to be educated out of their anti-black prejudices and their suspicion of anything leftist or liberal. South Africa needs to experience *glasnost*, which as Gorbachev puts it, is about 'openness' and the 'truthful and unbiased analysis of problems and a rejection of anything outdated' (1987, p. 44).

Is this possible in South Africa? According to Gorbachev, 'at sharp turns of history, in revolutionary situations, the people demonstrate a remarkable ability to listen, understand and respond **if they are told the truth**' (1987, p. 57, our emphasis). However, as he himself admits, 'the greatest difficulty in our restructuring effort lies in our thinking which has been moulded over the past years. Everyone from the General Secretary (his position when writing) **has to alter his thinking**' (ibid., p. 65, brackets and emphasis ours).

In rejecting the prospect of apartheid ending before 1996 we do not discount the possibility of the National Party's conducting long and erratic negotiations with elements in the mass democratic movement during the early 1990s. At best, this process will eventually bear fruit and facilitate a South African *glasnost* to prepare the population, both black and white, for the demands the transitional phase will make on every citizen.

Speculation on the second question — the nature and length of the transitional period — is even more difficult as it will be determined by a variety of imponderable factors. Nevertheless, given that the period will be crucial and decisive in the path of South African history, the lack of discussion on this question in academic and political circles should be deplored.

From a constitutional point of view, a major task during the transitional period will be to introduce a legitimate form of democracy which enables everyone to participate in decision-making processes. We must not, however, underestimate the public financial implications of such a process of democratization. When parliamentary bargaining power is granted to people previously deprived of it, their representatives will be tempted to use such power as a means of redressing the problems of poverty and underdevelopment. A real danger exists that the demands for welfare spending on the poorer sections of the population will over-strain the tax capacity of the South African economy.

Apart from the democratization process, the rebuilding of the South African economy must be a high priority during the transitional phase. It is reasonable to suspect that the present decline in the economy, caused predominantly by internal instability and growing international isolation, will continue during the final phase of apartheid. In all probability, a sustainable high economic growth rate will only be feasible once the mass democratic movement and the international community are satisfied that a decisive turning away from apartheid and towards a democratic future has taken place. It would however be unrealistic to expect a large inflow of foreign capital and entrepreneurship soon thereafter. Likewise it is improbable that international firms, which left South Africa under pressure from profitability and disinvestment, would return immediately if at all.

Strong economic revival and sustainable growth will only be possible if the international community sponsors a large Marshall Aid programme. Given that many third world countries have a dire need for this kind of aid, a case must be presented not for South Africa alone, but for the whole subcontinent. This could potentially be linked to a programme of building a subcontinental community market.

As in the Soviet Union, the transitional phase in South Africa will require a three-pronged policy of *glasnost* (to re-educate the population about the real nature of transitional problems), *perestroika* (reconstruction or rebuilding of the economy) and *demokratizasiya*. The crucial question concerns the synchronization of the processes of economic reconstruction and political democratization. Which one should get preference? While economic growth and redistribution may prove to be conflicting policy aims in the early stages of transition, they may become complementary in due time when investment in human capital starts to have a positive effect on productivity. Nevertheless, the trade-off between economic reconstruction and growth on the one hand, and democratization and redistribution on the other, will be one of the greatest policy challenges facing a future non-racial government in South Africa.

Notes

1   This essay is a joint venture which draws on ideas and arguments expressed in Terreblanche (1988 and 1989) and in a chapter of Nattrass' draft doctoral dissertation.

2   By virtue of the British parliament's South Africa Act of 1909 political control was placed in white hands. However, blacks and so-called 'coloureds' had limited voting rights in Natal and the Cape.

3   It is important to remember that foreign shareholders were an important element in the power structure and exerted a great influence on the structuring of apartheid society. In 1918 the proportion of mining dividends paid abroad was approximately 80 per cent.

4   The number of items on the tariff schedule jumped from 192 to 371 after the Pact government initiated its protection policy (Botha, 1973, p. 337).

5   The cheapness of black labour was ensured by the rigid application of Stallardist principles and the stunting of the black and non-racial labour movement by the 1924 Industrial Conciliation Act which denied blacks the right to trade union membership.

6   According to Van der Horst, between 1924 and 1933 the number of whites employed by the Railways rose from 4 760 to 17 783, while the number of blacks fell from 37 564 to 22 008. Likewise, in central and local government the proportion of whites rose from 45 per cent to 64 per cent (1942, p. 251, 264).

7   In 1934, the National Party and the South African Party fused to become the United South African National Party. The Labour Party, which had lost 10 of its 18 seats in the 1929 election, was by this stage politically insignificant. Hardline nationalists under Malan who rejected the fusion, formed the 'Gesuiwerde' (purified) National Party in 1935 and set about mobilizing the Afrikaner nationalist support which was to sweep it to power in 1948.

8   With the resignation of Hertzog, Smuts was forced to rely on the political support of liberals such as Finance Minister Hofmeyr. This had a major effect on social policy, especially in the sphere of labour.

9   Afrikaner proletarianization was quickened by the bankrupcy of many small farmers in the 1920s and 1930s which served to create a severe poverty problem. According to the Carnegie Commission of 1932, one-third of the Afrikaner population was desperately poor and another third classified as poor (Terreblanche, 1988, p. 367). Those who had migrated to the cities lacked the necessary skills to compete with

cheap black and coloured labour. They found it difficult to adapt to the unfriendly English-dominated cities and thus responded enthusiastically to the call of Afrikaner nationalism.

10 According to Adam & Giliomee, the proliferation of bureacracies and administrative structures which accompanied the institutionalization of apartheid largely solved the 'poor white' problem by offering them preferential access to jobs thus created (1979, pp. 160–176).

11 The original legislation passed in 1951 was overturned by an Appeal Court in 1952 which ruled that it infringed the 1909 South Africa Act, as it had been passed with less than a two-thirds majority. In 1955 the Senate was enlarged from 44 to 89 members to supply the government with the required majority in a joint sitting of the House of Assembly and the Senate. In 1956 the coloureds were removed from the common voters role. The whole process served to alienate English from Afrikaners and the (mainly Afrikaans-speaking) coloureds from the white Afrikaners in power.

12 The militant 'Youth League' of the ANC, which was formed in 1943, devised a strategy of mass action centred on the use of community boycotts and civil disobedience. The election of the Nationalists to power in 1948 convinced the ANC that their traditional focus on petitions and peaceful lobbying was redundant. As a result, the Youth League gained control of the ANC with a 'programme of action' which was to form the basis of the Defiance Campaign of the 1950s.

13 The resulting Treason Trial, which dragged on for five years, ended in aquittal for all the accused.

14 Section 10 of the Black (Urban Areas) Consolidation Act of 1945 stipulates that only those (and their dependants) born in 'white' areas, or who have worked for one employer for ten years, or several employers for 15 years, may remain in a 'white' area for longer than 72 hours.

15 In the 1989 elections, 80 per cent of the white electorate and 92 per cent of white Afrikaners voted for parties which still subscribe to apartheid or more recently to the 'group approach' of South African politics.

References

Adam, H. & Giliomee, H., *Ethnic Power Mobilized. Can South Africa Change?*, Yale University Press: New Haven, 1979.

Botha, D., 'On Tariff Policy: The Formative Years', in *The South African Journal of Economics*, December, 1973.

Boyle, K., *South Africa: Imprisonment Under the Pass Laws*, Amnesty International Report, United States of America, 1986.

Bradlow, E., *Immigration into the Union 1910–48: Policies and Attitudes*, M.A Thesis, University of Cape Town, 1978.

Carter, G., Gerhart, G. & Karis, T., *From Protest to Challenge*, vol. 3, Hoover: Stanford, 1977.

Cilliers, S. & Groenewald, C., 'Urban Growth in South Africa: 1936–2000', Department of Sociology, University of Stellenbosch, 1982.

Davenport, T., *South Africa: A Modern History*, Macmillan: London, 1987.

Gorbachev, M., *Perestroika, New Thinking for our Country and the World*, Collins: London, 1987.

Hanlon, J., *Beggar Your Neighbours*, Catholic Institute for International Relations: Indiana, 1986.

Hemson, D., 'Trade Unionism and the Struggle for Liberation in South Africa', in *Capital and Class*, no. 6, 1978.

Horwitz, R., *The Political Economy of South Africa*, Weidenfeld and Nicholson: London, 1967.

Johnstone, F., *Race, Class and Gold*, Routledge and Kegan Paul: London, 1976.

Landsdowne Commission, *Report of the Witwatersrand Mine Natives Wages Commission on the Remuneration and Conditions of Employment of Natives on Witwatersrand Gold Mines*, UG no. 21, 1944

Lipton, M., *Capitalism and Apartheid: South Africa 1910–1986*, Wildwood House: Aldershot, 1986.

Lodge, T., *Black Politics in South Africa Since 1945*, Ravan Press: Johannesburg, 1983.

Marks, S. & Trapido, S., 'The Politics of Race, Class and Nationalism in Twentieth Century South Africa', *mimeo*, Queen Elizabeth House: Oxford, 1987.

O'Meara, D., *Volkskapitalisme: Class and Ideology in the Development of Afrikaner Nationalism 1934–1948*, Ravan Press: Johannesburg, 1983.

Terreblanche, S., 'White South African Relations: A Reluctant Alliance', in *International Relations*, vol. 9, no. 4, 1988.

Terreblanche, S., 'The South African Drama: From "Union" and High Hope in 1910 Towards "Disintegration" and Despair in 1990?', Paper read at the 54th Annual Meeting of the Johannesburg Social Welfare Association, Johannesburg, June 1989.

Wilson, F., *Labour on the South African Gold Mines*, SPROCAS, Johannesburg, 1975.

Wolpe, H., 'Capitalism and Cheap Labour Power in South Africa: From Segregation to Apartheid', in *Economy and Society*, vol. 1, no. 4, 1972.

Van der Berg, S., 'Long Term Economic Trends and Development in South Africa', in *African Affairs*, April 1989.

Van der Horst, S., *Native Labour in South Africa*, Oxford University Press: London, 1942.

The case for a social democratic compromise

2

Pieter J. du Pré le Roux

Introduction

In this chapter it is argued that a South African version of social democracy is the only system, under the present circumstances, capable of ensuring political stability and economic progress in this troubled country.[1] The siege economy and radical socialism — the two options which in my opinion are most likely to be realized and in that order — understandably have a strong appeal to different constituencies in South Africa, but neither is capable of delivering what is promised.

The case for a social democracy is firstly based on **historical evidence**. The existing social democracies[2] have been more successful in eliminating economic and political domination, whilst at the same time maintaining high rates of growth relative to either the more radical socialist or the more conservative capitalist systems. However, valid points of criticism can also be raised against some aspects of these social democracies. This chapter argues that South African circumstances require the evolution of a version of social democracy with a more radical approach to issues such as land redistribution and the democratic control of elected representatives.

There are also pragmatic considerations favouring a South African social democracy. At present it is the only type of system which could emerge from a negotiated settlement. Both the socialists and the free marketeers who favour a settlement would rather see the conflict escalate than settle for the opponent's economic system. Many within these opposing groups may, however, reluctantly accept a social democracy as a compromise solution, rather than see the continued destruction of South Africa's economy and the escalation of military conflict into a full-blown civil war.

A third argument for a South African social democracy is the contention that it would be far more successful in eliminating racial domination and in enhancing the power of black South Africans than the traditional socialist systems. Old-style Marxists would dispute this, but they have a very unsophisticated understanding of power and domination.

Although I have no doubt that a social democracy would best serve the interests of most people in our land, there are a number of reasons why it is unlikely that this system will emerge from the present confrontations. But the future is not predetermined. In the end, significant groups of actors may opt for a social democracy, even if only reluctantly, and South Africa could then realize her not-insignificant economic potential.

Many liberal South Africans believe in the 'free marketeer' solution to South Africa's economic woes. This 'solution' does not merely imply a free market (an institution which is an important pillar of social democracy) but also a night-watch government which refuses to intervene on any level to rectify market failures and historical injustices. In the specific historical circumstances in which South Africa finds itself, this solution has as little chance of success as the tricameral parliament. It is foolish to believe that black South Africans would tolerate a perpetuation of white economic domination once white political domination has been brought to an end.

The changing nature of social democracies

In this section an attempt is made to explain the concept 'social democracy' by describing it in terms of the actual systems which have evolved in countries where social democratic parties have held sway. One cannot turn to the blueprints contained in the original party programmes. Social democracies as they exist in Europe today have turned out to be of a radically different nature from what was foreseen at the birth of the social democratic movement.

During the first few decades of this century (and until very recently in the case of some countries) the end goal was to achieve fully-fledged socialism, including the nationalization of larger enterprises. Social democrats broke ranks with the more radical socialist groups, not in rejecting this goal, but in arguing that socialism could be established gradually through democratic processes. Revolutionary changes, the social democrats argued, would be counter-productive.

Today virtually all social democratic parties have turned their backs on this end goal as an essential component of a socialist and democratic society. In his speech to the meeting of the Socialist International held in Stockholm in June 1989, the Swedish Prime Minister, Ingmar Carlson, argued that the goal of social democracy is to establish political control over the means of production, and not necessarily collective ownership. 'He just about declared collective ownership dead,' a Swedish newspaper concluded, quoting the following comments:

> What we have seen in eastern Europe, for example, shows that a formal take-over of the means of production did not in any way guarantee the realization of the socialist goals of liberty, equality and solidarity.

In the communist system, as in the case of unbridled capitalism, people are suppressed by power cliques over whom they have no influence. They are exploited to realize goals which were set without their participation (*Svenska Dagbladet*, 1989, p. 5).[3]

But if socialism for the modern social democrat is not primarily the collective ownership of the means of production, what does it in fact entail? In general the intention is to ensure democratic participation in setting the priorities for society in both the social and the economic spheres. Social democracy is a system committed to a process whereby an attempt is made to develop a consensus on economic policies acceptable to a wide spectrum of groups and classes in a society. The twin goals of this exercise are to **enhance overall economic welfare** and to create a much greater degree of economic equality, or to put it differently, to **eliminate economic domination**.

In the practice of European social democracies this approach has found its expression in **welfare state** measures providing national health and social security for all; **social investments** ensuring equal access to good education and health services; **intervention in the labour markets** to regulate negotiations between the trade unions and industry and commerce; **consumer protection** legislation; legislation to **protect the environment**; and many other interventions in and modifications of the market economy.

Socialism in the dictionary of modern-day social democrats does not primarily imply the socialization of the means of production; neither does it imply central or indicative planning. Indeed, social democrats have been more inclined to trust market signals with regard to the relative efficiency of different industries than have many more conservative governments. Social democrats are concerned with how the economic benefits are distributed, rather than with who owns the means of production. In practice, the new goal of ensuring a greater degree of equity in the distribution of income and wealth, and a greater degree of democratic control has primarily been realized by redistribution out of growth.

Although there was a time when many of them would deny it, social democratic parties accept that there is a trade-off between redistribution and economic growth. However, in the early phases of social democracies, much of the redistribution took the form of social investments with a high economic return, such as the establishment of efficient education and health systems. There is much to indicate that these investments increased the productive capacity of social democratic countries in the long term and thus contributed to higher rates of growth. Gunnar Myrdal somewhat over-optimistically claimed that social investment in education and housing, which improved the 'quality of the factors of production', had no negative consequences for growth:

> By ... raising the level of national productivity the reforms have themselves pro-vided the additional resources required for making them economically feasible and for securing at the same time further continued social reform policy (Myrdal, 1957, p. 47).

Even in the fully developed social democracies, where a very significant pro-portion of the economic redistribution which takes place clearly does not have economic returns, the commitment to full employment implies that economic growth remains a major goal. Indeed, one of the reasons for the rapid emer-gence of the Greens in Germany and later in the Scandinavian countries, was the reluctance of the social democratic parties to sacrifice economic growth for the sake of ecological considerations.

Socialism for social democrats implies a system in which the trade unions play a central role in determining the economic scenario. Although there is no significant longer-term indicative planning similar to that of the French and the Japanese, possible annual growth rates and the effect of different rates of increase on wage packets are carefully calculated when wage demands are considered. In Sweden, because of the very high premium placed upon full em-ployment, trade unions even acquiesced in falling real wages during the 1980s, in order to increase the economic growth rate. As a consequence, unemploy-ment in Sweden is today under 2 per cent. It does not follow that consensus is regularly reached in central negotiations between the trade unions, the em-ployer organizations and the state. Nevertheless, because of the central role that the analysis of macro-economic potential plays in wage negotiations, a short-term consensus is not uncommon, and differences when they do arise are often marginal, even though the longer-term goals may differ substantially.

Although most pricing in social democratic countries is left to the market, a number of central prices such as the interest rate and the exchange rates are controlled. In some social democracies, part of the financial sector has also been nationalized. The rules of tax-free investment funds enable the govern-ment to encourage private sector investments in a counter-cyclical fashion. Various degrees of control are exerted over foreign exchange dealings and for-eign multinationals have at times been limited to 50 per cent control of their subsidiaries in social democratic countries. Fairly convincing arguments have been put forward to show that a number of these interventions are no longer as successful as they used to be, and that some of them may be counter-productive at this stage of development. Nevertheless, the evidence seems to be quite clear that at certain stages most, if not all, of these measures benefited economic development.

In social democratic countries labour unions play a central role, not only in setting the overall macro-economic agenda, but also in determining the day-to-day working conditions on the factory floor. In recent years trade unions in most social democratic countries have, in terms of co-determination or a *mitbestimmung* approach, been given access to the boardrooms. During the past decade or two, democratization of economic management has, within the country and within firms (rather than collective ownership) become the cornerstone of the socialism of social democratic countries.

An evaluation of right and left-wing critiques of social democracy

Right and left wingers have standard objections with which they dispose of any suggestion that South Africans should consider a social democratic compromise rather than their respective versions of the true faith. It is necessary first to respond to these general arguments before the case for a social democracy for present day South Africa is developed. Although some of the questions raised by the critics do deserve serious answers, the inability of both sides in the debate to learn from the history of the twentieth century, and their dogmatic adherence to outdated nineteenth century social science concepts, would have been amusing had the commitments and actions which flow from these ideas not been so potentially catastrophic for our country.

In analysing the free marketeers' and the radical socialists' criticism of the social democratic model, no attempt is made to deal with the substantive aspects of these alternatives. The temptation to attack the philosophy and the alternative model of the free marketeers has been resisted, for there is no possibility whatsoever that this model will be implemented in South Africa under present conditions. Some of the theoretical underpinnings of the Marxist socialist model are questioned, but even though this type of model is most likely to emerge if a compromise is not reached in the next couple of years, it is not possible within the limits of this essay to systematically discuss the problems associated with it.[4]

The free marketeer critique of social democracy

In an obvious reference to Childs' (1936) *Sweden, the Middle Way*, Hayek (1944, p. 33) attacked the conviction 'that it must be possible to find some Middle Way' by claiming that:

> Both competition and central direction become poor and inefficient tools if they are incomplete; ... a mixture of the two means neither will really work and ... the results will be worse than if either system had been consistently relied upon.

The success of social democracies in the past 50 years has shown that this particular mix does work, and from the perspective of the great mass of people it has worked much better than the centrally planned economies and those free market economies in which government showed no concern whatsoever to correct market failures. Sweden, the first country to successfully implement Keynesian demand and anti-cyclical investment policies, avoided the depths of the depression in the 1930s and the high levels of unemployment of the 1970s. Although it is accepted that in the modern world economy Keynesian policies applied in one country only can have but limited success, the principle of democratic reflection on the economy and correction of market failures (where the economic instruments permit such intervention) continues to be applied with a considerable degree of success. To adhere dogmatically to Hayek's assertion, as some present day free marketeers do, is to ignore the history of the past 50 years.

More sophisticated conservatives have accepted the argument that social democracies have worked, but reject the suggestion that they therefore present a suitable model for South Africa. They argue that only mature economies can afford the luxury of such a system.

This argument is clearly correct if a plea for a social democracy is taken to imply that the same types and levels of welfare expenditure found in developed countries must apply in South Africa. However, 60–70 years ago, real per capita income in Sweden was not dramatically different from South Africa's today. A social democracy in South Africa would give priority to exactly those types of social welfare and investment expenditure which were high on the agenda when social democratic parties began to have an influence on policies in northern Europe. (In addition, because of the legacy of the apartheid economy, more radical measures — some of which are referred to below — will need to be considered.)

A third set of objections from the right has to do with the general contention that social democracies, although they show a great concern for market failures, ignore the consequences of government failures. More specifically, it is argued that the **high level of taxes** needed to finance social democratic expenditures present a **formidable disincentive** to engage in economic activity; that **private enterprises** are far **more efficient than state-run enterprises** and, more generally, that the share of the **government** in the economy is, under social democracies, reaching a level where it **smothers all economic activity** *inter alia* because the private sector is crowded out of the financial markets.

Recent adjustments and modifications in the policies of social democratic parties indicate that social democratic governments accept that these points of criticism have some validity.

With regard to the higher marginal tax rates, social democrats have often taken their cue from the arguments expressed by Keynes in a famous passage in his *General Theory*:

For my own part, I believe that there is social and psychological justification for significant inequalities of incomes and wealth, but not for such large disparities as exist today. There are valuable human activities which require the motive of money-making and the environment of private wealth-ownership for their full fruition ... But it is not necessary for the stimulation of these activities and the satisfaction of these proclivities that the game should be played for such high stakes as at present. Much lower stakes will serve the purpose equally well, as soon as the players are accustomed to them (Keynes, 1936, p. 376).

The basic premise that the stakes for the higher income groups can be substantially lower than they would be under a free marketeer regime without there being any significant disincentive on work, is accepted by all social democrats. It is the basis of progressive income tax policies all over the world. On the basis of experience in social democratic countries, it is today, however, increasingly admitted that marginal tax rates should not be much higher than 50 per cent. Marginal income tax rates of 80 per cent or even 90 per cent can clearly become significant disincentives. Rates of this magnitude also encourage large-scale tax avoidance and evasion, as bitter experience has taught some of the social democratic regimes. In recent years marginal income tax rates have thus been brought down. Social democratic countries have, however, continued to exploit other avenues of redistribution, such as higher inheritance taxes and progressive rates on property, which do not have the same marked negative consequences as do high marginal rates of taxation on income.

The validity of some of the arguments in favour of privatization has also been accepted by most social democratic parties, and some social democratic governments have themselves had vigorous privatization programmes, but only in those areas where privatization seemed to be in the interest of all. At the same time, there is still a strong conviction among social democrats that many activities can be handled more efficiently by governments than by private enterprise. The centralized pension scheme in the Scandinavian countries can, for example, be shown to be far more cost-effective than the multitude of individual pension schemes one finds in South Africa. In some instances there is a strong case in favour of a mix of privately owned and state or co-operatively owned enterprises. The co-operatively owned supermarkets and the government-owned postal bank in Sweden are, social democrats admit, more efficient because they face private competition. At the same time their participation in the market prevents the formation of cartels (at a high cost for the consumer) by the big oligopolies that dominate these sectors. On the basis of the experience of the social democratic countries, one can thus reject the dogmatic assertion of the free marketeers that all state-owned enterprise ought to be privatized.

Both right-wing and left-wing critics of social democracies have argued that the share of government in the gross national product has reached a level at which economic growth is being seriously undermined. In the early 1970s, left-wing critics of social democratic systems argued that there was no remedy to the fiscal crisis — short of an overthrow of the capitalist system. They argued that social democracy bought legitimacy for capitalism by the welfare state measures, but with government spending amounting to virtually 60 per cent of the net national product in the case of some countries, this process could be taken no further. It was economically impossible to further tax capital, and politically impossible to roll back the welfare state.

During the subsequent decade some social democratic governments seemed to have succeeded where their radical critics predicted that they would fail. The Australian Labour Party strongly embraced privatization to roll back the state. The Swedish economy was given a respite by the labour unions acquiescing, as noted, in a stagnant and even falling real wage. The success of some social democratic governments in reducing the role of the state confounded the predictions of left-wing critics, but was oil on the fire of the right-wing faith that the role of the government must be drastically limited.

In response to the general argument in favour of limited government, social democrats again argue in favour of a Middle Way. Social democratic parties world-wide accept that there is a real danger of destroying the economy by over-extending the role of the state. On the other hand, the conservative contention that the share of the state should not exceed one quarter of the national income, is rejected as having no scientific foundation. After all, many social democratic countries have shown sustainable high rates of growth, even though the government's share in income has often been more than 50 per cent (see Wilson's chapter).

There is clearly no simple correlation between the share of the national income directed to government expenditure and the growth rate. The efficiency of a country's civil service, and the type of expenditure undertaken, are factors of far greater importance than the actual level of expenditure (for example, expenditure on imported military hardware is very unlikely to have the same economic returns as expenditure on basic health, primary education and a better transport system). To place absolute ceilings on the share which the government may have in the economy, as the free marketeers are proposing, is to deny the government the role of redressing past injustices and dealing with the large-scale problems of poverty in South Africa. Political stability and economic growth require that 'human capital' investments be made in the interest of those who have for so long been excluded from the benefits of the economy.

A right-wing argument against social democracies (often also made in somewhat different language by Marxists who wish to justify the undemocratic nature of socialist regimes) is the following:

... where in the world have you seen a country making a successful industrial take-off under a system of complete voting equality. It most certainly did not happen in Germany or Japan. Nor did England or the United States have equality of vote during industrial take-off. For if all have the same say during such a period, they devour all the products of the society and no savings can be effected to ensure industrial growth (Rupert, 1962).

This argument, which has also been put forward by Lord Bevan and others (Myrdal, 1957, p. 46), might under certain circumstances have had some valid-ity. Particularly in the early stages of development, authoritarian regimes have at times been able to mobilize a surplus for reinvestment which might not have been possible under a democracy. However, under the present circumstances in South Africa, as Dr Rupert himself seems to accept, the lack of political partic-ipation by the great majority of South Africans has become a serious obstacle to growth. The political instability and international pressures on South Africa will not abate until democracy has been extended to all. For the same reasons, the inward industrialization strategy will have little success, even though it is economically more progressive than the free marketeer strategy. The denial of democracy, where it is a goal to which many of those who are excluded are committed, undermines the effective functioning of the economic system.

General arguments that social democracy cannot work, or cannot work in a country which is not fully developed, ignore the historic evidence. On the other hand, arguments by free marketeers which point out failures in government have, in those instances where they have clearly had validity, been taken seriously by social democrats. As a consequence the social democracies are today far less centralist than intended even only a couple of decades ago.

The radical critique of social democracy

During the 1970s and early 1980s predictions of the imminent collapse of welfare states were rife amongst left-wing critics of the Middle Way. It is indeed ironic that the 1980s turned out to be the age of the crisis for traditional socialism. However this does not mean that the radical criticism of social democracy can be disposed of simply by arguing that the socialist countries have not been doing well.

Three types of criticism have been levelled at social democratic systems from within Marxist circles. The first has to do with the contention that the social democracies cannot successfully realize the goals they have set for themselves. The second is based on the claim that social democracies are statist and un-democratic, and the third accuses social democrats of masking reality from the workers so that they do not perceive the injustices of welfare capitalism and the truths of Marxism.

The social democratic claim that their system is the **most efficient in elimi-nating domination and exploitation** is contested by Marxist critics. The predic-tion that social democracies would be destroyed by the fiscal crisis has already been dealt with. Clearly it did not come true. However, social democrats dealt with the crisis by reversing trends which had become well established over years. In some instances the share of wages in national income had to be diminished; enterprises under control of the state were privatized; the long-term trend of steady per capita increases in state expenditure on welfare had to be reversed. The fiscal crisis was overcome, but in the process the hope of left-wing social democrats, that the slow evolutionary march forward would in the end still lead to full scale socialization of the means of production, has taken a severe knock.

Marxists could respond by pointing out that the social democracies have survived the fiscal crisis only by sacrificing the socialist ideal of eliminating capitalist exploitation. And this is clearly the case if one defines exploitation and domination in nineteenth century Marxist terms, for Marxist exploitation continues to exist when one has private ownership of the means of production. However, for social democrats the concern is not whether a surplus accrues to private owners of the means of production or not, but whether the work-ers' standard of living improves and whether their control over their working conditions is enhanced.

The problems social democrats have with the Marxist conception of exploita-tion, power and domination are similar to those raised by Anthony Giddens (1979, 1981, 1985) in his monumental attempt to develop a synthesis of the valid insights of the various social theoretical traditions.

Exploitation is a concept which, according to the position adopted by social democrats, should have a more encompassing notion than is to be found in Marxist analysis. Exploitation is domination,[5] both in the political and in the economic spheres, that is harnessed to sectional interests. Indeed, as Ingmar Carlson also argued at the Socialist International referred to earlier, flagrant domination of one group by others continues in the communist countries in spite of the nationalization of the means of production. Furthermore, history has shown that economic exploitation has less to do with who owns the means of production than with who controls the allocation of the surplus. From their understanding of exploitation and domination, it follows that the extension of bourgeois democracy, rather than its elimination, should be given a high priority. Hence the high premium social democrats place on a pluralist democracy.

The social democrats do not only contest the Marxist conviction that domi-nation is exclusively a question of class domination. They also reject the Marxist conception of the struggle for power as a zero sum game. For example, in the economic sphere a successful compromise between the different classes can re-sult in the economic power of all groups being enhanced. Economic growth can be to the benefit of both the capitalist and the workers. The old Marxist faith that the eventual immiserization of the workers is inevitable, is rejected as being in conflict with the history of the social democracies and as a vulgar functionalist hypothesis.

As a consequence of these differences, social democrats claim as victories adjustments in the system which Marxists would scorn as temporary gains or as co-option strategies of the capitalist classes. For example, for social democrats there is significant progress if workers are able to influence most of the major decisions a company takes and even veto those with which they cannot agree; and if their wages continue to increase, even if the rate of exploitation (in Marxist terms) simultaneously increases.[6]

The social democratic concepts of power, domination and exploitation are virtually identical to those of the new generation of sophisticated post-Marxist, post-Weberian social theorists. Marxist accusations that social democrats in fact perpetuate capitalist domination and exploitation only make sense if one accepts the nineteenth century Marxists' definitions of these concepts. The theoretical foundation on which old-style Marxism is built, is crumbling away. In the process the pragmatism of social democrats is, *ex post facto*, acquiring a great theoretical coherence. In practice social democrats developed an understanding of exploitation, power and domination which, though scorned by the Marxist purists, is now acquiring a theoretical rigour and dominance in the social sciences.

Whereas Marxists usually criticize social democracies for failing to bring economic exploitation to an end, Nicos Poulantzas (1983, p. 601) accused social democracies of weakness in the very area where they are usually regarded to be the strongest:

> ...social democracy and Stalinism...exhibit a fundamental complicity: both are marked by **statism** and profound distrust of mass initiatives, in short by suspicion of democratic demands.

If one reads this accusation to imply that the suspicion of popular demands in social democracies runs as deeply as it does in a Stalinist country, one cannot but respond to Poulantzas with a certain degree of incredulity. Social democracies have, whatever their shortcomings might be, shown a healthy respect for democratic procedures. However, Poulantzas does have a point (as do libertarian critics of social democracies) when he accuses social democracies of statism. The system of proportional representation prevalent in most social democratic countries, together with the significant influence of trade unions on wages, conditions of work and types of investments undertaken by the business sector, do indeed ensure that a far broader spectrum of people are involved in the making of decisions than is the case in many other democracies. However, particularly in those countries where social democratic parties have been in control for long periods of time, social democrats have implemented programmes and policies against the wishes of the majority, in the confidence that, when election comes, they will again be able to muster the support of the majority of voters.

The inability of the electorate to have a significant influence on those decisions not likely to influence the loyalty of the electorate at the next election, can only be overcome by the Swiss system of referendums and initiatives, for this enables them to challenge decisions of the government. A decentralization of power to local government is another precondition if the people rather than the state are to dominate. Statism is always a danger when government is not directly responsible to the people. In social democratic countries there is usually a fair degree of decentralization of decision-making to local governments, but social democratic parties have shied away from the referendum system which, in the final instance, places power in the hands of the people themselves. Although it is clearly absurd to lump them together with the Stalinists, social democracies are, in this respect, more statist than they ought to be in terms of their own ideals and goals.

A third line of attack from the left is to accuse social democracy of creating a false consciousness amongst the working classes.

> The working class does not create spontaneous Marxism in the same manner which it spontaneously creates various forms of defence organization against capitalistic exploitation. The need for such organization is, so to speak, easily perceived. Such is not the case with the basic Marxist truths (Johnsson *et al.*, 1979, p. 42).

The workers do not realize that their perception is limited, for, as Johnsson and his co-authors admit: 'The social democratic policy works, it gives results, obvious and concrete in separate instances ..' (ibid., p. 43). But, of course, from a Marxist perspective, this apparent success is misleading. Workers accept the social democratic compromise and fail to discover Marxist truths. For Johnsson the situation can be rectified by theoretical work. Other Marxists use these types of arguments to justify the need for a socialist revolution. It is argued that the false consciousness of workers can only be destroyed by creating a different socialist reality.

The practical experience of social democratic countries as regards this type of argument clearly counts for nought. However, can the same be said for the experience of workers in existing socialist countries? Do the workers of Poland still need to discover Marxist truths? Johnsson's contention that the workers will fail to discover these truths is blatantly elitist. In most social democratic countries there are active Communist Parties, often with representation in parliament, and workers have been thoroughly exposed to the traditional Marxist perception of social reality. Marxism in these countries has been rejected for the very reason that workers are familiar with Marxist dogma and practice. They

are not ignorant of the position of workers in the existing socialist countries
(see Scharpf, 1979, p. 43).

Ideology does play a role when dominant groups justify their position. In
the case of social democracies, the arguments opposing democratic reforms
which will enable the electorate to launch initiatives or veto governmental
decisions, can be shown to be of an ideological nature. But to reject the social
democratic compromise as ideological, and to assume that the Marxist 'truths',
which have served to justify the totalitarian rule of most communist regimes are
not ideological, is to refuse to apply valid Marxist insights to Marxist theories.

Social democrats remain committed to socialist ideals: equality, the elimination of economic and political domination, the eradication of capitalist
exploitation. In terms of the outcome of the process, a social democracy can
justifiably be termed 'socialist'. If, however, systems are classified according to
the mode of production rather than the economic outcome, social democracies
may justifiably be branded 'capitalist', even though of a very reformed variety.

The radical critique of social democracies, as they have emerged, is not
convincing. Undoubtedly, the accusation that social democracies are statist
— an accusation which has also been levied by the right — does have some
validity. Marxists are also correct when they argue that social democracies have
reformed capitalism rather than destroyed it. But to contend that these reforms
have not eliminated most forms of economic exploitation, and to deny that
both economic and political power has been spread more equally and with
much greater benefit to the ordinary worker in the social democracies than in
any other system, is to be blinded by outdated, theoretical nineteenth century
concepts. It is to deny that the very ideals which Marxism planted in the hearts
of the social democrats have been largely realized.

The case for a South African
social democracy

This chapter argues that a South African version of social democracy is the only
system that has the potential to deal efficiently with the economic crisis faced
by South Africa. It does not contend that a social democracy will invariably be
the only workable economic system: given different historical circumstances,
the economic priorities of many groups and classes may well be better satisfied
by other economic systems. But under present conditions both those who in
the long term wish to see a free marketeer system and those who favour a truly
socialist South Africa, could with integrity support a social democracy as a short
to medium-term solution.

The nature of the political and economic crisis confronting South Africa
today is such that only a social democracy could come to grips with the underlying problems. After a decade or two there may be a case for arguing, if

one is a free marketeer, the case for a Thatcherite type of counter-revolution, or, should one find oneself on the other end of a spectrum, for a more radical socialist programme.

The balance of forces in South Africa are such that neither side can dictate the economic nature of a settlement. Should the ANC and the Mass Democratic Movement insist that a settlement on the economic front must imply a fairly large-scale nationalization of industry, mining, commerce and agriculture, the white establishment would rather face international sanctions and an increase in the military onslaught, than a negotiated settlement.

A radical socialist solution can of course be implemented if a total victory is gained, but this will only be at the end of a long and drawn-out war waged on both economic and military fronts. At that stage the destruction of the economy would be such that the state may have little choice but to take over much of industry and commerce. The unemployment rate would be so high (50–60 per cent), the housing backlog so immense, malnourishment so rife and public health in such total disarray, that social democratic measures could not hope to meet the aspirations of the people within a reasonable period of time. For these and other reasons discussed elsewhere (le Roux, 1988, pp. 217–18), an old-style socialist system is most likely to emerge if we are to wait for the day that the white political and business establishments no longer have the power to put forward minimum demands for a settlement. Those whites willing to fight to the bitter end because they fear a one-party Marxist state, will be creating the conditions under which such a state is most likely to emerge. As Giddens (1979) has argued so persuasively, we create our own future, but not with the consequences we intend.

The argument that a traditional socialist type of economy, or a mixed economy with a strong bias towards traditional socialism, would be opposed to the bitter end, applies *mutatis mutandis* to a free market economy in which the government would play a limited role. A settlement on the condition that there is a constitutional guarantee that government expenditure may not exceed 25 per cent, would not be acceptable. For black South Africans apartheid is a system both of political and economic domination. They want to end political domination in order to bring an end to economic domination as well. They would rather fight a long and drawn-out battle than accept any preconditions which deny them the right to redress economic injustices rapidly.

If there is to be a settlement soon, it will have to be along social democratic lines. History has taught us this system can radically limit both economic and political exploitation and domination, and at the same time maintain a high rate of economic growth. Although capitalists would for obvious reasons prefer a free market economy in which their position was much more dominant, they could live with this type of compromise. It is, therefore, a system which is likely to meet the minimum aspirations of all concerned.

Clearly a social democracy would broadly be modelled on the existing social democracies. But it would be foolish to attempt to predict its exact nature, for a social democracy is not a clearly defined system. It would emerge from the process of negotiations before and after liberation. A South African social democracy would be likely to resemble to its European predecessors in many respects. For example, during the initial phases social investment would be concentrated in areas of high return such as education, primary health care and basic housing. Although some of these investments could possibly be financed by savings made as a result of dismantling apartheid structures, there would also be a need for additional finance. As in the case of other social democracies, this would be found by imposing capital gains taxes, higher inheritance taxes, and other taxes on wealth. Care would, however, have to be taken not to raise taxation to a level where it could undermine the growth potential of the economy, for much of the required redistribution would have to take place out of growth.

In some respects, a South African social democracy is likely to be more radical than the established social democracies. Firstly, given the great degree of political conscientization which has taken place during the past decade, direct access to political power via a referendum system allowing for popular initiatives and vetoes could well be part of this system. Secondly, given the history of injustices, certain measures of retribution may take place particularly with regard to the land issue. Demands that the land of absentee landlords be redistributed to black farmers and co-operatives may well be implemented, and financial awards may be paid to those who were removed under the Group Areas Act from prime land.

Although a S. African social democracy may seem to be far too radical from the perspective of many of those who find themselves in the white establishment, and far too conservative from the perspective of the Marxist revolutionary, there is little doubt that it would be a system which could function to the benefit of all. If S. Africa were to again achieve an annual average GNP growth rate of above 5 per cent, and taxes were so structured that approximately 1 per cent of this rate of growth benefited the (mostly white) middle classes (some growth in income being necessary in order to stem the emigration of skilled workers), then the income of the (mostly black) poor, who presently receive only one-third of national income, could grow at an average rate in excess of 10 per cent per annum. Direct food subsidies, nutrition clinics, etc. could furthermore target support to those whose position was so desperate that a 10 per cent per annum increase would not suffice to meet basic needs. Clearly those at the bottom of the ladder would benefit more dramatically than those at the top. But virtually all[7] would benefit relative to what their position would be if there were an extended siege economy followed by a radical socialist system.

It cannot be assumed that South Africa would necessarily grow at the average annual rate of 5 per cent or more (which is required if the social democratic compromise is to work). Certain conditions would have to be met. *Inter alia*, an important precondition to settlement should be a firm commitment to specific types of support from the international community, for example, the rescheduling of some and the writing off of other portions of South Africa's international debt, and the preferential access of her agricultural products to the European Community Market. After settlement there will be little interest in South Africa, and very little of the expected international support will materialize. Furthermore, the level of growth rate needed will only be realized if those within South African trade unions who are presently nurtured on a radical socialist faith, are willing and able to play the constructive role required of them in a social democratic regime. Finally, if the business community does not truly commit itself to this type of compromise, and continues with its large scale disinvestment, it will not be possible for South Africa to realize her economic potential, and the social democratic compromise could fall to pieces.

It is unlikely that a social democracy will be implemented in South Africa under present circumstances. White South Africans are often the captives of their own racist or capitalist ideologies. They either believe that a democracy in an African context could not work, or that no system but a free marketeer version of capitalism could overcome South Africa's economic problems. However, given that the choice available to them is either a siege economy or a social democratic compromise, it is clear that an increasing number of whites are willing to consider a social democracy. Indeed, if a social democratic compromise should unambiguously be offered to them, they may well opt for it, given the international pressures for a settlement.

On the other hand, given the very significant role the Communist Party has played in the resistance movements, it is not surprising that most of the Marxist objections to a social democracy raised in this chapter are prevalent in resistance circles. However, partly as a consequence of what is happening in the Soviet Union, perceptions within the ANC and the Communist Party have been changing and consequently it is difficult to predict what the feelings of the majority of the ANC executive would be, although it is likely that a social democratic compromise, if sincerely offered, would be acceptable to the broad masses. The ANC executive may however find it virtually impossible to take the initiative and suggest this type of settlement, for, should it be rejected, the more radical opposition to the left of the ANC would be able gain support at the expense of what is today undoubtedly the dominant resistance movement.

Conclusion

The majority of South Africans may potentially be willing to accept a social democracy, even if only reluctantly and as a second choice, but the political dynamics of the situation are such that it is not likely that this compromise will be reached. Whites fear a settlement, because they believe it will be on more radical terms. The liberation movements, on the other hand, find it difficult to offer these moderate terms, even though they may well be acceptable to the masses, for fear that they will lose support to those with more radical objectives if their offer should not be accepted.

Although the political obstacles to an accord being reached cannot be overcome by academic discussions, work which challenges the certainties of opponents of a social democracy may remove some of the ideological obstacles to a potential settlement. Hence this attempt to question the conventional wisdom of those to the left and to the right. The calculated risk of opting for a social democracy is greatly to be preferred to the economic and human costs of a siege economy. Only those on the right and the left who subscribe to the dogmatic certainties of naïve nineteenth century social theories can reject this conclusion.

Jill Nattrass argued in the conclusion to her book, *The South African Economy, its Growth and Change* (1981, p. 344):

> The challenge to South Africans will be to make this solution work, to face up to the tough compromises that will have to be made by all parties and to plot a course that can be navigated between the Scylla of dictatorship and the Charybdis of revolution.

The question is whether we will be able to meet this challenge after liberation.

Notes

1 I first put forward some of the economic arguments for this type of system at the 1982 conference of the Economic Society of South Africa (le Roux, 1981) after having read Jill Nattrass' arguments in favour of what she called the social democratic reform option as opposed to National Party reform (Nattrass, 1981, pp. 339–43). See also the HSRC report (Godsell & le Roux, 1986) for arguments in favour of a participating economy which in fact amounted to a version of social democracy. Jill was a member of this committee. Her sharp intellect and strong commitment to honesty and rigour in academic research brought qualities to the intellectual debate which are far too seldom found. I dedicate this chapter to her memory.

2 Sweden and the other Scandinavian countries are the classical examples of social democracies. Holland, Belgium and Austria have also had long periods under social democratic governments. Even in Germany, where the social democrats have been in opposition more than in government, social democrats have had a very significant impact on policy. Canada, New Zealand and Australia, and a number of other countries could also, with some qualifications, be added to this list. In many respects Britain is atypical, *inter alia* because the trade unions were often of a very undemocratic nature. Indications are that Kinnock's Labour Party is moving closer to the social democratic tradition.

3 My own translation from Swedish.
4 The reader who still believes in old style socialism, is referred to the introductory chapters of *Perestroika* (Gorbachev, 1987) and to Alex Novec's scholarly *The Economics of Feasible Socialism* (1983).
5 Domination can, according to Giddens (1981, p. 60), take place in both the economic and the political sphere, and there can be domination both over human beings and over nature. Although an increasing number of social democrats share Giddens's ecological concern, the focus in most social democratic analysis remains on domination over human beings.
6 Given the fact that high and rising real wages usually call for increasing capital intensity, this usually means that the rate of exploitation in Marxist terms is higher in companies and in countries that pay higher wages. Conversely, given very reasonable assumptions regarding capital intensity (the organic composition of capital), the Marxist rate of exploitation is usually low in a country which is underdeveloped or in a company which pays low wages.
7 Clearly the social democratic compromise is not in the interest of the establishment politician who wishes to cling to power for another decade or two; nor is it in the interest of the radical politician who hopes to obtain the type of totalitarian powers a radical socialist regime would entail.

References

Childs, M.W., *Sweden: The Middle Way on Trial*, Yale University Press: New Haven, 1936.

Giddens, A., *Central Problems in Social Theory: Action, Structure and Contradiction in Social Analysis*, Macmillan: London & Basingstoke, 1979.

Giddens, A., *A Contemporary Critique of Historical Materialism, vol. 1: Power, Property and the State*, University of California Press: Berkeley and Los Angeles, 1981.

Giddens, A., *A Contemporary Critique of Historical Materialism, vol. 2: The Nation-State and Violence*, Polity Press: Cambridge, 1985.

Godsell, R.M. & le Roux, P., *Growth, Equity and Participation*, Human Sciences Research Council: Pretoria, 1986.

Gorbachev, M., *Perestroika, New Thinking for our Country and the World*, Collins: London, 1987.

Hayek, F.A., *The Road to Serfdom*, Routledge and Kegan Paul: London, 1944.

Johnsson, I., Nilsson, T. & Olofsson, G., 'Social Democracy and the Working Class on the Basis of Reformism', in Fry, J. (ed.), *The Limits of the Welfare State*, Saxon House: London, 1979.

Keynes, J.M., *The General Theory of Employment, Interest and Money*, Macmillan: London, 1936.

le Roux, P., 'Social Democracy: A Socio-Economic System for South Africa,' Paper delivered at the Conference of the Economic Society of South Africa, Durban, 17 December 1981.

le Roux, P., 'The Economics of Conflict and Negotiation', in Berger, P. & Godsell, B. (eds.), *The Future South Africa*, Tafelberg: Cape Town, 1988.

Myrdal, G., *Economic Theory and Underdeveloped Regions*, Methuen: London, 1957.

Nattrass, J., *The South African Economy: Its Growth and Change*, Oxford University Press: Cape Town, 1981.

Novec, A., *The Economics of Feasible Socialism*, George Allen and Unwin: London, 1983.

Poulantzas, N, 'Towards a Democratic Socialism', in Held, D. (ed.), *States and Society*, Martin Robertson: Oxford, in association with The Open University, 1983.

Rupert, A., 'I Plea for my Country and all its Peoples', Address to The African Affairs Society, New York, 26 April 1981.

Scharpf, F.W., *Sozial-demokratische Krisenpolitik in Europa*, Campus: Frankfurt/New York 1979.

Svenska Dagbladet, 'Socialistledare Kritiserar Kina för förföljelser', Wednesday 21 June 1989.

Apartheid ideology and economic development policy[1]

3

Colin McCarthy

Introduction

The need for equitable economic growth as a means of alleviating widespread poverty is unquestionable. Equally indisputable is the view that appropriate economic development policy can play an important role in achieving such equitable economic growth. Problems, however, arise when the content of 'appropriate policy' is to be defined. Agreement on ends is all too often accompanied by vehement disagreement over means.

This chapter focuses on two aspects of apartheid ideology which have had a very negative influence on development thinking and policy. The first is the view that South Africa should be balkanized and developed as a set of separate national entities. The second, a more ambiguous notion, is that South Africa should be viewed as a combination of the first and third worlds, rather than a purely third world country.

A balkanized South Africa

Segregationist policy, from Verwoerdian apartheid to the present tricameral constitution and ten homeland governments, was designed to perpetuate the dominant position of whites. The fact that black South Africans outnumber whites five to one lies behind the government policy of removing South African citizenship from blacks through the homeland policy. Over time this dream has somewhat concretized into political substance with four homelands accepting *de jure*, but internationally unrecognized, political independence.

From a conventional economist's point of view, these political manoeuvres appeared irrational because they sought to carve separate political entities from an economically integrated region. Although blacks were discriminated against (particularly in the labour market — see Terreblanche & Nattrass in this volume, Chapter 1) and drawn into economic activity as migrants and unequal partners with whites, the integrated nature of the South African economy had been accepted by pre-apartheid economic policy makers.

In the post-war period the policy of racial discrimination evolved from 'apartheid' to 'separate development'. In the political sphere this was reflected in the creation of separate national entities which, in the changing semantics of separate development, evolved into 'national states'. However, it was recognized that political sovereignty meant little without economic substance. Some provision was thus made for the economic development of these areas. Furthermore the propagation of the political idea that blacks were only temporary sojourners in white cities carried with it the responsibility of building a resource base in the homelands for returning migrants. Likewise the politically-inspired policy of restricting black urbanization in white areas necessitated the creation of employment in or within commuting distance of the homelands. It followed that, if black workers were not free to move to work, work had to be taken to them.

Nothing illustrates these efforts better than the policy of industrial decentralization. The policy is aimed at redirecting or relocating manufacturing concerns from the major industrial areas to designated decentralized points. In addition to taking work to workers, the economic rationale behind the policy is the contention that the metropolitan areas are over-concentrated such that the marginal social cost of industrial growth exceeds marginal private costs. However, rather than using differentiated taxes to internalize the social costs of additional urban industrial expansion, the policy uses liberal incentives to lower the private cost of establishing at a decentralized point. The idea is that when the cost of decentralization is lower than that of remaining or establishing in urban areas, industrialists will find it lucrative to decentralize.

Measuring the success of homeland development is not the subject of this chapter. However, if the more rapid growth of homeland GDP relative to GNP[2] is taken as a criterion, it would on the surface appear that a remarkable measure of success has been achieved. The GNP : GDP ratio of all the homelands combined decreased from 7,6 in 1970 to 2,5 in 1980 and 2,7 in 1985 (Halbach, 1988a, p. 517). Considering the sharp increase in the real wages of black mineworkers since 1973[3] which by all expectations should have had a pronounced positive influence on the GNP (via the remittances of migrants), the fall in the GNP : GDP ratio is remarkable. However, there are clear indications that the more rapid growth in GDP was less a result of grassroots economic development and more the result of financial transfers by the South African government for the financing of government services and education. During the 1970s economic growth in the homelands depended mainly on the growth in transfer payments to homeland bureaucracies (Halbach, 1988b, p. 143).

South Africa as a combination of the first and third world

International economic inequality became an important topic of debate in the post-war period, particularly in the 1960s in the wake of the decolonialization of

Africa. Successive 'development decades' initiated by the United Nations and its Conference on Trade and Development, pertinently focused attention on the North/South economic divide. The debate and discussions reached a peak with the Brandt Commission on international development issues. The existence of and the need to ameliorate inequality in the international distribution of wealth were vigorously stated in the Commission's report (Independent Commission on International Development Issues, 1980).

In broad terms, the Brandt Report argued that the acute and growing poverty of third world countries can only be redressed by active government intervention in the economies of both first and third world countries. This interventionist stance met with a great deal of criticism from neo-classical economists who believed the free market held the solution to poverty and that the '*dirigiste* dogma' (Lal, 1983) of the Brandt report was counter-productive.

In South Africa the international debate on North/South issues was noted and, belatedly (but not surprisingly), applied to the issue of the unequal distribution of wealth in the country. Sampie Terreblanche played a leading role in this regard, arguing that South Africa is a microcosm of the world situation with the black community symbolizing the 'have-nots' of the third world and the affluent white population symbolizing the rich first world (1975; 1977, pp. 151–152; 1980, pp. 273–85; 1982). The Terreblanche hypothesis sought to show up the tensions that exist between South Africa's 'first and third world people' (differentiated on the basis of their access to economic resources and democratic processes) in a social and economic structure that created and maintains the third world component in a dependent relation. Effective democratization of South African society would, under these circumstances, require structural change in economic and political relationships, and government intervention (à la Brandt) to redress inequality through appropriate redistribution policies (see also McCarthy, 1982, pp. 1–12).

However, as the idea of conceptualizing South Africa as a combination of the first and third worlds gained ground, a subtle justification for apartheid and an explanation of the tension and polarization in South African society was devised.[4] The reasoning was simple: the world at large experienced tensions between the 'haves' and the 'have-nots' with the former not doing nearly enough to alleviate the poverty of the latter.[5] It was argued that South Africa was a microcosm of the world at large with the significant difference that the 'first world' population was more attuned to the need to redress the poverty and lack of development of the 'third world' population.

The underlying thesis is that South Africa is unique in having both first and third world components and that unique problems demand unique solutions. Although it would be admitted that poverty is a problem and that in per capita terms South Africa could not be placed in the league of the rich industrialized world, the general contention remains that South Africa, by virtue of her highly developed component, is a developed country in the Western mould.

In general, proponents of the two-world view of South Africa fail to recognize that the South African economy differs little from other third world economies (particularly those in the higher income category), in having a dominant modern industrial sector side by side with large, less productive traditional and informal sectors. In fact, according to the indicators of industrial development and economic sophistication summarized in Table 3.1, South Africa is actually worse off than selected developing countries. This may seem to run counter to casual observation, but then South Africa is unique in having apartheid which hides poverty from the affluent observer.

Table 3.1:

INDICATORS OF INDUSTRIAL DEVELOPMENT
FOR SELECTED DEVELOPING COUNTRIES, 1986

	RSA	Brazil	Mexico	S/Korea	India
Per capita GNP (US Dollars)	1 850	1 810	1 860	2 370	290
% Share of manufacturing in GDP	22	28	26	30	19
% Share of machinery and transport equipment in manufacturing	16	24	14	23	26
% Share of machinery and transport equipment in merchandise exports	3	15	18	33	10

SOURCE:
World Development Report, 1988. World Bank: OUP.

It is important to note that the first world/third world distinction is frequently presented in racial terms, where 'first world' refers to whites and 'third world' to black citizens.[6] At the risk of appearing pedantic, one must nevertheless emphasize the fallacious nature of this semantic schizophrenia. If it is accepted that a country is either (according to standard definitions) a first or a third world country, then it follows that all citizens of a country should be described accordingly. For example, Brazil is a third world country and all its people, affluent and poor, white and black, are therefore third world citizens. In fact, the large gap in levels of income between people and in development between sectors, is a key element in defining a third world country. Regarding whites in South Africa as first world and blacks as third world people is absurd and should be seen for what it is — racist and degrading.

In view of the foregoing, it is concluded that the first world/third world divide is an invalid analogy for poverty and inequality in South Africa. This is particularly so if the underlying contention is that South Africa is unique because of this alleged division.

Ramifications of South African development ideology

If the perceptions and concepts discussed above had only been interesting and eccentric elements of discourse in a country given to ostentatious semantics, no real harm would have been done. Unfortunately, these views (and the surreptitious inferences drawn from them) have had important ramifications for economic development via their influence on development models and policy.

Balkanization

The real economic effect of geographic partition for the sake of political 'separate development' becomes clear when the integrated nature of the economy is considered. Trade, capital and labour flows and infrastructure are the building blocks of South Africa's integrated economy. According to neo-classical theory, optimum development requires that each identifiable region be developed according to its comparative cost advantages, through a free flow of capital and labour in search of profitable opportunities and employment. In this context, the goal of regional policy should be to stimulate economic activity in particular areas, with due regard for comparative advantage and the overall structure of the economy.

The policy of separate development, with its ethnic homelands and governments, seeks to segregate the integrated economy for reasons which are far from economic. For instance, political analysts often argue that the homeland policy is primarily a strategy of divide-and-rule, devised to undermine the political aspirations of the black majority. Similarly, supporters of separate development often maintain that the nationalism necessary for its success can only be fostered in geographically-defined areas. For these reasons, regions (the old 'native reserves'/'bantustans'/'homelands'), which were and still are clearly not self-contained economic regions, have become elevated to 'national states'.

The transformation of regionalism into nationalism has had important results for regional development policy. One outcome has been the misplaced emphasis on industrial development in regions which lack the resources and infrastructure for sustainable industrial growth. In this respect, political expediency even prevailed over certain official economic views. In the regional industrial decentralization programme of the time, it was persuasively argued that manufacturing industry should not be the sole agent of regional development, but that development efforts should encompass all sectors. In the *Manual on the Implementation of Regional Development Incentives*, a coherent regional development strategy was seen as requiring 'the utilization of the full development potential of each region including the agricultural, mining, services and industrial sectors' (1985,

p. 12). In the 1982 White Paper on regional industrial development strategy, the need for a balanced approach to regional development was accepted:

> Regional economic development comprises far more than merely industrial development and ... the development problems facing many of the less developed states can only be addressed effectively if attention is focused primarily on the mining sector, the services sector and especially the agricultural sector (1982, p. 2).

The good intentions never materialized and at present regional development efforts are still heavily biased in favour of the attraction of modern, mainly large-scale, manufacturing establishments to selected industrial growth points. Industrial decentralization remains the thrust of regional development policy.

Cogent reasons exist for the popularity of manufacturing industry as an instrument of development. Firstly, an association between manufacturing and economic development exists to the extent that development is defined in terms of degrees of industrialization. This association, and the national independence which industry is seen to bestow on a country, have made industrialization an important ingredient of economic and political nationalism. Secondly, many manufacturing industries are not locality-bound and can therefore be influenced by policy measures to situate in specific regions. In this sense, manufacturing is an autonomous source of development that does not, like primary production, depend on the existence of natural resources. Services, again, are mainly a derived source of development which are reliant on autonomous development in other sectors. Thirdly, manufacturing is considered to be more productive in terms of value added per unit of labour and capital, and has the added advantage of transmitting or multiplying development through extensive forward and backward linkages.

The second and third reasons are usually at the heart of the preference for using manufacturing growth in regional development policy. In South Africa, however, the homeland policy converted regional economic development needs into national issues. For example, the need to develop the eastern Cape has been translated into the development of the Ciskei and Transkei as national entities. Consequently the first reason presented above took hold and industrial development became the method and measure of regional development.

The emphasis placed on national entities in South African regional development is an important reason for the proliferation of officially designated development points, since such industrial development areas had to be allocated to each homeland regardless of their ability to sustain industrial growth. The large number of points in turn is an important reason why decentralized industrial growth turned out to be less successful than originally hoped for. Another reason is the absence of a basis for sustainable growth. Employment opportunities in manufacturing, in areas where comparative cost advantages have been ignored, can often only be maintained by perpetual subsidization.

Confusing regional and national issues not only caused sectoral distortions in regional development, but have also influenced the institutional arrangements that support development policy. The existence of hard political boundaries obviously restricts the co-ordinated development of a region. Furthermore, the exclusion of the 'independent homelands' from official statistics makes it almost impossible to gain a reliable picture of the economy as a whole and thus also to plan appropriately.

Since all regions demarcated in the current regional development programme (except Region A in the western Cape) comprise more than one national entity, a complicated and rather cumbersome organizational structure has resulted. This includes the District Development Associations, Regional Development Associations, Regional Liaison Committees, Regional Development Advisory Committees, the National Regional Development Advisory Council, and the homeland Councils of Ministers and Heads of State. The whole complicated structure has done little more than produce a new and varied breed of acronyms which leaves the uninitiated bewildered. Judging by results, the system appears to have had little success in expediting regional development in South Africa's integrated (but politically balkanized) economy (Halbach, 1988a, p. 508).

The high administrative cost of the homeland system of government is a further negative result of balkanization. The standard reaction to this charge is that homeland governments are merely entrusted (in a decentralized fashion) with the provision of services which would have been catered for anyway. However, even a superficial consideration of the duplication of government functions in the homelands and the tricameral system with its departments for 'Own Affairs', plus all the trappings of government and multitudes of ministers,[7] will suffice to bring home the excessive cost of the swollen bureaucracy and political apparatus.

A final point regarding the ramifications of political balkanization concerns the restrictions which it effectively placed on the process of black urbanization and on the provision of adequate urban facilities. This aspect is discussed below as an inference of the two-world paradigm. At this point it will suffice to note that the large deviation between the geographic distribution of production and the distribution of the population (Coetzee & Ligthelm, 1986, p. 164) was exacerbated by policy aimed at developing regions as national units and restricting the mobility of black people.

The two-world paradigm

The view that South Africa is a microcosm of the first and third worlds has had a less explicit, but nevertheless profound, influence on development policy and the economic growth path. This is particularly the case where it ties in with the policy of separate development as a form of moral vindication. It would not be wholly inappropriate to regard the way in which the two-world paradigm has been appropriated as an *ex post facto* justification of, and underlying theoretical framework for, Grand Apartheid.

It is not surprising that the concepts and analytical tools of development economics have a far greater currency in South African academic and policy circles than those of regional economics. When economically backward areas and poor people are regarded as the third world in our midst, it is understandable that policy-makers respond with policy prescriptions suitable for third world problems. The fact that affluent white regions (and the policy-makers themselves) are part and parcel of the problem, escapes them. With all the best motivation in the world they set about 'uplifting' the poorer areas.

In this paradigm, poverty exists beyond the frontiers of affluence. Development workers are intellectually and financially involved in using the principles of development economics to develop the 'have-nots' (blacks) of South Africa's third world. This begs the question about the relationship between white affluence and black poverty and carries with it distinct paternalistic overtones. As Kotze *et al.* note: 'In South Africa, the concept of "development" has the meaning of government planning and caring for that part of the population that is not categorized as "white" and which allegedly cannot care for themselves' (1988, p. 17).

It is not surprising that development economics has become one of the most popular fields of study for South African students of economics. There is also a strong tendency to work 'development' into the curricula of other disciplines.[8] Obviously an emphasis on development studies in a third world country such as South Africa is to be welcomed and encouraged. Unfortunately, as the discipline has been interpreted, the concern is frequently not with poverty in an integrated third world type economy; the approach in many instances (especially within official agencies) is to view the development of South Africa's 'third world' from the perspective of its 'first world'.

Development studies, aimed at an investigation of South Africa's 'third world', have become the intellectual growth industry of the day. Apart from a few notable exceptions, a perusal of a recent listing of development agencies in South Africa points to a multitude of organizations which are located within the two-world approach, or at worst, separate development ideology proper (HSRC, 1988, pp. 94–152).

The two-world paradigm can clearly be used to support the balkanization of South Africa and to justify the conversion of regional development issues into national/political development priorities. The large number of ethnic development corporations that are active in the field of regional development all have an explicit national mission, namely to initiate and finance development efforts in respective homelands. These corporations and institutions, such as the Southern African Development Bank and the myriad of official bodies active in the field of regional development, are part of South Africa's 'first world' initiative to develop her 'third world' regions as national units.

As argued above, the content given to the first world/third world divide frequently adopts a racial form with the first world referring to whites and the third world to blacks. 'First world' efforts to develop South Africa's 'third world' therefore extend beyond the regional or national sphere, and may include all efforts that seek to enhance the material well-being of blacks, from education and training to housing.

The major outcome of the two-world paradigm has been the adoption of an inappropriate model for evaluating the economic performance of the country. The first world orientation in policy-making circles has lead to a persistent tendency to evaluate first world economic issues when searching for policy guidelines. Canadian, Australian, American and British investigative reports, for example, are standard workhorses in the field of monetary and fiscal policy. Judging by their speeches, there are few cabinet ministers who have not at some time or another compared South Africa with the developed world. Furthermore, when standards or development indicators are seen to be inadequate or underperforming, this is monotonously blamed on the existence of a 'third world' in a 'first world' environment.

Popular consciousness is further moulded along these lines by newspapers which invariably contain reports comparing South Africa with developed countries. For example, a major daily recently carried a feature article on inflation in South Africa by its Financial Editor who concluded that 'when it comes to price increases, none of the Western industrial countries can beat South Africa' (Tommey, quoted in *The Argus*, 21 January 1989, p. 3). In this apocalyptic report where price rises in South Africa were compared with those in Britain, Japan, Germany and New Zealand, the author derogatively observed that 'to find price increases comparable to those in South Africa, one has to look to the South American "Banana Republics"' (*loc. cit.*). Likewise, *Die Burger* recently argued that poor productivity and inadequate goods and services can *inter alia* be attributed to 'the country's large third world component' (15 March 1989, p. 14).

In the academic world, a northwardly bias is equally pervasive. Economists and other social scientists troop off in steady streams for sabbatical sojourns at universities in Britain, the United States and western Europe. Sometimes it is to study development problems of third world countries, but frequently it is to engross themselves in theoretical models appropriate only to first world economies.

The failure to appreciate the intrinsically third world nature of the South African economy is reflected in the debate on deregulation. In this debate, a prominent argument is that the standards and regulations used in controlling

commerce and industry are typically those that one would expect in rich industrialized countries. But when the needs and development of the country's 'third
world' component are considered, development and initiative are unnecessarily
stifled by these constructs.

The high standards are the result of a perception in government and affluent
circles that South Africa is a first world country which should behave according
to and be judged by the standards of the rich industrialized world. Unless the
orientation in thinking is changed towards an acceptance of the intrinsically
third world nature of the South African economy, all comment on this issue
will remain a huff and a puff, with little meaningful deregulation.

The two-world view of the South African economy also played a major role
in entrenching the effort to prevent the 'third world' from intruding on the
'first world'. Grand Apartheid and ethnic nationalism sought, and in important
respects still seek, to keep blacks in the homelands. However, black urbanization
proved to be a phenomenon which could not be easily contained. In the absence
of adequate provision of urban housing (another offshoot of policy based on
the perception that blacks were temporary urbanites), urbanization lead to
the proliferation of urban squatting. While the likes of squatter areas such
as Crossroads grew, the belief that South Africa could avoid the third world
bane of rapid urbanization was stubbornly maintained. In a sense, the desire to
keep the third world in its place (ideally the impoverished rural areas) could be
detected. As long as the third world could be kept 'beyond the tarmac road', the
illusion of a first world economy and society could be maintained. As regards
the accommodation of urban blacks with Section 10 rights, the 'bricks and
mortar' philosophy reigned supreme; appropriate and affordable housing was
unacceptable, amongst other reasons because it did not fit in with first world
standards.

Conclusion

The argument presented in this chapter is neither original nor all that fundamental. It is also not intended to be critical of the growing concern with
poverty and the fate of economically under-privileged people and regions in
South Africa. The purpose was merely to tell the story of ideologically motivated, skewed economic perceptions in a society whose main actors like to
think of South Africa as a developed country afflicted with a third world sector.

The central theme is that dominant perceptions in the official development
agencies and the academic community are constructed on a view of the economy which does not reflect reality. South Africa is a typical third world country
with an integrated economy. Grandiose and costly schemes which balkanize the
country and result in the 'nationalization' of regional problems are politically
reprehensible and economically misguided. As long as South Africa is regarded

as a microcosm of the first and third worlds (the most recent and subtle justification of apartheid), resources will be wasted on inappropriate development. The end result will be an increasingly divided and polarized society with a declining economy and escalating poverty.

Notes

1 This chapter was written in recognition of Jill Nattrass' life-long opposition to apartheid and the economic policies which it inspired.

2 The GDP (Gross Domestic Product) defines the level of economic activity within the borders of a country whereas the GNP (Gross National Product) quantifies income earned by all factors of production belonging to a country regardless of whether it is earned in or outside the country. The 'citizens' of homelands who work as migrants earn wages in South Africa which are included in the homeland GNP but not the GDP. Given the importance of migrant earnings, it is not surprising that the GNP of the homelands exceeds the GDP by a wide margin. A fall in the GNP:GDP ratio shows domestic economic activity is increasing relative to the importance of remittances.

3 Since 1973, the real earnings of black mineworkers have increased fourfold, following a relative constancy in these earnings since early this century (see Van der Berg, 1989 and Hofmeyr in this volume).

4 Viewing South Africa as a combination of first and third world components does not necessarily imply a right-wing political programme. The two-world paradigm is common amongst many well-meaning development workers across the ideological spectrum. The radical analysis of South Africa as a form of 'colonialism of a special type' (see Wolpe, 1988) for example, rests on a vision of South Africa as fundamentally divided between white colonizers and colonizing regions and black colonized people and regions. The two-world paradigm addressed in this chapter refers to the dominant official ideology which has shaped policy in South Africa, and to the academic ideas which have wittingly and unwittingly given it further substance.

5 The United Nations had resolved that developed countries should contribute 0,7 per cent of their GNP to the developing countries in the form of official development assistance. In 1978, the industrialized members of the OECD (Organization for Economic Co-operation and Development) contributed an average of only 0,35 per cent of GNP as official development assistance (Independent Commission on International Development Issues, 1980, p. 224). Against this background, it was easy to argue that the South African 'first world' was doing much more to assist in the development of its 'third world'.

6 According to Kotze et al., 'the reigning official development paradigm in South Africa is based on a clear-cut distinction between those who are developed/modern/civilized/Western and those who are underdeveloped/traditional/tribal/African. The distinction is rationalized in terms of cultural differences: the traditional African mode of thinking and doing is the retarding factor' (1988, p. 18).

7 Consider for example the 14 ministers of health, five ministers of defence supervising five defence forces, five state presidents and no less than nine prime ministers of sorts — that is, the leaders of the self governing states and the chairmen of the three ministers councils in the tricameral parliament.

8 In a recent survey of the state of thinking on 'development' in South Africa, 19 subject
   fields were identified, with the author making it clear that the list is not exhaustive
   but a 'first selection of disciplines which are regarded to be of immediate priority'
   (Beukes, 1987, p. 218).

References

Beukes, E.P., 'Research Needs in Respect of Development in Southern Africa, in Coetzee,
    J.K. (ed.), *Development is for People*. Southern Books: Johannesburg, 1987.

Coetzee, S. & Ligthelm, A., 'Development Profiles and Existing Strategies', in Coetzee,
    J. (ed.) *Development is for the People*, Macmillan: Johannesburg, 1986.

Halbach, A., 'The South African Homeland Policy and its Consequences: An Evaluation
    of Separate Development', in *Development Southern Africa*, vol. 5, no. 4, 1988a.

Halbach, A., *Sudafrika und Seine Homelands Strukturen und Problemen der Getrennten
    Entwicklung*, Weltforum Verlag: Munich, 1988b.

HSRC (Human Sciences Research Council), *Prodder's Development Annual*, Pretoria,
    1988.

Independent Commission on International Development Issues (Brandt Commission),
    North-South: Programme for Survival, Pan Books: London, 1980.

Kotze, J., Van der Waal, C. & Fischer, A., 'Development and Research', in *Prodder's
    Development Annual*, Human Sciences Research Council: Pretoria, 1988.

Lal, D., *The Povery of Development Economics*, Hobart Paperback no. 16, The Institute
    of Economic Affairs: London, 1983.

McCarthy, C., 'The First World-Third World Analysis of South African Economic
    Development Policy: Relevance and Implications', in *RSA 2000*, vol. 4, no. 1, 1982.

RSA., *White Paper on the Information Document about the Promotion of Industrial Develop-
    ment as an Element of a Co-ordinated Regional Development Strategy for Southern Africa*,
    Pretoria, 1982.

Secretariat for Multi-lateral Co-operation in Southern Africa. *Manual on the Implementa-
    tion of the Regional Development Incentives*, Introduced on 1 April 1982, October 1985.

Terreblanche, S., 'Suid-Afrika's se Dubbele Hoedanigheid', Unpublished paper read at
    a Day of the Covenant meeting in Cape Town, 1975.

Terreblanche, S., *Gemeenskapsarmoede — Perspektief op Chroniese Armoede in die Kleur-
    linggemeenskap na Aanleiding van die Erika Theron-Verslag*, Tafelberg Publishers:
    Cape Town, 1977.

Terreblanche, S., *Die Wording van die Westerse Ekonomie — Structurele Analise met 'n
    Toepassing op die Suid-Afrikaanse Situasie*, Academica: Cape Town, 1980.

Terreblanche, S., 'Die Interdependenz zwischen der Suidafrikanischen Wirtschaf und der
    Wirtschaftlichen Entwicklung in Afrika und der Westlichen Welt', Unpublished pa-
    per read at a seminar for economic journalists, Boppard, Federal Republic of Germany,
    January 1982.

Van Der Berg, S., 'Long Term Economic Trends and Development Prospects in South
    Africa', *African Affairs*, April 1989.

Wolpe, H., *Race, Class and the Apartheid State*, UNESCO: Paris, 1988.

World Bank, *World Development Report*, Oxford University Press: New York, 1988.

Towards an understanding of bantustan politics

4

Johann Graaff

Introduction [1]

The somewhat comical events which made up the Bophuthatswana coup and counter-coup on Wednesday, 10 February 1988, provided the opportunity for numerous academics, reporters and politicians to parade similarly comic theories about what had happened. The government mouthpiece in the Cape, *Die Burger*, reported that the ANC was probably involved in the failed coup. For Professor Mike Hough from Pretoria University the coup was a huge surprise. Bophuthatswana had, after all, been seen as a model homeland. Nevertheless, he observed, military coups were a quite widespread phenomenon in Africa, although they had not occurred in South Africa before. (He had apparently forgotten the four previous coups and attempted coups in the Ciskei and Transkei). Brian Pottinger of the *Sunday Times* put it well:

> The standard response from many white South Africans is simply to shrug shoulders and say 'that's Africa' — the suggestion being that there is something inherent in the people of the continent that tends to corruption, incompetence and instability... Since the Second World War, after all, there have been 71 coups in Africa. The Transkei contributed merely another two and Bophuthatswana an attempted 74th (*Sunday Times*, 21 February 1988).

Two days later Pik Botha, Minister of Foreign Affairs, was at great pains to explain the differences between the Transkei coup (which Pretoria probably knew about, but did not interfere with) and the Bophuthatswana coup (which they did not know about, but did interfere with). 'The most important factor is that the Transkei government did not ask us for assistance — they did not even inform us' (*Cape Times*, 12 February 1988).

For some members of the South African police, military and intelligence, the surprise was more unpleasant. 'Widespread "backside-kicking" was apparently taking place in at least one intelligence-gathering organization as a result of its analysts' failure to forecast the rebel action' (*Cape Times*, 12 February 1988).

For more critical commentators, on the other hand, the event was viewed with quite evident pleasure. 'No longer is it possible to pretend there is more than a bogus independence in the "independent" states', said the *Sunday Tri-bune*. 'However naïve the perpetrators of the coup may have been in expecting any sort of sympathy or co-operation from the puppet master of Bophuthatswana, at least their actions revealed the extent of the puppeteer's mastery' (14 February 1988). The *Weekly Mail* noted P W Botha's 'tell-tale slip': 'We are tonight back in full control.' He hastily added: 'The president of Bophuthatswana is in full control' (12 February 1988).

For Professor Keenan of Wits University, there was something much more conspiratorial to Pretoria's intervention. They feared that much worse corruption would be revealed. President Mangope had 'played a major role in the anti-sanctions lobby abroad and been a charismatic defender of the homelands policy, which suited the South Africa government perfectly' (*Sunday Tribune*, 14 February 1988).

This chapter argues that both the conservative and radical kinds of theory illustrated here need to be sharply reassessed.

For a start, there are important reasons for saying that bantustan[2] leaders are not puppets in the sense used above. Nor does everything they do 'suit the South Africa government perfectly'. There is much about the bantustans which is both surprising and embarrassing to the South African Government. Contrary to much radical theory, the interests of bantustan leaders are in important ways at odds with those of Pretoria and South African capital in general. Bantustans are themselves capitalist state-type institutions (despite their history of extreme powerlessness and vulnerability to intervention) with particular interests and a monopoly of the means of violence and of taxation. Their state institutions suffer from a serious legitimacy crisis which drives their incumbents to ugly methods of survival and their class origins make them wholly dependent on the state for capital accumulation. They have for a considerable time been starved of financial aid. Their position on a tightrope between Pretoria and their voters periodically calls for public stances which are hostile to Pretoria. They have, in short, both the motives and the means to be thoroughly recalcitrant at times.

Whereas radicals may see bantustan leaders as puppets of Pretoria or South African capital, conservative theories portray them as caught in the chains of 'African' tradition. These culturalist theories of politics are intuitively attractive but are so flawed by problems of definition and formulation that they remain ineffectual. In the hands of some writers they also serve ideological ends in softening the moral opprobrium directed at apartheid.

Bantustans — dependent and stagnant states?

For some time Frankian dependency theory has both explicitly and implicitly been the basis of the view of bantustans as puppets of the South African regime. It started with Colin Bundy in 1972 whose debt to André Gunder Frank was quite explicit.[3] Writing about late nineteenth and early twentieth century South Africa, Bundy argued that, contrary to popular and academic liberal belief about black entrepreneurial ability, a substantial number of black peasants did very well as commercial farmers in the eastern Cape. The impact of industrial development on the Reef was to eliminate such farmers (since the mines needed labour), and to hold the reserves in a position of economic stagnation. This theme was carried forward by numerous writers in the 1970s, among them the contributors to Palmer & Parsons's reader, *The Roots of Rural Poverty in Central and Southern Africa* (1977).

For dependency writers of this period, the way out of underdevelopment lay in policies of self-reliant or autocentric development. Hence the notion that the reserves ought to develop an independent 'autocentric' momentum. One of Roger Southall's main points of critique against the bantustan system, for example, is that:

> there is little opportunity of Transkeian entrepreneurs embarking upon a path of autonomous industrial development... the pattern and structure of the industrial programme have done little to decrease Transkei's dependence upon the white economy, and would seem to have little capacity for encouraging self-sustaining development in the future (Southall, 1982, p. 240).

In the dependency framework, alongside the economic ideas of stagnation and dependence is that of tight control at the political level. Whether comprador, nationalist or populist, third world ruling classes were inevitably 'captured' by foreign capital or transnational corporations. Post-colonial ruling classes were both unable and unwilling to oppose the interests of the metropolitan bourgeoisie. Translated into South African terms, bantustan leaders became puppets, 'paid functionaries', 'camp commandants of the bantustan labour camps' etc.[4] In a certain ineluctable way, the insidious contagion of apartheid infected those in contact with it, and left them, much like Dracula's victims, drained of moral fibre and the will to resist.

Much has happened in the 1980s in the bantustan states to shake up older dependency notions of stagnation and the captured bourgeoisie. For a start, bantustan analysts have noted significant nodes of economic growth arising at selected spots both within and on the borders of bantustans. However isolated, exploitative, non-generative or dependent on incentives these might be, we need today to take account of places like Isithebe, Pietersburg-Seshego, Dimbaza, the Natal Midlands etc. (Tomlinson & Addleson, 1987).

More significant to the argument of this chapter, however, have been developments at a political level. For a ruling class which is supposed to be captured and bound hand and foot, bantustan leaders have exhibited a cavalier disregard for their puppet-masters. Bophuthatswana and Transkei have shared the distinction of being both financially bankrupt and wracked by military coups. Ciskei has had attempted coups and has abolished company tax.

The considerable differences between individual bantustan responses indicate the inadequacy of simple determinist explanations. What is needed is a theory of bantustan politics in general, and of the bantustan state in particular.

To this end this chapter touches on various debates in Marxist theory. These include the question of the 'relative autonomy' of the state from its economic base and the relationship of the state to class relations. Such issues acquire special interest in third world situations where the indigenous bourgeoisie have often been seen as 'captured' by the metropolitan or foreign bourgeoisie.

Alternative Marxist theories of the state

The state in developed countries

The relationship between the state and the capitalist class has been a hotly debated issue in Marxist theory. Some early Marxist writers conceived of the state as doing little more than performing certain useful functions for the capitalist system (a functionalist notion), or alternatively, as acting in the name, if not at the behest of, the dominant class or class fractions (an instrumentalist notion). This latter notion of the state is often thought to be well expressed by Marx and Engels: 'The executive of the modern state is but a committee for managing the common affairs of the whole bourgeoisie' (quoted in Gulalp, 1987, p. 289).

Later Marxist writers have been concerned to break out of these functionalist and instrumentalist straitjackets for the state. Thus Poulantzas argued for the idea of the state as a site of struggle between fractions of the dominant classes. 'The State's autonomy ... is concretely manifested in the diverse contradictory measures that each of these classes and fractions, through its specific presence in the State and the resulting play of contradictions, manages to have integrated into State policy' (quoted in Gulalp, 1987, p. 295).

Miliband, in an important contribution to the debate, specified the mechanisms and structural constraints of the state's autonomy. He wrote:

> ... an accurate and realistic 'model' of the relationship between the dominant class in advanced capitalist societies and the State is one of the partnership between two different, separate forces, linked to each other by many threads, yet each having its own separate spheres of concern' (quoted in Gulalp, 1987, p. 300).

Theories of the post-colonial state

Theorizing about the relative autonomy of the state has overflowed into third world political writing. There has, in consequence, been considerable debate on the 'post-colonial state' among writers like Alavi (1972), Beckman (1980, 1981, 1982), Leys (1976, 1978), Saul (1979), Samoff (1983), and von Freyhold (1976), to name but the most influential. Much of the Marxist writing is premised upon a view of the state as 'captured', 'instrumentalist' or 'functionalist'. There are however a number of important principles which liberate notions of the state from these crude premises. These will be dealt with in the following paragraphs.

Basic to a Marxist conception of the capitalist state is, to use Giddens' term, the extrusion of coercion from the labour contract. The legal and constitutional protection of individual rights means that a capitalist employer, unlike a feudal lord, has no claim over the personal life of his employee. It is the state which is concerned with 'maintaining law and order' under capitalism. The right to physical coercion, that is, 'the monopoly of the means of violence', rests with state institutions — the police, the army, the security forces and the courts. In short the capitalist state, by virtue of being capitalist, acquires substantial independent power via its monopoly of the means of legal violence and of taxation. In the modern, industrial, capitalist state, the means of violence, surveillance, and control, have been exponentially expanded by the state's capacity for collecting and storing information on, and monitoring the behaviour of its citizens (Giddens, 1981). In a capitalist system we are dealing with a state institution which has quite different resources, in both quality and quantity, from governing institutions in feudal or tribal systems.

If the state has its own resources, it also has its own interests and concerns which distinguish it from other ruling classes. Nevertheless, state interests should not be seen to differ too widely from those of the ruling classes. In their concern to remain in power, it is in the interest of state managers to ensure 'developmental' conditions for the expansion of capital in general. Different sets of state managers may pursue these ends in different ways, but in the end they are bound by what Alavi (1972) calls a 'structural imperative'. In concrete terms this might mean a concern for the development of infrastructure, education, health, energy, transport etc. The strength of the state depends, after all, on the strength of the economy. State managers must in their own interests work for economic growth.

As a result, the self-interest of state managers tends to converge with the interests of the capitalist class. Miliband described this relationship as a 'partnership' with the bourgeois classes; 'two different, separate forces, linked to each other by many threads, yet each having its own separate spheres of concern' (quoted in Gulalp, 1987).

A strong assumption underlying much writing on the post-colonial state is that the state and foreign bourgeoisie are of necessity in conflict, which is why the state needs to be 'captured'. This assumption is not correct. As Beckman writes of Nigeria:

> ... the Nigerian state is not a comprador state in the sense that it is primarily an agent of social forces external to the society. **These forces have been internalized**. Nor is it a 'national' state in the sense of being a carrier of national resistance to foreign domination. The relations of domination originating from outside **have been built into the fabric of domestic class relations** (Beckman, 1982, p. 50; my own emphasis).

Given the presence of a number of contending classes in the arena, there is also the possibility of shifting alliances and conflicts between them. In this situation, says Alavi (1972), the state is able to play an independent and mediating role in the conflicts between other classes.

What is also important about the post-colonial state however, is that the ruling classes are dependent on that state for their access to power and wealth. In consequence, they do not 'capture' the state from a position of power outside of it. The accumulation of resources on their part is almost completely dependent on their control of state institutions. In fact, they more often move from state positions to capture resources outside of it. In these circumstances, Sandbrook says, 'class relations ... are determined by relations of power, not production' (Sandbrook, 1985, p. 72).

The post-colonial state in Africa

There are in addition certain features of the post-colonial state in Africa which should be taken into account. African polities are artificial entities in a number of ways (Sandbrook, 1985). Colonial rule set ethnic groups against each other and operated for the most part by authoritarian methods. There is very little tradition of constitutional government. Development has been confined to urban enclaves, leaving the country not proletarianized, but peasantized. It has eroded the authority of traditional leaders. The moral authority of government leaders does not stretch very far into the countryside.

These circumstances all lead to critical steps being taken on the road to authoritarian and corrupt patron-client rule by individual strongmen, or what Sandbrook (1985) calls 'neo-patrimonialism'. Deprived of the usual economic and normative foundations on which first world leaders build their rule, and consequently driven by insecurity, third world and particularly African leaders must resort to other means.

Ensuring compliance and loyalty among citizens and bureaucrats in these circumstances becomes a matter of force, patronage, paranoia, nepotism, clientelism, bribery, personality cults and delivering tangible developmental benefits.

Where government funds are scarce, even development and bribery become more difficult. What remains are the ingredients for a particularly unlovely governmental form (Sandbrook, 1985).

Conclusion

In contrast to earlier Marxist views, it has been argued that the capitalist state as an institution is not necessarily in service of either the ruling classes (the instrumentalist view) or the economic system (the functionalist view). State managers have different interests and resources from those of the private sector. They control the means of coercion and of taxation. Their concern, and a very varied concern it is, is for the economy as a whole, rather than for individual interest groups. That does not mean they can do as they like. Not only do their interests **tend** to overlap with those of the ruling classes in general, but there is significant power exercised on them by the ruling classes.

This picture of the capitalist state is significantly modified by African conditions. African governments do not have the usual means of ensuring loyalty and compliance among their followers. Moreover, state incumbents are very dependent on their positions for gaining access to wealth. All this makes it extremely difficult for them to contemplate giving up power. So they end up using authoritarian and corrupt methods to retain power.

Bantustans as state-type organizations?

In the attempt to develop a theory of bantustan politics and the bantustan state, the question that needs to be asked is whether there is any conceptual advantage to be gained by seeing bantustans as capitalist states or state-type institutions. Is insight into bantustan government actions gained by viewing their resources and interests as similar to those of other post-colonial capitalist states, or should they be regarded as nothing more than beefed-up Tribal Councils or Black Local Authorities? (Mangope for Mayor!)

Monopoly control of violence and taxation

Bantustans enjoy a legal monopoly over the means of violence within their designated territorial spheres. The military-security apparatus handed over at 'independence' was by no stretch of the imagination overdeveloped. Pretoria had not built up armies or police forces for each bantustan area. However bantustan leaders have put considerable effort into developing their own military-security apparatuses with the help of Pretoria, ex-Rhodesians and Israelis. Where these have been seen as inadequate, bantustans have in one or two cases resorted to vigilante organizations.

Although bantustans have no control over money supply, exchange rates, interest rates etc., and have no central or reserve bank, they do enjoy a monopoly of taxation, which entails control over amounts (in 1986/7) ranging from R493 million in the case of the Ciskei to R1 052 million in the case of the Transkei.[5] This implies a concern not only for the collection of tax income, but also the nurturing of tax bases. In three bantustans this involves a considerable interest in, and co-operation with, the tourist-casino business — an interesting division of labour between Pretoria and the bantustans. It further means a concern for the complicated formulae by which Pretoria's Customs Union contributions to the bantustans are calculated, as well as the funding prescriptions of the World Bank-lookalike, the Development Bank of South Africa (DBSA). In Bophuthatswana's case there is also concern for the price of platinum.

In all, budgetary resources and concerns are quite similar to other post-colonial states.

However, to this must be added a strong **colonial** element in the funding provided directly by Pretoria under the head of 'statutory agreements'. This source of funding was intended to cover the money central government and provincial administrations had spent in maintaining services in the year of independence. The amount grew extremely slowly until 1985/6, and inflation was not taken into account in calculating the amount from year to year. More important than the arbitrary and cynical nature of this formula is the fact that bantustan governments, starved of funds to maintain basic services, have resorted to private sector loans. This has been relatively easy since Pretoria stands surety for these loans.

The irony of the situation is that **pre-colonial** financial arrangements have resulted in **post-colonial** debt-crisis situations. In 1984/5 government debt of the four 'independent' bantustans had risen to R1,4 billion.

A poverty of legitimacy

Bantustan leaders operate on a very fragile legitimacy base. Unlike many post-colonial African leaders, none have emerged from pre-existing political movements with grassroots bases. In fact, the aim of creating bantustans was precisely to bypass the existing black political movements like the ANC. The ideal of 'orderly progress to independence', so prized by National Party politicians, is exactly the condition which has deprived bantustan polities of political coherence.

Most bantustan leaders have risen and are dependent for support from traditional authority systems which have been seriously undermined by incorporation into Pretoria's administrative grid. Chiefs and headmen have been arbitrarily appointed or replaced on the grounds of their compliance with Pretoria's policies. They are, in important respects, paid functionaries stripped of any meaningful administrative power. Although this may be too simplified a view, bantustan leaders are, and have a right to be, anxious about their political support-base.

State incumbent or petite bourgeoisie?

Another important question in theorizing bantustan politics is the relationship of the bantustan leaders to the means of production, or their class position. Charney (1988) argues that the South African black urban (non-bantustan) elite displays the traits of a typical Poulantzian petite bourgeoisie, oscillating between the working and ruling classes, now supporting Black Consciousness ideologies, now the ANC.[6] They are unreliable, fissiparous, co-optible and compromised. Mare & Hamilton (1987) also describe the Inkatha superstructure as petit bourgeois, aspiring to bourgeois status. But that is far too simple.

Shula Marks's analysis of the 'ambiguities of dependence' (Marks, 1986) explains more accurately ideological shifts among black elites. She argues that, whether they are traditional authorities, christianized petite bourgeoisie, or trade union organizers, the position of South African black elites is fraught with multiple ambiguities that have to do with blackness (Biko's 'two-faced' blacks), nationalism, the survival of traditional authority in an urban context, and the position of administrators caught between white rulers and black voters.

The relationship of the bantustan leaders to the means of production is crucially mediated by, and secondary to, their access to state positions. Put more simply, even when they have traditional origins, most bantustan leaders originally had very little economic base beyond their ownership of cattle and sheep. Most other incumbents have been professionals, teachers, clerks, at most traders. Their access to wealth, such as commercial farming land, trading concerns, directorships, and housing has been very dependent on their control of political power.

The opportunities for robust development of a South African black bourgeoisie are to be found outside the bantustans in the metropolitan and large urban areas. Urban concentrations, which are something more than dormitory areas, are a very recent phenomenon inside bantustans. There seems to be little chance that the bourgeoisie which has been able (belatedly) to grow in non-bantustan urban areas will feed back into bantustan politics and development. The crystallization of bourgeois classes has, contrary to the apparent intention of official policy, been smothered inside bantustans.

In this situation, a very recognizable neo-patrimonialist pattern of insecure and authoritarian post-colonial government follows. The management of the state cannot be put up for competition in democratic elections. It becomes, in fact, both downright dangerous and unprofitable to be in opposition. Compliance with government rule must be ensured by patronage, nepotism, bribery, emergency regulations, developmental benefits and force. Development funds are either quite scarce or determined by DBSA criteria. This decreases opportunities for both development and bribery. Much like other post-colonial governments of the neo-patrimonialist variety, bantustan governments must rely on ugly methods of survival.

Bantustan leaders are, as a result, very vulnerable and very sensitive to threats to their legitimacy. Anti-Pretoria rhetoric on issues like territorial consolidation, the addition of extra land, population resettlement, South African citizenship for bantustan residents and financing should not be seen as an opportunistic and transparent ploy to improve their images both internally and internationally. While they are clearly dependent for their very existence as leaders on the maintenance of the bantustans, their status as leaders is very seriously threatened by the way in which Pretoria manages and manipulates them. They are a bit like abandoned sailors paddling furiously to keep a very leaky boat afloat. They cannot abandon the boat. But they can be extremely bitter at how many holes there are in it.[7]

With such poorly crystallized classes, and in the absence of any 'independence' struggle, political parties tend to lie in the shadow of prominent personalities rather than follow policy differences. For example, almost all political parties supported taking bantustan 'independence' in the beginning (Trevisan, 1984, p. 116). They are powerless, listless organizations operating as an extension of, and justification for, what happens in government offices.

> The reality is that the decisions are taken by the leader who at most has to obtain the consensus of the political elite. Such consensus is generally not difficult to obtain given the almost total inexistence (sic) of organized political opposition in the bantustans (Trevisan, 1984, p. 129).

From this perspective it is easier to understand why bantustan leaders find the prospect of international recognition so irresistible. It offers the chance of breaking out of Pretoria's stranglehold, at least in a financial sense. It also offers prestige.

What keeps this chimera alive is a string of thoroughly dishonest uhuru-hoppers[8] who pretend to sell both international recognition and finance. Bophuthatswana's famous uhuru-hopper, Shabtai Kalmanovitz, appears to have convinced Pretoria and Sol Kerzner as well as Mangope of the value of his wares. *Africa Confidential* (vols. 27–9) seems convinced that Bophuthatswana has attained added importance over other bantustans by providing a conduit through which sanctions-busting and casino negotiations might more easily be pursued. Hence Pretoria's overkill reaction to the wobbly coup attempt in Mmabatho. Mangope is more than just the golden boy of bantustan development, and this might give him a significant bargaining resource against Pretoria.

Bantustans as black local authorities?

Why go to the trouble of dragging out Marxist theories of the state when local government models would suffice? That would, if nothing else, diminish the dignity of bantustans by writing them down/off as glorified Black Local Authorities.

This section examines the alternative of viewing bantustans simply as beefed-up local authorities. This is, after all, exactly what they were after military defeat by colonial powers in the nineteenth century. The Glen Grey Act of 1894 established a system of elected councils in the Ciskei which was gradually extended throughout the Transkei, and eventually became the United Transkeian Territorial General Council (the Bunga). The explicit aim of this system was to strip traditional chiefs of their tributary, judicial, tax and state (ability to declare war) powers. A grid of 26 magistrates was put in place to bypass the chief and to administer the territory through village headmen. Councils and the over-arching Bunga, in which chiefs sat, had little more than advisory powers and negligible budgets (Hammond Tooke, 1975; Carter *et al.*, 1967).

The Black Authorities Act of 1951 brought the chief back into the administrative network and restored some of his traditional powers but at the same time subjected his legitimacy to contamination by association with the apartheid system. There are many instances of chiefs being deposed and replaced with individuals who enjoyed no hereditary claim to authority. In 1959 the Promotion of Bantu Self-government Act instituted Territorial Authorities with legislative assemblies dominated by a majority of nominated chiefs. This majority has frequently been useful to counter the effect of election defeats for incumbents. These Territorial Authorities rapidly accumulated administrative powers during the 1960s and 1970s. In the late 1970s and early 1980s, four Territorial Authorities acquired the additional trappings of 'statehood'.

This well-known history is repeated here to emphasize two points. First, it is often said (on the basis of these facts) that chiefs enjoy minimal political legitimacy, and that a political and administrative system built on this base must be exceedingly wobbly. That conclusion is too easy.

There is no doubt that a great many chiefs in both independent and self-governing bantustans are corrupt, lazy, indigent, impecunious, powerless, discredited, and deeply resented by their people. On the other hand, there are many instances of chiefs being at the centre of resistance to the ravages of separate development. The resistance to pass laws, Bantu Authorities and land conservation in the late 1950s (in Pondoland, Zeerust and Sekhukhuneland) all centred round chiefs (Lodge, 1983, ch. 11). Resistance to population resettlement in the 1970s and 1980s at, to name just a few places in the western Transvaal, Magopa, Mathopestad, Leeuwfontein, and Braklaagte, has likewise integrally involved chiefs. At other places chiefs have regained power by access to alternative financial resources like platinum royalties in the Pilanesberg area, land rentals in expanding peri-urban areas, commercial farming, trading licences etc. Zulu chieftainship has in places assumed the mantle of Inkatha warlord. Nor have chiefs been tightly encapsulated into rural areas. They have co-operated and allied themselves with trade unions and mass democratic organizations (Marks, 1986).

The institution of chieftaincy has in significant degree adapted to changing circumstance, acquired urban trappings, and responded to new needs. Inkatha may be the beneficiary of state repression, but it is a good example of a reinvigorated, adapted traditional institution. The massive spread of informal settlements on metropolitan fringes has immensely extended that adaptive process. It should not be assumed that chiefs automatically support bantustan governments. Chieftainship, whether we still care to call it traditional or not, is far too ambiguous a force to dismiss as devoid of political legitimacy.

Beinart (1985, p. 97) makes a stronger point. Chiefs, both as leaders and symbols of popular resistance to white rule, exercised a significant constraint on white power. 'Certainly', he says, 'capital and state... had only limited power to shape social relationships in those areas which were left under African occupation.' Even in the pre-independence period it is too facile to speak of puppets.

Another point is that over a period of 15 years the administrative and political structure of bantustans has changed radically from a penniless advisory council system occupying itself with nothing weightier than cattle-dipping and fencing, to an institution imbued with a fully differentiated state bureaucratic-military machinery, budgetary resources upwards of R1 billion to back it up, and concerns and anxieties ranging from foreign affairs to winning elections. The implications of statehood could not be more starkly illustrated. Bantustan structures cannot be dismissed as glorified Black Local Authorities. A theory of the state is required.

Disentangling state and nation-state

A great deal of confusion in thinking about bantustans derives from the criteria used for defining what an 'independent' state is. A 'proper' state is required to have a high level of discreteness and sovereignty *vis-à-vis* other states. Zimbabwe is a country with clearly delineated boundaries which unambiguously separate it from its surrounding neighbours. Within its borders it exercises unquestioned authority and control.

This is what is frequently held to be wrong with bantustans as states. They are impossibly fragmented geographically. Their territorial boundaries are extraordinarily porous, because substantial parts of their 'citizenry' spend more time outside their boundaries than inside. In fact, the activities of Pretoria's administration are usually more relevant and more pressing to their day-to-day lives than are those of Mmabatho or Umtata. Conversely the ties between a Mmabatho or a Bisho and Pretoria are so dense and powerful that it is difficult to discern any embryonic sovereignty or independence.

This approach to bantustans confuses the ideas of state and nation-state and makes the notion of nation-state do too much work as a unit of analysis.

A different metaphor is required. The focus on countries as discrete territorial units needs to be replaced by the concept of nodes in a regional network. Such nodes, which might consist of cities, transnational companies, regions or continents, are connected to each other by multiple strands. These networks are layered onto each other, separable only by analytical crystallization.[9]

This image has advantages for analysis of bantustans. It focuses on states as institutions, anchored at a particular geographical location, spreading their tentacles outwards as far as they can both within and beyond their designated territorial limits. Their control might not effectively cover their whole territory. On the other hand they might have tighter bonds with nodes outside of those boundaries than with remote parts inside them.

It is obvious, for example, that the interaction between the Odi/Moretele regions of Bophuthatswana and the Pretoria-Witwatersrand-Vereeniging (PWV) complex is far more dense and powerful than that with their political capital, Mmabatho. Conversely, the links between Mmabatho and Pretoria are far stronger than those between Mmabatho and Thaba'Nchu.

With the notion of a state institution as a power-node with a network which transcends territorial boundaries, the idea of bantustan leaders as state managers can be retained, while that of bantustans as nation states is abandoned. Bantustans have state institutions. They are not nation states. It is more helpful from this view to speak of Bisho's relations with Pretoria than of Ciskei's relations with South Africa.

This conceptual shift avoids the moral dilemma of radical writers (Innes & O'Meara, 1976). They do not wish to have their theories seen to imply that they 'accept the South African regime's own definition that the independent bantustans are in fact states, and thus (albeit unintentionally) serve to legitimize state ideology and, more importantly, the fragmentation of the Republic into its white core and black peripheral "states" (with all the oppressive consequences that go with that)' (Southall, 1982, p. 9).

Radical writers need not tie themselves into knots about bantustan independence and separateness at all. It is a non-issue.

Bantustan leaders as children of Africa: the role of culture

The picture thusfar drawn of the way in which bantustan governments work could be called a structural one. It picks out the situational constraints and inducements on people to act in a certain way as the salient ones. It says, crudely, put people in similar contexts and they will act in similar ways.

There is, however, a powerful stream of conservative writing which questions this view. Such writers focus attention on culture instead of structure in explaining political behaviour. They say, for example, that individuals are socialized into a universe of subjective values, symbols, beliefs, or norms which define the context within which political structures operate. This subjective realm has an important impact on the objective behaviour of political actors. Relevant in this regard are people's attitudes to trust, hierarchy, liberty and community loyalty (Jeppe, 1988).

Translated into African terms, these writers argue that 'Western' constitutional arrangements are incompatible with African culture. This explains why governments have been so unstable in Africa, and democracy so rare. Political institutions should be closer to 'traditional' African patterns of government.

> The concept of an institutionalized opposition is altogether incomprehensible and irreconcilable with the social (kinship and communal) values as well as the hereditary principles and religious values about leadership (Jeppe, 1988, p. 10).

> 'The typical dominant one-party or no-party political system of Africa is a further political characteristic which conforms with indigenous political culture...' (Jeppe, 1988, p. 21).

In formal language, this theory says that culture is the prime determinant of both political behaviour and political structure. It is not structure which determines culture (Almond & Verba, 1980).

This type of analysis lies easily alongside an emphasis on the importance of ethnicity in political life, and has often been used to justify the existence of separate ethnic bantustans to cope with inter-racial conflict in South Africa (Carter, Karis & Stultz, 1967). In popular terms these ideas can shade into simple racism. 'Give Africans political power and you get Idi Amin'.

No social scientists worth their salt would deny that culture is an important element in social and political life. However the 'culture-determines-structure' thesis as posed above is, even on its own terms, full of holes. Firstly, there is no single African political culture. African polities, for example, range from the militarized and highly stratified kingdom of Shaka Zulu based on kinship groups and age-cohorts, to the acephalous, weakly stratified communities of central Nigeria.

Secondly, African political leaders often have very untraditional origins. They have been brought up and educated in elite urban, even metropolitan, environments. To say that their constituents are rural people, and that the leaders are therefore 'forced to accommodate Afrocentric political values and processes' (Jeppe, 1988, p. 21) is to disguise a structuralist argument as a cultural one. Urban and urbanized politicians respond to traditionalism out of necessity and constraint, not from the strength of their own traditional values.

Not all cultural theorists are necessarily conservative. For example, Charney (1987) comes to a culturalist conclusion by, as in most of his writings, a Poulantzian route. In many African societies, he says, political activity is expressed in tribal language ('lineage-type discourse') and clientelist behaviour. That is because exchange relations (the capitalist mode of production) have not completely displaced the lineage mode of production; the typically-capitalist separation between economic and political instances has **not** been totally carried through. In these circumstances the ruling class utilizes tribal language to legitimize the state and disguise exploitation.

That is a highly functionalist view of culture and discourse. And what is to be made of this kind of language and behaviour in an urban context? Have exchange relations not yet penetrated into factories and townships, particularly in a South African context where pre-capitalist formations have been virtually eliminated? More importantly, does the use of tribal language indicate tribal structures? Laclau suggests a far more acceptable interpretation when he refers to rural 'symbols and ideological values' which migrants bring with them to the city.

Superficially this would appear to be the survival of old elements, but in reality, behind this survival is concealed a transformation: these rural elements are simply raw material which the ideological practice of the new migrant transforms in order to express new antagonisms. In this sense, *the persistence of certain ideological elements can express exactly the opposite of traditionalism: a refusal to accept capitalist legality*' (quoted in Marks, 1986, p. 113; my emphasis).

Conclusion

Elsewhere I have argued that 'independent' bantustans need to be seen in a quite different light from 'self-governing' ones (Graaff, 1984). The granting of 'independence' shifted the control conduit from the old, 'verkrampte' Department of (then) Plural Affairs/ Corporation for Economic Development (CED) combination to the 'verligte' Department of Foreign Affairs/ DBSA. That move represented a transfer of control from the right wing to the left wing of the Nationalist Party, a significant shift. It also meant freedom of access to the private sector, particularly to Sol Kerzner's tourist industry, and in Bophuthatswana's case, to income from JCI's and Gencor's platinum groups and a variety of light industries located to the north of Pretoria.

With this backing, Bophuthatswana was able to bypass restrictions laid down by the ultra-conservative white mineworkers' union, the western Transvaal farming lobby, the Dutch Reformed Church etc., and introduce both casinos and significant changes in the apartheid structure. They could, for example, abolish Group Areas, integrate schools, write a Bill of Rights into the constitution (for what that is worth today) and introduce a non-racial apprenticeship training system (*cf.* also Hirsch, 1987, on the Ciskei).

This view of 'independent Bantustans' attempted to go beyond the functionalist and instrumentalist writing about bantustans which had prevailed until then. It was pointed out that, while control from Pretoria undoubtedly existed, the stringency of that control varied considerably across different areas. It was tightest in areas like defence, security, and the mass media (Bop. TV). It was much looser in areas like education, agricultural and urban development. (Since the revelations about corruption and inefficiency, control is today far tighter in developmental areas). But that view remained functionalist since the Bophuthatswana state acquired its capacity for change through an alliance with one fraction of the South African state.

That view needs to be supplemented by a perspective which takes into account the resources, interests and anxieties which go into administering a post-colonial capitalist state with an extremely fragile legitimacy basis and significant colonial elements. There is a serious danger that bantustan leaders will be dismissed as mirror-images of a corrupt, immoral, authoritarian and contagious apartheid regime. 'What else would one expect from puppets?'

Bantustan leaders' activities need to be understood within the context of other kinds of structural constraints. The incumbents of bantustan 'governments' have been placed, however artificially or cynically, in a situation where they are structurally constrained to behave as if they were managers of recognizable capitalist states. This is, to some degree, what Pretoria intended, and their plan has succeeded. There is, however, a great deal happening which they neither intended nor foresaw.

Notes

1 I am indebted to Doreen Atkinson, Willie Breytenbach and Francine de Clercq for extremely helpful comment on earlier drafts of this paper.

2 Terminological note: I use the word 'bantustan' throughout to indicate a moral position. I reject the moral and analytical wrapping of official terminology, such as 'national states'. The term 'homeland' is problematic since for a great many people, bantustans are places to which they have been moved by force, or from which they have been prevented from moving. These places can only by a strenuous effort of the imagination be called home–lands.

3 In his 1977 article Bundy saw white Transkeian traders as 'the most important single agents of economic change, the influential envoys of the advanced economy... Trader and peasant enacted in microcosm the adverse terms of trade of a colonial relationship.' (Bundy, 1977, p. 213).

4 *cf.* Innes & O'Meara, 1976; Molteno, 1977. Southall (1982) talks, *inter alia*, of Transkei's leaders being bound hand and foot.

5 The following section draws heavily on an unpublished *mimeo* by David Bridgmann. He provided invaluable help in the initial formulation of this chapter.

6 That appears to be a very economistic interpretation, even of Poulantzas. Wolpe (1988) argues that, for Poulantzas, relationship to the means of production is a very 'abstract' determination of class, and that the 'concrete' content of class action will be determined by practice, discourse and organization.

7 During the independence run up, Mangope had the following to say about Pretoria's treatment of him. 'We ... have recently experienced the full blast of ... painful humiliation and disillusionment ... it is the question mark about the motives of the ... Government which is trying to trick us into an independence which smells of fraud' (Trevisan, 1984, p. 151).

8 'Uhuru-hopper' is a term coined, as far as I know, in the bantustans, to describe the dishonest types who hop from one newly independent country to another exploiting the naïvety of inexperienced leaders.

9 This, and much of the following discussion, is drawn from Giddens's (1981) discussion of 'time-space edges' as opposed to sociological units of analysis. He strongly emphasizes the state/nation-state distinction, as well as the important role which cities, as power-containers, played in the evolution of modern capitalist states.

References

Alavi, H., ' The State in Post-colonial Societies — Pakhistan and Bangladesh', *New Left Review*, vol. 74, 1972.

Almond, G. & Verba, S., *The Civic Culture Revisited*, Little, Brown & Co.: Boston, 1980.

Beckman, B., 'Imperialism and Capitalist Transformation: Critique of a Kenyan Debate', *Review of African Political Economy*, no. 19, 1980.

Beckman, B., 'Imperialism and the "National Bourgeoisie" ', *Review of African Political Economy*, vol. 22, 1981.

Beckman, B., ' Whose State? State and Capitalist Development in Nigeria', *Review of African Political Economy*, vol. 23, 1982.

Beinart, W., 'Chieftaincy and the Concept of Articulation: South Africa ca. 1900–50', *Canadian Journal of African Affairs* vol. 19, no. 1, 1980.

Bundy, C., 'The Emergence and Decline of a South African Peasantry', *African Affairs*, vol. 71, no. 285, 1972.

Bundy, C., 'The Transkei Peasantry c. 1890–1914: "Passing through a Period of Stress" ', in Palmer, R. & Parsons, L., *The Roots of Poverty in Central and Southern Africa*, UCLA Press: Berkeley, 1977.

Carter, G., Karis, T. & Stultz, N., *South Africa's Transkei: The Politics of Domestic Colonialism*, North Western University Press: Evanston, 1967.

Charney, C., 'Political Power and Social Class in the NeoColonial African State', *Review of African Political Economy*, vol. 38, 1987.

Charney, C., 'Janus in Black Face? The African Petite Bourgeoisie in South Africa', Paper delivered to Association of Sociologists in South Africa Congress, Durban, 1988.

Giddens, A., *A Contemporary Critique of Historical Materialism*, Macmillan: London/ UCLA Press: Berkeley, 1981.

Graaff, J. F. de V., 'Function, Dependency and Reformist Potential: the Case of Bophuthatswana', Paper delivered to the Congress of the Development Society of Southern Africa, Bloemfontein, 1984.

Gulalp, H., 'Capital Accumulation, Classes and the Relative Autonomy of the State', *Science & Society*, vol. 51, no. 3, 1987.

Hammond Tooke, W.D., *Command or Consensus: The Development of Transkeian Local Government*, David Philip: Cape Town, 1975.

Hirsch, A., 'The Industrialization of Dimbaza: Population Relocation and Industrial Decentralization in a Bantustan', in Tomlinson, R. & Addleson, M. (eds.) *Regional Restructuring under Apartheid: Urban and Regional Policies in Contemporary South Africa*, Ravan: Johannesburg, 1987.

Innes, D. & O'Meara, D., 'Class Formation and Ideology: The Transkei Region', *Review of African Political Economy*, vol. 7, 1976.

Jeppe, W.J.O., 'African Political Culture: The Neglected Component of Political Development', Paper delivered to Development Society Congress, Durban, July, 1988.

Leys, C., 'The "Overdeveloped" Post-colonial State: a Re-evaluation', *Review of African Political Economy*, 5 January–April, 1976.

Leys, C., 'Capital Accumulation, Class Formation and Dependency — the Significance of the Kenyan Case', in Miliband & Saville (eds.), *The Socialist Register*, Merlin Press: London, 1978.

Lodge, T., *Black Politics in South Africa Since 1945*, Ravan: Johannesburg, 1983.

Mare, G. & Hamilton, G., *An Appetite for Power: Buthelezi's Inkatha and South Africa*, Ravan: Johannesburg, 1987.

Marks, S., *The Ambiguities of Dependence: Class, Nationalism and the State in 20th Century Natal*, Ravan: Johannesburg, 1986.

Molteno, F., 'The Historical Signficance of the Bantustan Strategy', *Social Dynamics*, vol. 3, no. 2, 1977.

Palmer, R. & Parsons, L., *The Roots of Rural Poverty in Central and Southern Africa*, UCLA Press: Berkeley, 1977.

Samoff, J., 'Bureaucrats, Politicians and Power in Tanzania', *Journal African Studies*, vol. 10, no. 3, 1983.

Sandbrook, R., *The Politics of Africa's Stagnation*, Cambridge University Press: Cambridge, 1985.

Saul, J., 'The State in Postcolonial Societies: Tanzania' in Saul, J. (ed.), *The State and Revolution in Eastern Africa*, Heinemann Educational Books: London, 1979.

Southall, R., *South Africa's Transkei: the Political Economy of an 'Independent' Bantustan'*, Heinemann: London, 1982.

Tomlinson, R. & Addleson, M. (eds.), *Regional Restructuring under Apartheid: Urban and Regional Policies in Contemporary South Africa*, Ravan Press: Johannesburg, 1987.

Trevisan, I., 'Independent Homelands: An Analysis of Selected Issues in South Africa — Homeland Relations', Unpublished MA Thesis, University of Cape Town: Cape Town, 1984

von Freyhold, M., 'The Post-Colonial State and its Tanzanian Version', *Review of African Political Economy*, 1976.

Wolpe, H., 'Race, Class and State in South Africa', UNO, Geneva, 1988.

From booster to brake? Apartheid and economic growth in comparative perspective

5

Terence Moll

Boswell — Sir Alexander Dick tells me, that he remembers having a thousand people in a year to dine at his house ...

Johnson — That, Sir, is about three a day.

Boswell — How your statement lessens the idea.

Johnson — That, Sir, is the good of counting. It brings every thing to a certainty, which before floated in the mind indefinitely.

From *Boswell's Life of Johnson*, 18 April 1783.

Introduction

Jill Nattrass was expert at such counting — at using statistics to illustrate elementary points, concretize and test hypotheses, and demonstrate the weaknesses of her opponents' arguments. This is clear from her 1981 book, *The South African Economy*, but was even more vivid in conversation and debate with her. Here I attempt to apply her statistical approach to an aspect of the historical relation between the apartheid system and economic growth in South Africa, one of her favourite themes (Nattrass, 1981, ch. 11).

A group of radical/Marxist writers in the 1970s wished to invert the 'liberal' argument that apartheid had served to hamper economic growth. They asserted that apartheid was a unique system of social control designed to boost economic growth and industrialization in South Africa. This was done, they suggested, by the efficient assurance of an ample supply of low-wage black labour for capitalist firms (Wolpe, 1972; Legassick, 1974a; Milkman, 1982, pp. 405–408).

Economic growth statistics were a polemical trump card in this debate. According to Legassick, for example, 'it is clear that South African economic growth since 1948 has proceeded apace — exceeded in the 1960s only by that of Japan' (1974a, p. 6; 1974b, p. 269; Johnson, 1977, p. 28).[1] Allegedly spectacular growth in South Africa in the 1950s and 1960s was attributed to the apartheid system. The exact mechanisms at work were not fully spelled out, but the argument appears to be that exceptionally vicious exploitation of cheap black labour lowered capitalist costs and led to high profit rates, high investment levels and rapid growth (Davies, 1979, p. 334; Davies *et al.*, 1984, pp. 20–22; a more complex view is Curtis, 1984).[2]

The mid-1980s economic slump in South Africa saw the emergence of an elaboration of the radical theory. This was formulated in an effort to understand how apartheid had assisted economic growth until around 1973 but had begun to constrain it thereafter (Gelb, 1987, pp. 33–4; also Legassick, 1985, p. 590f). The current economic decline in South Africa was seen as an organic 'crisis', an argument based on evidence of low growth rates and investment levels and falling real incomes (Sutcliffe, 1986). Lipton followed a similar approach from the centre, arguing that the costs of apartheid to the economic system after about 1970 began exceeding the benefits thereof (1985, ch. 6). These are variants of what may be termed the 'from booster to brake' theory of the relationship between apartheid and economic growth.[3]

Aspects of the radical approach can be tested in various ways. In this collection (Chapter 7), Nicoli Nattrass looks at trends in manufacturing profit rates in post-war South Africa and concludes that they have been falling since the 1940s, contrary to some radical claims. My chapter, adopting an indirect route, looks rather at the empirical implications of certain radical assumptions. If the 'booster to brake' version of the economic effects of apartheid presented above is sound, South Africa should have enjoyed rapid economic growth after 1948, and her economic performance should have fallen away markedly in the 1970s compared to other developing countries.

The debate should however be seen in context. Firstly, after the war South Africa enjoyed exceedingly favourable conditions for economic development. A decade and a half of steady industrial growth had left her with a range of manufacturing industries. Savings were not a major constraint, as whites — the recipients of most personal income — saved consistently, and ample capital inflows were readily available. An economic and administrative infrastructure was in place and there was a supply of skilled white workers and low-wage black workers. Gold and diamond mining provided stable sources of demand for other sectors as well as revenue for the state, whilst providing foreign exchange to finance machinery imports necessary for import-substituting industrialization. Critically speaking, South Africa had a stable political system.[4]

Secondly, the South African economy had grown rapidly in the 1930s and 1940s. Du Piesanie estimated an average growth rate for the real GDP of 4 per cent per annum between 1929 and 1950 (1968, p. 41), which is higher than comparable figures for most developed and developing countries (compare to Maddison, 1970, Appendix B; 1982, Appendix A).

Hence, for the 'booster' phase of radical theory to survive, the South African economy should have spurted way ahead of similar developing countries which lacked the claimed exploitative efficiency of apartheid in the 1950s and 1960s. The good pre-1950 economic record should have improved and South African economic indicators should have been singularly impressive until the early 1970s, as various radicals claimed (Gervasi, 1970, p. 1; more recently COSATU, 1987, p. 37). At this stage the 'brake' phase of the theory implies that apartheid began to constrain economic growth in South Africa. Growth indicators should then have deteriorated markedly compared both to South Africa's previous record and to those for similar developing countries.

A sample of countries similar to South Africa is used to test these claims below for the apartheid period. If growth rates do not follow the expected patterns then some of the assumptions of the 'booster to brake' version of radical theory should be questioned. In particular, either 'cheap labour' in the 1950s and 1960s was not that cheap after all, or its importance to economic growth was much less than the radical arguments supposed.

Comparing economic growth records of developing countries

There is considerable evidence that groups of countries with similar economic characteristics experience similar economic forces and constraints in the development process. Chenery, for example, suggested that these similar characteristics include population and per capita GDP (as indices for wealth and market structure and size), and the availability of natural resources (1979, ch. 1).[5]

A sample of (basically capitalist) countries which were, in these terms, comparable to South Africa in the post-war period is required to test the growth rate claims discussed above. The starting point of 1950 is used, since by this date the initial political and economic uncertainty associated with the coming to power of the Nationalist government was over. 1960 was taken as base year since it is early in the period and is the first year for which a full range of statistics is available. Statistics on both population and real per capita income were drawn from the results of the UN International Comparison Project (Summers & Heston, 1984). This was necessary in order to ensure that real purchasing power was being compared, thereby reducing the effects of dubious exchange rates (Kravis, 1984, pp. 27–32).

By using selection criteria based on 1960 population figures of greater than four million (SA = 17,3 million); and per capita real GDP at 1975 international prices (adjusted for changes in the terms of trade) of between $800 and $2 800 (SA = $1 538),[6] we end up with a group of 20 medium-sized and large middle-income developing countries.[7] They are listed in the notes to Table 5.1. Their 1960 populations ranged from 94,1 million (Japan) to 6,8 million (Ghana); and 1960 GDPs per capita at 1975 international prices from $2 751 (Australia) to $814 (Nigeria). South Africa was positioned tenth in terms of population, and eighth in terms of income per capita.

Terence Moll

Table 5.1:
ECONOMIC GROWTH IN DEVELOPED AND
MIDDLE-INCOME DEVELOPING COUNTRIES, 1950–85

Indicator and group of countries	Real GDP growth rates (percentage per annum) over periods:			
	1950–60	1960–70	1970–80	1980–85
Median, 10 developed countries	3,8	4,2	2,9	1,6
Median, 20 developing countries	4,6	5,3	4,4	1,3
South Africa	4,1	5,8	3,9	1,0

NOTES:
1 Corresponding to the above definition of medium-sized developing countries, developed countries are defined as those which in 1960 had pop ulations of greater than five million and per capita incomes at 1975 prices, adjusted for changes in the terms of trade, of greater than $2 800 (Summers & Heston, 1984). The 10 countries which fulfil these criteria are: Australia, Belgium, Canada, France, Germany, the Netherlands, Sweden, Switzerland, the United Kingdom and the United States.
2 The 20 developing countries ranked by descending 1960 GDP per capita are: (1) Austria; (2) Venezuela; (3) Italy; (4) Argentina; (5) Spain; (6) Japan; (7) Chile; (8) South Africa; (9) Greece; (10) Mexico; (11) Portugal; (12) Peru; (13) Sri Lanka; (14) Colombia; (15) Turkey; (16) Maylasia; (17) Ghana; (18) Algeria; (19) Brazil; (20) Nigeria.
SOURCE:
World Bank data (see Table 5.2).

These countries were comparable in terms of some of the generally-accepted factors associated with economic growth. They differed chiefly in terms of the availability of natural resources and their diverse political-economic systems. South Africa was among the most resource-rich of them, so if she successfully followed socio-economic policies conducive to economic growth, we would expect to find her consistently towards the top of the economic growth rankings. Two widely-used growth indicators, real GDP and real manufacturing output, are examined.

Patterns of economic growth since 1950
World economic growth after 1945 proceeded at an historically unprecedented pace. Between 1950 and 1973, real growth rates in advanced Western economies averaged over 4 per cent per annum (see Table 5.1). Those in the socialist countries were equally impressive. World trade, industrial exports and technological development all flourished. Moreover, this growth was remarkably steady, with no major recessions for a quarter of a century. The pattern of this post-war 'Golden Age' was of one rapid output and demand growth within a stable trade and institutional framework, inducing high investment levels and rapid growth

in productivity (Maddison, 1982, ch. 6).

Most indicators of growth in the advanced capitalist countries slowed down after the late 1960s or early 1970s — not only GDP and manufacturing growth, but labour and capital productivity growth rates, as well as technological advance and investment levels (Maddison, 1987). Further, many of the institutional structures which had previously encouraged growth (a stable exchange rate system; control over the world money supply; low inflationary expectations; declining trade barriers and state commitment to demand-management) began to break down.

Many developing countries also prospered after 1950 as world trade and demand soared. In some cases new economic possibilities were opened up by political independence (Johns, 1988, ch. 6), and systematic state-led development policies transformed these economies. Maddison attributed around 2 per cent per annum of post-war GDP growth in developing countries to state-led policy measures and resource mobilization (1970, pp. 57–60). Not only did output and export volumes grow steadily, but the structures of these economies shifted towards the dynamic industrial sectors and some services sectors (Chenery, 1979, ch. 1).

The group of fast-growing developing countries includes many which had experienced a degree of economic and industrial development before 1950 and were able to take advantage of world economic prosperity thereafter. Their political systems were reasonably economically-oriented and usually inclined towards active industrialization policies (see Reynolds, 1985, chs. 5–8). These are now mostly in the category of middle-income developing countries, whilst many low-income developing countries — with the notable exceptions of China and perhaps India — are falling yet further behind (Summers et al., 1981, pp. 20–23; Morawetz, 1977, ch. 1).

The developing countries were less immediately affected by the post-1973 slowdown than were developed countries. Most continued to grow in the 1970s and only in the last few years have they suffered generalized recession, linked to such factors as the second oil shock, declining terms of trade, the debt crisis, and so on (Griffith-Jones & Sunkel, 1986, ch. 1). Some have shown signs of sustainable adjustment and recovery since the mid-1980s (World Bank, 1986, chs. 1–2).

Table 5.1 summarizes the overall pattern of post-1950 economic growth for ten developed countries and our 20 middle-income developing countries. The latter grew rapidly by historical standards (compare to Maddison, 1970, ch. 1, and Appendix A), with a median growth rate over decade periods of 4,5 to 5 per cent per annum until 1980.[8] Over this period they grew faster on the whole than the developed countries shown.[9] Many developing countries then slid into generalized recession and the developed countries moved slightly ahead over the 1980–85 period, though this tendency may have reversed after 1985.

Developing country annual GDP growth rates since 1961 are summarized in Figure 5.1 (the World Bank source does not provide annual figures before that). To illustrate general growth tendencies, three lines are drawn: the median, the 25-percentile and the 75-percentile. In any year, the middle half of growth rates for the 20 countries lie between the latter two lines on the graph.

Figure 5.1:

YEAR-ON-YEAR GDP GROWTH RATES
FOR TWENTY DEVELOPING COUNTRIES

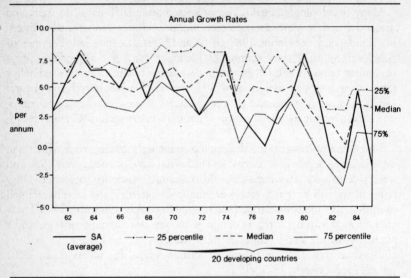

SOURCE:
World Bank data described in the sources to Table 5.2.

The median growth rate is fairly high in the 1960s, often over 5 per cent per annum, but falls away in the mid-1970s and again in the early 1980s. The spread between the 25-percentile line and the 75-percentile line increases in the 1970s, implying an increasingly divergent growth-experience within this group of countries. The slower-growing countries fell further behind after 1980, often experiencing negative economic growth in the last few years. The graph may however be misleading as some countries like Brazil and Japan tend to occupy the top of the graph, while others like Ghana and Argentina are consistently toward the bottom.

South Africa follows the developing country pattern, with steady growth from 1945 until 1973 and a slowdown since then (Moll, 1989a). The post-war peak was reached in the 1960s when real growth rates of 6 or 7 per cent per annum were achieved and state-directed industrialization policies appeared to be working. However, the growth pattern was reliant on gold exports, and roots of a later decline can be traced to both the regular balance of payments crises and the skills shortages which plagued the economy from the 1960s. After 1973 the economy experienced a downward spiral, relieved only by the gold boom which ended in 1981. Slower and more erratic growth rates interacted with political uncertainty, fluctuating investment levels and world economic factors, leading to absolute economic contraction in some years during the 1980s.

South Africa's record is not good compared to those of the middle-income developing countries shown in Table 5.1. Except for the 1960s, South Africa lies below the median — that is, in the bottom half of the group. Even in the halcyon 1960s decade South Africa did not excel, only rising above the 25-percentile line on the graph in 1967.

For methodological reasons, all such figures should be treated with caution. Hill suggests of OECD countries that for statistical reasons, differentials of around 1 per cent per annum are required before it can confidently be said that real GDP growth rates differed over a period (1971, pp. 79–80). Even with the unlikely assumption that South Africa's growth rate was underestimated by 1 per cent per annum compared to the other countries shown, her highest ranking within the decade would be only fourth during the 1960s.[10]

Growth rates in developing countries

These observations can be more carefully examined by comparing real GDP growth rates for the 20 countries over decade periods. Various sources of allegedly comparable figures are available for the sample of countries. Three widely-used sources which have been scrutinized by prominent researchers are:

* The United Nations Congress on Trade and Development (UNCTAD), which uses national accounts production data as supplied by collecting countries to the United Nations.
* The World Bank, whose 'own currency' figures are based on sources similar to the above but modified in various ways to make the figures more reliable and comparable.
* The United Nations International Comparison Project (ICP), which is expenditure-based and investigates domestic purchasing power, with extensive adjustments to make the date internationally comparable.

The figures are collected in different ways and have differing degrees of reliability. They are all compiled according to the UN System of National Accounts however, and should be less subject to errors of overstatement and chance than are those for poorer more agriculturally-dependent countries (*cf.* Kuznets, 1972).

Table 5.2 compares real growth rankings for South Africa over decade periods from the three sources. The results are reassuringly close, with South Africa's ranking in each period varying little between sources. South Africa performed moderately well in the 1960s — around eighth in the growth rankings — and indifferently in the 1950s and since 1970. Her overall 1950–85 ranking varies between twelfth and fifteenth (of 17 countries).

Table 5.2:

SOUTH AFRICA'S GDP GROWTH RANKING
AMONGST TWENTY DEVELOPING COUNTRIES

Source	South Africa's GDP growth ranking in period:				
	1950–60	1960–70	1970–80	1980–85	1950–85
1) UNCTAD	15	8	15	14	15
2) World Bank	14	8	13	12	(tie)13
3) ICP	15/17	7	14	14	12/17

NOTE:
Different base years for each country may be used for each period, having the effect of crudely chain-linking indexes. The ICP does not provide 1950 figures for three countries; these are excluded from the first and last columns. One UNCTAD figure in the first column is for 1951–60, and five World Bank figures for 1980–85 are for GNP growth rates.
SOURCES:
Figures calculated from: (1) 1950–60: UNCTAD, 1972, Table 6.2; 1960–70: UNCTAD, 1974, Table 6.2; 1970–80: UNCTAD, 1983, Table 6.2; 1980–85: UNCTAD, 1988, Table 6.2. (2) 1950–70: World Bank, 1976, Economic Data Sheet 1; 1970–80: World Bank, 1983 Economic Data Sheet 1; 1980–85: World Bank, 1987, country tables. (3) 1950–80: Summers & Heston, 1984, data tables; 1980–85: Summers & Heston, 1988, pp. 14–21.

As is well known, the official real output figures for South Africa are distorted because the official gold mining output indicator (ounces of fine gold produced) is partly a policy variable, linked to the gold price (Boyle, 1982, ch. 6). When the real gold price rises, poorer ore is mined and the output of fine gold may fall — even when employment, investment levels and nominal gold earnings have risen. Since 1970, the real gold price has risen considerably and output of fine gold has fallen by about one third.

One way of investigating how the real productive capacity of the gold sector has grown is to use tons of gold-bearing ore milled as the indicator of real output for this subsector (Lombard & Stadler, 1980, p. 7). Using the 'gold-recalculated' method of estimating real economic activity; real GDP growth rates fall on the average before 1970 (when the real gold price was falling and richer ore was being mined) and rise thereafter. The differentials between the conventional and recalculated GDP measures are quite largely due to the importance of the gold mining sector in nominal GDP, averaging 0,25 per cent per annum before 1970 and 0,6 per cent per annum since 1970.

Using World Bank national accounts figures, South Africa's gold-recalculated GDP growth ranking falls before 1970 and rises since that date. The new results are shown in Table 5.3. This more realistic evaluation of the long-term growth-record of the economy has intriguing effects on South Africa's position in the growth table. South Africa's overall ranking rises by one place to twelfth; her rankings before 1970 fall by a place; but for the 1980–85 period South Africa jumps from twelfth to eighth place. The latter result is partly a statistical aberration due to gold's large share of nominal GDP in 1980 and partly because eight average growth rate figures for the period cluster between 0,8 and 1,7 per cent per annum. The table does suggest however that South Africa's growth record since 1970 has been respectable compared to those of other developing countries.

Table 5.3:
SOUTH AFRICA'S GOLD-RECALCULATED GDP GROWTH RANKING AMONGST TWENTY DEVELOPING COUNTRIES

			Period:		
	1950–60	1960–70	1970–80	1980–85	1950–85
South Africa's recalculated GDP growth ranking	15	9	12	8	12

NOTE:
Figures for South Africa — following the World Bank approach — are calculated at the following base-years: 1950–70: 1963; 1970–80: 1975; 1980–5: 1980.
SOURCES:
World Bank figures: see Table 5.2 sources. South Africa figures: taken from Moll (1989b, ch. 3)

As a crosscheck on the above, manufacturing growth rates are considered. This sector is critical in the development process (Weiss, 1988, ch. 1) and produces outputs which are more measurable and homogeneous than GDP as a whole. Its growth can thus serve as another indicator of general economic performance.

South Africa's comparative manufacturing growth performance is illustrated in Table 5.4. This table is drawn up from several sources but they give similar results where they overlap. Growth rates are again compared over decades, but begin with the year 1953 when censuses of industrial production were carried out worldwide.

For developing countries as a whole, this table suggests rapid manufacturing growth until 1970, a slowdown in the 1970s, and stagnation since. South Africa's manufacturing output growth ranking, as compared with its GDP

Table 5.4:
SOUTH AFRICA'S MANUFACTURING OUTPUT GROWTH RANKING AMONGST TWENTY DEVELOPING COUNTRIES

| | Period: | | | |
Indicator	1953–60	1960–70	1970–80	1980–85
Manufacturing output growth rates (percentage per annum):				
20 developing countries (median):	8,5	7,2	5,3	0,3
South Africa:	5,3	8,0	5,4	0,3
South Africa's manufacturing output growth rate ranking:	12/13	8/18	10	16

NOTE:
Different base-years have been used for countries over different periods. Seven countries do not provide detailed manufacturing output figures for 1953, and two do not for 1960.
SOURCES:
1953–60: UN 1970, Table 48; 1960–70, Japan and Brazil: UN 1975, Table 48; 1960–70, other countries, and 1970–80: World Bank, 1983, Economic Data Sheet 1; 1980–85: World Bank, 1987, country tables.

growth ranking, is much the same for the 1950s and 1960s, slightly higher for the 1970s and lower in the 1980s.[11] In short, it seems the claims sometimes made about apartheid boosting industrialization and manufacturing growth in South Africa (Gervasi, 1970, ch. 1; Kaplan, 1977, ch. 8) are dubious when viewed comparatively.

Conclusion

Jill Nattrass once commented that she sympathized with radical ideals but thought radicals did not have enough 'respect for the facts'. This analysis of the empirical claims of the 'booster to brake' version of radical theory supports her criticism. Compared to a group of roughly-similar developing countries, South Africa does not follow the economic growth patterns the theory predicts.

There is little support for the proposition that the apartheid system led to exceptional economic growth in South Africa after 1948. This is even the case in the 1963–72 period — described as 'the real golden age of apartheid for those class forces which benefited from the system' (Davies *et al.*, 1984, p. 28). Even if apartheid did assure a low-wage black labour supply and perhaps raised short-term profit levels, there may have been too many other factors at work for this to be transformed into rapid economic growth.

More generally, economic growth is a complex thing and theories which isolate any single factor as crucial to it are preliminary at best (*cf.* Reynolds, 1985, chs. 15–16). Radicals could move on from concentrating on black labour control and wages to an investigation of other factors central to, or accompanying, economic growth. Fruitful areas of research include exports and the balance of payments, state economic policy and planning, the effects of apartheid on labour productivity, the financial structure, technology, and the economic effects of restraints on black urbanization and black business. It is likely that post-1948 state policy in many of these areas — often directly linked to the social forces behind apartheid — was dysfunctional to economic growth. The obvious evils of apartheid and the clear functionality of aspects of apartheid to particular capitalist interests at certain times appear to have shifted radical attention away from some central economic problems associated with it.

On the 'brake' side the evidence is also unfavourable. South Africa's overall growth-ranking of around thirteenth in the sample of middle-income developing countries for the 1950–85 period is consistent across decades, apart from a small improvement in the 1960s, and shows no marked decline after 1970. In fact, it improves slightly if the gold sector is dealt with more appropriately than by using the conventional measures of real output.

South Africa's economic 'crisis' of the 1980s deserves reinterpretation. Rather than a crisis of apartheid per se, it is part of a slump which affected middle-income developing countries worldwide and South Africa has not suffered particularly badly, as Tables 5.2 and 5.3 indicate. South Africa's real GDP growth of 1 per cent per annum between 1980 and 1985 (as conventionally measured) is a far milder index of crisis than are the corresponding figures for Nigeria (3,4 per cent per annum), Argentina (2,4 per cent per annum), or Venezuela (2,3 per cent per annum).[12]

Further, most of the factors regarded as responsible for South Africa's economic 'crisis' over the past decade — foreign debt, falling export prices and deteriorating terms of trade, low investment levels, capital flight, etc. — have been common in middle-income developing countries, especially those in Latin America (Sachs, 1985). This crisis should thus be viewed as part of a widespread phenomenon affecting many developing countries, rather than as a unique local happening.

The central message of all this is straightforward — South Africa should be analysed as part of the world economy. It flourishes when external conditions are favourable, and slumps when external conditions are poor. In these respects South Africa is a typical developing country. Typically, again, countries like South Africa can use the international environment to their own advantage, provided they follow cunning economic policies (cf. Riedel, 1987, p. 88). South Africa has not succeeded in this respect over the past few years.

External conditions appear to be the vital factor influencing future growth in South Africa. Many other developing countries have achieved structural adjustments and have begun shifting from import substitution to a more external orientation as a means of reducing inefficiencies, raising export earnings and moving towards a new and sustainable growth path. Political factors and the sanctions movement bar South Africa from taking this route. The necessary export markets, finance, technology and internal political stability are most unlikely to materialize. From this viewpoint the South African economic crisis — as distinct from that affecting developing countries as a whole — may only be beginning.

Notes

1 It is disturbing that he — and others writing in this vein — provided no references for this critical assertion. It presumably derives from such a source as Hóbart Houghton (1973, p. 209). He also omitted references and may have been comparing South Africa only with (some) developed Western economies, as was done by Innes, who claimed that over the 1950–66 period South Africa grew faster than 'all other' industrial countries, except for Japan (1984, pp. 188, 222; also Harsch, 1980, p. 107; Fransman, 1982, p. 243). This is theoretically questionable and empirically incorrect. For if South Africa is regarded as 'industrial', the same applies to Greece and Spain, which both grew faster than South Africa in the 1950s and 1960s, as did Austria and Italy in the 1950s (Table 5.2 sources).

2 This theme is elaborated in two unpublished theses, Bloch (1980, pp. 214–24) and Kaplan (1977, ch. 8).

3 Only the economic growth question is investigated in this chapter. Space does not allow analysis of other aspects of radical research.

4 The political protests of the 1950s can hardly be compared to the Algerian civil war and violent political fluctuations in countries like Argentina, Brazil, Chile, Ghana, Peru and Turkey.

5 He also stresses capital inflows and state economic policy (for example inward versus outward orientation). For present purposes they can be regarded as endogenous variables.

6 The 1975 base-year was more typical for prices in South Africa than the 1980 base-year used in Summers & Heston (1988).

7 This term is used to group the countries by size and income as of 1960. Some of the better performers have moved up and out of this group by the 1980s (partly aided by low population growth rates), while two — Ghana and Sri Lanka — are now low-income countries. Three countries were excluded from the original sample of 23. Angola, which became independent only in the 1970s, has suffered massive economic decline and continual civil war since then, and lacks the political stability necessary for long-term economic development. Iran and Iraq are regarded by the World Bank as 'capital-surplus oil exporters' (1980, p. 111) and especially favourable economic circumstances have applied to them.

8 Medians are used to avoid distortions caused by the use of averages where there are occasional radical fluctuations, for example the 1960–62 decline in Algerian GDP of 36,5 per cent during the civil war, and recovery of 29,5 per cent the following year. All growth rates calculated below are exponential and GDP is measured at factor cost where possible.

9 This is not necessarily the case for GDP per capita growth rates however, as population growth rates in the developing countries were higher.

10 South Africa's position is minimally affected if the selection criteria or the time-periods are varied. My ongoing research suggests that the South African economic record is even poorer when compared in closer detail to records of countries like Brazil, Turkey and Peru which have socio-economic similarities to South Africa.

11 Figures for the 1950s are deceptive as several countries not shown may well have had slower manufacturing growth than South Africa. Manufacturing growth rates should however be treated with caution as the figures for 11 countries in the 1980s lie between 0,5 per cent and –0,5 per cent per annum.

12 Other socio-economic indicators for these countries — declining investment levels, falling real wages, unemployment, increasing poverty — are also more severe than those for South Africa.

References

Bloch, G., *The Development of Manufacturing Industry in South Africa 1939–69*. Unpublished M.A. (Economic History) Thesis, University of Cape Town: Cape Town, 1980.

Boyle, G.A., 1980. *The Theory of Wasting Assets with Reference to the Regulation and Pricing of Gold in the South African Gold Mining Industry*. Unpublished M.A. (Economics) Thesis, University of Cape Town: Cape Town, 1982.

Chenery, H., *Structural Change and Development Policy*. Oxford University Press: Oxford, 1979.

COSATU (Congress of South African Trade Unions), *Political Economy: South Africa in Crisis*. COSATU Education: Johannesburg, 1987.

Curtis, F., 'Contradiction and Uneven Development in South Africa: The Constrained Allocation of African Labour-Power,' in *Journal of Modern African Studies*, vol. 22, no. 3, September 1984.

Davies, R. H., *Capital, State and White Labour in South Africa 1900–1960*. Harvester: Sussex, 1979.

Davies, R. H., O'Meara D. & Dlamini S., *The Struggle for South Africa*, vol. 1, Zed: London, 1984.

Du Piesanie, C. J., *Die Bepaling en die Gebruik van Kapitaalopbrengsverhoudings*. Unpublished M.A. (Economics) Thesis, University of Pretoria: Pretoria, 1968.

Fransman, M., 'Capital Accumulation in South Africa,' in Fransman, M.(ed.), *Industry and Accumulation in Africa*, Heinemann: London *et al.* 1982.

Gelb, S., 'Making Sense of the Crisis,' in *Transformation* no. 5, (Department of Economic History, University of Natal, Durban), 1987.

Gervasi, S., *Industrialization, Foreign Capital and Forced Labour in South Africa*. United Nations, (Ser. A/10): New York, 1970.

Griffith-Jones, S. & Sunkel, O., *Debt and Development Crises in Latin America: The End of an Illusion*. Clarendon: Oxford, 1986.

Harsch, E., *South Africa: White Rule, Black Revolt*. Monad Press: New York, 1980.

Hill, T.P., *The Measurement of Real Product*. OECD: Brussels, 1971.

Hobart Houghton, D., *The South African Economy*. Oxford University Press: Cape Town, 1973.

Innes, D., *Anglo American and the Rise of Modern South Africa*. Heinemann: London *et al.*, 1984.

Johns, R.A., *Colonial Trade and International Exchange*. Pinter: London & New York, 1988.

Johnson, R.W., *How Long will South Africa Survive?* Macmillan: London & Basingstoke: 1977.

Kaplan, D., *Class Conflict, Capital Accumulation and the State: An Historical Materialist Analysis of the State in 20th Century South Africa*. Unpublished D.Phil. Thesis, University of Sussex: Brighton, 1977.

Kravis, I. B., 'Comparative Studies of National Income and Prices,' in *Journal of Economic Literature*, vol. 22, no. 1, March, 1984.

Kuznets, S., 'Problems in Comparing Recent Growth Rates for Developed and Less-developed Countries,' in *Economic Development and Cultural Change*, vol. 20, no. 2, January, 1972.

Legassick, M., 'Legislation, Ideology and Economy in Post-1948 South Africa,' in *Journal of Southern African Studies*, vol. 1, no. 1, October, 1974a.

Legassick, M., 'South Africa: Capital Accumulation and Violence,' in *Economy and Society*, vol. 3, no. 3, August, 1974b.

Legassick, M., 'South Africa in Crisis: What Route to Democracy?' in *African Affairs*, vol. 84, no. 337, October, 1985.

Lipton, M., *Capitalism and Apartheid*. Gower: Aldershot, Hants, 1985.

Lombard, J. & Stadler, J.J., *The Role of Mining in the South African Economy*. Bureau for Economic Policy and Analysis, University of Pretoria: Pretoria, 1980.

Maddison, A., *Economic Progress and Policy in Developing Countries*. Allen & Unwin: London, 1970.

Maddison, A., *Phases of Capitalist Development*. Oxford University Press: Oxford, 1982.

Maddison, A., 'Growth and Slowdown in Advanced Capitalist Economies: Techniques of Quantitative Assessment,' in *Journal of Economic Literature*, vol. 25, no. 2, June, 1987.

Milkman, R., 'Apartheid, Economic Growth, and US Foreign Policy in South Africa,' in Murray, M. (ed.), *South African Capitalism and Black Political Opposition*, Schenkman: Cambridge, Mass., 1982.

Moll, T., ' "Probably the Best Laager in the World": The Record and Prospects of the South African Economy,' in Brewer, J.D. (ed.), *Can South Africa Survive?*, Macmillan: London & Basingstoke, 1989a.

Moll, T., *Essays on Economic Growth and Structural Change in South Africa*, (provisional title), Ph.D. Thesis in progress, St. John's College: Cambridge, 1989b.

Morawetz, D., *Twenty-Five Years of Economic Development 1950 to 1975*. Johns Hopkins University Press: Baltimore & London, 1977.

Nattrass, J., *The South African Economy: Its Growth and Change*. Oxford University Press: Cape Town, 1981.

Reynolds, L., *Economic Growth in the Third World, 1950–1980*. Yale University Press: New Haven, 1985.

Riedel, J., *Myths and Reality of External Constraints on Development*. Gower: Aldershot, Hants, 1987.

Sachs, J.D., 'External Debt and Macroeconomic Performance in Latin America and East Asia,' in *Brookings Papers on Economic Activity*, no. 2, 1985.

Summers, R. & Heston, A., 'Improved International Comparisons of Real Product and its Composition: 1950–1980,' in *Review of Income and Wealth*, vol. 30, no. 2, June 1984.

Summers, R. & Heston, A., 'A New Set of International Comparisons of Real Product and Price Levels Estimates for 130 Countries, 1950–1985,' in *Review of Income and Wealth*, vol. 34, no. 1, March 1988.

Summers, R. I., Kravis, B. & Heston, A., 'Inequality Among Nations: 1950 and 1975,' in Bairoch, Levy-Leboyer, P. & M. (eds.), *Disparities in Economic Development Since the Industrial Revolution*, Macmillan: London & Basingstoke, 1981.

Sutcliffe, M., 'The Crisis in South Africa: Material Conditions and the Reformist Response,' in *Geoforum*, vol. 17, no. 2, 1986.

United Nations, *United Nations Statistical Yearbook 1969*, New York, 1970.

United Nations, *United Nations Statistical Yearbook 1974*, New York, 1975.

UNCTAD (United Nations Congress on Trade and Development): 1972, *Handbook of International Trade and Development Statistics*. New York: United Nations, 1972.

UNCTAD (United Nations Congress on Trade and Development): 1974, *Handbook of International Trade and Development Statistics, Supplement 1973*. United Nations: New York, 1974.

UNCTAD (United Nations Congress on Trade and Development): 1983, *Handbook of International Trade and Development Statistics*. United Nations: New York, 1983.

UNCTAD (United Nations Congress on Trade and Development): 1988, *Handbook of International Trade and Development Statistics, 1988 Supplement*. United Nations: New York, 1988.

Weiss, J., *Industry in Developing Countries*. Croom Helm: London *et al.*, 1988.

Wolpe, H., 'Capitalism and Cheap Labour-power in South Africa: From Segregation to Apartheid,' in *Economy and Society*, vol. 1, no. 4, November 1972.

World Bank, *World Tables 1976*, Johns Hopkins University Press: Baltimore & London, 1976.

World Bank, *World Development Report 1980*, World Bank: Washington, 1980.

World Bank, *World Tables 1983*, Third Edition. Johns Hopkins University Press: Baltimore & London, 1983.

World Bank, *World Development Report 1986*, World Bank: Washington, 1986.

World Bank, *World Tables 1987*, Fourth Edition, Johns Hopkins University Press: Baltimore & London, 1987.

Economic growth, income distribution and social change

6

Mike McGrath

Introduction

At the centre of Jill Nattrass' research in the 1970s were the issues of economic growth and economic justice in the South African economy. At that time there was a wide-ranging academic debate underway about the relationship between the apartheid political system and economic growth, and about the potential which economic growth possesses for stimulating political and social reforms. The participants in the debate were grouped into two broad schools of thought, which have been referred to as the 'liberal orthodoxy' and the 'Marxist revisionist'. The positions adopted by these two groups have been reviewed by several writers (Fisher *et al.*, 1978; Kantor & Kenny, 1976; Wright, 1977). In summary, the liberal interpretation of the effects of apartheid is that it is a force acting to produce a sub-optimal allocation of resources, and one which has retarded South Africa's economic growth potential. The market is seen as an agent acting to produce efficient resource allocation, and the institutions of apartheid are thought to prevent the market from allocating the labour force optimally. They are seen as preventing the black population from developing its potential, by restricting access to education and by perpetuating the migrant labour system. The institutional framework, it is argued, has a corrosive effect upon economic growth, and future economic growth could be retarded if a lack of confidence in the political stability of South Africa curtails domestic and foreign investment. The protection which white labour has received has led to vast wage and income differentials between whites and blacks, which would be diminished were the market allowed to operate efficiently. Future economic growth will ultimately lead to a breakdown of discriminatory economic and political practices. Some writers see the breakdown of these practices as a pre-condition for growth in the long run, and by O'Dowd (1974) as an inevitable result of economic growth.

The sentiments expressed by the revisionists were almost the converse of those held by the liberals. According to the 'revisionists', racialism has legitimized the exploitation of blacks, and the 'labour repressive' nature of the economy has allowed both a rapid accumulation of capital and a high standard of living for the white working class. Writers of these persuasions see white supremacy and white prosperity as being suitably reinforcing, and argue that apartheid has led to high growth rates in the economy. They argue that any social changes which will occur as a result of the need to rationalize the operation of the economy's markets will be merely cosmetic in character, and will not fundamentally change the inegalitarian form of capitalism which exists in South Africa.

A third 'school' of South African authors emerged within this debate and Jill Nattrass was one of its leading contributors (Nattrass, 1978; Wilson, 1975; Schlemmer, 1978). This grouping argues that the relationship between growth and social and political reform lies between the two polar positions mentioned above. They argue that future growth will require social and political change, and that the existing distribution of economic welfare is contrary to the goals of economic stability and future development. Writers in this school recognize that the implementation of political reforms which have legitimacy need not occur, but if the path of legitimate political change is not taken, economic stagnation will be the most likely outcome. A scenario of this sort can be found in Nattrass' analysis of growth and political change (1981).

Within this debate the issue of income distribution is of crucial importance, and this paper examines the growth record of the economy and trends in the distribution of incomes. The analysis of the data is set against the background of Nattrass' theoretical analysis of economic growth and political changes.

Economic growth and political change

Jill Nattrass analysed three hypothetical growth paths (Nattrass, 1978; Nattrass, 1981, pp. 274–96). In her first model, though a modern and traditional sector coexist, the economy is in full employment. Growth in the modern sector causes an increase in competition for labour, and wage rates rise. The modern sector absorbs labour faster than the traditional sector, which decreases in relative importance, and the benefits from growth are rapidly shared with labour. The implication of this development path is that labour's bargaining power is increasing rapidly, and continued development in the situation requires political and social changes in order to ensure the co-operation of workers on the economic front. In this situation, the balance of economic forces is altered. Workers' real incomes rise, allowing positive savings, and income inequality is reduced. This alternative thus resembles the final phase for the Kuznets's 'inverted U' in which inequalities begin to narrow at a high level of development. Nattrass calls this the 'development from full employment' model (1978).

The second, called the 'development-development' model, corresponds to the 'Lewis-Fei-and-Ranis' labour surplus development models. A labour surplus exists in the traditional sector and growth of the modern sector is initially able

to proceed without raising wages. During this period, inequalities between capitalists and workers widen, but rising profits are channeled into new investment
and increased levels of employment in the modern sector. As long as employment growth in the modern sector is more rapid than the growth of the labour
supplies in the traditional sector, a position will be reached at which labour
becomes scarce, and development will proceed thereafter as in the 'development from full employment' growth path. A narrowing of inequalities will then
occur in the manner envisaged by Kuznets (1955) and Lewis (1954). Once the
labour surplus has been eliminated on the 'development-development' growth
path, the bargaining power of labour will be increased, political changes will
come about, and in this period labour will be in a position to press for social and
political reforms. These pressures will reinforce the tendency for inequalities to
narrow as a result of a shortage of labour.

In the debate about growth and change in South Africa, the orthodox
liberal school gives a perspective which is very similar to the 'development-
development' path, since they view growth as eventually leading to full employment, a more egalitarian income distribution, and social and political
change.

The third alternative, which Nattrass calls the 'development-underdevelop-
ment' path (1978), is associated with writers in the Marxist tradition, who
argue that growth in the capitalist mode requires and generates poverty in
the traditional sector. Rapid growth of the capitalist sector is possible because
the surplus of the traditional sector can be appropriated for investment in
the capitalist sector, by a combination of economic and political methods. The
result is that the growth paths of the two sectors alter, with capital accumulation
increasing in the developing sector, and declining in the other. In this model, the
surplus labour is not absorbed by economic growth, and political power may be
used continually, augmenting market forces, to undermine labour's bargaining
power. The use of increasingly capital-intensive methods of production may
also dampen the ability of the economy to absorb surplus labour. As the process
continues, standards of living fall in the traditional sector, and its inhabitants
become more dependent on the modern sector. Modern sector wage rates
may also fall, and the gains from growth will accrue almost exclusively to the
capitalist class. Continued growth may eventually cause a shortage of labour,
and a move to the 'development-development' path, but the underdevelopment
school predicts eventual stagnation of both sectors. The revisionist writers see
the South African economy developing along this growth path, and do not
foresee continued growth resulting in redistribution or political change.

In her analysis (1978), Nattrass made the important point that there is
nothing inevitable about any of the growth paths. An economy on any one
path such as the development path can easily move to the underdevelopment
path should the rate of accumulation decrease, labour-saving technological

changes take place on a sufficient scale, or population growth rates increase; or if the social and political changes required to accommodate the rising power of workers do not occur.

Nattrass' analysis serves as an important bridge between the empirical research on growth in developing countries and the political changes which usually take place as economies mature. In Nattrass' words:

> The basic axiom on which the arguments developed in this paper rest *is that although political and social change may be independent of economic growth, sustained economic growth is not independent of social and political change* (Nattrass, 1978, p. 77).

Apartheid and economic growth

From the early days of apartheid up to the present time, there have been pleas from liberal economists for its abandonment, on the grounds that the continuance of its policies represents a misallocation of scarce economic resources, and that consequently all South Africans would be better off without them. Until fairly recently these pleas fell upon deaf ears; or if heard often resulted in retribution by the state against the plaintiff. It was extremely difficult to sell the view that the apartheid policies from 1948 had retarded South Africa's economic growth, when the evidence pointed to the policies accelerating economic growth and strengthening the relative position of whites.

The growth performance of the economy since the period of union is shown in Table 6.1. The period of most rapid growth of GDP was over the years 1948–70, although high real growth rates had been achieved between 1928 and 1973. Per capita income growth achieved its highest rate in the period 1948–73, rising in this period to 2,7 per cent per annum. Many factors contributed to the higher economic growth in the period 1948–73, amongst them the stimulus given to import substitution industry by the Second World War; the improvement in South Africa's terms of trade as a result of the devaluations over the period; and the exploitation of new mineral deposits. It is, however, not a simple matter to prove that apartheid was economically irrational, given this high growth performance.

Profits also grew rapidly under the apartheid system. Real profits (gross operating surplus) achieved their highest growth rate between 1948 and 1973. The growth of real white wages in the mining, manufacturing and construction sectors of the economy was also high. The growth rate of white average wages more than doubled in the mining industry and rose almost three times as fast in manufacturing and construction under the Nationalist government than was the case over the period up to 1940. Black real wage rates on the other hand show a totally different pattern, remaining almost stagnant in the mining industry right up to the end of 1970. The performance of black real wage rates

Table 6.1:
SOUTH AFRICA'S ECONOMIC GROWTH PERFORMANCE 1911–87

			Annual real growth rates			
				Manufacturing and construction**		
Period	Gross domestic product per capita	Gross domestic surplus (profits)	Gross operating per man	Average wage per man	White wage per man	Black wage per man
1911–28	2,1	0,0	2,0			
1928–40	4,2	2,0	4,0	1,2	1,2	2,1
1940–48	4,6	2,4	3,0			
1948–73	5,3	2,7	4,3	1,2	3,0	1,3
1973–80	3,2	0,3	* 6,5	0,7	–0,1	3,5
1980–87	1,1	–1,4	–2,2	0,7	–0,3	2,2

NOTES:
*1973–79, 2,6 per cent per annum. ** After 1973, non-Primary Sectors
SOURCES:
Estimated from: *South African Statistics*, 1974,1976,1978; Steenkamp, 1962; van der Horst, 1971.

in the manufacturing and construction sectors is even more significant. The growth rate of wages in these sectors taken together over the period 1911–40 was on average 2,0 per cent, and black real wages rose every year over the period 1936–48. After 1948 this growth rate fell however, and was almost zero for the first 12 years of National Party control. Black real wages, in manufacturing and construction together, fell for the five years 1948–53 and only started to rise above the 1948 level in 1960, giving an average growth rate of 1,3 per cent per annum for the period 1948–73.

Putting all this information together, it seems that over the period in which the policies of apartheid were implemented by the National Party, the rate of growth of South African output, of total profits and of white real wage rates, were all high compared to the growth rates experienced over the period 1911–40, whilst the rate of growth of real black wages was significantly lower than it had been in the earlier period.[1] Under the institution of apartheid, economic growth thus appeared to cause the market to operate like a malevolent invisible hand, working to the advantage of white workers and capitalists, and widening wage differentials between white and black workers.

The period after 1973 is dramatically different. In the mid-1970s the oil price increases and slowing in growth of world trade filtered through to the South African economy, which had been partly buffered before 1975 by an increased gold price. In 1973 black worker militancy also reappeared and led to ongoing industrial unrest, while the quality of investment changed with an increase in public sector investment, and the share of the government sector in GDP started to rise. As Table 6.1 shows, the growth rate of the economy declined from 1973–80, then fell dramatically in the years after 1980, and in per capita terms incomes stagnated and then fell. Profits continued to grow in real terms in the 1970s, but at a reduced rate, and then fell in the 1980s. The South African economy, which had once been a magnet for foreign capital, and which had yielded high rates of return on foreign investment, now ceased to be attractive, and its creditworthiness collapsed. The culmination of this process came in 1985 with the debt standstill being imposed under the pressure from American banks for the repayment of short-term loans to South African banks.

The South African economy now became cut off from sources of foreign capital, and its growth in times of boom became constrained to rates of less than 3 per cent per annum. Repressive constraints on the growth of domestic absorption were imposed by the state in order to repay foreign debt in staggered negotiated amounts.

The relative worsening in the growth performance of the South African economy is clearly shown in Table 6.2. From this table it can be seen that since 1980 growth in the South African economy has also been subject to greater variability than many other countries, including 15 of the most heavily indebted countries. From 1980–87 the South African economy grew at 1,9 per cent per annum, compared with 1,8 per cent for the indebted countries, 2,2 per cent for industrial countries and 3,0 per cent for developing countries.[2] Over this period, among developing countries, the exporters of manufactured goods in general enjoyed considerably higher rates of growth, to be followed by primary product exporters, and then fuel exporters. South Africa's growth performance falls between the primary product exporters and the fuel-exporting economies.

Table 6.2:
COMPARATIVE REAL GDP PERCENTAGE GROWTH RATES, 1980/87

	Developing countries	Indebted countries	Industrial countries	South Africa
1980	3,4	5,4	2,6	5,6
1981	1,8	0,1	0,4	4,8
1982	1,7	–0,5	0,5	–0,8
1983	1,9	–2,7	2,3	–2,1
1984	4,0	2,3	3,6	5,1
1985	3,5	3,9	3,0	–1,2
1986	4,2	3,8	2,2	1,0
1987	3,4	2,4	2,8	2,6
Average	3,0	1,8	2,2	1,9

SOURCE:
McGrath & Holden, 1989.

The fluctuation in the gold price contributed to the variability in South Africa's GDP over this period. However, the poor growth performance of the South African economy cannot be solely attributed to changes in the price of gold. Capital outflows, low investment, inflation and political conflict have all had an effect on the performance of the South African economy.

Further, as Table 6.1 shows, with the shift to a lower growth path, the real growth rate of profit decreased, and real wage growth per man also fell sharply. However, the distribution of the decreased growth of real wages was unexpected, given the historical record, for it was white workers who experienced falling real wages after 1973, while black real wages rose.

The racial distribution of income[3]

Time-series estimates of income inequality for the economy do not exist, with an estimate of the Gini coefficient only available for the year 1975. In that year the Gini coefficient for the South African economy took a value of 0,68, which is higher than the Gini coefficient estimated for any economy for which family or household income data is available. The degree of inequality in South Africa's distribution is revealed when the Gini of 0,68 for South Africa is compared with the Gini coefficients for the developed Western economies, which range between 0,35 and 0,40. Unfortunately, adequate data is not available for the estimation of economy-wide inequality for earlier or later years. The extent of inequality is, however, highly dependent on the wide disparities that exist in the relative levels of income of the race groups, and a time-series of racial incomes per capita can be estimated back as far as 1946/47.

The distribution of incomes by race group is probably best measured by a disparity ratio, which shows the ratio of the per capita incomes of whites to the per capita income of the black group in question.

During the period 1946/47 to 1970 the results shown in Table 6.3 reveal that the white:black per capita income disparity ratio rose from 10,6 in 1946/47 to 15,0 in 1970. During the same period, the disparity between white and coloured per capita incomes narrowed slightly, whereas the gap between white and Indian per capita incomes widened up to 1960, and then diminished slightly. The table also shows that the real per capita incomes of all the races grew continuously during this 23-year period, with the exception of Indian per capita incomes over the period from 1946/47 to 1960. White, coloured and Indian per capita incomes grew at an average annual compound rate of over 2 per cent per annum during the period. Black per capita incomes grew at the very slow compound rate of less than 1 per cent per annum. The growth rate of black incomes in this period may not, however, be at all significant, for many assumptions were needed for the estimates from which it was derived, and small changes in these assumptions can completely remove the estimated growth of black incomes.

All the growth rates were higher in the 1960s, which is understandable, since this was a decade of rapid economic growth, and this lends credibility to the estimates of income for these years.

Table 6.3:
RACIAL PER CAPITA INCOMES AND DISPARITY RATIOS

| | Incomes per capita in constant July 1984 rands | | | | | Disparity ratio white to other | | | | |
	1946/47	1960	1970	1975	1980	1946/47	1960	1970	1975	1980
White	4 218	5 139	7 373	8 946	8 501	–	–	–	–	–
Coloured	674	810	1 226	1 540	1 619	6,3	6,3	6,0	5,8	5,3
Indian	990	897	1 443	1 998	2 165	4,3	5,7	5,1	4,5	3,9
Black	398	433	490	717	657	10,6	11,9	15,0	12,5	12,9

In the period 1970–75, estimated black per capita incomes grew most rapidly, rising in real terms by 7,7 per cent per annum. White per capita incomes grew at 3,9 per cent per annum, which was the slowest of all the race groups. The result of this period of (relatively) higher growth rates in black incomes was that the disparities between white and black incomes per capita were narrowed.

The weak performance of the economy over most of the period between 1975 and 1979 is reflected in income growth, for there was a fall in both the real per capita incomes of whites and those of blacks. Indian and coloured real per capita incomes grew at positive rates of 1,6 and 1,0 per cent per annum respectively. The per capita racial disparity ratios between whites and coloureds, and whites and Indians, continued to narrow, although the inequalities that still remain are disturbingly high. The white to black disparity ratio widened once more between 1975 and 1980, and in 1980 this ratio was still greater than it had been in 1946/47 and 1960.

Economic growth in the post-war period thus resulted in increased per capita incomes for all race groups, although relative inequalities between whites and blacks were increased over the whole period because white per capita incomes grew faster than black per capita incomes. Coloured and Indian per capita incomes grew at a faster rate than white incomes and the disparities between the incomes of these groups were narrowed.

Separate time-series of data are available for incomes of blacks from subsistence agricultural production, transfer payments from the state, and modern sector employment. To explain the growth in black incomes, these sources must be examined. Unfortunately a consistent time-series is not available on incomes in informal sector activities. The physical output of the subsistence agricultural sector of the black states appears to have remained at a relatively constant level from the late 1940s to the mid-1970s, and has declined continuously in per capita terms as the population density of the black states has risen. The sources of the growth of black per capita incomes must therefore be sought in the modern sector. Transfer payments from the state to blacks grew rapidly in real terms over the period 1945–80. State pension benefits and other forms of transfer payments, such as pensions for the blind and the disabled, were first granted to blacks by the Pension Laws Amendment Act of 1948. Notwithstanding this high rate of increase, these transfer payments were not a major factor contributing to the growth of black incomes, because even in 1980 they accounted for a mere 3 per cent of total black incomes. The growth in total black incomes must thus have been largely attributable to increases in modern sector employment and increases in real wage rates. A consistent series of data on modern sector employment and wages (excluding domestic service) can be assembled for the years after 1960. Data for selected years between 1960 and 1980 are shown in Table 6.4.

The time-series of Table 6.4 reveals that economic growth has benefited blacks through higher real wage rates, in addition to higher levels of employment. Over the whole period from 1960 to 1980, the black real wage rate rose faster than the real wage rate of any of the other race groups. The rate of growth of black employment over the 20 year period was, however, no higher than the growth of white employment, and was lower than the growth rates in employment of coloureds and Indians. Over the post-1960 period the growth rate of the black population was 2,9 per cent per annum, and this exceeded the growth rate of employment in the modern sector, with the level of black unemployment and under-employment increasing as a consequence. Rising real wage rates accounted for 65 per cent of the increase in black earnings in the whole period from 1960 to 1980, and in the intermediate years never accounted for less than 45 per cent of the increase in black earnings. Despite the high levels of black unemployment and under-employment that have been estimated, black real wage rates grew at the exceptionally high rate of 7,3 per cent per annum from 1970 to 1975. The following section provides an analysis of the forces contributing to these changes, but a reduction in the overall labour surplus of the economy does not, regrettably, appear to have been one of the factors that caused real black wages to increase. The economy was certainly not on the growth path of the 'development-development' model previously outlined.

A feature of the distribution of income in South Africa is wide urban-rural inequalities. Very marked inequalities exist in black household incomes in the urban and rural areas, and when household incomes are expressed in per capita terms, these inequalities become even more noticeable. Table 6.5 shows average household and per capita incomes in various regions in 1975. This table highlights the very marked income inequality that has come to exist between regions for the black population. Per capita incomes of black households in the metropolitan regions were 2,2 times as great as per capita incomes in the black states, and 3,7 times the per capita incomes of the black households in

Table 6.4:
EMPLOYMENT AND REAL WAGES OF RACE GROUPS IN MODERN SECTOR EMPLOYMENT (EXCLUDING DOMESTIC SERVICE) IN 1960, 1970, 1975 AND 1980*
(WAGE RATES** IN CONSTANT JULY 1984 RAND)

Year	White		Coloured	
	Employment	Real wage rate	Employment	Real wage rate
1960	813 606	10 588	316 111	2 700
	(3,0)	(3,5)	(5,1)	(2,7)
1970	1 097 030	14 932	517 851	3 541
	(2,3)	(1,2)	(3,4)	(4,1)
1975	1 230 420	15 850	612 493	4 338
	(1,9)	(−0,7)	(2,3)	(0,3)
1980	1 352 980	15 301	687 224	4 400
Growth rate				
1960–80	(2,6)	(1,9)	(4,0)	(2,5)

Year	Indian		Black	
	Employment	Real wage rate	Employment	Real wage rate
1960	64 343	3 639	1 899 250	1 310
	(6,9)	(2,6)	(2,7)	(3,5)
1970	125 382	4 722	2 490 170	1 856
	(3,2)	(5,0)	(3,3)	(7,3)
1975	146 971	6 038	2 926 660	2 644
	(3,2)	(2,0)	(1,7)	(1,7)
1980	172 243	6 652	3 182 290	2 992
Growth rate				
1960–80	(5,0)	(3,1)	(2,6)	(4,2)

NOTES:
* Figures in parentheses are percentage annual compound growth rates over the period.
** Wage rates exclude the value of payments made to employees in kind.

the white rural areas.

Remittances to the black states by migrants in the mid-1970s accounted for approximately 35 per cent of the income of the black states, after excluding commuter incomes earned in the metropolitan regions. Thus, the migrant labour system was a major source of income for the rural areas of the black states, and without it the urban-rural differential would be far greater. Paradoxically, however, the migrant labour system has been shown to have contributed historically to the cause of the low incomes of the black states. It is very clear, however, that any reduction in the rate of labour migration would have disastrous consequences in the short-term for households in the rural areas of the

Table 6.5:

AVERAGE MULTIPLE HOUSEHOLD INCOMES AND
PER CAPITA INCOMES OF BLACKS IN VARIOUS REGIONS IN 1975
(CONSTANT JULY 1984 RAND)

	Average household (rand)	Average household size	Per capita income (size)
Metropolitan regions	5 952	5,5	1 082
White rural areas	1 977	6,7	295
Black states	2 730	5,5	496

black states, unless alternative sources of income were created at the same time.

There is evidence to suggest that urban-rural inequalities in black incomes have increased with time.[4] The proportion of the black population living in households in the metropolitan areas increased from 14 per cent of the total domestic population in 1950 to 22 per cent of the total domestic population in 1980. As shown above, between 1960 and 1980, average real per capita black incomes grew by 2,4 per cent per annum. The growth rates of the real per capita black incomes in each of the major metropolitan areas were higher than this national rate in the period between the 1960s and 1980, ranging from 4,1 per cent per annum for Pretoria household members to a low level of 2,7 per cent per annum for Johannesburg. The real per capita incomes of black household members in Durban and the Witwatersrand grew at 3,5 per cent and 3,4 per cent respectively over the same period. This pattern continued in the 1980s, even though the economy had fallen to a path of income stagnation. For example between 1975 and 1985 in the Cape Peninsula, black real incomes per person increased by 3,1 per cent per annum, in Johannesburg by 1,5 per cent per annum, in Pretoria by 2,3 per cent per annum, and in Durban by 0,23 per cent per annum; while over the same period per capita incomes in the economy as a whole stagnated (see Table 6.1).

Since both the proportion of black households in the metropolitan regions and the rate of growth of their incomes have risen faster than the national average, the per capita differentials between black households in the metropolitan areas and in other areas of the economy will consequently have widened since the 1960s, and the share of the metropolitan areas in total black incomes will definitely have risen. Moreover, the slowing down in the rate of growth of black employment in the period from 1975 and 1980, coupled with a tightening of the application of influx control over this period, will have placed the greatest increase in the burden of unemployment on the already impoverished black states, and will have contributed to the widening of urban-rural income inequalities and intensified pressures for urbanization.

The slow erosion of apartheid in the economy

Since the mid-1970s a number of important changes have occurred in the South African labour market and in other institutions, which directly affect black incomes.[5]

The acceleration of changes in the labour market dates from the wave of strikes of 1973, and the various trade union groupings which surfaced as a result. Other pressures emanated abroad, leading to the various Codes of Conduct imposed on foreign firms. The codes generally required that companies adopt non-racial policies and actively promote the interests of their black employees. Many local firms did not lag far behind the multinationals, emboldened by the new climate and by the changing relative power of black and white workers. In 1981, various employer organizations came out in favour of a non-discriminating, unified industrial relations system, and encouraged negotiations with black trade unions. Local employer organizations also urged reform, recognizing that the dictates of continued economic growth and of white demography required blacks to be drawn rapidly into the skilled labour pool. With the growing assertiveness and alienation of urban blacks and the threat of international isolation, the concerns of employers broadened in the 1980s. Their leaders increasingly spoke out for social justice and political power-sharing as a means of avoiding revolution, while preventing capitalism from being identified with apartheid by black people.

Reflecting the new balance of power in industrial relations, the three largest employer organizations, including that run by Afrikaans-speaking businessmen, jointly issued a statement in 1985 expressing 'the deep concern of the private sector about the detention of certain trade union leaders'. The Federated Chamber of Industries produced a 'Business Charter of Social, Economic and Political Rights', effectively espousing the principles of a non-racial, liberal, democratic, capitalist society. Underlying collective stands of this sort was the concern to distance capitalism as an economic form from apartheid as a social form.

The growing tension in black society surfaced in urban revolt in 1976, and sympathetic black workers participated in a series of politically inspired 'stay-aways'. The government responded to the mounting pressures from white capitalists and black workers in 1977 by appointing one inquiry (the Wiehahn Commission) into all aspects of labour relations and another (the Riekert Commission) into other aspects of labour utilization. The general tenor of their recommendations was that racial discrimination should be removed from legislation and institutional practice.

The Riekert Commission recommended that urban blacks be granted greater freedom of movement and job opportunities. Insofar as its recommendations were implemented, the effect was to accentuate the distinction between urban 'insiders' (those blacks with rights to permanent urban residence, who posed the greater political threat) and 'outsiders' (the inhabitants of the rural homelands, best described as labour reserves, who could enter the urban areas only as temporary contact workers). The reversal of policy came only in 1986 when the government, concerned formally to 'deracialize' its laws, abolished the influx control legislation.

The Wiehahn Commission recommended that government should embrace the principle of freedom of association without qualification, and government accepted this recommendation in stages.

Union membership among blacks mushroomed after 1981, and by 1985 black membership of registered trade unions exceeded 800 000. Industrial conflict was heightened as the new unions and employers tested their bargaining strength. In 1985, 390 strikes were reported and 680 000 working days lost, representing a tenfold increase over 1979 in working days lost, although the level of strike activity was still low by international standards.

The Wiehahn Commission recommended the abolition of all forms of statutory job reservation and the phasing out was virtually completed by 1984. Wiehahn also advised against the continued statutory exclusion of blacks from apprenticeship training of artisans, partly because of the shortage of skilled artisans. Government accepted the recommendation but black apprenticeships did not expand dramatically, reaching only 12 per cent of the total in 1985. A later report of the Wiehahn Commission recommended the abolition of all forms of job reservation in mining, the sector in which it was most firmly entrenched by the (white) Mine Workers Union, and this was accepted in 1987.

The changes in the labour market generally occurred with the approval and support, and often on the initiative, of employers. In this they were pursuing their perceived interests. They did so more actively and less timidly than in the past because the cost-imposing opposition of whites was now being counterbalanced by cost-imposing pressures from blacks and, in the case of foreign companies, from abroad.

During the 1970s it became increasingly accepted by government as well as employers that, with the deceleration of growth in the white labour force, the continued rapid growth of the South African economy would require a great expansion of educational and training facilities for blacks. Black education began to expand rapidly in the 1970s and black secondary school enrolment grew by 20 per cent per annum over the decade.

Four official reports undertaken between 1979 and 1981 stressed the need to increase the supply of skilled black labour in order to avert skill shortages. Official projections of the demand for 'technological manpower' over the decade 1977–87, and the projected increase in the supply obtainable from white entrants, implied that the supply of blacks would have to grow over four times more rapidly than that of whites. In 1983, government accepted the principle

Table 6.6:

SELECTED OCCUPATIONAL AND RACIAL SHARES OF TOTAL EMPLOYMENT 1965, 1975 AND 1985

			As percentage of total employment		
			1965	*1975*	*1985*
A	Managerial, executive, administrative, professional, semi-professional and technical	Whites:	6,3	7,5	9,6
		Blacks:	2,2	3,4	4,3
		Total:	8,5	10,9	13,9
B	All non-manual	Whites:	18,4	18,7	20,9
		Blacks:	5,2	8,1	11,6
		Total:	23,6	26,8	32,4
C	All non-manual plus supervisors and artisans	Whites:	23,4	23,2	25,5
		Blacks:	6,0	9,7	14,1
		Total:	29,4	32,7	39,6
	All occupations	Whites:	32,3	29,7	29,3
		Blacks:	67,7	70,3	70,7
		Total:	100,0	100,0	100,0

SOURCE:
Knight & McGrath, 1987, p. 50.

that there should be racial equality of educational opportunities and standards. Despite these changes in educational policy, in 1985 the overwhelming majority of blacks already in the labour force were without post-primary education.

It is ironic that the Wiehahn, Riekert and other reforms to integrate the labour market occurred when the South African economy was stagnating. Table 6.6 is designed to quantify the extent of upward occupational mobility between 1965 and 1985, using three possible definitions of 'top jobs'. It can be seen that white and black jobs in all three occupational categories increased as a proportion of total employment in the two decades under review. For instance, 'C' jobs (skilled, non-manual) accounted for 29,4 per cent of the total in 1965, 32,7 per cent in 1975, and 39,6 per cent in 1985. Yet white employment, taken separately as a proportion of the total for all three categories, fell from 32,3 per cent in 1965 to 29,7 per cent in 1975, and to 29,3 per cent in 1985. Inevitably therefore, blacks in top jobs expressed as a proportion of total employment increased consistently in all three categories. The increase was of a similar order in the two decades but actually greater over the second decade in the non-manual and 'most skilled' non-manual occupations. Moreover, the figures understate the extent of black advancement between 1975–85 because the 1985 survey excludes the four 'homelands' which had become 'independent states' and it is in the self-governing homelands that black administrative and professional employment is concentrated.

A decomposition analysis to determine by race the effect of the grade composition of employment, and the effects on differences in pay structures, can shed light on the economic importance of the changes which have been outlined. The decomposition analysis revealed that the extent of racial pay discrimination was reduced by roughly half. In 1976 coloureds, Indians and blacks received respectively 37,8; 33,0 and 42,9 per cent less pay than whites on account of their race alone, in other words standardizing for sex and grade. The corresponding figures in 1985 were 21,2; 12,7 and 21,8 per cent respectively. The intensity of racial and sex discrimination did not differ significantly across the spectrum of occupational grades for the 1976 survey. However, the 1985 results show a tendency for discrimination to decrease as the skills required in the job rise, and as black worker numbers expressed as a proportion of all workers in a grade decline; indicating that the labour market had become more competitive at the higher occupational grades.

The decomposition analysis showed that racial differences in the distribution of workers among grades accounted for 57 per cent of the difference in racial mean wages in 1976 and for no less than 84 per cent in 1985. The residual, after standardizing for job grades and gender — which could reflect wage discrimination — represented 45 per cent of the wage difference in 1976, but only 21 per cent in 1985. In other words, differential grade attainment has become relatively more important, and segregated wage determination processes less important in explaining the racial wage gap in South Africa. The change in black and white mean wages between 1976 and 1985 has also been decomposed into the effects of changes in the occupational distribution and those of changes in the wage determination process. This exercise reveals that 89 per cent of the increase in white pay was due to the improvement of the white occupational distribution, while some 60 per cent of the increase in the black real wage was due to an improved grade composition of employment. Signs of an emerging integration of the labour market are quite clear. However, as Figures 6.1 and 6.2 show, black workers still remain crowded into less skilled occupations, while white workers dominate in the managerial, technical and supervisory grades of employment. Levels of educational attainment have now become the most important determinant of the occupational structures.

Largely as a result of the forces operating in the labour market, the black share of income continued to increase between 1980 and 1985, rising in 1985 (using the BMR's definition of income) to 29 per cent of total personal income. By 1985 all groups other than whites received almost 41 per cent of personal incomes, while in 1960 this group had received less than 30 per cent of the total.

Figure 6.1:

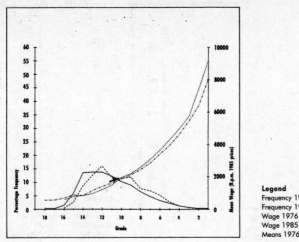

WAGE & FREQUENCY BY GRADE
1976 & 1985 — WHITES

SOURCE:
Knight & McGrath, 1987, p.22.

Future economic growth and income distribution

The growth record of the economy for the last 15 years, and the trends in income distribution, do not fit comfortably within the analytical framework of the 'liberals' or the 'revisionists'. The path of rapid economic growth has been shown to be far from inevitable. Political changes did not occur on a large enough scale to prevent political uncertainties and instabilities from eroding confidence and investment in the economy. In this regard Nattrass' analysis of growth and political changes proved highly perceptive. However, racial income inequalities were narrowed, despite the slow growth performance of the economy, because industrialists were forced to change their employment practices as blacks became more powerful as workers and consumers.

Income inequality still remains vast, but the economic power of the black group has grown to a significant level, and this undoubtedly is one of the factors influencing the changing attitude of government towards 'sharing' political power.

Government has also been forced by economic necessity to abandon many of its restrictive policies in response to the economic growth crisis. Faced with

Figure 6.2:

WAGE & FREQUENCY BY GRADE
1976 & 1985 — AFRICANS

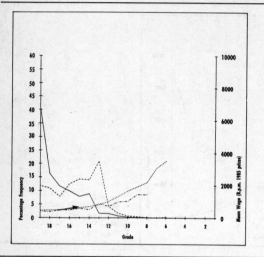

Legend
Frequency 1976 ———
Frequency 1985 - - - - -
Wage 1976 — · — · —
Wage 1985 · · · · · · · ·
Means 1976 to means 1985 ⟶

SOURCE:
Knight & McGrath, 1987, p.22.

the acceptance of the large and growing problem of structural unemployment, and with rapid urbanization following the abolition of influx control, the government has moved to allow more scope for informal sector growth, and has allowed greater freedom of competition in areas of the economy such as black transport. At the same time the government has prepared itself to expand the tax-base to capture a larger share of the growth in income from informal activities by adopting the Margo Commission's recommendation that the tax-base should be widened and that more reliance should be placed on indirect taxation.

The stagnation of the South African economy in the 1980s has eliminated any possibility of the economy absorbing all its economically active population into modern sector employment for years to come. It is, however, most probable that the trend to an integration of jobs and wage structures which started in the 1970s will continue. Thus within the metropolitan regions, the future is likely to show reducing inequality between the participants in modern sector occupations.

However, the incidence of poverty in the metropolitan regions will also increase. The slowing of growth of employment opportunities and the abolition of influx controls and restrictions on employment of black workers, have removed the protection which the migrant labour system gave to workers from rural areas, and this segment of the labour force will rapidly disappear. The termination of the migrant labour system will push these workers into the urban areas (most probably to be joined by their families at a later stage). Competition for unskilled jobs in urban areas will intensify, and unskilled wages will stagnate and may fall in real terms. Income shortfalls will be augmented by various subsistence-creating informal sector activities. Thus the wide urban-rural income gaps of the period prior to the 1970s will be transplaced to the urban areas.

The gains from economic growth have become more unequally distributed within the black population, and this process will continue to occur. Black households with access to modern sector jobs will most probably experience the greatest relative gains from economic growth. This group will remain a relatively small elite, and will most probably become a falling proportion of the black population.

Even if average wage differentials between whites and blacks continue to narrow during the coming decade, the gap in income from other sources will not begin to close for a long time, for it is to be expected that a substantial time will have to elapse before the income generated by the savings of blacks will contribute a substantial component of black incomes.

With its present economic institutions and situated on its current growth path, the South African economy will in the future continue to exhibit a distribution of incomes in which the present racial cleavages will exist, with the incomes of the white group dominating the upper deciles, although there will be a greater number of blacks in both the higher and the middle ranges. There is however now a consensus about the need for political reform as a precondition for South Africa to escape from its vicious circle of low economic growth and political instability.

Notes

1 See Nattrass' analysis of the growth of real wages in manufacturing (Chapter 7 in this volume). In that sector black real wages grew more rapidly than white real wages between 1960–74, but that pattern reversed between 1974–80. See Table 6.4 for white and black real wage growth for the economy as a whole.
2 See Moll in this volume for a more detailed comparative analysis.
3 The results of this section draw mainly on McGrath (1983).
4 Growth rates of incomes are estimated from selected Bureau of Market Research Income and Expenditure Surveys.
5 This section draws on the analysis of Knight & McGrath (1987).

References

Fisher, F., Schlemmer, L., & Webster, E., 'Economic Growth and its Relationship to Social and Political Change' in Schlemmer, L. & Webster, E. (eds.), *Change, Reform and Economic Growth in South Africa*, Ravan Press: Johannesburg, 1978.

Kantor, B.S. & Kenny, H.F., 'The Poverty of Neo-Marxism: The Case of South Africa', *Journal of Southern African Studies*, vol. 3, 1976.

Knight, J.B., & McGrath, M.D., 'The Erosion of Apartheid in the South African Labour Market: Measures and Mechanisms', Applied Economics Discussion Paper, no. 35, Oxford Institute of Economics and Statistics, September 1987.

Kuznets, S., 'Economic Growth and Income Inequality', *American Economic Review*, vol. 45, 1955.

Lewis, W.A., 'Economic Development with Unlimited Supplies of Labour', *The Manchester School*, vol. 22, 1954.

McGrath, M.D., *The Distribution of Personal Income in South Africa over the Period from 1945 to 1980*, Unpublished Ph.D Thesis, University of Natal: Durban, 1983.

McGrath, M.D., & Holden, M., 'Economic Outlook', *Indicator South Africa*, vol. 6, 1989.

Nattrass, J., 'Economic Development and Social and Political Change — A Suggested Theoretical Framework' in Schlemmer, L. & Webster, E. (eds.), *Change, Reform and Economic Growth in South Africa*, Ravan Press: Johannesburg, 1978.

Nattrass, J., *The South African Economy: Its Growth and Change*, Oxford University Press: Cape Town, 1981.

O'Dowd, M.C., 'South Africa in the Light of the Stages of Economic Growth', in Leftwich, A. (ed.), *South Africa, Economic Growth and Political Change*, Allison & Busby: London, 1974.

Schlemmer, L., 'Economy and Society in South Africa', in Schlemmer, L., & Webster, E. (eds.), *Change, Reform and Economic Growth in South Africa*, Ravan Press: Johannesburg, 1978.

Steenkamp, W.F.J., 'Bantu Wages in South Africa', *South African Journal of Economics*, vol. 30, June 1962.

van der Horst, S.T., *Native Labour in South Africa*, Frank Cass & Co.: London, 1981.

Wilson, F., 'The Political Implications for Blacks of Economic Changes Now Taking Place in South Africa', in Thompson, L. & Butter, J. (eds.), *Change in Contemporary South Africa*, California University Press: Berkeley, 1975.

Wright, H.M., *The Burden of the Present: Liberal Radical Controversy over South African History*, David Philip: Cape Town, 1977.

Economic power and profits in post-war manufacturing

Nicoli Nattrass

Introduction

One of Jill Nattrass' main concerns was the relationship between economic development and socio-political change (1978, 1981). According to her, development is stultified if socio-political structures fail to evolve sufficiently to 'meet the aspirations of the groups who are gaining economic power as a result of the economic growth process' (1981, p. 275). While recognizing that the nature and path of development reflects 'the underlying relative economic and political power structures that accompany all economic change' (ibid., p. 278), she was particularly concerned with the revolutionary potential of increased black earnings. In her view it was no accident that from the mid-1970s, increased black economic power (as indicated by income redistribution from whites to blacks) was accompanied by a process of institutional reform. It was also no surprise that social revolt escalated in the early 1980s in the face of the glaring inability of those reforms to match black aspirations.

Economic power, according to Jill Nattrass' framework, came from control over the factors of production (that is, capital and skills) and the political-institutional environment within which capitalism operated (ibid., p. 284). She also regarded labour's ability to disrupt the process of profit generation, via industrial action, as a key source of economic power.

There is, however, an important additional dimension to economic power and this is labour's ability to erode the rate of return on capital — that is, the profit rate (Armstrong *et al.*, 1984; Bowles *et al.*, 1986; Glyn *et al.*, 1987). This aspect was not investigated in any great detail. On the basis of a brief analysis of manufacturing census data she concluded that the 'increase in labour productivity was sufficient to fund the increase in real wages that took place over the post-war period without a reduction in the rate of return on capital' (1981, p. 184). It is thus not surprising that in the face of an apparently constant profit share and rate, she attached little significance to profit rate analysis as a tool for understanding economic power.

Her conclusion that labour was unable to gain a greater share of the surplus or erode capitalist profitability is, however, based on inappropriate data. The major problem with using the manufacturing census as a source is that the valuation of capital (in accordance with business accounting practices) is at historic cost rather than replacement value. Profit rates measured on capital valued at historic cost include two elements: an operating surplus (profit generated in production); and a revaluation surplus (profit obtained by holding a capital asset which remains physically unchanged over a period in which its price rises). The profit rate is thus biased upwards and falls uneasily between the nominal and real rates of return (Carlin, 1987, pp. 118–19). Thus in order to avoid the revaluation surplus (which originates from a redistribution of real wealth rather than in the production process), rates of return should be measured on capital valued at current replacement costs (Hill, 1979, pp. 11–12).

Using a more appropriate measure of capital (that is, net capital at current prices), a very different picture of trends in the profit share and rate emerges. As shown in Figure 7.1, the net rate of profit in the South African manufacturing sector has been on a strong trend decline over the post-war period, falling from 44 per cent in 1948 to 9 per cent in 1986. As this trend is reflected (although less severely) in the broader 'core' economy,[1] the analysis of manufacturing profitability can be regarded as representative of broad economic trends in South Africa.

Figure 7.1:
MANUFACTURING PROFITABILITY IN SOUTH AFRICA

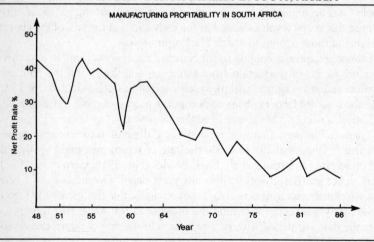

It is however important to stress that although South African profit rates fell in the post-war period, they remained substantially higher than those in the advanced capitalist countries (ACCs). International comparisons of profitability are fraught with difficulties owing to the lack of uniformity in international measurements of the capital stock (Hill, 1979). Nevertheless, the fact that the South African manufacturing profit rate has consistently remained over twice that in Europe, is worthy of comment. Table 7.1 provides an indication of relative manufacturing profit rates in some of the ACCs[2] and South Africa.

Table 7.1:
INTERNATIONAL MANUFACTURING NET PROFIT RATES

	1955	1960	1964	1970	1975	1981
ACCs	26,3	22,1	23,8	19,3	11,6	8,9
Europe	21,3	19,9	14,8	14,0	7,9	5,2
Germany	35,7	28,8	20,0	18,6	11,0	8,3
UK	18,8	17,5	14,6	9,6	3,9	1,7
Japan	20,7	43,8	41,4	46,5	10,4	13,3
USA	31,2	22,3	35,7	17,7	16,7	10,3
South Africa	39,3	35,3	31,1	23,6	15,1	15,2

SOURCE:
Armstrong et al., 1984, and own calculations for South Africa.

This essay examines the growth in the (net) rate of profit in South African manufacturing between 1948 and 1986. As this sheds light on the relative strength of workers (both black and white) and capitalists in South Africa, the analysis is presented as a contribution to Jill Nattrass' theory of economic power and social change. Furthermore, insofar as the vitality of the manufacturing sector is an important determinant of the long-term prosperity of the South African economy (Moll, 1988), an analysis of the manufacturing profit rates helps to shed light on the nature of accumulation in the post-war period. In this respect, the analysis has implications for political-economic interpretations of the relationship between apartheid and capitalism.

Periodizing the South African post-war economy

When analysing medium to long-term trends in an economy, it is important that the time period under consideration is divided into years which are on the same point of the business or growth cycle. Comparing peak with slump years distorts the long-term trend. Bearing this in mind, the post-war South African economy can be periodized according to the following 'peak-to-peak' cycles:[3] 1948–55, 1955–60, 1960–64, 1964–70, 1970–75, 1975–81, 1981–86. Various economic indicators for these periods are shown in Table 7.2.

As can be seen from Table 7.2, the rate of growth of output, employment and the capital stock all accelerated sharply in the early 1960s. In relation to the economy as a whole, manufacturing reflected these trends in an exaggerated

Table 7.2:

SELECTED ECONOMIC INDICATORS

						Average annual compound growth rates	
	1948 -55	1955 -60	1960 -64	1964 -70	1970 -75	1975 -81	1981 -86
Real GDP	4,6	4,0	6,0	5,5	4,0	3,0	0,3
Real manufacturing output	7,7	4,6	10,2	7,5	5,9	5,1	-2,4
Real man.investment	-0,7	5,5	25,1	4,3	7,1	7,8	-15,6
Real man. Net Capital Stock	8,3	5,2	8,3	8,3	8,6	6,5	3,3
Man. employment	5,2	0,3	6,1	5,0	4,1	1,8	-2,2
Total employment	2,7	1,3	2,9	2,9	2,4	1,3	-0,5
Rate of (CPI) inflation	5,5	2,2	1,8	3,4	9,4	12,6	14,7
$ Gold price	0	0	0	0	35,7	19,1	-4,4

SOURCES:
Various editions of *South African Statistics* and the *South African Reserve Bank Quarterly Bulletin* and unpublished material from the South African Reserve Bank, the Central Statistical Services and the Institute for Futures Research, Stellenbosch University. More detail is available on request.

manner with its share in value added rising from 18 per cent in 1948 to 24 per cent in 1981. The 1970s saw a slowdown in growth which stagnated to crisis proportions in the 1980s. Again, the manufacturing sector reflected these trends more severely. Manufacturing output declined in real terms and its contribution to value added dropped to 22 per cent in 1986.

In order to isolate which economic factors played important roles in shaping profitability trends, it is necessary, for mathematical reasons, to examine changes in the rate of growth of the profit rate rather than the absolute levels presented in Figure 7.1. The mathematical underpinnings behind the deconstruction are discussed on an intuitive level in the following section (and in more detail in the Appendix).

Deconstructing the rate of profit

The rate of profit (profits divided by capital) can be expressed as the product of the profit share (profits divided by total output) and the output:capital ratio. Thus the rate of profit that capitalists earn on their capital is a function of the proportion of total output accruing to them and the productivity of the capital employed by them.

$$\frac{P}{K} = \frac{P}{Y} \times \frac{Y}{K}$$

P = Profits (i.e. the net operating surplus at current prices)[4]
Y = Output (i.e. net value added at current prices)[5]
K = Capital stock (Net at current replacement value)[6]

In growth rate terms,[7] this can be approximated as:

$$\frac{\dot{P}}{K} = \frac{\dot{P}}{Y} + \frac{\dot{Y}}{K}$$

The deconstruction of South Africa's manufacturing profit rate over the post-war economic peak-to-peak cycles is given below:

	$\frac{\dot{P}}{K}$	=	$\frac{\dot{P}}{Y}$	+	$\frac{\dot{Y}}{K}$
1948–55	–1,8	=	0,7	+	(–2,5)
1955–60	–2,0	=	–0,6	+	(–1,4)
1960–64	–3,2	=	–2,9	+	(–0,3)
1964–70	–4,4	=	–2,2	+	(–2,3)
1970–75	–8,3	=	–3,0	+	(–5,8)
1975–81	0,2	=	3,5	+	(–3,3)
1981–86	–9,7	=	–4,3	+	(–6,0)

NOTE:
These approximations do not alwasy add up exactly (see note 7).

The profit share and the output:capital ratio can be deconstructed into further components:

The profit share
Given that value added (output) is the sum of wages and profits, the profit share can be expressed as one minus the wage share.

$$\frac{P}{Y} = 1 - \frac{W}{Y}$$

W = remuneration of employees

The performance of the wage and profit shares is constrained by the growth of the surplus available for distribution between wages and profits. Such surplus is a function of productivity increases and relative input costs. If input costs rise faster than output prices, the 'room' for wage or profit increases is less than that indicated by the growth in productivity.

Put simply, the profit share will fall (and the wage share rise) if wages increase faster than the surplus available for distribution. In other words, if the growth of wage income exceeds that of the total 'economic pie', then it follows that the pie slice accruing to capitalists will be eroded. Wages in this deconstruction are measured as 'product wages', that is, current wages deflated by the production price index so as to obtain a measure of the real cost to capitalists of employing labour.

The output:capital ratio

The output:capital ratio can be expressed as a function of the real gross output:capital ratio (which measures the productivity of capital) and a set of relative prices. The most important of these relative prices are the terms of trade between the manufacturing sector and the suppliers of capital goods, and input prices relative to output prices. As this essay concentrates on the labour market dynamics operating on profitability, trends in the output:capital ratio are discussed only cursorily.

South African manufacturing profit rates: 1948–86

The manufacturing profit rate has been falling at an increasing rate over peak-to-peak cycles from 1948 (except for the very slight recovery between 1975 and 1981). This has been because of declines in both the profit share (reflecting *inter alia* increased economic power for labour) and the output:capital ratio. These trends are discussed in more detail for each period, with the focus primarily on trends in average wages and employment growth.

The rate of profit: 1948–60

The period 1948–60 (which Lipton characterizes as the 'Consolidation of Apartheid'; 1986, p. 22) can be broken down into two peak-to-peak cycles which show declining profit rates but divergent trends in the profit share due to changing conditions.

Between 1948 and 1955 the rate of profit fell by 1,8 per cent per annum, despite a positive trend in the profit share. Between 1955 and 1960, adverse trends in both the output:capital ratio and the wage share contributed to a faster decrease in the profit rate.

The profit share

Between 1948 and 1955, the surplus available for distribution between wages and profits grew at only 0,1 per cent per annum. As product wages fell by 0,4 per cent per annum over the period, the wage share fell by 0,5 per cent per annum. Between 1955 and 1960 however, the growth of product wages exceeded that of the surplus and the wage share increased at the cost of the profit share.

The above trend suggests that, between 1948 and 1955, labour was relatively weak and unable to prevent the erosion of its share of output, whereas by the second half of the 1950s, it was able to secure gains at the expense of profits. However, while this was true in aggregate, the relative strength of workers differed markedly between the races.

The labour market in South Africa is highly segmented along skill and racial lines and is characterized by a shortage of skilled and semi-skilled (predominantly white) labour, and a surplus of unskilled (black) labour. Large-scale

urbanization of unskilled black workers took place during the war and this continued into the 1950s. This generated an ample supply of unskilled labour for
the urban manufacturing sector, at the expense of agriculture and the mining
industry. At the same time, the rapid expansion of industry exacerbated the
shortage of skilled labour, putting upward pressure on wages.

The downward pressure on unskilled wages and the upward pressure on
skilled wages was certainly exacerbated by the National Party's racial policies.
White workers were protected by job reservation against competition from black
workers aspiring to semi-skilled and skilled jobs. Repression meted out to the
black and non-racial trade union movement (for example, the 1950 Suppression
of Communism Act) was hardly conducive to the defence of the real level of
black wages. Nevertheless, despite the continuation of such repressive policies,
by the late 1950s black workers were making real wage gains, and the white:black
wage gap in manufacturing was rising less quickly than it had in the earlier
period.

Table 7.3:
EMPLOYMENT AND WAGES IN SA MANUFACTURING*: 1948–60

| | Average annual compound growth rates | | | | | | | |
| | 1948–55 | | | | 1955–60 | | | |
	White	Coloured & Indian	Black	Total	White	Coloured & Indian	Black	Total
Employment	3,2	4,7	6,5	5,2	–0,7	1,0	0,6	0,3
Real wages	3,4	0,3	–0,6	1,0	4,5	2,6	2,8	3,4
Product wages	1,9	–1,3	–2,1	–0,4	5,3	3,5	3,9	4,2
Surplus				0,1				3,8

* Average wages have been estimated so as to accord with remuneration statistics in the
national accounts. Detail available on request. Real wages are deflated by the consumer
price index. Product wages are deflated by the production price index. Surplus refers to
the surplus available for distribution between wages and profits.

As can be seen in Table 7.3, white wages rose more rapidly than black wages
in both periods, while black employment growth consistently outstripped that
of whites. Because the level and rate of growth of white wages was so much
higher than black wages between 1948 and 1960 (but particularly between 1948
and 1955), the white share of the wage bill increased from 61,7 per cent to
63,4 per cent, despite the decline in the white share of employment from 32,3 per
cent to 27 per cent.

Whereas average white wages grew in real terms at 3,9 per cent per annum
between 1948 and 1955, black workers were unable to defend their living
standards, and their real wages fell by 0,6 per cent per annum. Coloured/Indian
workers appeared to be in a stronger position (probably because they were better

educated and more skilled, and because coloured workers in the western Cape were afforded preferential access to employment by law). They experienced a small increase in real wages.

Between 1955 and 1960, white wages continued to rise relative to black wages, but this time black workers were able to secure real wage gains, thus indicating either upward mobility through the occupational structure or a tightening of the labour market situation (possibly exacerbated by industrial militancy) or a combination of both.

The trend in product wages is also illuminating. As pointed out above, product wages reflect the real cost to capitalists of employing labour. Between 1948 and 1955, black product wages fell sharply by 2,1 per cent per annum, coloured/Indian wages fell by 1,3 per cent per annum and white product wages rose by 1,9 per cent per annum. In each case, the trend in product wages was far more favourable to capitalists than would be suggested by trends in real wages. For example, between 1948 and 1955, coloured/Indian workers managed to secure real gains (in terms of purchasing power) at a time when their cost to capitalists was actually falling!

Given that the surplus rose by 0,1 per cent per annum between 1948 and 1955, and that overall average product wages fell by 0,4 per cent per annum, the rapid increase of white product wages was prevented from causing a profit (share) squeeze by the compensating declines in black and coloured/Indian product wages. This extremely interesting development lends weight to the neo-Marxist argument that white wage increases were more than compensated for by the decline in black wages.

Between 1955 and 1960, however, black product wages rose faster (albeit by only 0,1 per cent) than the surplus, thus contributing to the profit squeeze rather than alleviating the pressure caused by white wage increases. White workers, despite a small drop in employment, maintained their strong bargaining position and were able to maintain product wage gains well in excess of the growth in the surplus available.

The output:capital ratio

Over the period 1948–55, the output:capital ratio fell by 2,5 per cent per annum. The main contributing factors were the adverse relative price movements in the cost of inputs and capital. Of these two relative price trends, by far the most significant was the increase in input costs relative to value added prices — thus causing an input cost squeeze on profits.

The rise in relative input prices (which was the sharpest in the entire post-war period) was probably related to the transport and supply bottlenecks which dogged the late 1940s and early 1950s, and to increased import prices resulting from a currency devaluation in 1949 and the Korean war in the early 1950s. The question which immediately arises for our analysis of the profit rate decline, is why manufacturers were unable to pass on the rise in input prices to the consumer via higher value added prices?

A large part of the answer probably lies with the price controls which were instigated over the period in order to combat inflation. South African manufacturing has a very high import content. Consequently, faced with price controls in the domestic market and rising import prices, it is not surprising that the resulting relative price squeeze was enough to drag the rate of profit down in the face of positive trends in the profit share. Furthermore, the policy of import substitution and import licensing (which, according to Zarenda, was 'the main stimulus to production' in the post-war period up to 1957 (1977, p. 110)) may have had more negative effects on average profitability (by exacerbating imported input price rises) than positive effects (by protection of industry from international competition).

Between 1955 and 1960, decline in the output:capital ratio was slower than it had been in the preceding period; the main reason being the decrease in relative capital costs.

The rate of profit in the boom period: 1960–70

During the 1960s boom (when real GDP grew at 5,7 per cent per annum), the trend decline in the rate of profit continued to accelerate. The rate of profit fell from 35,3 per cent in 1960 to 27,2 per cent in 1970. In the early 1960s the main contributing factor was the sharp deterioration in the profit share, whereas by the late 1960s, this profit squeeze had declined slightly. In contrast, by the late 1960s, the decline in the output:capital ratio (which was minor in the earlier period) was contributing as much to the fall in profitability as was the profit share.

It is illuminating to compare the trends with those in the ACCs. During the 1960s, profit rates **rose** in the ACCs by 2,6 per cent per annum, due to **increases** in the profit share (0,7 per cent per annum) and in the output:capital ratio (2,0 per cent per annum) (Glyn, 1988, p. 233). While the ACCs experienced dynamic accumulation, the South African boom was showing distinct signs of being unsustainable. Whereas South African capitalists continued to earn higher absolute levels of profit than those earned in the ACCs, costs increased faster in South Africa and workers were better able to make gains at the expense of the profit rate.

The profit share

The profit share was squeezed in the entire period (although more severely between 1960 and 1964) by black and white product wages rising faster than the surplus available for distribution. Trends in the labour market are summarized in Table 7.4.

Table 7.4:
EMPLOYMENT AND WAGES IN SA MANUFACTURING*: 1964–70

| | Average annual compound growth rates | | | | | | | |
| | 1960–64 | | | | 1964–70 | | | |
	White	Coloured & Indian	Black	Total	White	Coloured & Indian	Black	Total
Employment	4,6	8,6	5,8	6,1	4,0	6,4	4,9	5,0
Real wages	4,9	2,1	5,9	4,0	3,2	1,5	1,9	2,2
Product wages	5,3	2,5	6,3	4,7	3,7	2,0	2,3	2,7
Surplus				2,9				1,6

* See notes to Table 7.3.

As in the earlier post-war periods, black employment grew faster than white throughout the 1960s. However, as regards the tendency for the rate of growth of white wages to exceed that of black wages, the period 1960–64 marks a sharp break. Over those four years, the white:black wage gap **fell** by 0,8 per cent per annum such that the white share of the wage bill declined from 63,4 per cent to 61,7 per cent (and the black share rose from 23,1 per cent to 24,4 per cent). However, between 1964 and 1970, this development was reversed. The white:black wage gap grew by 1,3 per cent per annum and the black share of the wage bill declined to 23,9 per cent despite the faster growth rate of black employment.

In the absence of data relating to the relationship between race, skill structure and differential rates for the job, it is difficult to explain why the growth of black wages was so rapid relative to white wages during the 1960–64 period and to its own growth in the following period. One could speculate that it may have had something to do with the technological changes embodied in new investment in the early 1960s (especially the foreign component) which was designed to operate on semi-skilled rather than artisan-based skilled labour (see Braverman, 1974). This would have increased the demand for black semi-skilled and unskilled labour, thus boosting black wages relative to white.[8]

However, further research is required to understand why the bargaining power of white workers appeared to be slipping in the early 1960s (while that of black workers was rising) and why the process was reversed in the mid- to late 1960s.

The output:capital ratio

Between 1960 and 1964, the output:capital ratio fell only slightly because the adverse trends in relative capital and input prices were almost entirely compensated for by a rapid rise in the real output:capital ratio. The rapid growth of manufacturing output over the period lies behind this development. However, by the late 1960s, continuing adverse trends in relative prices were once again reinforced by a fall in the real output:capital ratio (as the growth in output lagged behind that of the capital stock).

Gold-cushioned economic decline: 1970–81

For the period 1970–81 (which Lipton characterizes as 'the partial erosion of apartheid' (1986, p. 490)) the profit rate shows very divergent tendencies in the two peak-to-peak periods 1970–75 and 1975–81. Between 1970 and 1975 the profit rate dived at its most rapid rate since 1948. However, between 1975 and 1981, due to a sharp improvement in the profit share and an alleviation of cost pressures, the profit rate actually showed an slight upward tendency.

South African profit rates were less affected by the profit and cost squeezes which beset the ACCs after the oil price rises exacerbated the economic slow-down apparent from 1968.[9] South Africa was able to avoid excessive structural adjustment because the sharp increase in the gold price boosted her reserves, thereby cushioning her economic decline. With a delightful metaphorical flourish, Williams observed in 1975 that 'thanks to its virtual monopoly of the money commodity, the economy of South Africa stands revealed as the growing fingernail on the moribund corpse of capitalism' (p. 16). Given the above trends in profit rates, Williams can be forgiven for his thinking at the time.

However, South Africa to a great extent failed to reap the full growth potential of the leap in the gold price (Moll, 1989). Rather than channelling the additional foreign exchange resources into productive investment, consumption (and thus also inflation) was stimulated. As can be seen from Table 7.2, the gold price rose at an average annual rate of 35 per cent per annum in the early 1970s and at 19 per cent per annum between 1975 and 1981, whereas manufacturing investment over the decade grew at the relatively slow rate of just over 7 per cent per annum.

Table 7.5:
EMPLOYMENT AND WAGES IN SA MANUFACTURING*: 1970–81

| | Average annual compound growth rates | | | | | | | |
| | 1970–1975 | | | | 1975–1981 | | | |
	White	Coloured & Indian	Black	Total	White	Coloured & Indian	Black	Total
Employment	2,6	3,7	5,0	4,1	1,7	2,5	1,6	1,8
Real wages	2,4	4,9	6,3	3,0	0,4	1,1	2,6	1,1
Product wages	0,6	3,0	4,4	1,2	-0,4	0,4	1,9	0,5
Surplus				0,1				1,9

* See notes to Table 7.3.

The profit share

As is shown in Table 7.5, between 1970 and 1975 the profit share was squeezed because the product wages of all race groups (but especially blacks and to a lesser extent coloureds/Indians) rose a great deal faster than the surplus available for distribution.

Between 1975 and 1981, the rise in black wages remained in excess of the growth in surplus, but the fact that white product wages actually **declined** and coloured/Indian wages rose slower than the surplus meant than the share of profit was able to rise. Thus if we compare this period with the only other post-war period showing a falling wage share (that is, 1948–55), we see that this time it was the erosion of white (and to a lesser extent coloured/Indian) product wages that compensated for the rise in black product wages!

The white share of the wage bill declined from 61,7 per cent to 51 per cent between 1970 and 1975 and the white:black wage gap fell by 3,6 per cent per annum over the same period and by 2,3 per cent per annum between 1975 and 1981. The reasons for the decisive reversal in the relative fortunes of white and black workers from the early 1970s are to be found in the following developments. Firstly, the increased upward penetration of the occupational structure[10] by black workers, which was aided by the 'floating' of the colour bar from the mid-1960s (Lipton, 1986), the gradual removal of the colour bar from 1973 onwards and the 'process of restructuring work categories ... to create semi-skilled tasks for relatively unskilled workers — mainly blacks' (Wiehahn Commission quoted in Callinicos, 1988, p. 24). Secondly, the increased militancy of the black working class (as demonstrated dramatically by the 1973 Durban strikes) which in the context of the above developments, was bound to result in real gains.

Knight & McGrath (1987) found that the narrowing of the wage gap between 1976 and 1985 was principally a result of the growing proportion of blacks in higher-grade jobs and not the outcome of an increase in wage levels within occupational categories. The increased bargaining power of black workers in skilled and semi-skilled positions has been cited as one of the main reasons why the spontaneous Durban strikes of 1973 were successful (see Institute for Industrial Education, 1976, p. 145). However, as black wages rose throughout the economy in the early 1970s, it is likely that labour shortages extended beyond skilled categories over the period (see Hofmeyr's contribution in this volume).

One could argue that black wage increases in the early 1970s were in part a 'catching up' (of wages due) process, and in part the result of industrial muscle flexing. The (government-appointed) Kleu Study Group however, provides a different interpretation. On the grounds that 'social and political circumstances have given rise to a sharp increase in the wages and salaries of people of colour without a corresponding increase in productivity', it concluded that 'indicators are that ... labour in the manufacturing industry has been over-remunerated' (1985, pp. 160–1). Such conclusions are highly suspect. While it may be true that the rapid rise in black product wages squeezed profits, one can tell nothing about the relationship between the level of black wages and the marginal productivity of black workers. In the absence of any meaningful way of unpackaging the relative productivities of black and white workers, it is as valid to assume that workers were being paid their marginal product owed to them after the strikes, as it is to believe that they were before the strikes.

The output:capital ratio

The output:capital ratio declined markedly in both periods as a result of deteriorations in relative input and capital prices and in the real output:capital ratio. The cost-push inflation following the oil price rise probably lay at the root of the relative price trends, while the decline in the real output:capital ratio was the result of economic slowdown coupled with a still high level of investment in the early 1970s.

Why investment remained high is an interesting question. It probably has to do with the still high level of profits (by international standards), negative real interest rates in the 1970s,[11] fiscal investment subsidies since 1962, high levels of effective protection (which increased in the 1970s) and an over-valued exchange rate. All these had a price-distorting effect such that capital goods were artificially cheapened. Further research is needed to ascertain how much of the consistent decline in the output:capital ratio can be attributed to these developments.

The troubled and stagnant 1980s

At the end of 1981 South Africa entered a major recession from which she has yet to emerge. Per capita incomes have declined (McCarthy, 1987, p. 12) and the growth of the real GDP has been negligible. Manufacturing has been particularly badly affected. Between 1981 and 1986, real manufacturing investment fell by 15,6 per cent per annum, value added by 2,4 per cent per annum, and the share of manufacturing in the GDP declined from 24 per cent to 22 per cent.

These developments are reflected in the rate of profit which fell faster than in any other period.[12] While the ACCs managed to resuscitate productivity growth and once again achieve rising rates of profit,[13] South Africa's profitability performance continued to plummet. The decline in the gold price, the confidence-shaking effects of political crisis on investors, economic sanctions and disinvestment, along with misguided government monetary policies,[14] are key determinants of the sharply-deteriorating economic situation.

The profit share

Between 1981 and 1986, the profit share suffered the most severe squeeze of the post-war period.

Table 7.6:
EMPLOYMENT AND WAGES IN SA MANUFACTURING*: 1981–86

	White	*Coloured & Indian*	*Black*	*Total*
	Average annual compound growth rates			
Employment	−1,6	−1,6	−2,7	−2,2
Real wages	−2,0	0	1,7	0,2
Product wages	−0,9	1,2	2,8	0,8
Surplus				−0,9

* See notes to Table 7.3.

As can be seen from Table 7.6, the profit share decline was the result of black and coloured/Indian product wage growth in the face of a rapidly declining surplus. Unlike in the 1975–81 period, the decline in white product wages did not compensate for this trend. Rather, black employment fell faster than white employment and the rate at which the white:black wage gap was narrowing, slowed down.

Between 1981 and 1986, labour in South Africa was relatively more powerful than in the ACCs. Despite the absolute decline in output and employment, Indian/coloured and black product wage growth was positive. This drove down the profit share by 4,3 per cent per annum at a time when, in the ACCs, capitalists were able to secure a profit share growth of 4,2 per cent per annum.

The output:capital ratio

The output:capital ratio fell by 6 per cent per annum due to a severe decline in the real output:capital ratio (which outweighed positive developments in relative capital costs). The real output:capital ratio declined at such a rate because the capital stock grew at 3,3 per cent per annum while real output **fell** by 2,4 per cent per annum!

Conclusion

This essay shows that profit rates in the South African manufacturing sector have been on a severe trend decline from 1948 and that the downward slide of the profit rate actually increased during the 'apartheid boom' of the 1960s. This, along with the fact that the rising wage share explains a great deal of the fall, has implications for certain political-economic theories of South African development.

Revisionist-Marxist historians have argued that apartheid policies (rather than simply the process of capitalist accumulation) underlay allegedly buoyant profit rates during the 1960s. Saul & Gelb maintain that 'soaring profit rates during the 1960s boom' (1986, p. 73) were 'practically guaranteed by the apartheid state's policies' and that it was **on the basis** of apartheid's driving down of black wages (which **meant** rising profits) that the economy settled into a long-term expansion (1986, pp. 70–4).

Given that profit rates declined, largely as the result of the increasing economic power of (initially white but later black) workers, certain revisionist assumptions need re-assessing. Clearly, as the plummeting profit rate shows, severe pressures (or contradictions) were building up in the South African economy from 1948 and especially in the boom period. While profit rates were **absolutely** high enough to finance the boom, the growth/accumulation path was clearly unsustainable.

In this sense, it is of no help to divide the post-war political economy into periods in which apartheid provided the engine for growth and others in which the balance of costs and benefits was reversed (see for example Gelb, 1987). It is far more meaningful to conceptualize apartheid as simultaneously allowing for high profits and exacerbating (if not causing) the decline in profitability via the labour market and cost pressures generated by the system. There was never any honeymoon period for the marriage of apartheid and capitalism in terms of a **stable and reproducible growth path**. The roots of the 1980s economic crisis were manifesting themselves from the 1960s (if not before) in the form of falling profitability.

The challenge to radical political economists is to unravel the complex and contradictory processes which allowed for high, but rapidly falling profit rates in South Africa. Interesting questions include why profit rates were so much higher in South Africa, why the pressures which built up in the South African economy were so much more severe than in the ACCs, and whether or not apartheid policies alleviated or exacerbated the downward dive of the profit rate. In order to rise to this challenge, certain radical assumptions concerning the role of labour markets and the nature of the South African state need re-evaluating.

Marxist economic analyses of South Africa argued (implicitly or explicitly) that the alleged buoyancy of the profit rate was the result of a depressed wage share, which in turn was the outcome of a high rate of exploitation premised on the control, disorganization and repression of black labour (see for example Wolpe, 1972; Hindson, 1987). However, as we have seen, with the exception of the periods 1948–55 and 1975–81, the wage share **rose**.

While recognizing that apartheid policies brought with them costs to capitalists in the form of protected white labour, bureaucratic impediments to the hiring of migrants from the reserves, and shortages of semi-skilled and skilled labour, revisionists accepted (almost as an article of faith) that until the early 1970s, these detrimental aspects were offset by the depressive effect that apartheid policies had on black labour costs.

The effects of labour-market segmentation and differentiation on black wages are considerably more ambiguous than was generally acknowledged. Influx control limited employment options for blacks, increased the costs of dismissal, and (together with direct constraints on trade unions) inhibited workplace organization. All of these served to reduce black workers' bargaining power. But labour-market differentiation did not necessarily depress wages.[15] Influx control served also to protect the wages of 'legal' black urban residents, who were not subject to competition from a burgeoning army of urban squatters. Considerably more research needs to be undertaken into the links between occupational mobility, influx control, and wage determination in black labour markets.

The figures in this essay show that during the period 1948–55, wage rates and shares moved in the direction predicted by radical theories. However, from 1955 the wage share rose (except for 1975–81) due to black product wages rising consistently faster than the surplus available for distribution. This increased black bargaining power not only squeezed profits but also accelerated the erosion of racial distinctions in the labour market and set up pressures for change in the political sphere (see Nattrass, 1981 and more recently, Wolpe, 1988). It is thus vital that this change be reflected in our theoretical understanding of the post-war South African political economy.

Insofar as state policies may have actively contributed to the decrease in the output:capital ratio, the idea that the state acted in the interests of manufacturing and monopoly capital from the 1960s (see Davies et al., 1976, p. 28) needs qualification.

State economic strategies which encouraged the 'over-accumulation' of capital by artificially cheapening it through taxation, exchange and interest rate policies, had distinctly ambiguous effects. Whereas investment and growth may well have been stimulated, the rate of profit was undermined to the extent that these policies contributed to a declining output:capital ratio. Furthermore, state price-control policies (especially in the 1950s and 1960s) which prevented producers from passing rising input and capital costs on to the consumer, also contributed to declining profitability.

Even policies designed to protect and encourage industry backfired in important respects. For example, the Kleu Study Group argued (1985, p. 42) that high rates of (tariff) protection led to large numbers of entrants into the protected industries. This resulted in increased competitive pressures in some cases, and to excessive product differentiation in other cases (which reduced profits because the internal market was too small to allow for production runs of a size sufficient to be economical). Likewise, the economic pressures for structural change in manufacturing (towards high-productivity intermediate and capital goods sectors) were dulled by state policies which effectively subsidized the importation of advanced machinery (Kaplan, 1987). Consequently, it is possible that the government's import-substitution policy indirectly created the conditions for a cost squeeze on profits.

In this way one could make the case that despite the growth-stimulating effects of import substitution, the interests of capitalism (although not necessarily the short-term interests of individual capitalists) were undermined by the South African state. No doubt the adverse effects of these policies on profitability were unintended outcomes. Nevertheless, the political dimensions both to labour policies and the monetary and fiscal instruments which cheapened the cost of capital (see McCarthy, 1987; Biggs, 1982) should never be overlooked. South African macro-economic and labour policies tended to be highly contradictory attempts to marry the requirements of capitalist growth with the demands of capitalists, white workers and an ideology of racial segregation.

Radical interpretations of South African political-economic history have provided an important challenge to liberal economists who hold the conviction that government intervention in general and apartheid policies in particular were detrimental to economic growth. The Marxist focus on the growth-stimulating aspects of apartheid labour policies has served an important theoretical function. However, it is vital that political-economic analyses move beyond this framework and focus on broader, more ambiguous aspects of South Africa's growth path (see Moll's contribution to this volume).

As Wolpe has recently argued in an important radical contribution, the relationship between capitalism and apartheid should be understood as 'simultaneously functional and contradictory' (1988, p. 8). More empirical research needs to be done before the dynamics of this fascinating but complex relationship can be understood.

Notes

1 The 'core' economy includes mining, manufacturing, construction, electricity, gas and water, commerce, catering and accommodation and transport, storage and communication. The profit rate in this broadly-defined sector dropped from 20 per cent in 1948 to 9 per cent in 1986. During the 1960s boom, the profit rate declined at 1 per cent per annum.

2 This is a weighted average of the seven largest capitalist economies: the USA, the UK, Canada, France, Germany, Italy and Japan.

3 Peak years are defined as the year before the annual growth of the GDP falls below that of the five year moving average.

4 These figures were supplied by the South African Reserve Bank.

5 These figures were derived from data provided by the South African Reserve Bank and published in the national accounts.

6 The data was provided by the South African Reserve Bank.

7 Dots symbolize that the expression is a growth rate. Expressing the change in the rate of profit as an addition of the growth rate of the profit share and the growth of the output:capital ratio is an approximation which is adequate for small rates of change.

8 One would also expect coloured/Indian wages to have been boosted for similiar reasons. It requires further research to ascertain why this is not the case.

9 Between 1970 and 1975, profitability in the ACCs dropped by 9,7 per cent per annum (Armstrong *et al.*, 1984, p. 464–5) as opposed to 8,3 per cent in South Africa. However, between 1973 and 1975, ACC manufacturing profitability declined by 23,6 per cent per annum (ibid.) whereas it fell by only 12,1 per cent per annum in South Africa.

10 This tendency is evident for the non-agricultural sector of the economy. For example, between 1970 and 1980 the proportion of whites in professional, technical and related jobs fell from 68,3 per cent to 59,7 per cent while that of blacks rose from 21,1 per cent to 28,5 per cent. Likewise, the proportion of whites in clerical jobs fell from 72,9 per cent to 61,0 per cent while that of blacks increased from 15,9 per cent to 24,2 per cent (Nedbank, 1981, p. 38–9).

11 Given the high inflation rates of the 1970s (which averaged 12,6 per cent in 1970–75 and 14,7 per cent in 1975–81) the average Reserve Bank Discount Rates (of 6,9 per cent and 9 per cent respectively) were clearly negative in real terms.

12 Given that 1981–86 is more a severe sustained slump than a 'peak-to-peak' period, it is possible that the decline in the rate of profit is over-estimated in that it is expressed in terms of the entire capital stock — some of which would be lying idle. However, if one adjusts the capital stock so that only used capacity enters the equation, the profit rate still shows a substantial decline of 8,2 per cent per annum.

13 Between 1981 and 1985, manufacturing profitability in the ACCs rose at 3,7 per cent per annum (Glyn, 1988, p. 238).

14 According to Cassim, the *malaise* of the South African economy in the 1980's is 'iatrogenic' — that is, caused by a disease induced in it by physicians (1988, p. 2). In this respect he cites the financial reforms which liberalized interest rates (fuelling a massive recession as the cost of credit sky-rocketed) and the abolition of the financial rand which resulted in a sharp deterioration in the Balance of Payments.

15 The **fact** of the existence of institutionalized labour market segmentation and channelling is not sufficient to establish the case that it cheapened the cost of labour to industry. Bell provides a convincing case for the reverse effect. He maintains that one of the major reasons for the decentralization of industry to growth points (where restrictions on black labour do not apply) was precisely to circumvent regional and racial forms of labour market segmentation which were eroding profitability (1986, pp. 285–9).

Appendix

Deconstructing the rate of profit

The rate of profit (P/K) can usefully be deconstructed into the profit share (P/Y) and the output:capital ratio (Y/K). The methodology is an adaptation of that used by Glyn *et al.* (1987) and Glyn (1988).

$$\frac{\dot{P}}{K} = \frac{\dot{P}}{Y} + \frac{\dot{Y}}{K}$$

P = profits (i.e. the net operating surplus at current prices)
Y = output (i.e. net value added at current prices)

K = capital stock (net at current replacement value).

The profit share

The profit share is best deconstructed in terms of the wage share in value added (W/Y) and the labour market, price and technological factors affecting it.

$$\frac{P}{Y} = 1 - \frac{W}{Y} \quad where \quad \frac{W}{Y} = \frac{W}{Pq.L} \times \frac{Pyc.L}{Y} \times \frac{Pq}{Pyc}$$

W = remuneration of employees
Pq = price index of gross output (the production price index)
L = employment
Pyc = the net GDP deflator[1]

In growth rate terms this becomes:

$$\frac{\dot{W}}{Y} = \frac{\dot{W}}{Pq.L} - \frac{\dot{Y}}{Pyc.L} - \frac{\dot{Pyc}}{Pq}$$

The wage share rises or falls depending on whether product wages (the first term in the wage share deconstruction) rise faster or slower than the surplus available for distribution (that is, the latter two terms in the deconstruction). The surplus is estimated as the growth of productivity (the second term) adjusted by relative value added : input prices (the third term) so as to take into account input price effects on the 'room' available for wage and profit increases.

The output:capital ratio

The output:capital ratio can be deconstructed in the following way:

$$\frac{Y}{K} = \frac{GYC}{GKC} \times \frac{Pyc}{Pkc}$$

Where Pkc = net/gross capital stock deflator[2]
GYC = gross value added in constant prices
GKC = gross capital Stock in constant prices.

$$\frac{\dot{Y}}{K} = \frac{\dot{GYC}}{GKC} + \frac{\dot{Pyc}}{Pkc}$$

The first term (GYC/GKC) is the real gross output:capital ratio which measures the average productivity of capital. A fall in the ratio indicates that the average unit of capital is producing less output. Changes in the output:capital ratio (Y/K) are also a function of several capital cost effects[3] which are summarized by the second term in the deconstruction.

The above deconstruction for South African manufacturing is provided in Table 7.7.

Nicoli Nattrass

Table 7.7:

DECONSTRUCTING THE SOUTH AFRICAN MANUFACTURING RATE OF PROFIT

		Average annual compound growth rates						
		1948 -55	1955 -60	1960 -64	1964 -70	1970 -75	1975 -81	1981 -86
1	**Profit Share**	0,7	−0,6	−2,9	−2,2	−3,0	3,5	−4,3
2	Productivity	2,5	4,2	3,9	2,4	1,7	3,2	−0,2
3	Effect of input costs	−2,4	−0,4	−1,0	−0,8	−1,6	−1,3	−0,7
4	Surplus (2+3)	0,1	3,8	2,9	1,6	0,1	1,9	−0,9
5	Wage share	−0,5	0,4	1,6	1,0	1,1	−1,3	1,7
6	Product wage (4+5)	−0,4	4,2	4,7	2,7	1,2	0,5	0,8
7	**Output:Capital (8+9)**	−2,5	−1,4	−0,3	−2,3	−5,8	−3,3	−6,0
8	Gross real output/capital	−0,5	−0,7	2,0	−0,7	−2,6	−2,5	−4,2
9	Rel. capital costs	−2,0	−0,7	−2,3	−1,6	−3,3	−0,8	−1,9
11	**Profit Rate (1+7)**	−1,8	−2,0	−3,2	−4,4	−8,3	0,2	−9,7

SOURCES:
See notes to Table 7.2.

Notes

1 The net GDP deflator is the current price net domestic product divided by the current proce gross domestic product. It thus includes the effect of price changes and the changing weight of capital consumption

2 The net gross capital stock deflator is: current price capital stock divided by constant price gross capital stock.
This measure thus includes the effect of capital price changes and the changing average age of the capital stock.

3 $(Pyc)/(Pkc)$ can be deconstructed further as $((Pyc)/(Pq))+((Pq)/(Pkc))$. The first term represents relative value added : input prices and the second term represents relative gross-output : capital goods prices, that is, the terms of trade between the manufacturing sector and the suppliers of capital goods. As the domestic product and capital stock deflators are constructed to take into account the changing weight of capital consumption in value added and the changing age composition of the capital stock respectively, changes in these latter variables are also captured by these ratios.

References

Armstrong, P., Glyn, A. & Harrison, J., *Capitalism Since World War 2*, Fontana: London, 1984.

Bell, T., 'The Role of Regional Policy in South Africa', in *The Journal of Southern African Studies*, vol. 12, no. 2, 1986.

Biggs, F., 'Aspects of Combining Capital and Labour in South Africa' in *Studies in Economics and Econometrics*, no. 13, 1982.

Bowles, S., Gordon, D. & Weisskopf, T., 'Power and Profits', in *Review of Radical Political Economics*, nos. 1–2, 1986.

Braverman, H., *Labour and Monopoly Capitalism: The Degradation of Work in the Twentieth Century*, Monthly Review Press: London, 1974.

Carlin, W., *The Development of the Factor Distribution of Income and Profitability in West Germany*, D.Phil: Oxford, 1987.

Cassim, F., 'Growth, Crisis and Change in the South African Economy', in *After Apartheid: Renewal of the South African Economy*, Centre for Southern African Studies, University of York and James Curry, 1988.

Callinicos, A., *South Africa: Between Reform and Revolution*, Bookmarks: London, 1988.

Davies, R., Kaplan, D., Morris, M. & O' Meara, D., 'Class Struggle and the Periodization of the South African State in South Africa', in *Review of African Political Economy*, no. 7, 1976.

Davies, R. & Lewis, D., 'Industrial Relations Legislation: One of Capital's Defences', in *Review of African Political Economy*, no. 7, 1976.

Gelb, S., 'Making Sense of the Crisis', in *Transformation*, no. 5, 1987.

Glyn, A. & Sutcliffe, R., *British Capitalism, Workers and the Profit Squeeze*, Penguin: Harmondsworth, 1972.

Glyn, A., Hughes., A, Lipietz., A. & Singh, A., 'The Rise and Fall of the Golden Age', *Cambridge University Department of Applied Mathematics*: Cambridge, England, 1987.

Glyn, A., 'Behind the Profitability Trends', in *Keisai Kenkyu*, July 1988.

Hill, T., *Profits and Rates of Return*, OECD: Paris, 1979.

Hindson, D., *Pass Controls and the Urban African Proletariat*, Ravan Press: Johannesburg, 1987.

Institute for Industrial Education, *The Durban Strikes*, The Institute for Industrial Education: Durban and Johannesburg, 1976.

Kaplan, D., 'Machinery and Industry: The Causes and Consequences of Constrained Development of the South African Machine Tools Industry', in *Social Dynamics*, vol. 13, no. 1, 1987.

Kleu Study Group., *Report of The Study Group of Industrial Development Strategy*, Government Printers: Pretoria, 1985.

Knight, J. & McGrath, M., 'The Erosion of Apartheid in the South African Labour Market', Unpublished *mimeo*, Institute of Economics and Statistics: Oxford, 1987.

Lipton, M., *Capitalism and Apartheid: South Africa, 1910–86*, Wildwood House: Aldershot, 1986.

McCarthy, C., 'The Structural Development of South African Manufacturing Industry — A Policy Perspective', Paper presented to the Economic Society, Pretoria, 1987.

Moll, T.C., 'Mishap or Crisis? The Apartheid Economy's Recent Performance in Historical Perspective', Seminar paper presented at the African Studies Institute, University of the Witwatersrand, June 1988.

Moll, T.C., ' "Probably the Best Lager in the World": The Record and Prospects of the South African Economy', in Brewer, J. (ed.), *Can South Africa Survive? Five Minutes to Midnight*, Macmillan Press: London, 1989.

Nattrass, J., 'Economic Development and Social and Political Change' in Schlemmer, L. & Webster, E. (eds.), *Change, Reform and Economic Growth in South Africa*, Ravan Press: Johannesburg, 1978.

Nattrass, J., *The South African Economy: Its Growth and Change*, Oxford University Press: Cape Town, 1981.

128 Nicoli Nattrass

Nattrass, N., 'Capitalism, Apartheid and Plummeting Profit Rates: Trends in South African Manufacturing from 1948 to 1986. Paper presented to the Southern Africa History and Politics Seminar, Oxford University, 30 January, 1989.

Nedbank, *South Africa: An Appraisal*, Nedbank Group: Johannesburg, 1981.

Saul, J. & Gelb, S., *The Crisis in South Africa*, ZED Press: New York, 1986.

Williams, M., 'An Analysis of South African Capitalism — Neo-Ricardian or Marxism?', in *Bulletin of the Conference of Socialist Economists*, vol. 1, no. 4, 1975.

Wolpe, H., 'Capitalism and Cheap Labour Power in South Africa: From Segregation to Apartheid', in *Economy and Society*, vol. 1, no. 4, 1972.

Wolpe, H., *Race, Class and the Apartheid State*, UNESCO: 1988.

Zarenda, H., 'The Policy of State Intervention in the Establishment and Development of Manufacturing Industries in South Africa', Masters Dissertation, University of the Witwatersrand: Johannesburg, 1977.

Black wages: the post-war experience[1]

Julian Hofmeyr

8

Introduction

The distribution of income in society, along with its implications for growth and social justice, has long fascinated economists. It is not surprising that in South Africa this particular debate should have focused on the distribution of income between races. The work of Jill Nattrass was of particular interest in this respect (Nattrass, 1978; Nattrass, 1981). She was concerned with actual wage differentials between the races and the relationship between economic growth and progressive change in South Africa. The question of whether economic development was premised on or undermined racial inequality in South Africa was very close to her heart. It is as a contribution to the debate on these issues that this essay has been written. The origins of the closing wage differential between blacks and whites from the 1970s is discussed, and it is argued that economic forces arising out of the process of economic development underlay the relative improvement of black wages.

Up until 1970, studies of income distribution in South Africa show that the white share had remained roughly constant at around 70 per cent for at least 50 years (see McGrath, 1977 for an overview). Over the next decade, however, the white share fell dramatically to just over 60 per cent, while that of blacks rose from roughly 20 per cent to nearly 30 per cent (Devereux, 1983, p. 36). In view of the previous long and enduring constancy of racial shares of income, this is an astonishing finding.

Since there is no reason to suppose that the distribution of wealth changed significantly over this period, one can safely conclude that the change was the result of a redistribution of wage income. Between 1970 and 1984, the black share of the modern sector[2] wage bill rose from 20 to nearly 30 per cent. The main reason for this was the rapid rise in black wages relative to those of whites: over this period, black wages almost doubled in real terms, while white wages rose by only 9 per cent.

Wage trends

Figure 8.1 shows how average annual wages in the mining, manufacturing and modern sectors have increased for the various race groups. Unlike the modern sector series (which goes only as far back as 1970) it was possible to construct a series for mining and manufacturing dating from 1945. The wage scale is logarithmic so that equal percentage changes appear the same whatever the wage level.

Figure 8.1: INCREASE IN AVERAGE WAGE ANNUAL WAGES IN THE MINING, MANUFACTURING AND MODERN SECTORS (VARIOUS RACE GROUPS)

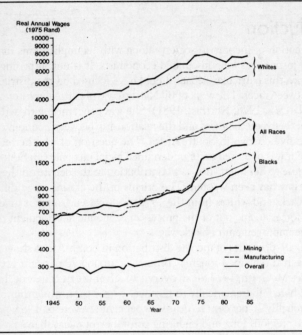

NOTES:
Modern Sector excludes agriculture and domestic service.
The basis of estimation was changed as from 1960, resulting in a substantial discontinuity; figures corresponding to both bases have therefore been given. Apart from this, there are various other discontinuities owing to definitional changes etc.. The effects of these on average wages are small however and they have been ignored. The independence of the TVBC states from 1975 onwards introduces further discontinuities; however, the effects should be minimal as the amount of industrial activity in these areas is relatively small.
SOURCES:
RSA 1964, 1976, 1982, 1984a, 1984b, 1985, 1987.

As can be seen from the Figure 8.1, white wages stagnated while black wages rose steadily between 1970 and 1984, after a period of very high growth in the early 1970s. The most spectacular sectoral trend was that of black wages in the mining industry. After stagnating between 1945 and 1963, they rose gently until 1971 when they accelerated sharply, almost trebling within four years. Thereafter they rose strongly, but at a less rapid rate. White mining wages, by contrast, stagnated and even fell after 1974.

Wages for blacks in manufacturing followed a very different course. They stagnated until 1960 and then began to climb. After about five years of fairly rapid growth (3,8 per cent per annum), the rate of increase slowed. After 1972, the rate of increase picked up again (apart from a slowdown between 1976 and 1979) until 1984. After 1984, the trend was reversed and real wages actually dropped.

In order to evaluate why the above wage trends should have occurred, it is necessary to gain an understanding of both the performance of the economy and the institutional changes taking place at the time.

The performance of the economy

Between 1946 and 1960, the South African economy grew at an average rate of 4,4 per cent per annum, with only minor fluctuations. This compared favourably with a population growth of 2,4 per cent per annum over the period. During the 1960s, South Africa's growth performance was spectacular: 5,5 per cent per annum over the decade with not a single year below 4,2 per cent. As with the previous period, the population growth of 3,1 per cent was far below that of the economy.

The second half of the 1970s and the 1980s tell a different story. After a brief slowdown in 1972, the economy picked up, only to plunge into a recession which, at its lowest point in 1977, witnessed a growth rate of only 0,1 per cent. The economy gradually improved its growth performance in the late 1970s, peaking in 1980 with a recorded growth rate of 7,3 per cent for the year. The respite, however, was short-lived. Between 1980 and 1983, the economy grew at only 0,5 per cent per annum. There was growth of 5 per cent in 1984 followed by a further contraction in 1986.

From 1975 (which really marks the end of the post-war boom) to 1985, average economic growth was 2,4 per cent per annum. As this was slower than the rate of population growth, per capita incomes in South Africa declined over this period.

The growth of modern sector employment (excluding agriculture), relative to population, followed a similar course. The figures are tabulated in Table 8.1. [3] Employment growth was significantly higher over the substantial period 1921 to 1975, with the exception of 1951 to 1960 when it was only slightly below. If mining and services are excluded in addition to agriculture, the effect is further enhanced, and employment growth is substantially greater than population growth for the entire period. This is true for all races and the effect is accentuated when whites are excluded.

Table 8.1:
POPULATION & EMPLOYMENT GROWTH (PERCENTAGE PER ANNUM)

	Population	Employment		
		(a)	(b)	(c)
1921–51				
All Races	2,01	3,31	4,47	5,36
Blacks	2,00			
Non-white	2,06	3,16	4,60	5,40
1951–60				
All races	2,59	2,31	3,60	2,76
Blacks	2,71	2,21	4,20	3,39
1960–70				
All races	3,09	3,55	4,39	4,67
Blacks	3,39	3,52	4,97	5,11
1970–75				
All races		3,70	4,34	4,03
Blacks		4,10	5,40	4,85
1975–85				
All races		0,67	0,21	0,07
Blacks		0,22	–0,27	–0,34

NOTES:
(a) 1921–51: Includes mining, manufacturing, construction, electricity and South African Transport Services.
   1951–70: Modern sector excluding agriculture
   1970–85: Modern sector excluding agriculture and domestic services
(b) 1921–51: As for (a), but excluding mining
   1951–85: Modern sector excluding agriculture, mining and services.
(c) Manufacturing only.

SOURCES:
(a) Population: RSA (1987), Table 1.1.1.1
(b) Employment: 1921–51: RSA (1982), p.7.4
   1951–70: RSA (1982), p.7.5
   1971–85: RSA (1987), Table 2.2.1

When examining the employment performance of the modern sector, there is some justification for excluding agriculture, mining and services since access to employment in these sectors has either not been subject to influx control or much less so than the others. Moreover, a substantial proportion of the mining labour force came from beyond South Africa's borders. With the exception of some professional occupations such as nursing and teaching which are included in services, these sectors act to a large extent as a 'residual' or last resort for those who cannot find jobs in the rest of the modern sector, where wages were, on the whole, much higher, at least until the 1970s (as will be seen in due course). It is therefore plausible to divide the economy into a high-wage core providing 'prime' jobs, and a lower-wage periphery providing 'secondary' jobs. The core can then be thought of as 'driving' the economy, development being the process of increasingly moving the population from the low-wage secondary labour market into the high-wage primary one. In so doing, a scarcity of labour is created for the secondary sector, forcing up the wages there, and ultimately bringing about the unification of the sectors. Parallelling this would be a movement away from subsistence agriculture and the raising of average incomes there.

In this sense, then, the performance of the South African economy was highly satisfactory over a sustained period, which came to an end only in 1975. Although there have been some years of high growth subsequent to this, the violent fluctuations and depth of the recessions has meant that overall performance has not been adequate in terms of these criteria.

The post-war boom

What then was the cause of the rise in black wages which took place after 1970? It is contended that, although institutional factors played their part, the fundamental cause was a labour shortage (even at the unskilled level), brought about by the sustained high growth of the post-war boom. It will also be argued that even the institutional changes were, directly or indirectly, a result of the high growth rate and the strains this induced in the economy.

It may be hypothesized that, in undergoing development, the modern sector of an economy initially faces a virtually unlimited supply of labour which is prepared to work at the going industrial wage.[4]

This labour comes from the so-called traditional sector, typically homeland agriculture in the South African case. As the development process proceeds, demand for labour in the modern sector increases rapidly at a constant real wage, until eventually the supply of labour prepared to work at this wage dries up,[5] and the only way further labour can be extracted from the traditional sector is by raising wages. At this point, labour has become a scarce resource and can no longer be said to be in surplus.

The wage trends in Figure 8.1 suggest that such a model would provide a plausible explanation for the sudden rise in black wages in the 1960s and 1970s. In other words, the pool of surplus labour available to the modern sector dried up sometime in the 1960s, and thereafter labour scarcity in the face of a growing demand forced wages up.

This argument essentially relies on the operation of market forces, that is, it is couched in terms of supply and demand. A different type of explanation can be counterposed. Such an argument would rely on non-market or institutional factors. Several such factors can be suggested: overseas influence on multinationals, government and trade union pressure, moral suasion etc. However, while many of these factors are important for large urban employers, it is difficult to conceive of them having much effect on rural or small employers. This is particularly so in South Africa, where for a long time it was government policy to keep labour cheap for farmers by preventing competition from urban employers. Thus if industrial wages had risen for non-market reasons, this should have led to urban employment expanding more slowly than otherwise, and an increasing number of persons being available for employment at lower wages by employers who felt they could get away with paying less. This would, in particular, apply to employers in the secondary labour market, such as farmers and the mines. It would therefore be expected that there would be a widening gap between wages in the prime urban labour market and those in mining and agriculture. If, however, an increasing labour shortage resulting from economic growth was pushing up wages in the prime labour market, then the same should have been happening in the secondary market, unless the institutional structures segmenting the market were so impenetrable as to prevent any significant leakage. A finding that market forces were pushing up these wages in spite of segmentation would be a very strong conclusion. In the next section, we shall examine what happened in these sectors.

The gold mines

As documented by Wilson (1976) the South African gold mines occupy a unique position with respect to the black labour market. Firstly, they developed an extensive recruiting network for foreign labour, which extended from neighbouring countries to those as far away as Zambia and Malawi. Secondly, the gold mines have historically been constrained by a gold price which was determined on world markets and which, in addition, was maintained constant in dollar terms for many years. Inflationary pressure thus implied that the real revenue per ounce of gold decreased over a long period and hence put the mines under pressure to contain or even reduce costs in order to maintain profits.

Given that expensive white labour (which accounted for more than two-thirds of the wage bill and for which other sectors were also competing) could not be replaced by cheaper black labour for institutional reasons, it is not surprising that the mines resorted to every means possible to keep black labour costs down. This they did by making extensive use of migrant labour and by spreading their recruiting net ever wider to avoid competition with other employers. As can be seen from Figure 8.1, this policy resulted in an increasing gap not only between black and white wages on the mines, but also between black wages in mining and those in manufacturing, at least after 1960.

As the gap widened, the proportion of South African blacks in the mine labour force began to drop, from about 35 per cent in the mid-1960s to a low point of 20 per cent in 1973. The political risks of being entirely dependent on foreign labour so alarmed the mines that when the gold price was released from its straitjacket in 1971 and began to rise (it quadrupled in rand terms from 1971 to 1974), they decided to increase the South African component of their labour force, principally by raising wages to levels competitive with those in manufacturing. They also expanded their internal recruiting network and instituted a public relations drive to promote work on the mines.

According to Wilson (1976), the mines' resolve was strengthened by three particular events. September 1973 saw the first of a series of violent compound confrontations which spread to most parts of the industry over the following 32 months and led to 172 deaths. In 1974 the Malawian government suspended further recruitment for the South African mines after an aircraft carrying Malawian migrants crashed in Botswana; with the result that the number of miners recruited from areas north of latitude 22°S dropped by 55 000 in 1974. Also in 1974, the overthrow of the Caetano government in Portugal presaged the independence of Moçambique, and a Marxist Frelimo government, which was likely to adopt a hostile attitude towards South Africa, came to power.

The impact of the change in mining wage and recruitment policy was dramatic. By 1979, the proportion of South African blacks (using 1910 boundaries) had almost trebled, rising to 57 per cent of the workforce. The question which immediately arises is where these workers came from. It is conceivable that some were drawn back from industry. By 1979, the average cash wage on the mines had risen to 75 per cent of that in manufacturing (as compared to 34 per cent in 1971) and, in addition, miners received free food and accommodation. However, as compound life leaves a great deal to be desired, and as work on the mines is dangerous and unpleasant, it is unlikely that someone who had once acquired a legal job in manufacturing would willingly have swapped it for one on the mines.

Rather, it is likely that the bulk of these workers came from the ranks of the unemployed and the agricultural sector, both subsistence and modern. Regular black employment in commercial agriculture decreased from 710 000 in 1965 to 565 000 in 1976. While there are many reasons for this decline, one would expect to find some evidence of labour shortages in agriculture if the hypothesis concerning competition from the mines and industry is valid. There is indeed plentiful anecdotal evidence of labour shortages in commercial agriculture at about this time, particularly in the sugar farming areas of Natal which draw their labour from the Transkei, thus bringing them into direct competition with the mines (Wilson, Kooy & Hendrie, 1977, pp. 15–17). The following section investigates this question in more detail.

Agriculture

Because of the isolation of the agricultural labour market from that of industry, agricultural wages (even taking into account free accommodation, rations etc.) have always compared unfavourably with those in manufacturing. However, to the extent that segmentation breaks down under pressures of growth, one would expect farm wages to be affected, although possibly with a lag.

Data on agricultural wages are somewhat fragmented and it is necessary to piece together a picture of what has happened. The longest series are kept by the Directorate of Agricultural Production Economics and are derived from production cost surveys of the five main grain-producing areas: Rûens and Swartland in the western Cape, north-western Orange Free State, Transvaal Highveld, and western Transvaal. These data are tabulated in Table 8.2. The two western Cape areas are somewhat atypical, having substantially higher wages than the rest. This can be attributed to the fact that the labour force is largely 'coloured' or mixed race (rather than black) and would, therefore, not have been subject to influx control. Thus farmers in the western Cape would have been exposed to competition from industry to a greater extent than elsewhere. In addition, the western Cape is relatively isolated from the rest of the country.

Wage levels in the other three areas are, however, remarkably similar — given the wide separation of the areas and the relative isolation of local markets for farm labour. It is significant that after a long period of relative constancy following the war, wages more than doubled in all three areas between the mid-1960s and the mid-1970s. Despite fluctuations about the new higher level, there is no discernible trend in wage levels after this period.

Central Statistical Services publish a wage series covering regular farm workers, but unfortunately the basis has changed from time to time and it is possible to construct a consistent series covering the critical period from 1965 to 1976 only. Real cash wages rose steadily over this period, starting off somewhat slowly from R143 per annum and rising more rapidly towards the end, when they reached R246 per annum. They rose 23,2 per cent from 1965 to 1971, and a further 39,6 per cent by 1976.

Wages in the sugar industry during the 1970s show similar trends. According to data collected by the South African Sugar Association (which, unlike the other sources, contains occupational detail), all categories of labour experienced substantial wage increases between 1972 and 1976 but the greatest increases went to the male-dominated grades, which were also paid substantially more than the others. The average increase for these grades was more than 40 per cent in real terms between the 1972/3 and 1975/6 seasons.[6] Thereafter real wages

Table 8.2:

WAGES FOR BLACKS
IN THE MAJOR GRAIN PRODUCING AREAS (1975 RAND)

	Transvaal Highveld		NW OFS		Swartland		W.Tvl		Rûens	
	Cash	Total	Cash	Total	Cash	Total	Cash	Total	Cash	Total
1938/39					149	319			87	99
1945/46	83	212	60	221						
1946/47	72	216	60	215						
1947/48	74	224	60	200	159	467			299	583
1948/49			64	193	164	460	83	239	299	593
1949/50			72	206	157	441	76	257	277	569
1950/51	68	229								
1951/52	63	212								
1952/53			76	265						
1953/54			82	274			110	315		
1954/55	89	248			189	550	63	295		
1955/56	85	234			204	545				
1956/57										
1957/58										
1958/59	63	222								
1959/60					190	513			325	563
1960/61			142	260	191	527			311	582
1961/62	101	221								
1962/63	101	228	67	270			69	292		
1963/64	96	224					74	240		
1964/65	111	258	77	293			104	337	382	635
1965/66	96	262	75	292					290	731
1966/67									386	730
1967/68									397	680
1968/69									411	646
1969/70	148	527	95	356			106	341	410	619
1970/71									386	621
1971/72									486	672
1972/73					362	744			563	515
1973/74									478	788
1974/75	211	442							479	881
1975/76							239	490	477	805
1976/77	254	559	221	511	332	829	186	595	499	876
1977/78	257	458	249	566	296	795	234	507	509	829
1978/79	237	479	159	582	342	765	227	686	484	791
1979/80	191	559	242	604	281	768	243	490	449	779
1980/81	289	588	332	638	336	815	249	533	497	919
1981/82	312	660	281	691	335	787	260	553	491	830
1982/83	296	609	249	560	346	749	241	567	483	803
1983/84	271	532	250	552	346	744	205	492	508	863
1984/85	310	551	222	580	375	820	269	542	526	807

NOTES:
Cash: Annual cash wages including bonuses
Total: Cash wages plus in-kind allowances valued at farmer's costs.
SOURCES:
Up to 1979/80: Fenyes, 1983, Tables 38,45–49.
Remainder: Directorate Agricultural Production Economics.

in all categories stagnated (with some fluctuations), although at substantially higher levels than in 1972/3.

The wage evidence in agriculture is thus consistent with the picture of a labour market still strongly segmented by the mid-1970s, but where competitive pressures were nonetheless forcing up wages, albeit in an uneven and irregular way. Even bearing in mind the often inadequate nature of agricultural wage statistics and the diverse, segmented labour market, it is still significant that such widely separated and varying types of agriculture all experienced substantial wage rises at the same time as mining and industry. It is also significant that once the economy and the rate of labour absorption by modern urban-based industry slowed down in the second half of the 1970s, the upward trend in agricultural wages petered out. This reinforces the argument that it was competitive pressures which forced wages up in the earlier period.

But how does all this square with those studies finding a substantial amount of black unemployment over the period? Knight (1978), who found that up to one-third of the black labour force was 'residual' (unemployed or underemployed in homeland agriculture), proposed the following model in order to reconcile these findings with the wage and anecdotal evidence suggesting that there was a shortage of labour. He argued that the unemployed refuse relatively low-paid jobs on the mines and in agriculture in order to be available to accept high-wage jobs in the urban core. Unemployment is thus seen as a search or queuing phenomenon. Knight's model therefore neatly reconciles the presence of large amounts of 'residual' labour with that of a labour scarcity in low-wage sectors which, as a result, were forced to raise wages in order to attract and retain labour. The scarcity is real, however, in the sense that employers in the low-wage sectors who had previously apparently been able to obtain as much labour as they wished without raising wages, could no longer do so. In other words, because economic opportunities had changed substantially as a consequence of growth, people who had previously been prepared to offer their labour at the lower wage now felt it worthwhile to withhold it in the hope of something better, forcing the lower wage up in the process. This situation was, however, to change dramatically after 1975.

The decade 1975–85

It is clear from Figure 8.1 that although black wages continued to rise after 1975, they did so at a somewhat lower rate. In addition, black employment in the modern sector (excluding agriculture) hardly grew at all. This is not surprising, given the poor performance of the economy after 1975. In fact it is surprising that wages grew at all, given the absence of labour market pressure.

The increase in average wage levels is the result of two different types of process: changes in the structure of wages — for example, a change in wage levels for specific occupations; and movement of the working population through that structure, in other words, upward penetration through the occupational levels. It is possible to examine the relative contributions of these two types of effect over this period because of the availability of urban survey data from the Bureau for Market Research (BMR) at the University of South Africa which relates individual and job characteristics to wage levels for the years 1975, 1980 and 1985.

The BMR data were analysed using regression techniques with a standard semi-logarithmic earnings function incorporating human capital, industry and occupation effects. A standard analysis such as that often used in studies of discrimination was then used to decompose the change in average wages into the various effects. Data from the different years were also combined with the use of time dummies, to obtain average rates of change in wage levels over the decade. In addition the data were analysed with and without the inclusion of benefits in kind. This made no important difference to the results.

It was found that unskilled black male workers suffered a significant real wage decline over the decade. Occupational differentials on the other hand increased but nonetheless all occupational wages for males suffered a real decline. This was least for skilled workers, followed by the clerical, professional and semi-skilled groups, in that order. Real wages for females increased however.

There were significant differences in sectoral pay in 1975 after accounting for other labour force characteristics. Manufacturing was the best-paid sector, and community services the worst.[7] However, by 1985, mining had become the best-paid sector, even if payments in kind are ignored. All sectoral wages increased relative to manufacturing such that by 1985 most other sectoral differences had disappeared. However, community services maintained its relative position and remained significantly worse paid than the rest.

As far as regional differences were concerned, the decade 1975–85 saw a unification of wages in the industrial heartland (Johannesburg and its surrounding areas) while other regions lagged behind. In particular, wages in Cape Town were not significantly different from those in Johannesburg in 1975, but were nearly 9 per cent below in 1985.

After accounting for other differences in characteristics, women were paid significantly less than men in both 1975 and 1985, but the difference was substantially smaller in 1985. However, it is not clear to what extent shorter average hours of work or changes in them contributed to these effects.

The decomposition analysis showed that changes in the structure of wages actually contributed negatively to the movement of average wages, whereas upward mobility through that structure accounted for all of the wage rise which occurred, in addition to compensating for the negative structural movement.

Specifically, upward penetration through the occupational levels and increasing levels of education of the workforce were the major positive effects contributing to movement through the structure. The increasing proportion of women in the labour force pulled the average down to some extent. The major factor contributing to the structural change was the fall in real wage levels, only partially offset by the increase in women's wages and decreasing sectoral differentials. Increasing occupational differentials made relatively little contribution.

The results from this analysis support and are consistent with the earlier argument that black wages are primarily determined by forces arising out of the process of economic growth.

Consider first the finding that for unskilled labour, wages in manufacturing dropped over the decade 1975–85, while occupational differentials increased (although not sufficiently to offset the drop in wage levels generally).[8] This is consistent with the poor performance of the economy over the period. In times of rising unemployment, the unskilled are least able to defend their economic position. However, even under these conditions, certain skills are likely to be in short supply, thus driving up the wages of those fortunate enough to posses such skills. The data divisions are too crude to detect such effects, but the fact that skilled wages suffered the smallest decline is consistent with this view.

That wages for professionals rose scarcely faster than those of semi-skilled workers is an unexpected finding. However, bearing in mind the large number of female professionals in the community services sector (nurses, teachers and the like), the result becomes less strange. The state is virtually a monopsony employer of nurses and teachers in the sense that their alternative employment options have (particularly in the past) been limited to unskilled or semi-skilled work.

The finding that movement up the occupational and educational ladders jointly made the largest contribution to the increase in average wages (whereas the changes in wages paid to specific occupations and educational levels made a negative contribution), is also significant to the argument. This accords with the poor overall performance of the South African economy which nevertheless was continuing to suffer from skill shortages in certain areas at certain times.

The closing of sectoral wage gaps suggests that the market was becoming more unified with the increasing erosion of segmentation, as controls on the movement of black labour became less important over the decade. Even the result for mining is consistent with this view: in a competitive labour market one would expect to find dangerous and unpleasant work (such as that in mining) more highly rewarded than safer and less arduous occupations.

The area results are also consistent with the view that the labour market was unifying. The fact that significant wage differences between the various areas constituting the industrial heartland tended to disappear over the decade clearly supports this view. That outlying areas were increasingly left behind can in all likelihood be explained by the poor economic performance over the decade, with outlying and more specialized areas tending to suffer first. The fact that wages in Cape Town were so high in 1975 probably reflects an artificial scarcity of labour, induced by the application of influx control, which was more strictly applied in the western Cape than elsewhere. It is likely that the relative decrease in wages in Cape Town over the decade reflects a decrease in the stringency of the application of these laws, and a resultant decrease in the artificial scarcity of labour. It may of course also simply reflect the fact that economic performance in Cape Town was that much poorer than elsewhere, and a declining demand for labour had allowed wages to drop relative to those in Johannesburg. The less-strict application of influx control may also explain why wages tended to fall in other outlying areas, most of which were closer to labour-supply areas than the industrial heartland.

Finally, one may be tempted to question what role increasing unionization and the growing militancy of unions played in wage setting. While there had been unofficial black unions for many years, they had little clout in the face of intimidation, harassment and non-recognition by employers and the state. It was really the publication of the report of the Wiehahn Commission in 1979, and its subsequent implementation, which set black unions on their feet. Strike action increased rapidly from 1980. Sutcliffe & Wellings (1985, p. 360) give figures to show that between 1975 and 1979, strike action in the manufacturing sector involved less than 20 workers per 1 000 on average. In 1980 this rose to about 45, in 1981 to 60, and in 1982 to 130. They report that the majority of strikes were over wage-related issues (p. 363). It is not clear to what extent strike action affected overall wage levels, although it may have been a factor in certain subsectors and establishments. The fact that the structure of real wages declined over the decade 1975–85 suggests that industrial action did not have a great effect over this period.

Growth and institutional change

Up to this point there has been relatively little mention of the roles played by institutional change and conflict in the raising of wage levels. In recent years, both have evidently made a contribution. Even here, however, it will be argued that the fundamental cause of raised wages was the sustained growth of the post-war boom.

One of the most comprehensive accounts of the processes contributing to the erosion of black-white wage differentials is given by Knight & McGrath (1987). They consider the following processes: industrial action and union-ization, foreign pressure, and changing employer, managerial and government attitudes.

Their account of industrial action and unionization begins with the Natal strikes of 1973/4. It includes an analysis of events leading up to the appointment of the Wiehahn Commission (RSA, 1979) and the implementation of its findings. They also discuss the subsequent rapid growth of black unionization and the militancy and politicization of the black labour movement in the 1980s.

According to Knight & McGrath, the build-up of foreign pressure (which they regard as a crucial factor behind the black wage increases) started in 1973 with a series of articles in the Guardian newspaper in Britain. These exposed the poor conditions of black employees in South African subsidiaries of British companies, and led to an enquiry by a House of Commons committee which recommended a code of practice for subsidiaries in South Africa. This development was echoed in Europe, and in America with the Sullivan Principles. The codes generally specified that firms should follow non-racial policies and provide training and promotional possibilities for black employees.

In their discussion of changing management and government attitudes, Knight & McGrath stress the increased acceptance by management and government of the ability of black people to perform skilled and managerial jobs, and of their right to form trade unions. Accompanying this was a reversal on the question of black education and training, with the consequent rapid expansion of both. There was also an increasing willingness on the part of employers to speak out in favour of reform in general, and of the government to provide it in areas such as job reservation and, more recently, influx control.

While the processes and changes documented are undoubtedly of great importance, Knight and McGrath's account is framed largely in institutional terms with the effects of economic growth mentioned only in passing. In my view, they do not place sufficient emphasis on the fundamental role of growth, at least as an initiator of many of the processes they detail.

The 1973 strikes followed a long period of industrial quiet. They occurred on an unprecedented scale in a wide variety of industries including government and semi-government bodies. It is highly significant that they took place **after** black wages had begun to rise. It is likely that the strikes accelerated this process, but it had already begun. In general, conflicts such as strikes arise because of a crisis of expectations brought on by a situation of uneven change (for example, in relative wages and working conditions), rather than because of bad conditions *per se*. After all, conditions had been bad for years and were on average no worse in Durban than elsewhere.

State and employer responses to the strikes were also significant. Unlike previous black strikes, the Natal strikes, although illegal, were handled with kid gloves (by South African standards). Instead of brutally repressing the strikes, arresting the ringleaders and dismissing substantial parts of the workforce, the police took little direct action and top management became involved in negotiations. This was even true of government departments (such as the postal services) involved in the strikes as employers. Although the strikers did not achieve their initial demands, they succeeded in significantly improving their wages and working conditions.[9]

Two inferences can be drawn: firstly, it seems likely that the strikes were a product rather than a cause of the changes taking place; and secondly, that black workers were in a position of unprecedented power (given the skill shortage and the unlikelihood of management being able to replace the entire workforce).

During the strikes, management found it difficult to negotiate with the strikers as there were no recognized structures or leaders. A realization that this was the legacy of decades of negative official and management attitudes to black worker organization, frequent intimidation of activists and the lack of recognition of the unions which existed, contributed to a change of heart by management. There was little doubt that recognized structures and formalized negotiation procedures were preferable to the situation which faced them during the Natal strikes.

It is likely that this chain of events contributed significantly to the decision to appoint the Wiehahn Commission, the findings reached by it and the government's subsequent acceptance of them. It may therefore be argued that even though the Wiehahn Commission and all its consequences took place after the post-war boom had ended, the processes set in train by the high growth accompanying that boom played a large part in triggering this sequence of events.

Even foreign pressure can be related to the dynamics unleashed by the process of economic development. It is significant that foreign pressure has usually come in waves which have been set in motion by some internal event or set of events. The 1973 and 1974 Natal strikes undoubtedly played a large part in the initial build-up of foreign pressure for improved conditions of employment. The riots (etc.) of 1976 also contributed to the pressures which were exerted in 1977 and thereafter (for example, the drawing up of the Sullivan Principles and European Code). However, even in this case, it is plausible to argue that high growth, the demand for educated manpower and the strains induced by the consequent rapid expansion of black education under an unyielding and doctrinaire approach on the part of the authorities, played a large part in the build-up of stress in the educational system, which triggered the Soweto uprising of 1976.

More obviously, economic imperatives generated by rapid growth clearly played an important role in changing employer, managerial and government attitudes to black advancement. Faced with an increasing shortage of skilled labour, management was forced to consider blacks for positions previously earmarked for whites. As a result of this experience, management adapted their attitudes (Knight & McGrath, 1987, p. 48). Furthermore, having come to accept blacks as a more settled, unionized component of the work force, it is not surprising that management has taken on board other concerns of blacks (such as housing) and has even challenged the government on some of its more reactionary policies and actions. The government's about-face on the question of black education and training is clearly also a consequence of the same set of processes.[10]

It is therefore clear that the high growth of the post-war boom was an important contributory factor, directly or indirectly, to most of the institutional and attitudinal changes leading to improvement in the relative position of blacks. Perhaps the most significant result of growth was a breaking down of old rigidities and, in particular, white perceptions of the potential of black people. The significance of the change in white attitudes to black advancement cannot be overstressed.

Conclusion

The picture that emerges is remarkably consistent. The long post-war boom with its high growth and strongly growing demand for labour in the high-wage core of the economy eventually resulted in a scarcity of labour, at first only for urban-based industry. This caused wages in the urban core to be forced up during the 1960s. To some extent, influx control (and other factors isolating farm labour) protected commercial agriculture from competitive pressures. In spite of influx control, the mines began to feel these pressures insofar as they were increasingly less able to attract South African blacks. They were able to resist the pressure for higher wages by spreading their recruiting net ever further beyond the borders of South Africa.

In the early 1970s, the rate of increase of urban wages accelerated dramatically, presumably because the shortage of labour was being felt ever more keenly. There is no doubt that urban industry was experiencing significant skill shortages at the time. However as the declining component of South African blacks on the mines indicates, these shortages must have extended even into the area of unskilled labour. In 1971 the mines took their dramatic decision to increase this component by raising wages, and this had a substantial effect on recruitment after 1973. As the needs of the mines and industry became more pressing, segmentation began to break down and, sometime between the mid-1960s and the early 1970s, large parts of commercial agriculture began to experience competitive pressures (at least for male labour) and were forced to raise wages significantly.

It is therefore clear that the high growth rate of the South African economy led to the disappearance of an overall surplus of certain types of black labour in large and significant parts of the economy. In particular, this would have applied to prime-age male labour who would have been eligible for work on the mines (whether skilled or unskilled). It is considerably less likely that it would have applied to groups such as women, to whom influx control laws were far more strictly applied.

The long period of sustained high growth produced severe strains in the economy, and these precipitated, or were at least a major contributor to, a whole sequence of events which forced employers, management and the state to change their attitudes significantly, particularly in regard to the questions of black advancement, education and unionization. Substantial institutional changes followed. Although the post-war boom ended before many of these could be implemented, a process of change had been started which acquired a momentum of its own. The result was a rise in the level of education of the black labour force, penetration up the occupational ladder, and the increasing unification of the labour market. There was also rapid growth of black unionization and labour militancy.

The performance of the economy changed dramatically in the second half of the 1970s. Commercial agriculture continued to shed labour, the homeland populations grew while the homelands became less able to support even a constant population, and the mines discovered that they could recruit as much South African labour as they wished. Overall, modern sector prime employment failed to keep pace with population. Without hypothesizing a large and growing role for a highly successful informal sector (which is implausible), it is difficult to maintain that labour demand continued to press against supply. The performance of agricultural wages is totally consistent with this: after the mid-1970s they effectively stagnated, and the gap between them and industrial wages grew until the onset of the post-1984 recession.

Despite the poor performance of the economy and the apparent disappearance of labour-market pressure, average wages for blacks in the modern sector — excluding agriculture — continued to increase (though at a slower pace) until at least 1984. The major factors contributing to this were: improvement in both educational levels and in upward movement through the occupational structure, the closing of sectoral wage gaps, and the increase in wages paid to women. Significantly, wages paid to specific occupations and for educational achievements actually fell in real terms, despite growing occupational differentials.

It is clear that market forces had a significant effect on average wages before 1975. However, it is unlikely that they played much direct part subsequently, except in regard to certain occupations requiring particular skills. Nonetheless, they had a significant indirect influence, acting via their effect on management and government attitudes to black advancement. This was reinforced by non-market forces such as foreign and trade union pressure. The direct effect of non-market forces on wage levels is unclear, but the results suggest that it was not great overall, at least before 1985.

Notes

1   This paper arose out of work carried out with the generous assistance of the Chairman's Fund Educational Trust of Anglo American/De Beers. The said bear no responsibility

for the views expressed or conclusions drawn. The author is also grateful to Professor Nel of the BMR for making available their data, and for comments on a preliminary draft by John Knight of the Institute of Economics and Statistics at Oxford and Nicoli Nattrass of the Department of Sociology, University of Stellenbosch.

2 Figures for the modern sector exclude agriculture and domestic services throughout this chapter.

3 The growth of population and employment is compared in Table 8.1. Due to changes in the borders of the Republic, a consistent population series is available only until 1970. However, if the figures for 1960–70 are simply extended to the period after 1970 they may be accepted as sufficiently accurate for the purposes required here. Further, uniform employment series are not available for the whole period and therefore various aggregates are given. For the period before 1951 the series covers only selected sectors. However, these constitute a substantial part of the urban industrial economy.

4 W. Arthur Lewis originally proposed a model of the development process along these lines in a now-famous article published in 1954.

5 There is no inevitability in this process; it is merely the outcome under a fairly plausible set of assumptions.

6 Data are available from only the 1972/73 season.

7 It should be remembered that the BMR sample is urban-based and therefore agriculture is almost totally unrepresented.

8 This is of course not true for women's average wages which increased over the period.

9 The material on the 1973 strikes is summarized from Institute for Industrial Education (1974).

10 Knight & McGrath do in fact attribute this set of processes to economic growth (p. 48).

References

Devereux, S., *South African Income Distribution 1900–80*, Saldru Working Paper No. 51, University of Cape Town: Cape Town, 1983.

Fenyes, T.I., *Die Benutting en Vergoeding van Plaasarbeid in die Suid-Afrikaanse Landbou*, Directorate Agricultural Production Economics, Department of Agriculture: Pretoria, 1983.

Hofmeyr, J.F., *The Rise in Black Wages in South Africa: 1975–1985, mimeo*, University of Natal: Durban, 1989.

Institute for Industrial Education, *The Durban Strikes 1973*, Ravan Press: Johannesburg, 1974.

Knight, J.B., 'Labour Allocation and Unemployment in South Africa', *Oxford Bulletin of the Institute of Economics and Statistics*, vol. 40, 1978.

Knight, J.B. & McGrath, M.D., 'An Analysis of Racial Wage Discrimination in South Africa', *Oxford Bulletin of the Institute of Economics and Statistics*, vol. 39, 1977.

Knight, J.B. & McGrath, M.D., *The Erosion of Apartheid in the South African Labour Market: Measures and Mechanisms*, Applied Economics Discussion Paper No. 35, Institute of Economics and Statistics: Oxford, 1987.

Lewis, W.A., 'Economic Development with Unlimited Supplies of Labour', *Manchester School of Economic and Social Studies*, vol. 22, 1954.

McGrath, M.D., *Racial Income Distribution in South Africa*, Black/White Income Gap Project Interim Research Report No. 2, University of Natal: Durban, 1977.

Nattrass, J., 'Economic Development and Social and Political Change' in Schlemmer, L. & Webster, E. (eds.), *Change, Reform and Economic Growth in South Africa*, Ravan Press: Johannesburg, 1978.

Nattrass, J., *The South African Economy: its Growth and Change*, Oxford University Press: Cape Town, 1981.

RSA, *Statistical Yearbook 1964*, Government Printer: Pretoria, 1964.

RSA, *South African Statistics 1976*, Government Printer: Pretoria: 1976

RSA, *Report of the Commission of Inquiry into Labour Legislation*, Part 1, RP 47/1979, Government Printer: Pretoria, 1979.

RSA, *South African Statistics 1980*, Government Printer: Pretoria, 1980.

RSA, *South African Statistics 1982*, Government Printer: Pretoria, 1982

RSA, *Bulletin of Statistics March 1984*, Government Printer: Pretoria, 1984a.

RSA, *Bulletin of Statistics December 1984*, Government Printer: Pretoria, 1984b.

RSA, *Bulletin of Statistics June 1985*, Government Printer: Pretoria, 1985.

RSA, *South African Labour Statistics 1987*, Government Printer: Pretoria, 1987.

Sutcliffe, M. & Wellings, P., 'Worker Militancy in South Africa: A Sociospatial Analysis of Trade Union Activism in the Manufacturing Sector', *Environment and Planning D: Society and Space*, vol. 3, 1985.

Wilson, F., *International Migration in Southern Africa*, SALDRU Working Paper No. 1, University of Cape Town: Cape Town, 1976.

Wilson, F., Kooy, A. & Hendrie, D. (eds.), *Farm Labour in South Africa*, David Philip: Cape Town, 1977.

Unions and industrial councils — why do unions' policies change?[1]

9

Mike Morris

Introduction

The struggle between workers and capitalists over the division of the economic surplus into wages and profits is a fundamental determinant of growth and socio-political change in capitalist societies. This is particularly the case in South Africa where trade unions are increasingly adopting militant economic and political stances. The outcome of this struggle is a function of many factors, including the pace of accumulation (in periods of rapid economic growth the demand for labour puts workers in a stronger bargaining position); state repression; the collective bargaining institutional framework; the nature and extent of trade union organization; and the tactical gains made in the process of bargaining.

In this volume Hofmeyr (Chapter 8) and Nattrass (Chapter 7) point to structural economic aspects of worker bargaining power in South Africa. What is missing from their analyses is the extent to which organizational requirements (and the structural/material conditions which shape the strategic options open to trade unions) affect the way in which workers exercise their bargaining power. This essay attempts to fill this gap by tracing the dialectic between the structural and organizational forces which underlay NUMSA's strategic about-face regarding national collective bargaining and the industrial council system in South Africa.

For those who have followed the history of trade union struggles, the changing nature of union policy towards national collective bargaining and industrial councils seems, at face value, either to exemplify flagrant inconsistency or rampant opportunism. After all, some of the unions which were the most consistently and vociferously opposed to the industrial council system — the Metal and Allied Workers Union (MAWU; now the National Union of Metalworkers of South Africa, NUMSA) and the General Workers Union (GWU; now the Transport and General Workers Union, T & GWU) — have in the past few years actively propagated the advantages of participating in these statutory collective bargaining structures.[2]

The general thrust of this chapter is to argue that unions (like all organizations which have mass membership and are responsive to their organizational needs) formulate their particular policies not simply by articulating an ideological vision, but fundamentally in terms of two major influences. Firstly, the material conditions that shape the political, economic and social environment within which the unions operate; and secondly, the organizational requirements which result from the changing fortunes of these unions.

In developing these points by focusing on the metal industry, this chapter shows how the organizational requirements in the early years of MAWU's history shaped the union's rank-and-file organizing strategy and democratic internal structure. The union's changing policy towards the industrial council system is rooted within these strategies and structures. Finally, the chapter explores how union policy towards that system operated (in terms of these strategies and structures) so as to advance workers economic interests and organizational development.

The basic premise in the argument is that, in the case of the Metal and Allied Workers Union, it is neither opportunism nor inconsistency that provides the key to understanding the radical policy alterations undergone by this union in its approach to the metal industrial council. Rather, it was the dialectic between a policy that operated with some success, and the changing conditions within which that policy could no longer yield results, that forced a radical revision of attitudes towards participation in the industrial council structure in the metal and engineering industry. With this in mind, the basic strategies and structures that were formed in the early years of the MAWU's existence are set out, and MAWU's relationship to the industrial council is periodized into three phases.

The early years of the independent trade union movement[3]

The Durban strikes of 1973 gave birth to the new trade union movement. By 1976 the advice centres and fledgling unions, under the impact of the heightened worker activity which characterized the mid-1970s, had become proper trade unions. These unions manifested a number of structural characteristics that were to shape their initial responses to the industrial conciliation system which they encountered.

They were numerically very small, with a total of only a few thousand members. These members were primarily unskilled and highly exploited black workers who faced very specific problems — gross disparities between their wage levels and those of skilled and semi-skilled white, Indian and coloured workers; and despotic and racially-biased labour relations on the shop floor.

The unions were regionally located and even those that claimed to be industrial unions were only so in name. Furthermore, whatever they called themselves, structurally they operated more like regional general unions. This applied even to those unions comprising the TUACC[4] (later to become the backbone of FOSATU[5]) which, although it was composed of industrial unions, operated more as a large general union with industrial sectors than as a federation comprising independent industrial unions.

Their weakness and lack of resources, combined with the lessons they drew from SACTU's[6] inability to make headway as a trade union federation in the 1950s, conditioned these unions to depend heavily on a plant-based organizational style. Because the limited resource base of these unions made it difficult to organize more than a single factory concentration of workers, the TUACC unions marshalled their limited resources to focus on single plants controlled by multinational companies. These companies were regarded as internationally more vulnerable, and the unions hoped to achieve a breakthrough through sustained shop floor pressure. This took the form of an organizational reliance on factory committees (called shop steward committees in most unions) which referred all issues back to the general membership for mandate and ratification.

Although these unions primarily organized black workers, they ideologically projected themselves as non-racial unions. This was a function of a number of influences on these unions: the importance of the political tradition of non-racialism; the significant role that many radical whites played in their emergence; an identification of racism with state departments that intervened whenever black workers sought to defend their own interests; the manner in which racism and ethnicity was used by the state, employers and the white unions to divide and weaken black workers; and finally the perceived need for unity on the shop floor.

These characteristics crystallized into three principles which became the hallmark of the new independent trade union movement:

non-racialism
worker control
shopfloor, plant-based organization.

These principles are often portrayed by commentators as abstract commitments to democratic principles. For the ordinary workers and the hard-pressed union organizers that held these unions together, these principles were very concrete. They were the only way they could guarantee the organizational strength to make any headway on union issues. These principles were thus strongly grounded in the organizational requirements of these unions.

Phase 1: 1975–82

These organizational principles clearly dominated the initial reactions of the independent trade union movement towards the industrial council system. Union perceptions of the industrial council system were coloured by their experience of industrial conciliation structures on the factory floor. The threat these structures posed to the organizational principles sustained both the independent trade union movement and the organizational problems and requirements confronting unions in this period.

The emergent underground unions perceived the industrial council system as fundamentally racist and bureaucratic. The system was too intertwined with, and dependent on, state involvement and hence — to the organizers — was fraught with the twin dangers of potentially co-opting them and alienating them from their worker constituency. Workers saw the industrial council structures as management-dominated, and the white racist craft unions as locked in a cosy relationship with the state (via the labour department) at the economic and political expense of the unskilled black workers. They perceived the industrial council procedures to be bolstering up the despotic labour relations practices and undermining their own rank-and-file plant-based disciplinary and grievance procedures. Predominantly craft unions were bargaining in these industrial council forums: the fact that they were unrepresentative of the unskilled black majority was an affront to these workers. This was reflected in the disparities in wage levels and personnel practices at plant level. For unions like MAWU, the manner in which deals were struck to the benefit of management and the craft-based Confederation of Metal and Building Unions (CMBU), but at the expense of the semi- and unskilled black working class, was very clear. Black unskilled workers experienced the industrial council system in an extremely concrete way every week when their pay packets reflected the industrial council deductions. The unfairness of what they regarded as some external institution deducting their money with seemingly little benefit to them was a source of continual aggravation.

The industrial council structures ran counter to the basic organizational principles underlying the independent trade union movement — that is, factory committees bargaining at the plant level, with the general membership being the primary decision-making body. Hence it was small wonder that the bargaining and conciliation structures instituted by the national industrial council were seen as a direct threat to, (and indeed designed to destroy) their own plant-based union structures. Since SEIFSA's[7] attitude to plant-level rights was to deny plant-based negotiating any legitimacy, this perception held by the independent unions was substantially correct. To unions like MAWU and the GWU (who were perhaps the most vociferous in their arguments against industrial councils), the industrial council system came to symbolize and epitomize the worst features of South Africa's racial despotic system.

There were also structural reasons why these unions could only view the industrial council system in the manner they did. As I have stressed, these unions were at this stage numerically small, regionally based and by no means representative (even at the regional level) of the industry they were operating in. The industrial council system was thus incomprehensible to these unions. It literally had no substantive meaning to them except as a mechanism for repression, dis-organization and domination. The entire *raison d'être* of the industrial council system — to facilitate national, industrial collective bargaining (leaving aside on whose terms and whether the structure was democratic or even facilitative of the trade union side of the table) — could not make any organizational sense to unions that were not confronting the issue of negotiation on a national, industrial, or even company bargaining level. The result was that the debates and arguments rationalizing the strategic alternatives were pitched at a highly abstract, principled and fundamentally political level.[8]

This explains why in this first phase the unions took up a directly con-frontationist position against the entire industrial council system, rejecting it completely. They were faced with the problem of struggling to establish a pres-ence and foothold in the industries they were organized in, rather than trying to consolidate national industrial bargaining presence. In addition they daily experienced the industrial council structure as a racist, bureaucratic system. Hence they motivated that shop floor bargaining was the only viable and prin-cipled alternative to full-scale incorporation of, and consequent domination by the statutory industrial relations system.

The aim of posing plant-based negotiations as the viable alternative to industrial council negotiations was however unsuccessful. Indeed the initial breakthroughs in the metal industry in Cape Town, where Trident Marine and Consani were 'forced/persuaded' or 'agreed' to negotiate wages and conditions of service with the General Workers Union (which not only refused to join the industrial council but was also unregistered) served mainly to **harden rather than soften** SEIFSA's attitude. In the final analysis, it was the 1981 rolling strike wave in the East Rand metal industry, which was aimed at securing wage bargaining at plant level (and initiated, but not really co-ordinated by MAWU), that set the scene for a shift in attitudes of both union and management. This initiated the transition to the next phase.

Phase 2: 1983–87

Management responded in two ways to this strike wave. On the plant level — the alternative terrain on which MAWU chose to fight its whole campaign — management's response was totally intransigent. However at the level of organized business, there was a strategically qualitative shift in approach. With-out revision on the issues of bargaining over wages and conditions of service, SEIFSA became more responsive to the demand for shop floor rights, **but not as an alternative** to the industrial council system. SEIFSA accepted some lim-ited plant-level rights being accorded to unions, for example: the recognition of shop stewards; time off for training; access to the plant; stop-order facilities; and some grievance and disciplinary rights — **but only** if they registered and joined the industrial council. Hence management altered its strategic position on plant-level bargaining as a direct response to the changing terrain of union struggles on the factory floor. This was clearly not a move to accept plant-level bargaining as an alternative to industrial council, but rather an attempt to maintain the industrial council as the sole basis for industry-wide collective bargaining over wages and conditions of service.

On the union side, MAWU's membership grew phenomenally as a direct consequence of this strike wave. This threw up new organizational priorities which in turn led to a strategic shift on the issue of participation in the industrial council. Instead of operating within the confines of a numerically small union, suddenly MAWU organizers — particularly in the Transvaal — found themselves with too many factories to service on the plant level. The organizers were literally unable to cope with the demands being placed on them and could not service the ever-expanding number of factories and workers. They desperately tried to maintain organizational contact, instead of adequately servicing each plant. In truth they spent their time running from strike-ridden factory to factory, offering advice, talking to a few shop stewards, arguing with management, hand-collecting union subscriptions and in the end not doing anything particularly effectively. Whilst this certainly nurtured self-sufficient shop stewards, it did nothing productive for the centralized co-ordination that a union necessarily requires. The union became incapable of maintaining a correspondence between its stated policy and the demands arising from so many factories.

MAWU was facing new organizational problems: too many factories but too few organizers; too many workers to service at plant level yet too few co-ordinating structures to achieve economies of scale in negotiations; the organizational necessity for centralized national interventions in contrast to the increasing emergence of factory sectionalism; and the need to assert the union's presence at the national industrial level but insufficient muscle to challenge the power and weight of SEIFSA.

In short, MAWU had radically and fundamentally altered its character from a small, regionally-based union to one with substantial membership, nationally spread throughout the whole industry, **but without the commensurate collective bargaining structures and focus to operate in this context**. It had become a union with a national industrially-based membership but it was not a **national industrial union**.

At the most basic level, there was a critical need for some national co-ordination of campaigns and uniformity of wages **between** factories. This could however only materialize if the union shifted from its structure as a set of discrete factories, each with their own particular problems and solutions, towards being an organization exhibiting national planning and co-ordination. Although this obviously required a qualitative shift in the union's strategic vision, the strike wave had also partially laid the foundation for this change to occur. The inability of the organizers to deal effectively with factory-based problems on the ground had also facilitated (on some levels) inter-factory unity and the embryonic development of inter-factory shop steward councils. The aftermath of these strikes thus revealed the need, and provided the potential basis, for a sense of national organizational and structural unity.

The inability to secure workers' demands in the 1982 strike wave forced a rethink on the union's part. It was apparent that the strategy of positing plant-level bargaining as the sole alternative to national collective bargaining through the industrial council system was no longer appropriate. The material conditions within which MAWU operated had radically altered, new organizational requirements were being thrown up, and a strategic shift was thus required on its part.

Despite the ordinary members' reaction of total resistance to the industrial council system, the troubled union leadership tentatively started to explore alternative ways of accommodating it on terms more favourable to them. The basic problem was how to devise a new strategy which maintained the organizational strengths of shop floor unionism, while still confronting the new problems being encountered. It was becoming apparent to many in leadership echelons in MAWU that the union had to either devise a new, more appropriate strategy on the basis of changed conditions; or would have to carry on facing a new reality with a familiar strategy, but one applicable to a previous period. There was neither uniformity of opinion nor a guarantee that the union would respond in the most rational, strategic manner — after all, the history of mass organizations is replete with missed opportunities, principled failures and glorious defeats. Organizations are not rational subjects: they are fissured by contradictions, struggles and conflicts, and past ways of viewing the world weigh heavily upon them.

Without going into the details of the process,[9] the outcome was a strategy which treated the issue of membership of the industrial council in organizational and tactical, rather than principled, terms. It was recognized that the union was still too weak to make any real impact on the balance of power in the industrial council at industry level. However, if there was a need to weld the union into a nationally coherent entity, then the centralized structure of the industrial council could be used to assist in this process. Abandoning the demand for plant-level bargaining was not required, because MAWU's relative weakness on a national industrial level, compared to capital's power within the industrial council system, meant that entry into the industrial council was necessarily coupled with plant-level bargaining.

The reason for going into the industrial council was thus primarily to use the forum as a means of co-ordinating a national wage campaign, presented formally at the industrial council, but fought out at the plant level. Plant-level bargaining was now not antithetical to industrial council structures, but was viewed rather as an ancillary addition. Participation in the industrial council structure was necessary in order to mobilize on a national basis and break out of the isolation of separate factory struggles. This would be achieved by posing a national wage demand without necessarily expecting to win it, but still having the power to fight out at the plant level. Hence the demand was for the right to be a member of the industrial council and still to be able to bargain at plant level in order to secure higher wages than those set at the yearly industrial council negotiations.

The strategy had shifted: the structure of plant-level bargaining was no longer posed as an **alternative** to participating in a national collective bargaining structure, but as a bargaining supplement to participation in the industrial council system. In short, plant-level bargaining was not intended to substitute participation in the industrial council system, since its role was not seen as equivalent to the union's role within the industrial council system.

So MAWU's relationship to the industrial council became ambiguous. The union took the forum seriously but not necessarily in the sense in which the industrial council saw itself, that is, as a collective bargaining mechanism.[10] MAWU's strategy was to participate in this bargaining process but not in the same manner in which they participated at plant level, where the expectation was that an agreed wage settlement would be reached after negotiation and struggle. The union used the processes of formulating a national demand and of reporting back through large, regionally-based cross-factory general meetings and joint shop steward councils. This was the mechanism for welding together a consciousness amongst workers that the union was more than a collection of individual factories. In addition, in the creative way in which it used the bargaining team within the industrial council, and reported back to standing meetings of a shop steward council representing nearly every factory in the union, MAWU moulded this consciousness into a national organization ancillary to and supportive of the union's national executive committee.

The stress on the bargaining team's role was an important part of the strategy. Even though the balance of power favoured capital in the industrial council, the manner in which the MAWU negotiating team participated radically altered the **form** in which power relations were expressed in this system. This was very much a conscious part of the union's strategy. The entrenched objections which workers and union officials had for the industrial council system had often stemmed from a revulsion for the overly bureaucratic, formal, white-official dominated negotiating procedures prevalent therein. MAWU's deliberate use of a large team of black worker negotiators, sometimes speaking in the vernacular and drawing on their concrete experience rather than relying on economic statistics, was a clear attempt to shake up and facilitate the democratization of the formal structures of this collective bargaining forum.

This strategy worked initially because the union knew that the other side of its national industrial weakness was that its negotiating team could argue and bargain without having to come to any agreement at all. MAWU turned their limited options in the industrial council negotiating forum to their own organizational advantage. They had little option but to vocalize their members' demands and express their opposition to the deals that the CMBU (and the other small unions with black members) in the industry were willing to strike, and to refuse to be party to the agreements. Since MAWU did not, as yet, constitute the majority grouping on the trade union side of the industrial council negotiating forum, this strategy allowed them to have their (somewhat limited) cake and eat it. They could be the main antagonists within the forum and yet not have to take responsibility for the inadequate agreement that emerged from the negotiations in the Industrial Council, with which their members were not happy.

Furthermore, there was reasonable certainty that the other parties would insist that the Minister of Manpower gazette the main agreement, because their own constituencies would not accept wage increases being deferred. This would leave the way open for MAWU to pursue the strategy of taking up their own substantive demands at plant level. Thus MAWU could participate without abandoning the fundamental commitment to rank-and-file democratic organization which had been the basis of its strength in the past. This also allowed the union to expand its membership amongst previously unorganized workers, since it could clearly be seen as the uncompromised, but also serious, champion of the workers in the metal industry.

Phase 3: Post-1987

The strategy of participating in the industrial council but not in the settlement process, and of using the industrial council for organizing but still placing the primary emphasis on wage bargaining at the plant level, fitted the requirements of the second period. It quickly came up against its own limits, however. The strategy's very success in expanding union membership and consolidating the unions' national framework threw up new organizational requirements. The rapid growth in MAWU's membership in the engineering industry and its merger with MICWU and NAAWU[11] to form NUMSA, expanded the metal union's membership to 150 000, making it by far the largest union in the metal, engineering and automobile industries. This forced a reformulation of NUMSA's strategic vision with regard to the industrial council system. The obvious question that had to be faced was: given the success of the previous phase's strategy in expanding membership and welding together a national union, what would happen now that MAWU had become the biggest union in the industrial council? Essentially it had to find a way to bargain at the national industrial level.

A number of possible divergent strategies were discussed. They could follow a path (which had some currency in the early days of MAWU's participation) of breaking up the central industrial council structure into subsectors. This possibility was rejected since it would have contradicted the very reason for getting involved in the industrial council system — that is, it would have weakened the organizational gains made during the second phase. Breaking up the bargaining unit into various subsectors would also have broken up NUMSA's recently acquired national internal coherence, as well as leaving the union numerically and organizationally very weak in a number of the subsectors. This would have been a backward step organizationally, and would have forced bargaining from a point of numerical weakness rather than strength. Once again the whole was greater than the sum of its parts.

Alternatively, the union could follow the path of the Paper, Wood and Allied Workers Union (PWAWU). Although this union had the absolute majority in the paper industrial council, and could have dictated the terms for that particular industrial council system, it decided to force the break-up in the paper industrial council. NUMSA, contrary to PWAWU, decided that trying to break up the metal industrial council would not be in its own long-term organizational interests. This would be squandering the centralized power that the union held in the bargaining forum, to score the dubious advantage of an ideological point. Furthermore, there were forces within management that favoured the disintegration of national industrial collective bargaining in order to undercut and weaken NUMSA's position in the industry.

A key NUMSA official, commenting on the changing circumstances facing the union, gave the first hints of an awareness of the need to adopt a new policy towards national collective bargaining and hence the industrial council system.

> Because of overtime pressure, some SEIFSA companies are now trying to pull out of the industrial council. They are telling workers that they will negotiate only at plant level. In this way they are trying to divide workers. They want workers only to worry about factory negotiations (interview in *South African Labour Bulletin*, vol. 7, no. 3, 1987).

Given the history of the struggles over the industrial council system, there was an obvious historical irony in this complaint. NUMSA was now fighting to defend the structural integrity of the industrial council system from certain managements whose sole purpose was to revert to plant-level bargaining in order to destroy the national organization of workers in the industry. These employers were intent on restoring their competitiveness in the market by escaping the national uniformity of wages and conditions of service that the industrial council was imposing on them.[12] This tied in with noises emanating from the Department of Manpower about the need to deregulate. By 1987 the Minister of Manpower seemed to be looking for excuses **not** to gazette the main agreement, not to extend it to smaller, decentralized firms, and to grant exemptions against the wishes of the majority parties in the industrial council.

The organizational imperatives facing the union had radically altered and the tactical choices available to them were correspondingly different from the previous period. NUMSA now had both the need and the capacity to bargain effectively at national industrial level, and this obviously altered union attitudes to bargaining within the industrial council system.

If NUMSA did **not** bargain to completion within the national industry bargaining forum of the industrial council, then the Minister was faced with the constant temptation not to gazette the main agreement. If the agreement was neither gazetted nor extended to bodies not party to the industrial council, then SEIFSA could well fall apart, since it would no longer benefit companies to join SEIFSA and its *raison d'être* would have disappeared. However if this occurred it would also mean the end of a statutory national industrial centralized bargaining system (that is, the industrial council), which in turn would mean the end of a minimum level of wage uniformity, and the cessation of protection from unfair competition by companies employing unorganized workers. This would have destroyed NUMSA's ability to act as a national union.

Whereas MAWU had joined the industrial council in order to consolidate itself as a national union without accepting the commensurate collective bargaining responsibilities of the forum, NUMSA's organizational requirements now forced it to maintain the statutory national collective bargaining system precisely in order to counter those tendencies undermining its legitimacy as a national union. This brought about an historically ironic, but understandable, partial congruence of interest between SEIFSA and NUMSA in preserving the industrial council against those employers wishing to push deregulation to its logical conclusion — the destruction of the industrial council itself.

The new phase heralded a complete reversal of union attitude towards the industrial council system. This did not mean that it was willing to agree at all costs within that bargaining forum, but rather that it would now follow through to conclusion the implications of bargaining collectively on a national industrial basis. It was therefore not a surprise that the 1988 wage talks resulted in a national industrial dispute and the possibility of the first-ever legal national wage strike in the metal industry, only averted by Ministerial action. In this case the Minister's hand was forced and the State strategy of not gazetting the agreement was inverted. If the Minister did not gazette the agreement which NUMSA had rejected, then he allowed a legal national strike to occur. If he did, then he undermined the legal basis of the strike, but in so doing maintained the national coherence of the union and allowed it to flex its muscles without having to test them.

As a result of their newly found national organizational strength, NUMSA forced SEIFSA (in the 1988 dispute) to bargain seriously within the industrial council structures. As a result of this, a new strategy is slowly emerging from NUMSA in this third phase. This is essentially concerned with attempting to develop policy on a number of important questions:

* How to defend the integrity of the industrial council with respect to **setting** national industrial wage rates. (This would require bargaining to completion within the industrial council system.)
* How to use company shop steward councils to bargain and set **procedural and other non-wage** issues. (This would require the elaboration of a company level bargaining forum.)
* How to use plant-level shop steward committees to bargain for and police the **implementation** of these agreements. (This would require maintenance of the importance of plant level shop steward structures, but also a new way of structuring them into the collective bargaining system.)

The introduction of company-level negotiation over procedural and non-wage substantive issues has been a fairly recent phenomenon. There are some important congruences of interest from both managements and the union in constructing this level. It facilitates the development of a common approach at both management and union levels in the different plants within the company, or within a single division in a company. It helps to co-ordinate issues amongst the various factories at plant level, and hence stops the wastage of resources which occurs if everything is dealt with at each separate plant. It creates a structured and recognized forum for management and the national union organizers in order to deal with issues at plant level which are not being dealt with by the line management and the local union structures. This is important, since management often demands that the union head offices intervene in a plant dispute. In the absence of formal correspondence between the union and the management at the national company level, it is often structurally difficult for such interventions and negotiations to occur fruitfully and legitimately. Furthermore, negotiating relations become haphazard and anarchic.

The problem is, how to institute this level so that national industrial level bargaining is supplemented and not undercut? The strategy of this third period is to attempt to integrate organizational requirements at the central level with the basis of the union's organizational strength on the shop floor; and to integrate wage bargaining at the central level with the maintenance of shop steward structures on the factory floor. The problem the union faces is how to use national bargaining to build plant structures whilst at the same time not allowing these plant structures to undercut national bargaining. In this strategy, plant-level union activities have not been abandoned nor counterposed to national collective bargaining activities, but they are no longer the central focus of wage bargaining.

Although this emergent policy attempts to integrate the different levels of collective bargaining into an interdependent strategy, it can be schematically summarized in the following terms:

The industrial council system will be used for national industrial wage bargaining, and therefore the system will be defended against those employers who wish to break it up;

Plant-level bargaining will be used for dealing with local issues, thus keeping the shop steward structures intact and ensuring that interventions at the central level are backed up by organizational muscle on the ground;

The second tier of company-level bargaining will be used for issues other than wages, to strengthen the centralized unity of the union, ensure a coherence and uniformity between plants of the same company, and deflect factory demands for wage bargaining at plant level onto company-level bargaining over other substantive issues.

In this way, the coherence and integrity of the national industrial wage bargaining structures can be protected, and the union can intervene on the basis of these local shop steward structures without making workers feel that their plant-level struggles and demands are being abandoned.

In the metal industry, the strategy emerging in this third phase with regard to the industrial council system reverses that of the second. In this most recent phase, plant-level structures play the role of organizationally backing up wage bargaining at the industrial council level, for they facilitate a powerful, coherent intervention within the national industrial wage bargaining structures. Without active shop steward structures on the factory floor, the wage bargaining strategy would collapse into bureaucratic, centralized union negotiations. Without a centralized national wage bargaining strategy, the shop floor structures would disintegrate into isolated, fragmented activities.[13] The whole would then be reduced to the sum of its parts.

Conclusion

Much discussion around union policies focuses primarily on the ideological differences and grand political visions espoused by the different factions within the trade union movement. Whilst such debate and controversy is undoubtedly of importance, the focus on these questions to the exclusion of the real organizational issues, which drive the serious unions, is detrimental to an understanding of the dynamics of this movement. One of the most important lessons to be learnt from this union movement is the emphasis it has placed on the concrete and the organizational mechanisms in order to make material and organizational gains. In this regard, the serious unions have not shied away from radically altering their policies and abandoning strongly-held ideological positions that ran counter to the concrete organizational requirements of the day.

NUMSA's relationship to the industrial council system over the past decade illustrates this most clearly.

The union movement is undoubtedly one of the most important social forces bringing about structural change in South Africa. Other such forces within the oppressed population could learn much from the historical struggles of this movement. However, unless the focus is sharply directed towards the organizational and concrete struggles undertaken by these unions, it is unlikely that much of lasting value will be transferred as lessons to these other social structures.

Notes

1 The ideas expressed in this chapter derive from my own previous trade union experience as well as intensive discussion at various times with a number of trade unionists on the issue of the industrial council system: Dave Lewis, Di Cooper, Msokoli Qotole, Pat Horn, Bobby Marie, Alec Erwin and Geoff Schreiner. I am particularly grateful to the comments made by Geoff Schreiner and Pat Horn on an earlier draft. It is as well to stress that whilst this article has benefited immensely from the viewpoints of these unionists, they are not responsible for the manner in which I have chosen to analyse the issue of the metal union's relationship to the industrial council system.

2 This chapter will concentrate on the Metal and Allied Workers Union's experience of the industrial council system. See Morris (1986) for a similar discussion of the General Workers Union's radical alteration in its approach to industrial councils as a result of changing organizational imperatives. See Davies (1976); Lewis (1985a & b); NUTW (1982) for additional information on industrial councils and union struggles.

3 See Steve Friedman (1987) for an overview of the trade union movement up until 1984.

4 Trade Union Advisory Co-ordinating Council.

5 Federation of South African Trade Unions.

6 South African Congress of Trade Unions.

7 Steel, Engineering Industries Federation of South Africa.

8 Much of the argument against the industrial council system occurred within the context of debates around registration. See SALB: vol. 5, nos. 6 & 7, 1980; vol. 7, no. 3, 1981; vol. 7, nos. 4 & 5, 1982; vol. 8, nos. 1–3, 1982. The articles by Dobson (1982), Hartman (1982); and Webster (1983) focus directly on the industrial council system and the metal industry.

9 See Eddie Webster (1983)for a complementary and more detailed analysis of this period.

10 It is just as well to point out that a reasonably strong case could be made that SEIFSA, whilst obviously welcoming MAWU's entry into the industrial council, did not negotiate with any seriousness with the union in this period.

11 Respectively, the Motor Industries Combined Workers Union and the National Automobile and Allied Workers Union.

12 This issue is wider and more complex than a simple response to the gains made by NUMSA in the metal industry. Some companies like Barlow Rand had a well

developed strategy, which they applied across industries, to negotiate everything in the smallest bargaining unit possible.

13 See the interview with Bernie Fanaroff in *SALB*, vol. 12, no. 4, 1987, p.41,. 'With the committee of chairmen, each is directly responsible for his own factory and workers in his factory will discipline him if he does wrong. The chairman himself has a much deeper understanding of what we are actually doing during the Industrial Council meetings'.

References

Davies, R., 'The Class Character of South Africa's Industrial Conciliation Legislation', *South African Labour Bulletin*, vol. 2, no. 6, 1976.

Dobson, P., 'The Industrial Council in the Metal and Engineering Industry', *South African Labour Bulletin*, vol. 8, no. 3, 1982.

FOSATU, 'Principles of Collective Bargaining', *South African Labour Bulletin*, vol. 8, no. 1, 1982.

Friedman, S., *Building Tomorrow Today*, Ravan Press: Johannesburg, 1987.

Hartman, N., 'Industrial Councils: Barriers to Labour Democracy', *South African Labour Bulletin*, vol. 8, no. 1, 1982.

Lewis, J., 'MAWU and the Industrial Council,' *South African Labour Bulletin*, vol. 11, no. 1, 1985a.

Lewis, J., 'PWAWU Deathblow to the Industrial Council?', *South African Labour Bulletin*, vol. 11, no. 1, 1985b.

Morris, M.L., 'The Stevedores and the GWU', *South African Labour Bulletin*, vol. 11, no. 5, 1986.

NUTW, 'Industrial Councils: New Dimensions to the Struggle in the Textile Industry', *South African Labour Bulletin*, vol. 8, no. 5, 1982.

Webster, E., 'MAWU and the Industrial Council: A Comment', *South African Labour Bulletin*, vol. 8, no. 5, 1983.

Unemployment and labour market issues — a beginner's guide[1]

10

Sean Archer, Norman Bromberger, Nicoli Nattrass and George Oldham

Introduction

The question of unemployment in South Africa has been hotly debated since the late 1970s (see review in Hofmeyr, 1985). Studies showing high and rising[2] levels of black unemployment from the early 1970s or earlier (see for example Simkins, 1978; Knight, 1978; Bell & Padayachee, 1984; and Bell, 1985) appeared to contradict evidence of labour shortage and increasing black wages in various sectors of the South African economy (Bromberger, 1978; Hofmeyr, 1985). Issues of conceptualization, measurement and explanation became blurred in the controversy, in part because ideological factors appeared to play a large role.

The absence of reliable estimates of unemployment and lack of any consensus as to how unemployment should be measured, further confounded the question. This chapter attempts to chart a path through the stumbling blocks identified in the debate, by clarifying the measurement concepts and pointing out where theoretical preconceptions intervened to produce widely ranging interpretations and estimates.

The concept of unemployment

The concept of unemployment is relatively old. Milton's phrase 'rove idle unimploid' dates from 1667 (Williams, 1976, p. 274). Over time, the meaning of the word has evolved from a broad application, to 'things not being put to use', then 'people not active in production', and finally to the specialized modern sense of 'not being employed for payment by another person or institution although seeking to be so'.

Examining the distinction between 'unemployed' and 'idle' is instructive. In current everyday usage, the former refers to a social situation — an inability to exchange labour for income in a collective activity — and the latter to a personal condition. In the first case individuals are not working because of economic and social forces beyond their control; in the second they have exercised a choice and are not working because they do not wish to. In other words, where able-bodied workers are **unemployed**, the fault lies with impersonal causes like local and world market conditions or possibly government actions; but where they are **idle**, their own decisions are the main cause and no question of the responsibility or blameworthiness of others arises.

In current economic discourse there is a parallel distinction between 'involuntary' and 'voluntary' unemployment. The normative connotations of these concepts have tended to cloud the debate. Those who place great faith in the ability of the market mechanism to create socially desirable outcomes are reluctant to accept that the system has failed to the degree implied by high levels of 'involuntary' unemployment. Likewise, researchers concerned with exposing the extent of poverty in South Africa and the plight of many without jobs, are understandably reluctant to accept an analysis of unemployment as 'voluntary' and hence the responsibility of the individual rather than the system or the state.

Standing puts his finger on the problem:

> The concept of unemployment is hard to define partly because it combines a condition (being without employment), a need (for work), an attitude (desire for work) and an activity (searching for work). Some question the applicability of the term if used to describe the position of someone satisfying the first criterion without satisfying one or more of the others. Hence the claim that many of the unemployed in both industrialized and low-income countries, are in fact voluntarily unemployed. If so, the associated social distress would be overstated and unemployment could be downgraded as a policy concern (1981, p. 563).

In the debate on South African unemployment, most energies were directed at the issue of 'voluntary' versus 'involuntary' unemployment (see Hofmeyr, 1985 pp. 155–6). Although the distinction is theoretically important to economists, it is often ambiguous and difficult to put into operation in the real world (Bell, 1985; Hofmeyr, 1985, p. 156). When it comes to interpreting unemployment statistics, the issue of whether the under-employed or 'voluntarily' unemployed are included, for instance those engaged part-time in low-productivity subsistence activities or those kept by geographical immobility or lack of skill outside the main wage-labour markets, is a contentious matter.

Unemployment — the statistic

Unemployment in South Africa has been measured in the recent past as lying between 4 and 52 per cent, depending on how and where the measurement was made (Wilson & Ramphele, 1989, pp. 88f). While regional differences in unemployment are certainly important, another major reason for the variation is likely to be statistical categories themselves. For example, Moll (1984, p. 238–57) has shown that depending on the definition of work adopted,[3] the rate of unemployment in the village of Lower Roza, Transkei, rose from 5,2 per cent to 26,3 per cent; and that if one included the discouraged unemployed (see below), the rates rose from 7,1 per cent to 36,8 per cent. Likewise, Prinsloo found that the unemployment rate in Cape Town and Durban varied from 9 to 17 per cent[4] depending on whether the discouraged unemployed were included in the definition of the labour force (discussed in Wilson & Ramphele, 1989, pp. 91–2). Consequently, clarity about the conventional statistical categories used in measuring unemployment is essential before commencing discussion of unemployment; and in particular, it is essential to take cognizance of the sensitivity of measured unemployment to the definitions used.

The estimated magnitude of unemployment in an economy is thus the outcome of conceptual and measurement decisions relating to the changing balance between **demand** for labour in production and the **supply** of labour (determined by alterations in birth and death rates; net migration flows; education; social policies; and customary beliefs and attitudes to paid work, for example, concerning the economic role of women). In capitalist economies, effective demand and the level and structure of wages plays a major role in balancing the supply and demand for labour. In planned economies, institutional means are harnessed to the same end. Although it is generally accepted that neither of the systems has been wholly successful in eliminating unemployment in the sense of providing jobs for all who want them, the full employment ideal has been approached more closely and is consistently under planning despite other problems of resource allocation in the system.

Total population, the broadest concept of labour supply, is the product of two demographic variables — birth and death rates — and of migration flows across national frontiers. As the population includes many too young and too old to work, those of working age are usually taken as between the ages of 15 and 64. This **'source population'** or **'working age cohort'** is the outcome of the time structure of previous births and deaths. A proportion of this category — the residual after excluding students, women occupied solely in domestic duties, the retired, and persons living entirely on their own means or wholly dependent on others, constitutes the **economically active population**. When expressed as a ratio to the total population, this yields the **crude activity rate**. Although many researchers regard the economically active population as identical to the **labour force**, a narrower measure can be obtained by subtracting employers, own-account workers, unpaid family workers and members of producers' co-operatives from the economically active population. Finally, the **participation rate** is obtained by expressing the labour force (narrowly or broadly defined) as a percentage of those of working age.

In this conventional approach, which identifies employment with wage employment, the labour force by definition comprises the sum of persons employed in wage labour plus the unemployed. The magnitude of unemployment thus depends on how many jobs the economy can generate, given the way in which work is conceptualized operationally, and therefore how the labour force is defined. Those deemed to be living entirely within their own means (or the means of others) by choice, in the sense that they are not actively seeking work, are excluded from the labour force and hence also from the category of unemployed. Likewise, a housewife falls outside this concept of the labour force and hence outside the categories of employed and unemployed. This happens despite the fact that she may be engaged in production, either through subsistence activities or in raising future members of the workforce. The vision of work in the official conventions is a proletarian one in that by assumption people either work for wages or do nothing productive since they lack the necessary resources to utilize their labour in work. This definition has been criticized as too exclusive and therefore not appropriate for developing countries where subsistence, peasant and informal production occur on a large scale, since people still have significant access to land and related resources and the capital requirements for small business are a minimal constraint.

It is incongruous to regard discouraged work-seekers — those who desire paid employment but believe it is impossible to find and therefore do not expend energy searching for it — as 'voluntarily' unemployed and not part of the labour force. Similarly there are many people, as Ardington (1984, p. 64) found for the Nkandla district, who do not regard themselves as unemployed because they never considered employment as an achievable goal. For these reasons, many research workers are uncomfortable with extending the concept of 'voluntary unemployment' beyond frictional unemployment (that which occurs as the result of lags during job switches). However, as shown below there is an influential argument which maintains that all those without jobs are voluntarily unemployed in the straightforward sense that they refuse to work at the going market rate. In one unqualified version of this view, the labour force is synonymous with the number of employed people plus the frictionally unemployed, thus making the magnitude of unemployment in South Africa a 'mythical problem' (Kantor, 1980, p. 144). In addition Gerson (1981) argues that the long-term rate of employment is the 'natural rate' which includes frictional unemployment and structural unemployment resulting from contrived imbalances in the economy which prevent full employment of certain types of labour.

Thus the estimated rate of unemployment will depend on how the labour supply is conceptualized for measurement. For example, if the whole working-age cohort is identified with the labour force, then very high rates of measured unemployment will result. Referring to the 'potential economically active population' as the labour force, Sarakinsky & Keenan, for instance, report unemployment rates of 55 per cent in areas such as Thaba Nchu and Lebowa (1986, p. 21). This methodology erroneously presumes that everyone of working age can and wants to work. One needs rather to multiply the working age population by the participation rate to obtain an acceptable estimate of the labour supply. If one then subtracts the number of formal sector jobs from the labour supply (defined this time as the total economically active population enumerated in the census), it appears that in 1980 there were 3,3 million people unemployed in South Africa, giving an unemployment rate of 30 per cent (President's Council, 1987, p. 11). However even this method, though similar to that of Simkins (1978) and Knight (1978), **includes** as unemployed some work status categories left out of the narrower definition of the labour force, for instance unpaid family and own-account workers (see above), as well as individuals in unenumerated informal production and the under-employed in agriculture.

Kantor & Gerson argue for other reasons that the latter methodology misspecifies the labour supply and that what has been termed involuntary unemployment can be explained via search theory, described in the next section, and low labour force participation due to restrictions on the mobility of labour and prevailing low wages (discussed in Hofmeyr, 1985, p. 24). According to Gerson, Simkins' methodology measures 'poverty rather than unemployment' (1982, p. 130).

Using a more narrow definition of the labour force, the Current Population Survey (CPS) netted only those jobless people who had taken active steps to find employment in the four weeks preceding the interview. Applying this criterion resulted in measured unemployment rates of roughly 13 per cent in October 1977 and 7 per cent in January 1982 — the peak of the 1978/82 upswing (Oldham & Bromberger 1989, p. 13). Although there are always some who choose not to work under almost any labour market circumstances, the original CPS categorization is too strict as it excludes the discouraged unemployed work-seekers. For this reason the International Labour Organization (ILO) recommends, particularly for developing countries, that an extended definition of unemployment be constructed which includes people currently available for work but not actively seeking it; for reasons such as the belief that work is unavailable, a lack of knowledge of where to find work, illness or short-term lay-off (ILO, 1982, p. 48).

Moll's study cited earlier implies that, on an extended definition, unemployment in South Africa could be between 37 per cent and 46 per cent greater than the conventional measure adopted by the CPS (1984, p. 252). However, after the CPS introduced an expanded definition of unemployment by dropping the work-seeking requirement in 1987, its data indicates that the inclusion of discouraged work-seekers results in less than a 2 percentage point increase in the rate of black male unemployment to 11,9 per cent (Nattrass, 1989, p. 12). These findings of the CPS should, however, be interpreted with caution as Moll (1984) and Meth (1988) warn of methodological problems and inconsistencies in the CPS procedure, from the survey stage of the research through to the analysis.

In conclusion, it should be noted that a particular weakness of the labour force concept as conventionally defined is that it ignores the extensive under-utilization of labour so characteristic of developing countries.[5] This includes visible under-employment (people working restricted hours who wish to work longer) and invisible under-employment (people working full hours whose skills and capabilities are not however being fully utilized). Yet the substantial statistical difficulties inherent in identifying and estimating under-employment make it highly problematic to measure by conventional means. Extensive household surveys might do the job but are prohibitively expensive to conduct on a periodic basis.

There have been other attempts in South Africa to get to grips with this question. Simkins developed the concept of 'full-time job equivalents', in which, if a person could obtain only a part-time job for say 10 hours a week, then that person was counted as one-quarter employed and three-quarters unemployed (discussed in Wilson & Ramphele, 1989, p. 85). Using a 'fully developed poverty approach', Bromberger applied the under-employment notion to South Africa in order to identify low-wage, low-productivity employment (1978, p. 15). Individuals are regarded as under-employed if they do not earn an income sufficient to meet their defined basic needs. Neither of these approaches are wholly convincing to those economists who object to this blurring of unemployment, under-employment and poverty categories. These attempts however remain illuminating for those interested in the relationship between unemployment and poverty.

Unemployment — the theoretical input

As we have seen, differing conceptual, methodological and theoretical positions can muddy the statistical waters when it comes to measuring unemployment. This would seem particularly true of the South African debate and for this reason it is essential to gain a broad understanding of the nature of the opposing theoretical traditions.

One pure version of neo-classical analysis starts from the modelling premise that the world comprises a series of smoothly-functioning, always-clearing markets. Supply and demand quantities are equated by price so that unexploited opportunities for mutually beneficial trading simply cannot arise. In the labour market this means that increased demand for labour, *ceteris paribus*, bids up the price (wage), thereby drawing more people into the labour force and into employment (and vice versa). In this view, individuals are either simultaneously in the labour force and wage employment, or between jobs or out of the labour force. In other words, in the abstract model, extensive unemployment is not a possibility in that those without jobs are simply not prepared to work at the going rate and hence must be defined as non-participatory and out of the labour force.

The only way unemployment can emerge in this paradigm, is for market failure to occur. If there do exist individuals who would be prepared to work at the going market rate, then it follows that the market mechanism, which should have adjusted by allowing the wage to fall, has failed. By inference, unemployment exists only because the wage has not fallen far enough to make wage employment undesirable. Interesting questions that as a consequence suggest themselves to neo-classical economists are why the labour market exhibits prices which are 'sticky in a downwards direction' and whether job-seekers have unrealistically high wage expectations (see Hofmeyr, 1984).

A substantial economic literature attempts to explain such labour market failure; for instance, job-search behaviour has often been put forward as an explanation of unemployment. Because information about jobs is imperfectly known and costly to obtain, it is hypothesized that the rational work-seeker will not accept the first job offered, but will use the job search process, keeping him or her out of full-time employment, as an information-gathering exercise. Search will continue until the cost of search becomes greater than the expected gains. Such a process increases the rate of apparent unemployment in the short term, for instance during a cyclical downturn.

This perception assumes that work-seekers do in fact have the means to finance their job search. While this is no doubt true of some aspirant wage workers, it is by no means true for all potential work-seekers in South Africa. Wilson & Ramphele emphasize that the cost of job search is often prohibitive — especially for those in rural areas where the cost of transport to the cities is high (1989, p. 86).

Another theoretical attempt to explain why wages do not fall far enough to eliminate unemployment is the 'efficiency wage' hypothesis. Here it is argued that firms set 'efficiency wages' above the market clearing level so as to reduce turnover and to increase labour productivity (Stiglitz, 1976). Unemployed workers will thus queue for these jobs, yet their presence will not induce firms to engage in wage cutting. A similar phenomenon is held to occur if the labour market is segmented for institutional or structural reasons — that is, where parallel and different job hierarchies exist at varying wage levels. Job-seekers may rationally turn down jobs in the low-paying segments in favour of queuing for jobs in the higher paying sectors. A type of disequilibrium is thus built into the labour market insofar as there is a shortage of jobs of the preferred type (Berry & Sabot, 1978).

Knight (1978) has presented an argument of this kind for South Africa. In an attempt to reconcile labour shortages in mining and agriculture with the existence of unemployment, he suggests that homeland men refuse employment in the primary sector in order to wait for less certain employment in manufacturing at much higher wages, which he argues were determined in part by political and institutional factors. A more recent and extended analysis by

Hofmeyr continued this theoretical tradition in contending that a model based on choice in a segmented labour-market best explains unemployment in South Africa (1985).

Neo-Keynesian theories of unemployment focus on business cycle conditions, primarily the state of aggregate demand, rather than on rational choice and market distortions. The crucial difference between a Keynesian and neo-classical perspective is that in the former it is held to be possible for the economy to operate at a less than full employment level of output. Wages are taken to be sticky downwards and attention is focused on the economic conditions shaping the environment within which potential work-seekers make the decisions theorized about by neo-classical economists.

In South Africa, the work of Bell & Padayachee (1984), which explains unemployment in terms of the slowing down of the growth rate of output (itself primarily a function of world trade and a fluctuating gold price), and the work of Simkins (1978, 1982) fall broadly within this perspective. They estimate the number of unemployed in South Africa in the early 1980s to have been in the region of 2,5 million people.

Other 'structural' analyses of unemployment locate the problem rather in the particular nature of the South African growth path.[6] The limited supply of skilled labour — exacerbated by the colour-bar, closed-shop agreements, and educational inequality — is argued to have slowed down the growth rate, encouraged capital intensity, reduced the rate of job creation and thereby caused unemployment (Maree, 1978; Work for the Future Conference Committee, 1981; and Nattrass, 1983). In other words, apartheid policies have introduced factor price distortions, which by increasing the supply price of skilled labour, have pushed South Africa off a more appropriate labour-intensive growth path. Other apartheid institutions such as influx control and the suppression of black business are portrayed as contributing to the unemployment problem.

Radical analyses of structural unemployment occur in the context of a critique of capitalism, according to which the level of employment and wages is explained by the dynamics of national and international capital accumulation, class struggle and exploitation (Erwin, 1978); while the role of state policy in exacerbating the problem has also been addressed (Lewis, 1989). Unemployment is defined synonymously with joblessness rather than in accordance with the conventional measures discussed above (Maree, 1978, p. 16), so that whether a person is looking for a job, has unrealistically high expectations, or is a victim of a temporary downswing, is of lesser interest to the radical analyst. The important issue is identified as how and why the capitalist system cannot provide work for all, which may explain why such broad definitions of the labour force are used, yielding extremely high estimates of unemployment in South Africa. The best known of these is Sarakinsky & Keenen's estimate of

6,5 million unemployed (1986, p. 22).

Conclusion

Since the mid-1970s, South Africa's labour force has grown faster than has employment.[7] It seems generally accepted that there are fewer wage jobs available annually than the number of school leavers; and it is also accepted that the number of blacks without formal sector employment is high and rising, and that the problem is worse for women and rural-dwellers. Furthermore, most observers would agree that low-income groups in South Africa do not choose and cannot afford to be 'idle' in the sense of non-productively engaged: poverty is a widespread and integral feature of South African life (see Wilson in this volume).

What divides economists is a concern with how this situation should best be approached theoretically, and therefore how individuals should be categorized according to the prescribed notion of unemployment that results from theoretical presuppositions. The two questions are, we have seen, intertwined and probably complicated by ideological considerations.

The clearest lesson to be learned from this sketch is that it is singularly important to pay attention to what is being measured as unemployment, and to locate all arguments about causation in the theoretical traditions which inform them. Once these issues have been clarified, it may be easier to select the analyses pertinent to the question at hand. At the same time, recognizing the legitimacy of a question does not mean suspending a critical evaluation of the answers typically given by those who pose it.

Our contention is that the many questions one can ask do involve differing perceptions of unemployment. For instance, if one is interested in the way individuals accept and reject jobs in the labour market, then the question of individual choice (albeit in a constrained environment) is appropriate. It must be accepted that even in the 1980s where real per capita incomes are falling and the rate of formal job creation is negligible, the supply of labour is a function of the wage offered. Many people continue to reject low-wage job offers[8] for a variety of reasons, including expectations of future higher wages, family responsibilities, or income-earning opportunities in the informal sector. Any proposed understanding of unemployment which does not allow for a degree of employment refusal is seriously incomplete.

But if the question being addressed concerns poverty and access to income, then the concepts of under-employment and subsistence and informal production would also be relevant. The narrow definition of unemployment, encompassing only those actively seeking wage employment, would result in incomplete estimates which would therefore be inappropriate to a broad illumination of poverty. Of particular importance to this kind of question would be the size of the informal sector and the survival strategies of those without formal jobs. Whether a person 'chose' to remain out of wage-paid employment, given the costs and perceived benefits of job search, would be of secondary importance in this perspective.

Finally, where the pertinent question is why the economy has failed to generate sufficient formal job-slots to absorb new entrants into the labour market, the structuralist and radical approaches may be the most promising. Here the central issue is the net level of job creation rather than whether or not people are refusing to work at the existing wage rate.

It now seems likely that a great deal of the heat generated in the unemployment debate stems from a lack of clarity about what precisely was being measured and how the divergent statistics generated may nevertheless shed light on different questions. Although in the final analysis the major theoretical traditions are incompatible, at present there may be additional room for people working in the unemployment field to learn positively rather than negatively from one another.

Notes

1 It has not proved feasible to include separate essays from all invited authors, so this chapter contains selections from individual contributions presented in memory of Jill Nattrass. She was probably unique amongst South African economists in attempting consciously to bridge the disciplinary and ideological divides amongst all those concerned with issues of development and political economy. This essay is a contribution to that line of endeavour which she represented and fostered with such energy in her professional life.

2 The upward trend in unemployment is not always constant. For example, unemployment between 1973 and 1976 was lower (by a few percentage points) than it had been between 1968 and 1972 (Bell, 1985).

3 The definition of work corresponding to the low estimate of unemployment includes all activities which earn money income for the household, and subsistence activities which provide food (Moll, 1985, p. 248). The definition of work applicable to the high estimate of unemployment includes the top 60 per cent of market-oriented informal earners (ibid., p. 250). Work as conventionally measured usually refers only to those engaged in wage labour.

4 The estimates are for Durban and Cape Town taken together.

5 The CPS goes some way towards overcoming this problem by publishing a series of hours worked, even though it counts as employed only those who work for more than five hours a week. A puzzling aspect of this data is the consistently low tally of people working short hours.

6 For a critique of structural analyses of unemployment in South Africa, see Gerson, 1982.

7 Van der Berg & Smit estimate that between 1975 and 1988, the labour force (measured as the Economically Active Population based on census material with a few

adjustments) increased by 3,9 million whereas employment grew by only 0,9 million (1989, p. 4).

8 For example, in an unpublished survey conducted in 1989 in areas adjacent to Pieter-maritzburg, it was found that none of those women who were not employed or looking for work were willing to accept a hypothetical wage of R3 a day, but 21 per cent became willing to work at R6 a day and 41 per cent were willing to work for R7,50 for a three-hour day at a local public works project. It is instructive to note that over 50 per cent did not accept the highest hypothetical offer — even though it was offered as a local job and hence without attached transport costs and other inconveniences.

References

Ardington, E.M., 'Poverty and Development in a Rural Area of KwaZulu', Development Studies Working Paper No. 9, University of Natal: Durban, 1984.

Bell, T., & Padayachee, V., 'Unemployment in South Africa: Trends, Causes and Cures', *Development Southern Africa*, vol. 3, 1984.

Bell, T., 'Issues in South African Unemployment', *South African Journal of Economics*, vol. 53, 1985.

Berry, A. & Sabot, R., 'Labour Market Performance in Developing Countries: A Survey', *World Development*, vol. 6, 1978.

Bromberger, N., 'Unemployment in South Africa: A Survey of Research', *Social Dynamics*, vol. 4, 1978.

Erwin, A., 'An Essay on Structural Unemployment', *South African Labour Bulletin*, vol. 4, no. 4, 1978.

Gerson, J., 'The Question of Unemployment in South Africa', *South African Journal of Economics*, vol. 49, 1981.

Gerson, J., 'The Unemployment Issue', in Kantor, B. & Rees, D. (eds.), *South African Economic Issues*, Juta: Cape Town, 1982.

Hofmeyr, J., 'Black Unemployment. A Case Study in a Peri-Urban Area in Natal', Carnegie Conference Paper no. 123, 1984.

Hofmeyr, J., *Labour Market Participation and Unemployment*, HSRC Investigation into Manpower Issues: Regional Development Studies no. 1, 1985.

International Labour Organization (ILO), *Statistics of Labour Force, Employment, Unemployment and Underemployment*, Report 2, Prepared for the 13th International Conference of Labour Statisticians, Geneva, 1982.

Kantor, B., 'South Africa's Mythical Problem: Blacks; Is there Unemployment?', *Businessmens' Law*, vol. 9, 1980.

Knight, J. 'Labour Allocation and Unemployment in South Africa', *Oxford Bulletin of Economics and Statistics*, vol. 40, May 1978.

Lewis, D., 'Economic Policy and Unemployment', Paper presented at the *Economic History Seminar*, University of Cape Town, August 1989.

Maree, J., 'The Dimensions and Causes of Unemployment and Underemployment in South Africa', *South African Labour Bulletin*, vol. 4, no. 4, 1978.

Meth, C., *Sorry Wrong Number. A Critical Examination of South African Labour Force Estimates, 1970–1987*, Research Monograph no. 4, Economic Research Unit, University of Natal: Durban, 1988.

Moll, T., *Planning with South African Labour Statistics: The Politics of Ignorance*, MA Thesis, University of Natal: Durban, 1984.

Nattrass J., 'Approaches to the Problem of Unemployment in South Africa', Paper presented at the Manpower and Management Foundation of Southern Africa Conference, November 1983.

Nattrass, N., 'Economic and Sociological Approaches to Unemployment', *Centre for Social and Development Studies*, Working Paper no. 19, 1989.

Oldham, G. & Bromberger, N., *Unemployment in South Africa*, Paper presented to the Economic Society Conference of South Africa, September 1989.

President's Council, *Report of the Committee for Economic Affairs on a Strategy for Employment Creation and Labour Intensive Development*, PC1/1987.

Sarakinsky, M. & Keenen, J., 'Unemployment in South Africa', *South African Labour Bulletin*, vol. 32, no. 1, 1986.

Simkins, C., 'Measuring and Predicting Unemployment in South Africa 1960–1977', in Simkins, C. & Clarke, D., *Structural Unemployment in South Africa*, University of Natal Press: Pietermaritzburg, 1978.

Simkins, C., 'Structural Unemployment Revisited: A Revision and Updating of Earlier Estimates Incorporating New Data from the Current Population Survey and the 1980 Population Census', *South African Labour and Development Research Unit Working Paper*, University of Cape Town, 1982.

Standing, G., 'The Notion of Voluntary Unemployment', *International Labour Review*, Sept–Oct, 1981.

Stiglitz, J., 'The Efficiency Wage Hypothesis: Surplus Labour and the Distribution of Income in LDCs', *Oxford Economic Papers*, vol. 28, 1976.

Van der Berg, S. & Smit, B., 'The Economic Environment and Employment Creation in South Africa', Paper presented to the Demographic Society of South Africa Congress, Stellenbosch, September 1989.

Williams, R., *Keywords*, Fontana: London, 1976.

Wilson, F. & Ramphele, M., *Uprooting Poverty. The South African Challenge*, David Phillip: Cape Town, 1989.

Work for the Future Conference Committee, *Work for the Future Conference Summary and Proposals*, Work for the Future Conference Committee, University of Natal: Durban, 1981.

The migrant labour system: changing dynamics in rural survival

11

Julian May

Introduction

During the early 1980s numerous researchers documented the poverty-stricken quality of life in the rural areas of South Africa's homelands. Today it is generally accepted that the vast majority of rural households have incomes which are below subsistence levels. The potential for agricultural production has moreover become so eroded that rural people rely chiefly upon remittances from migrants in the towns to meet their subsistence needs (Knight & Lenta, 1980; Nattrass & May, 1986). Rural people should thus be regarded as consumer communities who need to purchase the majority of their subsistence needs, rather than producer communities who can meet subsistence needs through the utilization of local resources (Derman & Poultney, 1983).

Until the early 1970s, rural/urban linkages were primarily characterized by oscillating labour migration. The decision to migrate and the length of stay in the urban areas was usefully theorized in terms of an interaction of push/pull forces (Wilson, 1972; Nattrass, 1976a). However, in subsequent years the predominance of oscillating migration has given way to rapid urbanization and growth in commuting. In these respects, the dynamics of rural/urban linkages could be usefully re-stated.

To this end this chapter investigates the processes which have undermined rural pull and urban push factors so extensively that rural/urban dynamics can no longer be interpreted in terms of a push/pull model of migrant labour. Changing socio-economic conditions in the homelands are discussed with reference to survey data on KwaZulu from Natal University's Rural Urban Studies Unit[1] Data Base. The results and their implications are interpreted in the light of the current debate on the migrant labour system in South Africa.

Oscillating migration, 1936–70

In her analysis of oscillating black labour migration, Jill Nattrass argued that:

the level, direction and rate of growth of the migration stream is a function of the interaction of four forces acting upon it: the urban or modern sector pull forces of job opportunities, increased rewards etc.; rural push forces arising from relative poverty or labour reallocation in the area; urban push forces in the form of the desires of employers to minimize their responsibilities to their labour force, and the rural pull forces arising from the social, political and economic ties that are maintained by the migrant with his home region (Nattrass, 1976a, p. 81).

The relative strength of these forces, she argued, was a function of the nature of the development path.

For the period 1936–70, conditions in rural and urban areas were such that it was useful to isolate these forces. While wages and employment opportunities for blacks generally increased, urban housing for black families was in short supply, with widespread lodging and backyard shack-dwelling, and social facilities virtually non-existent. In the rural areas output per capita is estimated to have remained constant between 1939 and 1946 and to have contributed approximately 40 to 50 per cent of subsistence food requirements (Simkins, 1981). Knight & Lenta (1980, p. 160) calculated that cereal production in the homelands remained roughly constant between 1926 and 1948 and declined thereafter.

In these conditions a push/pull analysis seemed appropriate as there were still relatively strong rural pull and urban push factors. Migrants, while perhaps not in the position to choose whether or not they would participate in the migrant labour system, could at least decide when and for what period they would migrate. Nattrass (1988, p. 42) notes that in 1936 there was a greater than 75 per cent probability that by the time a migrant was 45 years old, he would have withdrawn from the system and be living in the homelands. In this sense a development or life-cycle of the household could be identified in which the economic position of the rural household changed over time in accordance with the extent of the participation of household members in the migrant labour system and agricultural production. This in turn was related to the demographic structure of the household (Murray, 1981; Spiegel, 1980).

From 1946 to the mid-1950s this situation persisted and total output in the homelands remained constant although the growth of the population implied a decline in per capita terms. Per capita ownership of stock units showed a concomitant decline after 1948. Agricultural productivity in the homelands also began to decline rapidly in both absolute and per capita terms, and Knight & Lenta (1980, p. 160) calculate that by 1965/69, per capita cereal production was just over one-quarter of the 1924/26 level. With increasing poverty and greater dependence upon wage labour in the rural areas, Hindson (1987, p. 74) argues that from the 1960s intensified influx control legislation and urban removals sought to contain the urbanization which might otherwise have occurred. Accompanying these measures, preference in the allocation of hous-ing and employment served to create a differentiated black labour force, with a stabilized urban component and an oscillating migrant workforce. Finally, the state allocated considerable funds for the development of decentralized 'growth points' bordering the homelands. These measures attempted to to prop up urban push and rural pull forces.

The prevention of rapid black population growth in the cities, together with the expulsion of surplus urban-dwellers and the massive relocation or 'dumping' from both urban and rural white-designated areas to the homelands, created increasing social and economic differentials between urban and rural sectors, sharpening the relative poverty of the latter. One of the consequences of this was the rapid growth of rural settlements with extremely high population densities which have been termed 'displaced' urban settlements within the homelands (cf. Simkins, 1985; Graaff, 1986). Murray (1987) has estimated that about 56 per cent of the homeland population can be regarded as already being effectively urbanized in that they reside in such settlements without a productive or social base of a rural nature. The efforts of the state to maintain the migrant labour system undermined the material basis of migrant labour — agricultural production which supplemented household income — thereby pressurizing increasing numbers of unemployed to find ways of circumventing legislative controls to move back or nearer to the cities.

In view of this, it is not appropriate to infer that decisions concerning migration since the early 1970s have been taken in response to interacting push and pull forces. Moreover, in the short term at least, it is not clear that the majority of rural-to-urban migration is temporary or oscillating in nature, or that it is dominated by male breadwinners. It is no longer possible to distinguish a development cycle in rural households which reflects participation in the migrant labour system. Instead, it appears that there is an overwhelming push from the homeland areas which has the capacity to induce the prospective migrant to abandon his/her home and to locate at least a part of the family in an urban area, or more likely, its fringe. This issue is raised in the next section, where the present position of households in the homelands is examined. Information is derived from the results of micro-studies conducted in these areas.

Dependency and poverty, 1970 to the present

Surveys conducted over the last ten years in the homelands have revealed that dependence upon urban wages has reached the point where income from agriculture (including crops which are consumed by the household) is estimated to contribute less than 10 per cent of the total income for the majority of rural

households (Ardington, 1984; Gandar & Bromberger, 1984; May, 1987). Muller
(1987, p. 15) reports that in the Transkei, poorer households in both urban
and rural areas were more dependent upon remitted monies than wealthier
households, which derived the majority of their income from local wages earned
in teaching, nursing, state employment and so on. Local production contributed
less than 5 per cent of total income for all income groups. In KwaZulu, research
undertaken by the Rural Urban Studies Unit has shown similar results and
Table 11.1 provides this data, illustrating the relative importance of wages,
agricultural and informal sector income, and transfer payments for households
surveyed in rural areas, shack settlements and formal townships.[2]

Table 11.1:
RELATIVE IMPORTANCE OF SOURCES OF HOUSEHOLD INCOME

| | Percentage of total income | | |
Source	Rural areas	Shack areas	Townships
Wages & remittances	76,8	80,1	87,8
Agriculture & informal sector	8,1	6,0	4,5
Pensions & transfers	14,0	7,0	6,6
Miscellaneous	1,1	6,9	1,1
Average monthly income (R)	208,40	273,56	463,63
No. of cases	1110	392	810

SOURCE:
Rural Urban Studies Unit Data Base. Incomes have been standardized to 1985 prices
(see note 2).

Wages and remittances make up over three-quarters of rural household income, only a slightly smaller proportion than in the shack areas. In all areas,
but particularly in the rural areas, transfer payments, including charity and
pensions, make up the next most important source of income. Of the rural population sampled by the Rural Urban Studies Unit, 77 per cent had household
incomes which were below the relevant household subsistence level (a hypothetical minimum income necessary for subsistence) compared to 41 per cent
of those living in formal townships and 58 per cent living in shack settlements.
Seventy four per cent of the rural households reported that they did not have
a savings account of any type, and of those who did save, over half indicated
that this was in order to pay for the education of their children. This represents
an investment in an urban-orientated future in which education is seen as the
primary means of securing employment.

The comparative employment profile of rural, shack and township communities also reflects rural/urban differentials. Using survey data from KwaZulu as
an example, Table 11.2 shows the occupational breakdown for rural, township
and shack-dwellers.

Table 11.2:

EMPLOYMENT PROFILE OF THE
POTENTIALLY ECONOMICALLY ACTIVE* POPULATION

	Rural		Township		Shacks	
	Migrant	Resident	Migrant	Resident	Migrant	Resident
Employed	82,7	21,0	61,6	44,6	42,9	44,3
Not econ. active	3,7	45,0	12,0	18,7	26,2	20,0
Work-seeker	8,3	22,8	5,9	16,2	10,3	19,5
Schooling	5,3	11,2	20,5	20,5	20,6	16,2
Total Sample	3550	7796	342	3145	107	1254

* Population who are 18 to 64 years of age
SOURCE:
Rural Urban Studies Unit Data Base (see note 2).

The rural household comprises persons permanently resident in the rural areas and those temporarily absent as migrants. Twenty-one per cent of rural adult residents were either formally employed or were full-time farmers or otherwise self-employed. In contrast, over 80 per cent of migrants from these areas were employed. Seventy per cent of all rural household members who were employed were migrants living and working away from their homes. Of those in the rural areas who were employed, 44 per cent were full-time farmers or otherwise self-employed and 21 per cent were domestic, farm or casual labourers. Thus 65 per cent of the employed labour force in the rural areas were engaged in relatively unskilled and poorly paid work.

With respect to the composition of the migrant labour force, there has been an increase in the participation of women in the migrant labour system, which reflects the need for economic activities other than subsistence agriculture. In 1960 the percentage of females in the economically active age group who were absent as migrants was found to be 5,8 per cent, rising to 8,6 per cent in 1970 (Nattrass, 1976b). In 1985 the surveys in KwaZulu found a female absentee rate of 15,3 per cent. For South Africa as a whole, Nattrass (1988, p. 41) calculated that women formed 19 per cent of the migrant labour force.

In shack settlements and townships the proportion of those living temporarily away from their homes as migrant workers is far smaller than it is in rural areas (8 per cent, 10 per cent and 31 per cent respectively). Locally employed persons comprise approximately 40 per cent of residents.

Finally, the proportion of the urban population who are work-seekers was higher amongst resident shack-dwellers, stressing the importance of these areas in facilitating easier access to the job market through their proximity to the urban areas.

This survey data would appear to confirm that forces of economic necessity pushing families from rural areas have increased to the point where rural household subsistence is almost entirely derived from economic activities and employment in the urban areas. Employment opportunities in the rural areas are relatively scarce and the majority of those available are restricted to unskilled activities and self-employment. Those jobs which might offer better opportunities, such as teaching, nursing and extension services, tend to require higher levels of skill and education than the majority of rural-dwellers possess. These factors act to diminish economic forces which might attract migrants back to the rural areas, and increase the attraction of living in formal or informal urban settlements where a wider range of economic possibilities exist.

Urban push factors are more difficult to measure and are closely associated with rural pull forces which attract the migrant back to rural areas. Thus, while social conditions in the shack areas may be poor, whether these would act as a factor pushing a migrant back to the rural areas is largely dependent upon relative conditions and opportunities in the latter. Likewise, the risk of prosecution, demolition or political victimization in shack areas may also be offset by poverty and the absence of alternatives in the rural areas.

In contrast to the rural push forces precipitating out-migration, factors which previously pulled the migrant back from the cities have weakened both in relative and real terms. The gains that might be derived from maintaining a rural home are likely to be minimal if the potential for agricultural production is constricted by lack of access to agricultural factors of production such as land, capital and equipment. Furthermore in some parts of South Africa ownership of cattle is restricted by poverty, overcrowding, poor quality of grazing land or bureaucratic ruling (cf. Ardington, 1988; May, 1984; Stavrou et al., 1988). Another factor diminishing the relative attraction of rural areas relates to access to social facilities. Crowding or slum conditions in shack areas must be contrasted with the distances that have to be travelled in the rural areas. Table 11.3 compares travelling time to various amenities for rural, shack- and township-dwellers in KwaZulu.

This data shows that the travelling time to essential facilities such as a water source, schools and transport networks was up to five times greater in rural areas than in either townships or shack settlements. Only with regard to access to the postal service and to hospitals or clinics were there similarities between the rural and shack areas. Certainly in terms of access, relative social conditions are far less attractive in the rural areas than in a shack settlement despite visible over-crowding in the latter. In Mgaga on the edge of Durban, for example, although piped water is available, some 11 000 people share eight taps (Stewart, 1983). The incidence of violence in urban areas is however a factor which may contribute to urban push and it is possible that urban families may relocate their children at least to more rural areas so as to avoid conflict such as that which broke out in the Pietermaritzburg area during 1987.

From the economic point of view, a major attraction of maintaining a home

Table 11.3:

TRAVELLING TIME TO AMENITIES

Type of Amenity	Rural			Shacks			Township		
	0–5 mins	15–30 mins	30 mins	0–5 mins	15–30 mins	30 mins	0–5 mins	15–30 mins	30 mins
				Percentage of households in group					
Post	12,9	16,3	70,8	0,5	20,9	78,6	24,5	43,6	31,9
School	31,8	39,1	30,1	67,3	25,1	7,6	60,5	28,4	11,1
Bus	60,2	28,4	11,4	89,0	9,0	2,0	85,9	13,1	1,0
Shop	42,0	34,4	23,6	72,9	23,3	3,8	82,6	14,1	3,3
Water	59,0	22,9	18,1	84,6	12,2	3,2	100,0	0,0	0,0
Hospital/ clinic	5,8	8,6	85,6	1,6	2,1	96,3	8,4	17,4	74,2

SOURCE:
Rural Urban Studies Unit Data Base (see note 2).

in rural areas has been the lower accommodation cost compared to that of townships. However, housing costs in shack settlements (including rental, service costs and the cost of construction, repairs and improvements) compare favourably with rural costs and the Rural Urban Studies Unit surveys suggest that these are about one-eighth of the costs in townships. There are of course numerous hidden costs in shack settlements, including the lack of facilities, poor living conditions, the absence of security of tenure and the frequent need for some form of political protection. However many of these costs are also prevalent in rural areas and must be viewed against possible economic advantages in the shack areas.

A major factor strengthening urban pull, or perhaps more accurately, increasing the urbanization rate, has been the possibility of legal relocation within a homeland in an area sufficiently close to a centre of employment to allow for commuting to the metropolitan areas of the RSA. Workers are able to travel from their homes in rural or semi-urban areas in the homeland to their place of work in urban centres on a daily basis. Other commuters prefer to spend the working week as tenants in hostels, shack settlements or township housing, returning to their homes in the rural areas over the weekend. According to the Development Bank of South Africa, the total number of commuters from the homelands (including TBVC) increased from 698 000 in 1980 to 768 000 in 1985, yielding an annual growth rate of just under 2 per cent per annum (Development Bank, 1987a and b).

The surveys conducted by the Rural Urban Studies Unit[3] in KwaZulu found that in 30 per cent of rural households there was either a daily or weekly commuter (sample of 1 114 households). The very existence of transportation which allows for commuting is a factor inducing the relocation of the household as a whole to areas closer to the sources of employment.

Aside from improving access to formal employment, urbanization has a dynamic of its own. Data from the Rural Urban Studies Unit surveys indicates that informal sector participation in shack areas is higher than in the rural areas or townships. Just under 40 per cent of households in shack settlements are estimated to have at least one family member participating in the informal sector as against 31 per cent in the townships and 24 per cent in rural areas (May & Stavrou, 1988). This counters the potential risks of unemployment and offers unemployed members of the household a means of supplementary income generation which may well exceed that of subsistence farming.

An increase in factors pulling the prospective urban-dweller, together with his family, to areas nearer to the cities and towns which offer employment is confirmed by the survey material. In addition, the existence of land under tribal tenure around many South African cities has meant that legislative measures to push migrants and their families out of the cities have been circumvented. These changes can be seen to have manifested themselves in the specific form of urban expansion which has occurred around urban areas in South Africa over the last ten years.

Migration and urbanization

By the mid-1980s it was clear that influx control legislation would not significantly inhibit future black urbanization and that a rapid growth in shack areas, particularly in those homeland areas bordering white designated cities (most notably KwaZulu around Durban and Bophuthatswana around Pretoria), had pre-empted any rapid surge that might have occurred with the removal of influx control. Indeed the greater Durban area has been cited as one of the fastest-growing cities in the world.

Estimates of the urban growth rate in South Africa have varied widely over time and between researchers. Between 1946 and 1951, Hindson (1987, p. 55–71) calculated an average annual growth rate of 6,6 per cent for urban blacks, declining to 4,5 per cent between 1951 and 1960, and to 3,9 per cent between 1960 and 1970. However, he goes on to point out that these figures underestimate urbanization as they do not include the urban population in the homelands, and he cites an estimate made by Simkins of the annual growth of the homeland urban population as 33,5 per cent between 1960 and 1970 (1987, p. 71). Haarhof (1985) supports this figure, estimating the annual growth of the urbanized black population within the homelands to be 24,3 per cent between 1951 and 1980. Present estimates are also inconclusive as shown by Table 11.4.

Graaff (1986) argues a growth rate of 3,9 per cent per annum for all black urban areas, in contrast to Haarhof's estimate of 6,2 per cent. Estimates of

Table 11.4:
ESTIMATED ANNUAL BLACK POPULATION GROWTH RATES

Researcher	Growth Rates (Percentages)		
	Urban	Peri-urban	Rural
Cilliers & Groenewald (1982)	3,9	x	x
Graaff (1986)	3,9	5,5	1,6
Haarhof (1984)	6,2	6,0	–0,2
KFC (1988)	x	10,2	x
May & Stavrou (1988)	3,9	8,1	x
Simkins (1983)	4,1	5,1	0,9
Simkins (1985)	4,5	5,5	0,0

peri-urban growth rates are less diverse although the KwaZulu Finance Corporation's 1988 figures for numbers of shack-dwellers allow for the calculation of a growth rate of 10,2 per cent per annum for Durban's shack settlements between 1985 and 1987. May & Stavrou (1988), differentiating between very dense shack settlements in peri-urban areas and slightly more scattered settlements in areas which still contain elements of a rural economy, estimate a future overall growth rate of 8,1 per cent per annum for informal settlements around Durban.

Estimates of the growth rate of the rural black population tend to support the notion that permanent out-migration has become a significant feature of rural/urban dynamics. Haarhof (1984) goes so far as to suggest that the rural population is slowly declining in absolute terms; and a number of estimates are lower than the natural population growth rate.

What could account for the differing estimates of black urbanization is the particularly complex form of urban settlement in South Africa. Both Simkins (1985, p. 42) and later Graaff (1986, p. 8) have chosen to refer to a 'spectrum of settlement patterns' ranging from wholly rural through a number of intermediate points to wholly urban. Informal settlements are located towards the midpoint of this spectrum. In these areas located on the urban periphery, the vast majority of the employed are commuters, travelling on a daily basis from their residences in the homelands up to 60 kilometers to their place of work in the white-designated towns. Under the defunct influx controls such workers would have been treated no differently from migrant workers with regard to the right to legal employment in the metropolitan area. The removal of influx control has allowed for the relocation of rural families to a 'commuter belt' considerably larger than that previously sanctioned by the government and local authorities.[4]

Nattrass (1988, p. 42) acknowledged that as early as 1970 the probability of a migrant returning permanently to the homelands by the time he was 45 years old had declined to only 31 per cent. In an earlier publication she noted that migrant labour no longer operated in a selective manner in terms of age, sex and education, and was instead a necessary way of life for the whole rural economy in the homelands (Nattrass, 1977). This suggests that the interaction of push/pull factors which underlies the migrant labour system can also assist in understanding the partial collapse of this system into an essentially one-way flow of migration into a particular form of urban settlement. Typically this has been into a belt of informal settlements located on the fringe of white-designated towns or cities. The population of these settlements has been able to resist attempts to reinstate oscillating migration, either by virtue of their location in the homelands, such as those around Durban and Pretoria, or by the resilience of their inhabitants in the face of demolitions and forced removals, such as around Cape Town.

Conclusion

Increasing poverty and deteriorating agricultural production have undermined the role of the homelands in providing subsistence incomes for the families of migrant workers. At the same time, the social and economic costs of living permanently in urban areas have declined relative to the rural areas, with the growth of vast shack areas and the relaxation of certain measures controlling the rate of black urbanization. The interaction of these factors has led to a redefining of the previous rural/urban linkages, from predominantly oscillating migrant labour (that is the classic migrant labour system), to more frequent relocation of at least part of the rural household to the urban fringe. From this fringe the employed can commute, the unemployed can actively seek work and the self-employed can gain access to a potentially enormous market. This acts to push the migrant from rural areas to the formal and informal urban areas.

Whether this leads to the continuous expansion of shanty towns, poorly equipped with respect to essential facilities and difficult to upgrade, is dependent upon the prospects for an intermediate pattern of settlement which falls between shack settlements and formal townships. The various site-and-service projects and 'squatter upgrade' schemes which have often been supported by organizations such as the Urban Foundation and the various homeland development corporations, may go some of the way towards improving the living conditions experienced by urbanizing black families. What is indisputable is that this urbanization is based upon changing socio-economic dynamics which have been historically determined. Reimposing legislative measures to curtail black urbanization, whether into shack areas, dense 'rural' settlements on the urban fringe, or formal townships, cannot reformulate these dynamics.

Notes

1 The Rural Urban Studies Unit was originally established by Jill Nattrass in the Development Studies Unit at the University of Natal with a research grant made to her by the HSRC.
2 The research used to establish the data was undertaken between 1982 and 1985 by the Rural Urban Studies Unit using a standardized questionnaire. All income data is calculated in terms of 1985 prices. The following areas are included in this data base: Edendale; Emzumbe; Esikhaweni; Hlanganani; Imbali; Madadeni; Mapumulo; Mbongolwane; Mfolweni; Mgaga; Mondlo; Nondweni; Nqutu; Umlazi.
3 See note 2.
4 It remains to be seen whether the Control of Illegal Squatting Act of 1989 will reimpose effective controls on this growth.

References

Ardington, E.M., *Poverty and Development in a Rural Community in KwaZulu*, Carnegie Conference Paper no. 53, Cape Town, 1984.

Ardington, E.M., *Nkandla Revisited: A Longitudinal Study of the Strategies Adopted to Alleviate Poverty in a Rural Community*, Rural Urban Studies Working Paper no. 16, Centre for Social and Development Studies, University of Natal: Durban, 1988.

Cilliers, S.P. & Groenewald, C.J., *Urban Growth in South Africa, 1936–2000*, Research Unit for Development Sociology, Occasional Paper no. 5, University of Stellenbosch: Stellenbosch, 1982.

Derman, P.J. & Poultney, C., *The Social Dynamics of Smallhold Farming in the Siphondweni District of the Makathini Flats*, HSRC: Pretoria, 1983.

Development Bank of South Africa, 'Statistical Abstracts on Self-governing Territories in South Africa', compiled by The Institute for Development Research: Sandton, 1987a.

Development Bank of South Africa, 'SATBVC Countries Statistical Abstracts', compiled by The Institute for Development Research: Sandton, 1987b.

Graaff, J.F. de V., *The Present State of Urbanization in the South African Homelands and Some Future Scenarios*, Research Unit for Sociology of Development, Occasional Paper no. 11, University of Stellenbosch: Stellenbosch, 1986.

Gandar, M. & Bromberger, N., *Economic and Demographic Functioning of Rural Households: Mahlabatini District, KwaZulu*, Carnegie Conference Paper no. 56, Cape Town, 1984.

Haarhof, E., 'Black Urbanization in Natal/KwaZulu: 1980–2000', *Reality*, vol. 17, no. 3, 1985.

Hindson, D., *Pass Controls and the Urban African Proletariat*, Ravan Press: Johannesburg, 1987.

Knight, J.J. & Lenta, G., 'Has Capitalism Underdeveloped the Labour Reserves of South Africa?', *Oxford Bulletin of Economic Statistics*, vol. 42, no. 3, 1980.

KwaZulu Finance Corporation 'Urbanization: Present and Future Third World Realities', *The Developer*, no. 26, 1988.

May, J.D., 'Rural Poverty, Subsistence or Dependency', Unpublished M.Soc.Sci Thesis, 1984.

May, J.D., Migrant Labour in Transkei: Cause and Consequence at the Village Level, *Journal of Contemporary African Studies*, vol. 6, no. 1/2, 1987.

May, J.D. & Stavrou, S.E., *The Informal Sector: Socio-economic Dynamics and Growth in the Greater Durban Metropolitan Region*, Rural Urban Studies Unit Report no. 17, University of Natal: Durban, 1988.

Muller, N.D., *Rural and Urban Poverty and the Measurement of Development Performance in the Transkei*, Rural Urban Studies Unit Report no. 9, University of Natal: Durban, 1987.

Murray, C., *Families Divided: The Impact of Migrant Labour in Lesotho*, Ravan Press: Johannesburg, 1981.

Murray, C., 'Displaced Urbanization: South Africa's Rural Slum', *African Affairs*, July, 1987.

Nattrass, J., *The Migrant Labour System and South Africa's Economic Development, 1936–1970*, Unpublished Ph.D Thesis, University of Natal, 1976a.

Nattrass, J., 'The Migrant Labour System and South Africa's Economic Development', *South African Journal of Economics*, vol. 44, no. 1, 1976b.

Nattrass, J., *Migrant Labour and Underdevelopment: The Case of KwaZulu*, Black/White Income Gap Project, Interim Report no. 37, Department of Economics, University of Natal, 1977.

Nattrass, J., *The South African Economy: Its Growth and Change*, Oxford University Press: Cape Town, 1988.

Nattrass, J., & May, J.D., *Migration and Dependency: Sources and Levels of Income on KwaZulu*, Rural Urban Studies Unit Report no. 3, University of Natal: Durban, 1986.

Simkins, C., Agricultural Production in the African Reserves of South Africa, 1918–1969, *Journal of Southern African Studies*, vol. 7, 1981.

Simkins, C., 'Four Essays on the Past Present and Future Distribution of the Black Population of South Africa', *Southern African Labour & Development Research unit*: Cape Town, 1983

Simkins, C., 'Projecting African Population Distribution and Migration to the Year 2000', *RSA 2000: Dialogue with the Future*, vol. 7, no. 1, 1985.

Spiegel, A.D., 'Rural Differentiation and the Diffusion of Migrant Labour Remittances', in Meyer, P. (ed.), *Black Villagers in an Industrial Society*, Oxford University Press: Cape Town, 1980.

Stavrou, S.E., Mbona, D., Yokwe, X. & Mbona, C., *K5 - A Preliminary Study of an Informal Rural Settlement*, Rural Urban Studies Paper no. 12, Development Studies Unit, University of Natal: Durban, 1988.

Stewart, P., *A Study of Settlement Efficiency : Mfolweni and Mgaga*, Paper presented to the workshop on 'Black Urban Life in Durban in the Twentieth Century', October 27 and 29, Durban, 1983.

Wilson, F., *'Labour on South African Gold Mines 1911–69'* Cambridge University Press: London, 1972.

Economic and political aspects of urbanization and housing policy

12

Charles Simkins

Introduction

Three issues will dominate the discussion of the size and spatial distribution of urban populations in South Africa for the foreseeable future. These are:

* the determinants of black population distribution and migration and the extent to which these can and should be influenced by state policy;

* the intra-urban spatial distribution of the population by race and the pressures tending to change this, subject to the constraints of government regulation; and

* the terms on which it will be possible to house urban families unable to afford conventional housing, and the implications for private and public sector resource allocation.

In each case, underlying demographic and economic factors determine the context within which policies are defined. The context, the range of policy choices and the influences on these choices will be discussed.

Black population distribution and migration[1]

The most satisfactory work has recently been published by the Bureau of Market Research of UNISA (Sadie, 1988; van Zyl, 1988). Estimates of the population composition by race, sex and age in South Africa as whole since 1936 have been produced, as well as the size of the population by race in each district in 1985. These estimates enable one to assess the pattern of migration and population growth for the decade to date and to put this into the context of events since 1960.

Continuity and change between 1960 and 1985

Data from the 1985 Population Census are now available. As in the case of the 1980 Census, the degree of undercounting was severe. Central Statistical Services, the Human Sciences Research Council and university-based scholars have attempted to correct for this. This chapter makes use of Sadie's revised figures (1988).

Population distribution between 1960 and 1980[2]

In this chapter black population is differentiated according to whether it is to be found outside or inside homelands or within metropolitan, urban, small town, dense settlement or rural areas. Of interest is the fact that a number of metropolitan areas straddle a divide between the Republic of South Africa and a homeland.

Between 1960 and 1980 the population in the parts of the metropolitan areas outside the homelands grew at a compound rate of 2,6 per cent per annum, very close to the growth rate of the black population as a whole. Net migration[3] into these areas was therefore very small during the period, and was in fact negative during the 1960s. The population in towns outside the homelands grew at much the same rate — 2,4 per cent per annum.

During this period there was also a net emigration of 1,3 million from the farms outside the homelands. Even so, the farm population grew from 3,7 million to 4,2 million.

Taken as a whole, the homeland share of the RSA's total black population rose from 39 per cent to 52 per cent between 1960 and 1980. Some of this increase can be attributed to boundary changes, but the greater part resulted from population movement and a higher crude birth rate in the homelands than elsewhere. For analytical purposes it is possible to divide the homeland population in two ways — between proclaimed urban areas and other areas, and between areas which form part of functional metropolitan regions (whether proclaimed urban or not), proclaimed towns elsewhere, dense settlements and rural areas.

Between 1960 and 1980 the proportion of the homeland population living in proclaimed urban areas rose from 1 to 17 per cent. A substantial part of this increase is accounted for by boundary changes near Durban which resulted in KwaMashu and other urban areas being incorporated into KwaZulu.

The annual growth rate in the black population in the non-TBVC homeland parts of metropolitan regions[4] was 13,6 per cent between 1960 and 1970, and 5,1 per cent between 1970 and 1980. About 2,4 million people lived in both TBVC and non-TBVC homeland parts of the metropolitan areas in 1980 (1,1 million of these living in proclaimed urban areas), with a further 800 000 people in proclaimed towns elsewhere in the homelands. The remaining parts of the homelands collectively contained about 7,8 million people in 1980. There was a net in-migration of 1,7 million people into these areas between 1960 and 1980. It is difficult to apportion this population between dense settlements and rural areas, but Graaff's estimates (1987) imply that 1,7 million people lived in dense settlements outside the functional metropolitan regions in 1980.

These patterns should be seen against the background of the usually rapid pattern of rural-to-urban migration typical of a semi-developed country. The key feature of the 1960–80 period was a net migration of 400 000 black people into the rural areas (dense settlements in the homelands included). Given that there was high economic growth during most of this period, this containment of urbanization was a remarkable performance, and various aspects deserve comment.

In the first place, the growth of the dense settlements reflected the fact that the increase in the homelands population was not matched by an increase in access to agricultural land. The process of the establishment of these dense settlements is documented in Platzky & Walker (1985). Briefly, many of them were founded as a result of resettlement from 'black spots' in rural areas outside the homelands or as a result of agricultural 'betterment' schemes within the homelands. Residents of dense settlements rely on incomes generated in the urban areas (to which they have disadvantaged access) and transfer incomes, particularly pensions. In general, the closer dense settlements are to cities, the better off are their residents. The situation in the more remote settlements is appropriately described as marginal.

Secondly, this reversed net migration of 400 000 was not sufficient to stop urban population growth, although the growth in the urban areas outside the homelands was contained by two measures. Partly as a result of the closing down of black residential areas in some of the smaller towns, and the removal of their inhabitants to the homelands, there was a net emigration of about 150 000 people from the small towns between 1960 and 1980. Furthermore, rapid population growth in the metropolitan areas was confined to the homeland parts.

Developments in population distribution between 1980 and 1985

Table 12.1 sets out the distribution of the black population in 1980 and 1985 with a projection to the year 2000. It indicates that there was a dramatic increase in the rate of net emigration from the rural areas outside the homelands. Total net emigration over the five year period was nearly 1,6 million people. The result was an absolute drop in the farm population from 4,2 to 3,2 million — a phenomenon not seen at any time in the preceding 60 years. This drop was spread across all regions except the western Cape, where there was a very small rise. In percentage terms, the drop was small in the western Transvaal and the Orange Free State. It was particularly large in Natal and the northern Transvaal. A great deal more work would be needed to establish the reasons for this acceleration, including a study of the relative roles of pull and push factors. Nonetheless, some preliminary observations are possible.

The early 1980s saw a slight rise in farm employment, unlike the 1970s when this level dropped. The number of black workers in regular farm employment is reported by the Central Statistical Service's Agricultural Census/Survey to have risen from 548 000 to 595 000, an increase of 9 per cent. Defective measurement

Table 12.1:
THE DISTRIBUTION OF THE BLACK POPULATION IN 1980
AND 1985 WITH A PROJECTION TO THE YEAR 2000 (MILLIONS)

	1980	1985	2000
Outside homelands			
Metropolitan	4,55	5,39	10,51
Urban	1,49	1,52	2,38
Rural	4,12	3,16	3,16
Inside homelands			
Metropolitan	2,29	3,87	8,03
Urban	0,83	1,14	1,90
Dense settlement	1,69	2,11	3,29
Rural	6,11	7,17	7,82
TOTAL	21,08	24,36	37,09
Per cent in homelands	51,80	58,60	56,80

SOURCE:
Simkins (1989). All population figures in this section are taken from this source.

of Natal agricultural employment means that the real rise must have been somewhat lower, perhaps 4 or 5 per cent.[5] The combination of the slight rise in employment and the drop in population means that the (high) dependency ratio on the farms dropped (from 7,5 people per regular worker to 5,5), moving closer to the urban ratio. The rise in black formal sector employment outside agriculture and domestic service over the same period was 1,3 per cent.

The real wage per full-time agricultural worker dropped by about 2 per cent over the period. The only region with a significant rise in the wage rate was the western Cape. In the northern Cape, the western Transvaal and the Orange Free State (where 40 per cent of the black farm population are resident), real wages fell by close to 20 per cent. Elsewhere, they remained roughly constant or rose slightly. This compares with a 12 per cent real rise in black urban wages. Some of this difference is accounted for by an improving skill composition in urban employment.

The drop in dependency ratio is likely to have been caused by a mixture of push and pull factors, with pull predominating for young adults and push for the old. The small movements in employment and wages in the rural areas parallel those likely for unskilled workers in the urban areas. The drop in real wages in the northern Cape, western Transvaal and Orange Free State suggest that those areas will supply a relatively high number of out-migrants in the 1985–90 period. It is likely that the number of dependents per full-time worker will continue to drop: if this happens, the black population on the farms will stabilize or decline further, implying a rapid rate of out-migration, smaller in terms of numbers than that between 1980 and 1985.

Table 12.1 further indicates that net in-migration was greatest in the homeland parts of the metropolitan areas. The population in these areas grew by 11,3 per cent per annum between 1980 and 1985, net in-migration being estimated at 1,25 million people. The net in-migration to the Durban region accounted for half of the total; most of the rest went to the northern fringe of the Pretoria-Witwatersrand-Vereeniging area (PWV). Compared with the 1970s, in-migration into these areas sped up considerably. The consequence was a slowing in the rate of migration to the other parts of the homelands: homeland urban areas gained about 20 000 in-migrants, dense settlements about 15 000, and rural areas only about 10 000. This represents a transition to a pattern more closely approximating standard international experience than the pattern which was evident between 1960 and 1980. Nonetheless, in-migration into rural areas remains an aberrant phenomenon. It should also be noted that these population movements implied a further rise in the proportion of the black population living in the homelands, from 52 per cent in 1980 to 59 per cent in 1985.

It has on occasion been suggested that consent to 'independence' by homeland governments increases the marginalization of their populations in the sense of reducing their access to economic opportunities. In particular, at the time of the abolition of the pass laws it was suggested that people who were registered as citizens of the independent homelands would still be disadvantaged by their status as aliens. To date, no evidence has come to light of official use of the Aliens Act to discriminate against citizens of independent homelands on the urban labour market. Nonetheless, it is instructive to compare the growth rates of the dense settlements and rural populations (the populations most disadvantaged with respect to opportunities for formal employment) of the homelands between 1980 and 1985.

In general, there has been a higher growth of the rural and dense settlement populations in the independent homelands. The exception is the Transkei. That alone is informative — although we have no direct evidence of gross migration, the low growth in the Transkeian dense settlement and rural population must have been in large measure a result of the families of contract workers moving to Cape Town in this period. Alien or not, they managed to move. A look at the last entries in Table 12.2 gives us some further clues. The proportion of the homeland rural and dense settlement population living in dense settlements is lower in the independent homelands than in the other homelands. It also did not grow between 1980 and 1985 in the independent homelands, whereas it did in the case of the others. Corresponding to this was a higher rural settlement and a lower dense settlement population growth rate in the independent homelands. This implies greater agricultural potential in the independent homelands, itself a possible determinant of the decision to take independence in the first place. In other words, one must look for explanation of the inter-homeland differentials from the rural side. In addition, Transkei and Venda do not adjoin metropolitan areas. Of course, the fact that the percentage of black people living in all homeland rural areas and dense settlements rose from 35,6 per cent to 38,1 per cent must be ascribed to a limited general absorption of population by the cities.

Table 12.2:
GROWTH RATES OF THE RURAL AND DENSE SETTLEMENT POPULATIONS IN THE HOMELANDS 1980–85 (PER CENT PER ANNUM)

Independent homelands		*Other homelands*	
Transkei	2,3	QwaQwa	4,7
Bophuthatswana	8,3	KwaZulu	2,8
Venda	9,2	KaNgwane	2,0
Ciskei	5,0	Gazankulu	4,2
		Lebowa	2,8
All independent homelands		*All other homelands*	
All settlement	4,3	All settlement	2,9
Rural settlement	4,3	Rural settlement	2,3
Dense settlement	4,3	Dense settlement	4,7
Percentage of rural and dense settlement population in dense settlement			
All independent homelands		*All other homelands*	
1980	18,2	1980	24,4
1985	18,1	1985	26,7

SOURCE:
Simkins (1989).

Table 12.1 further shows net in-migration into the parts of the metropolitan areas outside the homelands to have increased in comparison with the pattern of the 1970s. A net movement of just over 125 000 people occurred, indicating a population increase rate of 3,4 per cent per annum. This was more than accounted for by net in-migration to Cape Town. There was a net out-migration of about 175 000 people from the non-homeland part of the PWV. Out-migration from the smaller towns continued the pattern of the 1970s.

Structural and policy determinants of population movements up to the year 2000

Structural determinants
South Africa seems increasingly likely to resume the rural-to-urban population movement characteristic of developing countries. What happened between 1960 and 1985 was an extraordinarily rapid rate of out-migration from

the rural areas outside the homelands. In 1950, 35 per cent of the black population lived in these areas; by 1985, the figure had dropped to 13 per cent. Nearly all of this net out-migration showed up as an increase in the homeland population. This was accommodated by a rise in the population density in the homeland rural areas; the creation and growth of dense settlements in the homelands; some growth in homeland urban areas; and most recently, a rapid increase in the population of the homeland parts of the metropolitan areas. Because the rural population outside the homelands has dropped to such a low level, it will become less important as a source of further out-migration. What will become more important is out-migration from the homeland rural areas. Nonetheless, the distribution of the population is such that, unless urban population growth is very rapid, the homeland rural population will continue to increase, but at a rate well below the rate of natural population increase. The projection in Table 12.1, for instance, implies a 0,6 per cent growth rate per annum in the homeland rural population and a net out-migration of 1,8 million over 15 years.

Policy determinants

The broad structural trend will be affected by three elements of policy.

Firstly, the policies required to slow the rate of emigration from rural areas outside the homelands would be the removal of racial disabilities as far as ownership and tenancy in these areas are concerned. Legal changes would have to be accompanied by an effective development programme if sizeable demographic effects were to be achieved. In contrast, although there are signs of informal changes towards a more market-oriented system of land tenure in the homelands, any attempt to promote this by giving it formal legal expression would almost certainly have the effect of dislodging households with precarious grazing or arable rights. If rural push is to be minimized, a policy of opening up the non-homeland rural areas to the black population will have to be combined with a cautious modernization programme in the homelands.

Secondly, a changed policy towards the small towns could lead to their playing a greater role in accommodating black population increase. Since small town jobs in aggregate increase almost as fast as city jobs, the present pattern of net out-migration should be changed to one of net in-migration. Of course, rates of growth would vary widely across towns. Some small towns serve as the market centres of slowly growing or declining agricultural districts. Others with an industrial base or close to rapidly growing population centres would have a more dynamic future. In national terms, however, the contribution of small towns to population absorption would be modest, given that less than 7 per cent of the black population lives in them at present.

Finally, as far as the metropolitan areas are concerned, the issue is not so much their aggregate rate of growth as the partition of population increase between the parts inside and outside the homelands. The appearance of informal settlements in Cape Town and Port Elizabeth was an important step in the opening of the non-homeland parts to black settlement; the abolition of the pass laws was a second, and the announcement of areas for black township development in the PWV was a third. In general, one can expect the growth rate in the non-homeland and homeland parts of the metropolitan areas to move closer together. How fast this will happen will depend on how fast solutions are found to the low-cost housing problem on a freehold or leasehold basis. The projections in Table 12.1 show a population growth of 4,6 per cent per annum in the non-homeland parts of the metropolitan areas, and 5,0 per cent per annum in the homeland parts between 1980 and 2000.

Likely policy evolutions

It is clear that the government has so far had to make far fewer concessions on the platteland than in the cities. Indeed, as has already been indicated, the policy of keeping the black population to a minimum on farms outside the homelands has had astonishing success. There have also been removals of entire locations close to small towns to the homelands, a programme which has never been possible in the cities. From this point of view, the immediate future looks much like the recent past. But two demographic factors are likely to induce concessions in the future.

The first of these is the unwillingness of whites to stay in the rural areas. In 1980, there were 400 000 whites on the farms outside the homelands; by 1985, the figure had dropped to 370 000 (Simkins, 1989). This continues a long trend. It has been compensated for by an increase in farm size and capital intensity, both of which contribute to increasing rural polarization. This development means that a considerable number of possibilities for more efficient farming are impossible to implement.

The second factor is the pressure which massive emigration from the rural areas puts on the cities. Urban interests might well be served by policies designed to slow the rate of rural emigration by the changing of rules regarding access to land, backed by a new rural development policy. Working against these demographic-economic considerations, of course, is a powerful political conservatism among white farmers. This conservatism, however, is vulnerable since it is based more on tradition than on a rational assessment of interest. Under the demographic and economic circumstances, it is not impossible to devise policies which would create new possibilities for white farmers as well as aspirant black farmers.

The concessions in the urban areas will depend more on historical settlement patterns and political geography than any other factor. The proximity of KwaZulu to Durban and Pietermaritzburg, of the Ciskei to East London, and of

Bophuthatswana and KwaNdebele to the northern PWV will mean that settlement patterns will develop along existing lines in the foreseeable future. On the other hand, new townships outside the homelands will have to be created in Cape Town, Port Elizabeth, the Orange Free State goldfields and the southern PWV. In these cases, the battles will revolve around the precise location of these townships. Here, local interests will play a substantial role. For the top income stratum among black people, these battles will interact with the issue of access to free settlements and areas reserved for other groups.

The intra-urban distribution of the population

Theoretical considerations

In neo-classical analysis, agents maximize their utility by choosing a location and density of occupation subject to household budget, land price and transport cost constraints. In the simplest models, a city on a featureless plain with a single central business district is considered. The outcome of this model is circular symmetry. Occupation densities are completely and costlessly flexible. Where incomes are unequal, the poorest people locate closest to the CBD, occupying land at high densities. Along any radius, incomes increase with distance from the CBD.

There are two important implications for South African cities. Firstly, judging by the result of the neo-classical model, our cities are inside out, with the poorest people on the peripheries. This sub-optimal arrangement can be ascribed to the Group Areas Act. If the Act were to cease to exist, constraints on occupation rates and subdivision could function to maintain this pattern, at least in part. Secondly, if groups of people had aversions to living in proximity to members of other groups, the market would segregate the population. Suppose two such groups inhabited our model city. Then any ring (corresponding to a fixed level of household income) would consist of two portions solidly inhabited by members of either group. Taking all rings together, the areas occupied by the groups would form two slices, the edge of which would be determined by the income distributions of the groups. If the distributions changed, so would the size and shape of the slices.

Now suppose legislation fixes the boundaries within which a group can live. Even if the boundaries are exactly those which market forces would create at any one point in time, they are not necessarily those which these forces would create at subsequent times. Boundaries, therefore, constrain the system in a suboptimal configuration. Moreover, they create advantage for one group at the cost of disadvantage for another. The group with more space than the market would assign will face lower rents than its counterpart. Should these differentials become marked, economic incentives arise to contravene the law. Empirical analysis of landuse/transport interactions is complex and requires computer modelling. One such model, applied to Cape Town, indicates that if the Group Areas Act were lifted and there were no constraints on occupational density, areas close to the city centre would indeed change their racial complexion. On the basis of existing income distribution, white people in Cape Town would manage to inhabit much the same total area as at present. Coloured people would suffer a contraction of their physical living space as they became exposed to black competition (Simkins, 1988).

Empirical considerations — Factors causing changes to existing intra-urban use of the conventional housing stock

Table 12.3 is based upon changing population and income distributions for all races in metropolitan areas. It reports the implications (between the years 1980 and 2000) of households in metropolitan areas outside the homelands having the ability to afford to own or rent a dwelling worth R25 000 in 1985 prices (R40 000 in 1988 prices) — about the price of the cheapest available conventional house, though small flats in some areas cost less.

Table 12.3:

ABILITY TO AFFORD HOUSING
IN NON-HOMELAND METROPOLITAN AREAS (BY RACE); 1980 & 2000

	Whites	Coloureds	Asians	Blacks	Total
Population percentages able to:					
Own, 1985	62,5	18,4	20,9	13,2	
Rent only, 1985	22,9	28,5	29,7	27,1	
Own, 2000	62,9	37,4	59,9	16,9	
Rent only, 2000	22,7	31,7	23,3	30,8	
Number of households (thousands) able to:					
Own, 1985	612	67	35	126	840
Rent only, 1985	133	103	48	260	544
Own, 2000	702	191	126	317	1336
Rent only, 2000	214	157	50	577	998

Table 12.3 indicates that, whereas 78 per cent of potential home-owning households in the metropolitan areas were white in 1985, this figure will drop to 58 per cent by the year 2000. In contrast, 52 per cent of coloured, Indian or black households could afford to rent but not own the cheapest conventional houses in 1980 and this figure is expected to rise to 68 per cent in 2000.

Table 12.4:

CONSTRUCTION OF HOUSING UNITS, 1986 & 1987

	Private sector*		Public sector**	
	1986	1987	1986	1987
Whites	16 649	17 443	3 632	1 045
Coloureds	4 127	5 493	9 579	3 263
Asians	2 586	2 795	4 017	378
Blacks[1]	4 248	7 330	8 313	1 025

NOTE:

1 The Bureau for Economic Research at Stellenbosch believes that black housing activity is grossly under-reported with many of the newly created black local authorities' data going unreported. Business and Marketing Intelligence estimate that 24 112 black housing units were built outside the homelands by the private sector in 1987, and a further 11 465 inside the homelands. Of these, 8 978 were in the price range R40 000 and above and a further 5 029 in the price range R25 000 to R40 000 (*Weekly Mail*, 21 October 1988).

SOURCES:

* Central Statistical Services, Statistical News Release.

** Administration: House of Assembly — Department of Local Government, Housing and Works. These figures reflect the construction of family and welfare housing.

Table 12.3 is based upon the determinants of demand. Table 12.4 sets out the supply position in 1986 and 1987.

The average annual increase in supply of housing by the private sector between 1986 and 1987 can now be compared with the average annual increase in demand between 1985 and 2000 for ownership or rental of units valued at R40 000 or more, assuming a 3 per cent growth rate.

Table 12.5:

COMPARISON OF SUPPLY AND DEMAND FOR HOUSING

	Average annual increase in demand (metropolitan non-homeland)	Average annual increase in private sector supply (national non-homeland)
	1985–2000	1986–87
Whites	7 500	17 000
Coloureds	10 600	4 800
Asians	6 700	2 700
Blacks	25 700	*12 300

* This is based on the BMI figure for 1987.

Such a comparison must be treated with caution: the periods are not the same, and one is short-term while the other is long-term. Also, the demand figures cover only metropolitan areas. Nonetheless, in aggregate terms, there appears at present to be a situation in which the increment of supply outruns the increment of demand for whites, whereas the reverse is the case for the other three groups.

This is about as far as empirical analysis can take us, given our present state of knowledge. In order to develop the implications of these findings, one has to resume the argument at the theoretical and policy levels. This will establish a conjectural account of some of the processes at work and therefore the issues to be faced. Further research is required to confirm or modify this account.

The context and possible content of policy choices

Before discussing the policy options, attention should be drawn to two issues: the effects of inflation and the importance of the life-cycle in determining demand.

The operation of the private rental market in the conventional housing sector is of importance. Housing finance is provided in an inflationary environment, but still with the level of nominal mortgage payments appropriate to a non-inflationary situation. The results are twofold.

Firstly, home-owners who rely on mortgage finance find that the real value of a dwelling they can afford at any time is lower than the one that they could have afforded if the inflation rate were zero. On the other hand, they find that the reduction of their debt in real terms is more rapid. This encourages periodic trading-up.

Secondly, in markets not characterized by crowding, one gains access to a given quality of housing on a rental basis at a considerably lower income than on a purchase basis. If the average mortgage rate is 17 per cent and rentals are set at 10 per cent of the value of a house, rents will be about half the repayment rates on a 100 per cent mortgage bond plus rates. The implications are apparent from Table 12.3. In all cases, apart from whites in the years 1985 and 2000, and coloureds and Indians in the year 2000, the number of households able to rent but not buy a dwelling worth R40 000 at 1988 prices exceeds the number able to own such a dwelling. The scope for the development of the private rental market is great. Moreover, areas in which there are high proportions of rental units will become prime candidates for 'greying'.

The other issue of importance for policy changes is the fact that the desirability of different locations varies over the life-cycle of a household. Locations near the city may be particularly attractive to young single people and childless couples. The arrival of children may make relocation in the suburbs attractive. To the extent that schooling remains segregated, households containing children will have an incentive to live in own areas. The implication is that the demand for housing has to be analysed in terms of household type as well as household income.

The policy discussion can be conducted in terms of the options for the management of boundaries. Recall that, without special additional legislation, the market will lead to segregation if members of groups among the population prefer to live next to each other rather than next to members of other groups. Given evidence of such desires among at least part of the population, complete abolition of the Group Areas Act is consistent with considerable continued *de facto* segregation. Of course, the groups which are formed under market conditions will not necessarily be the same as those created by statute. Within statutorily uniform white groups, for instance, there are to be found predominantly Jewish or Afrikaner neighbourhoods. What black groups choose to do under market conditions largely remains to be seen.

As already indicated, boundaries can be expected to move with changing demographic and income distribution patterns. The government's alternative to determination of boundaries by the market is to retain state management of boundaries, but to allow flexibility through the declaration of free settlement areas. This creates the opportunity for decreasing the price differentials for housing of a given quality across racial groups. The free settlement policy provides no automatic mechanism for abolishing them entirely; progress will depend on administrative action by the state, which may be more or less sensitive to market conditions.

Critics of free settlement areas assert that under present conditions, free settlement areas will effectively become coloured, Indian and black areas. This will certainly be true if they contain only a small number of dwellings and the rate of housing supply in coloured, Indian and black own areas is not increased. Under such circumstances, whites will be outbid for the use of housing in these areas. To the extent that neither of these conditions hold, the conclusion becomes less clear-cut. The outcome will then start to depend more on the location of the free settlement areas.

Further, the critics state that the unwillingness to open other white group areas means that free settlement areas will have to bear the entire burden of adjustment, instead of this being spread more thinly. As stated, this proposition is true, but it may not be very significant. The higher the market value of houses in any white group area, the more it is protected against penetration by other groups simply by the facts of income distribution. Most of the emerging demand for housing by other groups can only be satisfied in the lowest-income white group areas. It is precisely here that white political resistance to penetration is the greatest. Proponents of free settlement areas therefore refer to a general need for political rather than market management of boundaries in these areas and between these areas and adjacent group areas.

The argument may be pushed one stage further. It appears to be the government's intention to demarcate free settlement areas and then let market processes define the boundaries between self-defined groups within these areas. Given the existing pressures, there will certainly be a process of boundary redefinition. In a well-informed, rational market, this process should proceed smoothly. The interaction of prices and preferences for certain kinds of neighbours would indicate to owners of property that they could improve their position by buying and selling. When all these transactions have been completed, the system would be at a new equilibrium. In the process, all the newcomers would have made clear gains, otherwise they would not have sought to enter the area. The position of existing residents is more complex. On the one hand, the proclamation of a free settlement area may mean the acquisition of undesired neighbours. On the other hand, a new source of demand for housing will push up prices and hence create capital gains.

But the assumptions of sound information and rationality in these markets can be questioned in situations where there is strong group sentiment. Experience from other countries suggests that on the basis of rumours and speculation, people can panic and sell. This could happen even within a free settlement area, as long as it was not very small. So the political management implied in the free settlement areas policy cannot be expected to manage all the problems of boundary shift. Within the political constraints, the market will play a major role. What the free settlement policy really seeks to do is to contain the pace of boundary shift and the adjustment process which goes with it. In fact, the ability of the policy to accomplish even that will depend on the speed with which free settlement investigations can be conducted, and how fast decisions can be made in existing white group areas where penetration by members of other groups is already taking place.

The issues in this field are complex. The pressures on the Group Areas Act have to be understood within the framework of a general equilibrium analysis (that is, by looking at the operation of a city or town as a whole). A number of important issues have been touched upon: the pace of housing development in 'own areas'; the pace of proclamation of free settlement areas; demographic shifts and shifts of income distribution; and the distribution of households across different stages of the household life-cycle. Some aspects of these relationships are very poorly understood. The issues are often obscured rather than illuminated by the policy debate, which polarizes positions rather than defining a full range of policy interventions. They will not yield to simplistic approaches. The very intractability of the problems can be expected to force more sophisticated understandings and proposals.

Housing the poor: the options

The extent of the problem in non-homeland metropolitan areas

Apart from conventional housing costing R40 000 (at 1988 prices) per unit or more, three other products are available — a modest conventional house or apartment costing between R25 000 and R40 000; a starter house costing between R15 000 and R25 000[7]; and a serviced site, costing R5 000 or more, on which households build their own dwelling over time.

Using the income distributions underlying Table 12.3, one can work out the number of non-homeland metropolitan households who cannot even afford to own a serviced site; those who can afford to own a serviced site but not a starter house; those who can afford to own a starter house but not a modest conventional house; and those who can afford to own a modest conventional house, but not a house worth R40 000. The results are presented in Table 12.6.

The options

Table 12.6 requires careful interpretation. In the first place, it should be borne in mind that the option of renting rather than purchasing housing complicates the picture. Most white people, rather than buy a starter house, would choose to rent a higher-value unit on the private market. Similarly, there are relatively few coloured and Indian metropolitan households living in self-built dwellings on serviced sites. Instead, many poorer households are accommodated in local authority rental stock.

Secondly, recall that the assumption underlying Table 12.6 is that the shape of the income distribution for each group will be the same in the year 2000 as it was in 1985: the effect of increased real incomes is assumed merely to shift the mean. With a high rate of in-migration from other areas (in the case of black people), this assumption is almost certain to be over optimistic. Accordingly, the demand for serviced sites will be higher than Table 12.6 indicates.

Nonetheless, Table 12.6 suggests that the mix of housing activity ought to be spread fairly evenly across the board. Leaving aside the additional units needed to satisfy demand in 1985, Tables 12.3 and 12.6 show that between 1985 and 2000, the non-homeland metropolitan population will be able to afford 496 000 new conventional homes, 314 000 new modest conventional homes, 303 000 new starter houses and 231 000 new serviced sites — an average of 90 000 new units per year. This is based on an assumption of 3 per cent real growth in personal incomes per annum. Should this growth rate be exceeded, a slightly larger number of units will be demanded and the mixture will become more affluent. Lower growth implies the converse.

Table 12.6:

AFFORDABILITY OF MODEST CONVENTIONAL HOUSES,
STARTER HOUSES AND SERVICED SITES, IN METROPOLITAN AREAS
OUTSIDE THE HOMELANDS, IN 1985 AND 2000

	Whites	Coloureds	Asians	Blacks
Percentage able to afford:				
Modest conventional				
1985	24,7	18,5	18,8	13,8
2000	24,6	23,7	26,7	18,0
Starter house				
1985	14,8	26,5	30,4	28,2
2000	14,5	26,4	15,7	28,5
Serviced sites				
1985	8,0	37,7	31,7	40,8
2000	8,0	18,3	9,6	36,8
Number households able to afford (thousands):				
Modest conventional				
1985	242	67	31	132
2000	275	118	56	337
Starter house				
1985	145	95	50	270
2000	162	135	33	533
Serviced sites				
1985	78	136	52	391
2000	89	91	20	688

Finally, one may note that the changing pattern of demand again creates pressures on the Group Areas Act. Unlike the situation in respect of the conventional housing market, where the issue is penetration of white groups areas by the members of other groups, the issue here is the penetration of coloured and Indian group areas by black people.

Policy issues

Achieving the required outputs will require policy changes in three important fields, namely the availability of land for residential development; subsidy policy; and finance.

For nearly two decades, government policy was firmly set against making land available outside the homelands for black residential development. Their position has recently softened. While the government still has a preference for the location of new residential areas in the homeland parts of the metropolitan areas, it is now recognized that in Cape Town, Port Elizabeth and the southern and central PWV, land will have to be made available outside the homelands. The issue is now one of the quantity and location of land upon which townships may be developed. The most important factor determining these decisions will be local political pressures. For these reasons, and also because of the price of land, it will be difficult to obtain well located land in the quantities required for site-and-service development.

Existing housing subsidy policy is inefficient in getting assistance to those who need it most and in stimulating the private sector to produce housing and sites. It subsidizes public housing far more heavily than private housing of the same price. It would be possible to provide every household in need of assistance (for instance, all those with incomes insufficient to buy a conventional house) with a lump sum subsidy of about R5 000 (at 1989 prices). This would be sufficient to pay for a modestly-serviced site in many locations, removing the need to finance purchases by poorer urban households. Reform of the present piecemeal system in this direction would powerfully aid housing delivery.

The results of Tables 12.3 and 12.6, together with the assumptions that a subsidy policy (of the sort just outlined) will be in force and that 90 per cent loans are needed, make it possible to estimate the average annual finance requirement associated with the construction of new houses/sites between 1985 and 2000.

Table 12.7:

AVERAGE ANNUAL HOUSING FINANCE REQUIREMENTS,
1985–2000 (1988 PRICES)

	Average price (R'000)	Subsidy (R'000)	90% loan (R'000)	Units ('000)	Finance (Rm)
Conventional	65	0	58,5	33,1	1 936
Modest conv.	32,5	5	25	20,9	523
Starter	20	5	13,5	20,2	273
Serviced site	10	5	4,5	15,4	69
Total					2 801
Total mortgage* (serviced sites excluded)					2 732

* Loan sizes for serviced sites are generally too small to be financed by mortgage loans. Other forms of finance will have to be made available for this section of the market.

Table 12.7 sets out the calculation: the annual average figure of R2,8 billion (at 1988 prices) required for mortgage finance compares with building loans (granted by building societies alone) of R1,16 billion in 1985; R1,80 billion in 1986; R2,92 billion in 1987; and R3,29 billion in 1988 (all at current prices). There is no major problem with the mobilizing of mortgage funds to meet the expected demand. There is not even a great deal of adjustment to be made even if all new modest conventional and starter houses were to be financed by means of mortgage loans. In this case, conventional houses can be expected to absorb 72 per cent of all mortgage advances for new dwellings between 1985 and 2000.

Although the absolute funding requirement is not large, there remain major problems in financing end-user purchases of serviced sites and starter housing. Apart from limited funds allocated to starter houses by some institutions, building societies and banks have never financed developments of this sort. The weight of tradition and nervousness about lending in the current political environment make these problems difficult to resolve. Furthermore, for small loans, the administrative costs of mortgage finance rise sharply in relation to repayments of the loan itself. Progress will only be made in this area if there is a greater involvement of banks and building societies in granting somewhat smaller loans than they do at present; granting loans against the surrender value of pension/provident funds which would require changed legislation; the creation of small loans companies; the offer of unsecured finance; and employer assistance.

Conclusion

Urbanization and housing are issues for which numerous policy options are available. Some of them involve adjustments which are relatively easy to make. Others imply more substantial changes. The important point is, however, that the issues are not unmanageable, and policy bargains can be struck. For them to actually be struck in a way which augments the welfare of urban residents, intelligent analysis and cool heads will be required.

Notes

1 The most satisfactory work has recently been published by the Bureau of Market Research, UNISA (Sadie, 1988; van Zyl, 1988). Estimates of the composition of the population by race, sex and age in South Africa as a whole since 1936 have been produced, as well as the size of the population by race in each district in 1985. These estimates enable one to assess the pattern of migration and population growth for the decade to date and to put this into context of events since 1960.

2 Unless otherwise indicated, the estimates are taken from Simkins (1983).

3 Net migration to or from a region can be calculated from population estimates on two dates. The net migration between these two dates (M) is given by the formula
$M = P_2 - P_1 (1 + g)$
where P_1 and P_2 are the populations at the beginning and end of the period, and g is the rate of the population increase.

4 These are the magisterial districts of Umlazi, Embumbulu, Ndwedwe, Ntuzuma, Empumulanga and Vulindlela in KwaZulu and all of KwaNdbele.

5 There was a large and implausible rise in agricultural employment in some districts, notably Lower Tugela, between the 1980 census and the 1985 survey.

6 The assumptions used in deriving this table are set out in the Appendix.

7 In a starter house the space provided and/or level of finishes of the house are minimal. Where the finishes are basic, the unit typically does not exceed 70 square metres and

where there are full finishes the unit typically does not exceed 40 square metres. Over time, the household extends and/or upgrades the basic unit. The level of services is often not as high as those in a conventional house.

Appendix

Sources of information and assumptions underlying Table 12.3

(a) The growth rate of personal income between 1985 and 2000 is assumed to be the same as that from 1970 to 1985, that is, 3 per cent in real terms per annum. The racial distribution of income in 1980, 1985 and 2000 is taken from Loubser (1988).

(b) Personal income in the metropolitan areas is taken from Nel & van Wyk (1984).

(c) Population estimates and projections are taken from Simkins (1989).

(d) It is assumed that the metropolitan/non-metropolitan personal income per capita ratio will remain constant between 1980 and 2000 for the almost entirely-urbanized white and Indian population. It is assumed to drop in the case of coloured and black people.

The shape of the income distributions (relative to the means) for the respective populations is assumed to remain constant between 1985 and 2000. The average household size is also assumed to stay constant. In the case of whites, the income distribution is obtained from the AMPS 1985 survey; in the case of other groups, it is a weighted mean of the metropolitan distributions as measured by the Bureau of Market Research in 1985. Affordability is calculated by assuming annual payments of 18 per cent of the value of a house (worth R25 000 at 1985 prices) in the case of ownership and 10 per cent in the case of rental. Based on an analysis of housing expenditure data, it is assumed that 20 per cent of household income will be spent on housing. This is slightly higher than actual white and Indian expenditures and considerably higher than present coloured and black patterns. It is expected that the coloured and black patterns will shift as privately-owned housing becomes more widespread among these groups. This gives minimum qualifying incomes, which are then located on the income distribution functions to read off the percentage of households qualifying.

References

AMPS Survey, South African Advertising Research Foundation: Johannesburg, 1985.

Graaff, J.F. de V., 'The Present State of Urbanization in the South African Homelands: Rethinking the Concepts and Predicting the Future.' *Development Southern Africa*, vol. 4, no. 1, February 1987.

Loubser, M., 'Income Elasticities of Black Metropolitan Households', Paper presented to the 28th AGM of the Bureau of Market Research, UNISA, Pretoria, 1988.

Nel, P.A., & van Wyk, H. de J., 'Personal Income of the Republic of South Africa and National States by Population Group and Magisterial District, 1960–80', Report no. 113, Bureau of Market Research, UNISA, Pretoria, 1984.

Platzky, L., & Walker, C., *The Surplus People*, Ravan Press: Johannesburg, 1985.

Sadie, J.L., 'A Reconstruction and Projection of Demographic Movements in the RSA and TBVC Countries', Report no. 148, Bureau of Market Research, UNISA, Pretoria, 1988.

Simkins, C., *Four Essays on the Past, Present and Future Distribution of the Black Population of South Africa*, S.A. Labour and Development Research Unit: Cape Town, 1983.

Simkins, C., 'The Structural and Economic Implications of Urbanisation', *Development Southern Africa*, vol. 5, no. 4, 1988.

Simkins, C., 'An Urban Foundation Demographic Model: Phase Three', Unpublished, 1989.

van Zyl, J.A., 'Adjustment of the 1985 Census Population of the RSA by District', Report no. 149, Bureau of Market Research, UNISA, Pretoria, 1988.

The black taxi revolution

Meshack Khosa

13

Introduction

The importance of small business development as a source of economic growth and as a means of furthering black economic empowerment in South Africa was one of Jill Nattrass' oldest and most enduring academic themes (1970, 1972, 1985, 1986). When advocating policy in support of small business development, she argued that racial discrimination, lack of access to capital, and a minefield of restrictive and inappropriate legislation were major obstacles to the growth of small black enterprises (1985). The development potential of small black business is also highly constrained by structural factors (see Nattrass in this volume, Chapter 14). That there is, however, room for rapid and successful small business development is illustrated by the phenomenal growth (which followed changes in legislation and the credit environment) of the black taxi paratransit[1] sector in South Africa.

This short chapter offers a preliminary reflection on the black taxi industry which, from small beginnings, has developed into a powerful feature of the South African urban economy. Over the past decade, the growth in the number of ten and fifteen-seater kombi taxis has revolutionized the urban transport sector. Even though kombi taxi fares are more expensive than bus and train fares, kombi taxis have become popular and fast means of transport for the growing numbers of urban black commuters.

The chapter is divided into four sections. The first section examines the situation pertaining to the black taxi sector in the 1980s and provides an indication of the phenomenal growth of black taxis in the past five years. The second more historical section outlines the emergence of the black taxi operation in South Africa. The third section discusses the black taxi industry in the 1980s and the emergence of the South African Black Taxi Association (SABTA). The final section examines a few positive and negative aspects of capital accumulation in the black taxi industry.

Black transport in the apartheid city

The presence of race zoning policies has made the black taxi industry unique to South Africa. In other third world countries (where a similar growth in the paratransit sector occurred from the 1970s) taxis are not effectively restricted to particular race groups.

The apartheid policies enshrined in the Natives (Urban Areas) Act of 1923 and the Group Areas Act of 1950 forced most black people to the fringes of urban areas. This artificially-wide separation of home from workplace has made commuting long distances an integral feature of life for South Africa's urban black population. Eighty per cent of black commuters spend 2,5 hours travelling to and from work daily and 20 per cent spend an average of 4,5 hours travelling (PC 97/1985).

Since the passing of the 1952 Bantu Services Levy Act, the state has subsidized black urban transport. In order to ensure an adequate and smooth flow of labour to industry and commerce in the urban core, the government continues to spend enormous sums of money on transport subsides. Sixty-eight per cent of black peak hour commuters travel by public transport, of whom 29 per cent travel by rail and 39 per cent by bus (Cameron & Lipman, 1987, pp. 10-11). Twenty-three per cent walk, cycle or use private means of transport and 9 per cent rely on kombi taxis (loc.cit). However, the shorter the commuting distance, the more popular the kombi taxi becomes as an option. Over distances up to 15 kilometres, 16 per cent of black peak hour commuters travel by kombi taxi (SAIRR, 1986). Between 16 and 30 kilometers this figure drops to 5 per cent and over 30 kilometers, to 2 per cent (ibid.). In addition to peak hour line-haulage, there are at least 1,2 million other black travellers of whom 400 000 use buses, 300 000 trains and the balance use kombi taxis (Cameron & Lipman, 1987).

Despite their relatively small share of the black urban transport market, kombi taxis are competing aggressively with conventional bus and rail services. As can be seen in Table 13.1, the number of passenger trips on trains and buses has declined in absolute terms between 1982/83 and 1984/5, while that in taxis has grown rapidly. Between 1985/86 and 1986/87, the number of passenger trips on buses and trains continued to decline by 13 and 7 per cent respectively (Business Day, 27 July 1988) thus fuelling the speculation that the black taxi explosion has been responsible.

Similarly, the meteoric growth in the number of taxis (especially pirate taxis) in comparison to the decline in train coaches and the sluggish growth in buses, points to the increasingly sharp competitive edge of the taxi sector. These developments have stimulated discussion as to whether taxis can replace the present often cumbersome and inefficient train and bus transportation network. The idea has great currency among the supporters of privatization and employment creation via small business development.

The kombi taxi sector has, however, nowhere near the capacity to capture the entire commuting labour force and in any case charges fares which are too expensive for the majority of commuters. The kombi taxi sector has skimmed off those commuters who can afford the quicker, safer, more comfortable mode

Table 13.1:
PASSENGER TRIPS AND TRANSPORT VEHICLES IN SOUTH AFRICA

	1982/83		1983/84		1984/85	
Passenger Trips (million)						
Train	722	(29%)	709	(28%)	685	(24%)
Bus	1 358	(55%)	1 295	(52%)	1 260	(50%)
Taxi	384	(16%)	475	(19%)	560	(22%)
Passenger Vehicles						
Train Coaches	10 909		10 709		10 709	
Buses	22 363		22 900		23 295	
Taxis- sedan	4 093		4 954		5 986	
- kombi	9 698		10 826		11 982	
- pirate	10 800		14 600		18 000	
Total taxis	24 591		30 380		35 968	

SOURCE:
SAIRR, 1986, p. 196.

of travel. The vast majority of black urban travellers will, for reasons of low incomes, continue to opt for the overcrowded, unreliable, dangerous and grossly uncomfortable (but subsidized) public transport sector.

The emergence of the black taxi operation

The phenomenon of black taxis can be traced to the turn of the century. From the early 1930s, black taxi operators were increasingly handicapped by a barrage of political and economic constraints. Nevertheless, they continued their services and by the 1970s it had become clear even to government officials that black taxis were offering an essential service.

The predecessors of the modern black taxi were the horse-drawn cabs which emerged in the late 1800s. By 1894 in Johannesburg, there were a few black cabbies operating mainly with a black clientele. As the Cab Owners Association was a non-racial organization and no restrictions existed on the transportation of passengers, black cabbies were able to ferry whites around the city. However, from 1897 onwards, the town council enforced separate cab ranks for different races. The white community, which by-and-large regarded blacks as 'social pests', demanded that black cabbies should have their licences confiscated (Van Onselen, 1982). In 1902, the council created two licensing categories: first class for whites and second class for blacks. All black cabbies had their licences relegated to second class and were thus barred from transporting whites. This set a trend which authorities later followed when licensing black taxis.

With the emergence of motorized taxis in 1909, horse-drawn cabs were moved out of the taxi ranks. At first, a few 'native' taxi ranks were provided in the downtown area but these were later relocated to the periphery. The council justified the move on the grounds of 'annoyance caused to residents in the neighbourhood...in the early hours of the morning due to laughter, loud talking and noises' (Minutes, Johannesburg City Council, 23 June 1931). The history of the provision and relocation of taxi ranks reflects the segregationist policies dominant in South Africa. It was only in the late 1970s that the trend changed and black taxi ranks were allocated in city centres.

From the 1920s, the government favoured trains as the means of transporting black workers. Nevertheless, several independent bus operators and taxi services emerged and flourished. In order to combat this competition, the government passed the Motor Carrier Transport Act of 1930 which created a (bus and rail) transport monopoly in major cities. In the absence of competition, travelling costs became inflated and the government was forced to intervene in order to regulate fares.

The move to transport monopoly was fought by various local taxi associations, but their campaigns were weakened by a lack of collective action. It was only in the 1980s that black taxi operators united under a national taxi association and in some townships forged deliberate links with the mass democratic movement. The amalgamation began in 1959 in the Witwatersrand with the creation of the Soweto Taxi Association. This was followed by the establishment of the United Soweto Owners Association in 1973 and other regional associations in the 1970s.

Black taxis in the 1980s

In May 1981, various regional taxi associations merged to form SABTA in order to promote solidarity with colleagues in other geographical areas, and to tackle common problems as a united front (*Taxi*, vol. 3, no. 2, 1982). The first SABTA president, Mr. Sojane, predicted that 'taxi owners will reach their glory with me' (*Taxi*, vol. 1, no. 8, 1981). By the end of 1982, SABTA had a registered membership of over 20 000. This rose to more than 50 000 in 1989. SABTA, as presently constituted, is an amalgamation of more than 300 local, 40 regional and five provincial taxi associations, each with their own management structures. SABTA has recently begun to cast its net wider and recruit members in the frontline states of Botswana, Lesotho, Swaziland, Zimbabwe, Moçambique and Namibia. It is important to note that SABTA represents short distance taxi operators. Long distance taxi operators are organized under the banner of South African Long Distance Taxi Association (SALDTA) which has a membership of 11 000, the majority of whom do not operate legally.

Although SABTA represents the interests of black taxi operators, 60 per cent of SABTA member vehicles are white-owned. Black operators usually pay monthly installments plus extra weekly charges to white owners. The issue of predominantly-white financial and corporate backing in the black taxi industry is addressed in the final section of the chapter.

The black taxi industry is far from homogeneous and can be differentiated on many levels. It can be divided into permit holders and non-permit holders. Country-wide there are over 40 000 licensed kombi taxis and more than 80 000 'pirate taxis'[2]. Of the permit holders, 95 per cent are SABTA members. The black taxi industry is also regionally biased. Of the 32 572 licences granted in 1988, 65 per cent were in the Johannesburg-Pretoria region (with the majority in Soweto)[3], 17 per cent in Potchefstroom and only 11 and 7 per cent respectively in the Durban and Cape regions (Weekly Mail, 15–22 December 1988). In addition, one can differentiate between fleet owners and owner-drivers, those with zonal licences to operate between townships and cities, and those with magisterial licences who are only legally allowed to provide services within a particular township.

A major turning point in the fortunes of the black taxi industry occurred in 1978 when, with the advent of the kombi, taxis were allowed to carry up to eight passengers instead of the previous maximum of four. This gain was however threatened when the Welgemoed Commission (reporting in 1983) proposed that kombis be banned and replaced by four-seater vehicles on the grounds that 'the kombi-taxi is in many ways a particularly strong competitor for the existing bus or train services' (quoted in McCaul, 1987, p. 438). It was only after vociferous and popular protests waged by the mass democratic movement and sections of the private sector that the government in 1985 withdrew the draft bill based on the report of the Welgemoed Commission.

In recent years, the government has adopted a more favourable attitude to the black taxi industry. This coincides, unsurprisingly, with plans to introduce privatization and deregulation in the transport sector. In 1987, the government went so far as to give licensing officials the right to legalize 16-seater taxis, subject to certain conditions.[4]

Whilst there is no quota limitation on entry into the taxi market, the success of a licence application depends on the applicant's justification as to why he or she can provide a better service than the existing transport facilities. Once in the market, taxi operators are unconstrained by any government regulations affecting fares. However, the local taxi associations tend to regulate the industry very closely. Zonal fare structures are set, which in a given area are independent of distance travelled. Thus for example, taxi fares from any point in Soweto to Johannesburg are fixed, but usually increased during weekends. Furthermore, at official taxi ranks, 'marshalls' not only collect money from passengers, but also ensure that only members of the rank operate.

Taxi commuting is not without its problems and has been associated with crime and gang-type wars over turf. According to a study done in Dobsonville, there was a high correlation between taxi drivers and criminal activity and the taxi rank was shown to be 'a hot-bed for criminality and an ideal social milieu for clandestine criminal behaviour' (Moabi, 1976, p. 127). The taxi industry is also associated with fast, reckless driving, a high frequency of road accidents, overcrowding, high fares, rude language and a general lack of etiquette amongst drivers. During peak periods, passengers are 'forced to squeeze into taxis like sardines' (*The Star*, 26 June 1984) and as one passenger succinctly puts it, 'to complain would not help because by so doing, you are adding fuel to the fire' (*Rand Daily Mail*, 4 July 1984). Taxi passengers are not consulted before fares are increased and taxi drivers have had a long history of ambiguous co-operation with civic and political organizations regarding days of protest.

However, residents and taxi operators often share a common enemy in the bus companies, particularly during bus boycotts. It has been alleged that taxi operators had a hand in arranging attacks on buses in a number of townships, to ensure that bus routes terminated on the outskirts (McCaul, 1987, p. 439). On other occasions, residents have protested in support of taxis. For instance, during the West Rand boycott of Greyhound Bus Lines in 1986, commuters demanded that the company's midibuses be withdrawn from the townships, that the company stop blocking residents' applications for taxi permits, and that it refund the taxi operators fined during the boycott for overloading (McCaul, ibid., p. 440). The above notwithstanding, it must be remembered that the relationship between taxi-operators and commuters is in the end mediated by the profit motive.

Capital accumulation in the black taxi industry

Today, the black taxi industry is a powerful force in the urban economy. Estimates reveal that taxi owners buy over 800 million litres of petrol per year and purchase over 3,5 million tyres per annum. The black taxi industry provides four major motor manufacturing companies with a turnover of more than R1 billion a year. The kombi taxi industry has a capital investment of about R3 billion (equivalent to two gold mines), and has created some 300 000 jobs (which is equivalent to 60 per cent of the entire gold mining industry).[5]

With the meteoric rise in the number of black taxis, advocates of free market principles were quick to point out that capitalism is colour-blind and argued that black taxi operators were actively and lucratively participating in the process of capital accumulation. However, this was not without the active involvement of big business and finance capital which in the early 1980s recognized the taxi industry as a new arena for investment. The birth of SABTA facilitated the merger of the 'aristocracy of finance' and black taxi operators, by providing a stable body to act as a guarantor in their investments. SABTA is thus able to offer its members benefits such as discounts on new vehicles, tyres and spare parts.

Major financial and banking institutions (such as Wesbank which specializes in vehicle finance, and Rand Merchant Bank) have entered the taxi industry and introduced concessions to SABTA members. According to a SABTA-Wesbank agreement, operators can get vehicles on a deposit of 20 per cent. This was facilitated by SABTA providing Wesbank with adequate securities to allow a relaxation by Wesbank of their normal credit requirements. Consequently, more and more urban black taxi operators find it easier to purchase or operate kombis. However, it must be remembered that it is almost impossible to join SABTA unless one already has a taxi. This limits the benefits of financial concessions (such as those negotiated between SABTA and Wesbank) to existing fleet operators.

Big businesses which have entered into deals with the black taxi trade include Toyota, Volkswagen, Nissan, and Unipart. SABTA has also succesfully forged links with multi-national corporations (such as Shell and Total) as is evident through SABTA's anti-sanctions campaigns.

A new range of vested interests in the kombi taxi industry has emerged. For example, SABTA entered into an agreement with Unipart which entitles its members to spare parts at a 50 per cent discount. SABTA membership also entitles operators to discounts at certain furniture shops and chain stores. Various companies clamour to do business with SABTA. For instance, Toyota, which claims to represent 40 per cent of the 10 to 16-seater taxi sales and sells on average 300 kombis a month to SABTA, contributes a small sum to SABTA's coffers for every taxi sold. Nissan, which sells about 100 kombis a month to SABTA, donated 32 new mini-buses to SABTA for use by its regional representatives in 1987 in order to promote the vehicles in the black townships. Volkswagen has introduced a new 14-seater kombi (which was developed in conjunction with SABTA) and hopes to boost its share of the taxi market by 20 per cent as a result.[6]

Similarly, in a bid to increase their market share, South African oil companies (Castrol and Cera Oil) not only launched new oils designed specifically for taxis, but also use special SABTA packaging and pay royalties for using SABTA's name. At present, SABTA owns 16 petrol stations located in black townships. In July 1987, Total (South Africa) entered into a preferential agreement with SABTA in terms of which local taxi associations were offered a direct shareholding in a number of existing and new service stations in black townships. The idea is that SABTA and Total jointly manage the service stations until such time as the local taxi operators acquire the necessary management skills. At this point, ownership will be transferred to the local taxi associations.

The marriage between big business and the taxi industry has not, however, been entirely a bed of roses. There are growing allegations that black taxi operators are often victims of fraud. For example, in March 1989, it was reported that about 1 000 kombis were sold in contravention of the Credit Agreement Act, resulting in a high rate of kombi confiscation and inflated profits for the agency concerned. It was necessary for SABTA to come to the rescue of many operators in a similar position. This latest taxi credit scam raises intriguing questions about the ambiguous role of credit in the paratransit revolution.

To add a further note of caution, the growth in economic power of black taxi operators has its dark side in terms of often exploitative labour practices. As black taxi operators increasingly secure fleets of kombis, they become taxi managers and employ workers in the capacity of drivers, cleaners, mechanics, taxi marshals, taxi receptionists, 'accountants' etc. These employees are often forced to work extremely long hours for a pittance. COSATU (the Congress of South African Trade Unions) has begun to organize the 'grossly exploited' workers employed by taxi operators as drivers (*Weekly Mail*, 2–9 February 1989). It is telling that SABTA has so far refused to enter into any negotiations with COSATU over the issue.

Conclusion

The story of the black taxi industry reflects both the political and economic repression of blacks in South Africa's history and the contradictory processes generated under South Africa's racial form of capitalism. Apartheid policies as applied to black cab drivers in central city areas severely stunted the growth of black entrepreneurship in the paratransit sector. However, the residential segregation of South Africa's urban landscape and the removal of black townships to the urban fringes, paradoxically re-created the conditions for the development of a dynamic black taxi industry. The dangerous, overcrowded and uncomfortable character of the public transport network provided by the apartheid state played into the hands of the black taxi industry which was able to draw off the richer commuters as a result.

Although the black taxi industry has allowed many operators to accumulate capital on a hitherto unprecedented scale, the full might of black economic muscle in this area was only realized after collective action was taken with the formation of SABTA. The formation of this national association enabled black taxi operators to bargain with big financial and corporate capital on a more equal footing and to harness the resources necessary for rapid growth.

However, whereas unity was a good thing for taxi operators, it was not necessarily always a good thing for the black commuters. Taxi associations allow for oligopolist pricing policies which eliminate competition and result in higher fares. What is good for taxis is not always good for the people who rely on them for transport to and from work. Similarly, while the growth of black economic power is clearly desirable, it carries with it distinctly negative aspects.

The exploitative relationship between black taxi owners and their drivers is one example.

Despite the fact that some taxi operators belong to the UDF affiliates, the potential for severe conflicts of interest between commuters and taxi operators and between taxi operators and their employees should sound a warning to those who believe that increasing black economic power is an unambiguously progressive move in the South African context. Capitalism is a contradictory and crisis-ridden system. Drawing black entrepreneurs and capitalists into that system inevitably draws them into contradictory or conflict relationships with other members of the community.

Notes

1 Paratransit is a term for transport services which lie somewhere between private passenger transport and conventional public transport in terms of price and quality of service.

2 In 1984, the *Financial Mail* estimated that there were 82 000 kombis carrying 500 000 black commuters daily, of which only 18 000 taxis were legal (10 February 1984).

3 It was reported in 1986 that about 7 000 taxis were in operation between Soweto and Johannesburg, and carried about 150 000 commuters daily. These figures indicate a dramatic rise from the estimated 6 000 people who used taxis daily in 1984 (*The Star*, 11 August 1984). Friday afternoons, Saturday mornings and pay-days are the busiest times for taxis.

4 To become a legal taxi operator one needs a public road carriers permit (which indicates the purpose of the permit and the locality in which services will be rendered), a certificate of vehicle fitness from the Traffic Department, a public drivers licence and third party insurance.

5 Sources for the data in this paragraph come from *Economist* 3/2/84, *Motorist* 1986, *Star* 19 June 1988, and *Weekly Mail* 15-22 December 1988.

6 Likewise, the South African Motor Manufacturing Association is alleged to be in collaboration with SABTA to develop a new Ford or Mitsubishi bus.

References

Cameron, J., & Lipman, V., 'Passenger Transport Policy Options: The Effect of Deregulation of the Combi-taxi and the withdrawal of Passenger Subsidies paid to Conventional Bus Operators', TT/140, *NITRR*, Pretoria, 1987.

McCaul, C., 'Crises and Restructuring in the Passenger Transport Sector', in Moss, G. & Obery, I. (eds.), *South African Review 4*, Ravan Press: Johannesburg, 1987.

Moabi, P.J., 'Deviance and the Urban African Taxi: A Sociological Analysis of the Taxi as a Deviant Opportunity Structure in Dobsonville', MA Dissertation, UNISA, Pretoria, 1976.

Nattrass, J., 'The Effect of Size upon the Financing of Business', in *The South African Journal of Economics*, vol. 38, no. 3, Sept. 1970.

Nattrass, J., 'The Effect of Credit Control upon the Financing of Business', in *The South African Journal of Economics*, vol. 40, no. 1, March 1972.

Nattrass, J., 'The Theoretical Basis for a Small Business Development Programme', Submission to the *President's Council*, in respect of the Development of Small Business and the Informal Sector, May 1985.

Nattrass, J., 'Black Business in a Changing Society', Address to NAFCOC, 1986.

PC 97/1985, *Report of the Committee for Constitutional Affairs of the President's Council on an Urbanization Strategy for the Republic of South Africa.*, Pretoria, Government Printer, 1986.

SAIRR, *South African Race Relations Survey*, SAIRR, Johannesburg, 1986.

Van Onselen, C., *Studies in the Social and Economic History of the Witwatersrand, 1886-1914, New Babylon and New Niniveh*, Ravan Press, Johannesburg, 1982.

The small black enterprise sector — a brief note of caution

14

Nicoli Nattrass

Introduction

The black taxi industry in South Africa has experienced revolutionary growth in the 1980s (see Khosa's contribution to this volume). This illustrates the great potential for growth that exists in the small formal and informal black enterprise sectors. However, as Khosa notes, rapid capital accumulation in the industry was facilitated by apartheid-structured cities and the formation of the umbrella organization SABTA. Most small businesses do not operate in similar advantageous environments and do not have the same potential for rapid growth. This point is often neglected by enthusiasts of small business. In government planning and policy circles particularly, there has been a tendency to extrapolate uncritically from individual success stories to the small business sector as a whole.

This short chapter is divided into two sections. The first outlines the shift in state policy regarding the small black enterprise sector in South Africa. Where pertinent, the reflection of key ideas in development economics theory and in the policy prescriptions of international development agencies is indicated. The second section points to some existing research on the informal sector in South Africa, and argues that prospects for rapid expansion and prosperity are poor for the majority of small (formal and informal) operators.

By the most basic definition, the informal sector operates outside official rules and regulations whereas formal sector enterprises do not. In a survey of 129 black businesses in Katlehong, it was found that 108 were unlicensed (Nattrass & Glass, 1984). By the criterion of legality, most small black businesses in South Africa are likely to be informal. However, as it is not clear what precisely is meant by the informal sector, and because many of the difficulties informal operators face are also those besetting small formal businesses, the discussion in the chapter widens in places to refer to the small enterprise sector in general.

The original perpetrator of the concept 'informal sector' defined it to include all self-employed people (Hart, 1973). However, as Davies has pointed out, such a definition 'precludes the possibility of workers being employed by informal operators ... (and) ... does not provide criteria by which the self-employed in the formal sector can be distinguished from those in the informal sector' (1979,

p. 88). Hart also outlined some of the expected characteristics of an informal sector operation such as 'small-scale' and 'labour intensive' and this tended to confuse the issue further. As Moser argues, 'it is difficult to tell whether it is the people or their activities which are being classified' (1978, p. 1052).

In development literature the informal sector particularly is regarded as a category within which to locate the poor. This is problematic as there are some rich informal operators (such as drug dealers) and many underpaid and exploited workers and entrepreneurs in the formal sector (see Peattie, 1987). Although formal small enterprises have better access to capital and markets and on average probably earn higher incomes than their informal counterparts, drawing a strict conceptual distinction between them is of limited use.

The change in state policy towards small black enterprises

Prior to the late 1970s, the attitude of planners and administrators in South Africa to small urban black businesses was generally hostile. Encouraging the expansion of black enterprise was seen as counter-productive on the grounds that it would accelerate rural-urban migration, overburden public services and compound the social and health problems associated with the informal sector (Wellings & Sutcliffe, 1984, p. 4). It suited the state better to channel black initiative to the bantustans in an attempt to shore up the political structures there by encouraging the establishment of a homeland petite bourgeoisie (Kahn, in Krige, 1985, p. 94).

However, from the early 1980s, the policy was transformed into one of acceptance, encouragement and upgrading of small black enterprise activity. By the late 1980s, it was estimated that there were at least 500 000 black-owned businesses, 100 000 black-owned taxis, 150 000 hawkers and vendors, 50 000 small shopkeepers and 70 000 small backyard manufacturers in South Africa (African Council of Hawkers and Informal Business, quoted in May & Stavrou, 1989, p. 33). Institutions such as the Urban Foundation and the Small Business Development Corporation provided further growth stimulus by focusing aid and attention on the more wealthy formal and even on a few informal black businesses.

This more favourable attitude to black business development dovetailed with the broader economic policy shift in favour of the market mechanism and away from excessive state economic regulation (McCarthy, 1982, p. 7). The 1987 government White Paper on *Privatisation and Deregulation in the RSA* reiterated the imperative for 'encouraging entrepreneurship' and stressed that 'the approach to regulation must therefore emphasize the promotion of economic activities and be less directed towards their control' (quoted in Rogerson & Hart, 1989, p. 30).

However, as Rogerson & Hart (1989) show, there is a gap between reform policy and its practical implementation on a local level. They point out that deregulation of hawking is limited in Port Elizabeth, being retarded by a hostile council in Pretoria, resisted in Johannesburg by formal sector enterprises who feel threatened, and restricted in Durban to particular geographical zones. They conclude that 'the future geographical landscape of reform and redistribution' will be profoundly affected by 'policy variations between those local authorities which cast off shackles and embrace urban accommodationist planning as opposed to those which cling to a philosophy of planning **against** urban growth' (ibid., p. 42).

The recognition of black urbanization as a permanent phenomenon and the issue of black unemployment as a pressing problem no doubt played a role in changing official attitudes to the small black business sector. The clear failure of Grand Apartheid to turn the tide of black urbanization, coupled with population growth well in excess of economic growth, forced a rethink on the issue of black economic initiative in urban areas. State planners were compelled to consider policies which individuals in the business sector and the universities had been advocating for some time.[1] Despite the uneven nature of policy on a local level, there is a clear trend away from persecution of the informal sector and an easing up of the restrictions on the small enterprise sector as a whole.

The growing recognition of the political advantages of a black petty capitalist class will probably facilitate the more widespread loosening up of repressive regulations. According to Reynders of the National Manpower Commission, encouraging black entrepreneurship would 'expand the base for township administration' (1977, p. 237) and 'prevent a further deterioration in black attitudes towards the free enterprise system' (ibid., p. 242). This was echoed by Vosloo, the chairman of the Small Business Development Corporation, who noted in 1985 that 'South Africa could expect second and third generation black urban residents to become a destabilizing factor in society if they were denied new business and job opportunities in the future' (quoted in Nattrass et al., 1986, p. 32). These particular advantages are no doubt becoming all the more attractive to the South African state in the 1980s as the townships erupt in political turmoil and fiscal crisis.

The role that the informal sector could play as a source of income and employment, and as a substitute for welfare provision (Wilkinson & Webster, 1982, p. 9) is frequently expounded in government circles. As Simon Brand (at the time Economic Advisor to the State President) argued, 'we should pay more attention to the employment potential of this sector. With full social security still a long way off the informal sector performs a valuable function' (quoted in Krige, 1985, p. 80). In this way, the informal sector is portrayed as a low-cost solution to South Africa's unemployment and welfare problems. As Bromley observed of government enthusiasm for the informal sector, it appears to offer 'the possibility of helping the poor without any major threat to the rich ... and is in this way a potential compromise between pressures for redistribution ... and the desire for stability on the part of the economic and political elites' (1978, p. 1036).

The idea that the informal sector can help solve the unemployment problem has two sides to it. Firstly, it involves the assumption that the informal sector (and the small business sector at large) will generate jobs on a substantial scale. This aspect is discussed later in this chapter. The second, more covert side is the way in which the informal sector has been used to justify and even reduce the measure of unemployment in society. Those not in formal employment are assumed to be employed in the informal sector, rather than unemployed as such.

This has its theoretical reflection in development economics, with job search explanations of urban unemployment in third world countries. Here it is assumed that jobs exist which job-seekers are not prepared to take, and so in this sense, unemployment is deemed to be voluntary. In addition to the few vacancies that usually exist in the industrial sector, job search theorists implicitly and explicitly include the informal sector in the range of possible jobs (see Harris & Sabot, 1982, p. 80). Consequently most of those who are openly without jobs of any description are regarded as refusing jobs in the formal and informal sectors. Furthermore, those eking out a living in the informal sector as a last-ditch survival strategy are regarded as 'employed', self-sufficient and outside the bounds of state welfare responsibility.

A less extreme version is the argument that people who are active in the informal sector (usually as a survival strategy) are still job-seekers who have entered the informal sector as a temporary measure (Fields, 1975). In this sense, the informal sector is seen as a soak pit for the unemployed which expands in times of austerity and contracts during economic upswings when the demand for labour is high. In this way the informal sector is conceptualized in such a way that unemployment appears simultaneously less extensive and less socially unacceptable.

The South African state has taken full advantage of these kinds of arguments which neatly class informal sector operators as 'employed' rather than 'unemployed'. For example, the 1984 White Paper on *A Strategy for the Creation of Employment Opportunities in the RSA*, argued that 'small business and what is known as the informal sector represent a significant part of total employment' (p. 9). Clearly there are informal sector operators who have chosen their occupation (in the sense that there were viable formal sector alternatives open to them) and are engaged in productive activity, yielding a return at least as good as the bottom rungs of the industrial wage structure. Leiman cites evidence to this effect for Zimbabwe (1988, pp. 4–5). However, as shown by most research in South Africa, this is not the case for the vast majority of informal sector operators.

The arguments in favour of informal sector upgrading and small business development in South Africa reflect those prevailing in international development agencies. According to the World Bank, small-scale enterprises should be encouraged as they are more labour intensive than their larger formal counterparts and generate more direct and indirect jobs per unit of capital invested (1978, p. 18). This is clearly echoed by the National Manpower Commission which argued that the informal sector, by virtue of its low capital:labour ratio, is a low-cost employment generator (1984, p. 10).

Although it is recognized that small enterprises account for between 50 and 90 per cent of employment but only 20 to 45 per cent of output in third world countries (ILO, 1984, p. 23), the importance of the sector as a means of countering poverty is stressed by the international development set. It is argued that in the developing world where capital is scarce, the informal sector mobilizes 'capital that would not otherwise have come into existence' (ILO, 1972, p. 21). Profits are often ploughed back into businesses in order to purchase equipment (Chuta & Liedholm, 1982, p. 109) and the development of indigenous, more appropriate technology is argued to be stimulated by small enterprise activity. Consequently the active encouragement and upgrading of informal sector activities is advocated in the ILO's World Employment Programme and the World Bank's Urban Poverty Programme.

The dominant conventional development ideology concerning the promotion of small formal and informal businesses sees the major obstacles to their expansion as a shortage of capital, a lack of access to existing marketing structures and unrealistic licensing requirements (Hart, 1973; Sethuraman, 1977). Another important problem facing small business is held to be the lack of entrepreneurial and management skills. Chuta argues in his study of small entrepreneurs in West Africa that 'management competence is a key determinant of business success and management capacity is strictly limited' (1983, p. 275). In terms of this perspective, the informal sector has the potential to unleash a very powerful developmental impetus in third world economies once these obstacles have been overcome. Training programmes, the development of marketing and buying co-operatives, group lending schemes and government-subsidized credit facilities are proposed as suitable means of overcoming constraints. This optimistic viewpoint is characteristic of the enthusiastic discovery of the informal sector by South African planners and development ideologues.

The potential of the informal sector

As McCarthy argues in this volume, the fundamental fallacy of the aforementioned kind of thinking in South Africa is that the insights of development economics are applied to black areas and welfare problems as if black South Africa were an isolated third world alongside a first world white South Africa. What may be true for a poor third world country, characterized by a weak manufacturing and natural resource base, is certainly not true for South Africa. South Africa is a third world country in terms of criteria such as per capita income and inequality, but sections of the economy are far from economically undeveloped. This makes the uncritical transplantation of classic development economics solutions to black unemployment and poverty highly problematic.

For example, in a study of the KwaZulu Development Corporation's small business development programme, it was argued that one of the major obstacles facing small black entrepreneurs attempting to enter the manufacturing sector was competition from sophisticated large-scale white producers (Nattrass, 1984). Once black businesses moved away from fairly limited, township-specific products (like coal and wood burners, backyard mechanic operations etc.) into activities with greater possibilities for expansion, they encountered vigorous competition with which, for the most part, they had neither the resources nor the experience to cope.

Krige argues that a major reason why informal sector manufacturing activity in KwaMashu is stunted is because 'the greater level of manufacturing development in South Africa leaves less space for informal sector manufacturing' (1985, p. 180). She found that only 3 per cent of her sample had grown large enough to employ labour (loc. cit.). Similarly, Dewar & Watson found in their survey of the informal sector in Cape Town that only 4 per cent employed more than three people (1981). In general, the evidence from available studies of small enterprises in South Africa suggests that although the costs of creating jobs are low, employment opportunities are limited and remuneration is very poor (see overview in Nattrass et al., 1986, pp. 64–7).

In this respect, the more radical Marxist-oriented scholarship in the development field is often more appropriate to the South African situation. In terms of this perspective, it is argued that the informal sector or 'marginal pole' is peripheral to and marginalized from the process of capital accumulation (Obregon, 1974). It simply provides people with low-cost goods such as shack housing, and the means to scratch out a living, and the capitalist economy with a means of absorbing the unemployment resulting from structural and cyclical phenomena. Informal sector activity at the bottom end of the spectrum in South Africa, such as garbage picking (De Kok, 1986) and car washing (Mbona, 1989), clearly fits the above description.

One of the most striking features of informal sector studies in South Africa is that low earnings are constantly reported for informal operators (see overviews in Krige, 1985, pp. 35–41; May & Stavrou, 1989, p. 25). Beavon & Rogerson for example found that only a very small minority of operators received incomes which were higher than the lowest echelon wage in the formal sector (1982).

Similarly, a survey of the informal sector in Inanda and Clermont found that half the enterprises sampled were earning less than R100 a month and only 2 per cent were earning over R800 (Nattrass & Glass, 1986). Once adjustments were made for depreciation and labour costs, the study found that the real rate of return on investment in the informal sector was less than that on many other low risk alternatives (ibid., p. 51).

The low rate of return on capital has important implications for free marketeer type analyses of credit provision for small enterprises. Neo-classical analysts blame market imperfections for the small entrepreneur's lack of access to capital. By this they mean that if interest rates were allowed to rise high enough to compensate the lending institution for the high level of risk associated with extending credit to small businesses, then small business would have access to credit — albeit at a higher price.

This has been argued recently for South Africa by Hesketh who maintains that the access to finance and the growth potential of small enterprises would be improved if the Usury Act was 'reviewed towards removing the interest rate ceiling' (1989, p. 38). This argument is problematic for two reasons. Firstly, if small enterprises operate with a low rate of return[2] (as most do), then the availability of expensive credit is at best meaningless (as businesses could not afford it) and at worst dangerous as it may push marginal businesses into bankruptcy as a result of the high interest repayments. Secondly, the theoretical basis of the argument is suspect. As Stiglitz & Weiss (1981) have shown, it is not always rational for banks to increase the rate of interest on risky loans as this encourages a higher rate of default. In other words, even in a free market situation, credit will still be rationed and small enterprises discriminated against.

In addition, where credit is left to the private sector, one finds that lending institutions have a preference for extending loans for the purchase of capital equipment. Lending on this basis 'provides an incentive for small scale firms to move away from the labour intensive methods that constitute an important argument in favour of their promotion' (World Bank, quoted in Nattrass et al., 1986, p. 85). If extending credit to the small enterprise sector is to have any meaningful impact in terms of alleviating poverty and unemployment, heavily subsidized public sector loans are necessary. It is important that the pitfalls of a market-regulated system (that is, interest rates leading to higher defaults and capital intensity) be avoided.

The most numerically significant component of South Africa's informal sector economy are street traders (see overview of evidence in Rogerson & Hart, 1989, p. 29). Petty trading such as hawking has very limited potential for expansion and is overwhelmingly undertaken as a survival strategy in the face of extensive unemployment and as a means of supplementing meagre formal sector wages.

Such petty commodity production as exists is regarded by radical theorists as exploited by and subordinate to the formal sector (Le Brun & Gerry, 1975; Moser, 1978; Tokman, 1978). With respect to the exploitative relationship between large-scale (formal) and small-scale (predominantly informal) sector enterprises, sub-contracting arrangements are targeted by radical analysts. It is argued that providing the formal sector with intermediate goods guarantees the informal sector a market, but it also places it in a very vulnerable position. Informal sector operators can be 'laid-off' with no comebacks or costs (Roberts, 1978, p. 117) and there is always the risk that the formal sector will break down the production process even further and pay proportionately lower prices to sub-contracted informal operators.

Empirical evidence can be found to support this gloomy prognosis. In a survey of sub-contracting by large firms to small firms in Brazil, no sign was found of large firms playing the role of foster parents to the smaller one, or of any technical assistance from the parent firms. Schmitz (quoted in Nattrass *et al.*, 1986, p. 89) states, 'Small contractors take the brunt of market fluctuations because their production is the first to be cut in slack periods. Under such circumstances, sub-contracting can hardly give the small producers a solid base from which to expand'.

Regarding the subordinate relationship of the (small-scale) informal sector to the (large-scale) formal sector, Le Brun & Gerry state, 'the fact that petty production is faced with advanced methods and technologies operating in the same exchange economy, effectively blocks the transition of petty capitalist production to capitalist commodity production' (1975, p. 24). Because informal sector enterprises exist outside of government protection and patronage, and have little or no access to credit (Weeks, 1973), they operate in a market where they have to pay significantly higher purchase prices and receive significantly lower sale prices than their formal sector counterparts. The small enterprise sector is thus seen to be caught in a squeeze where it buys goods from the larger (formal) sector at prices above their 'value' and sells to the same sector at prices below their 'value' (Moser, cited in Nattrass *et al.*, 1986, p. 21).

More importantly, the informal sector is squeezed on a structural level into market niches which the formal sector finds unprofitable. The most obvious of these niches are markets not yet flooded by mass-produced articles (Nattrass, 1987, p. 864) and production for the 'poor market' — low-cost goods made out of scrap materials and second-hand articles (Sandbrook, 1982, p. 160). However, the danger always exists that if such production becomes too profitable and shows growth potential, the formal sector will enter the market and, by virtue of its superior technology and access to resources, eliminate informal sector competition. Beinefeld refers to this as the 'growth-destruction impasse' (1975) facing petty-commodity producers.

Another option open to the small enterprise sector is to act as agents of larger formal sector firms. Hawkers who purchase their goods from formal traders and then resell them in the streets are in effect an extension service. In a study of relations between formal and informal operators, it was found that the degree of formal sector antagonism varied inversely with the amount of trade conducted with hawkers (Nattrass, 1987, p. 870). Clearly there is room for co-operation between large, formal and small-scale informal operators. However the potential for growth in such a structural situation is highly limited for informal operators.

This is not to say that there is no potential for growth in the informal sector or the small enterprise sector in general. The informal sector is extremely diverse and differentiated and there is a wide range of earnings in the sector and in important components of it (Mazumdar, 1976). Success stories, especially concerning informal sector enterprises with some initial access to capital and skilled labour, can be found in the development literature. In Nairobi for instance, informal sector enterprises have been known to multiply their capital by as much as six to ten times over an average of five years (Sethuraman, 1981, p. 35). In South Africa's case, given the historical repression of the black informal and formal small business sectors (see Nattrass *et al.*, 1986, pp. 33–9) the potential for the rapid expansion of black enterprise following changes to restrictive legislation and the provision of capital loans is substantial. The black taxi revolution documented by Khosa in this volume bears testimony to this. However, to make blanket generalizations about the development potential of the informal sector as a whole is very unwise. As argued above, the structural conditions facing small black (formal and informal) businesses are hostile to easy, sustained, rapid expansion.

The growing degree of economic concentration in South Africa's business sector and its implications for small business development is an issue which needs to be squarely faced. As Nattrass *et al.* argue:

> Once big business perceives small business as either a threat or an opportunity, then it is highly likely that it will use its economic muscle to its own advantage, through either eliminating the competition in the first instance, or through a take-over of the small business in the second. Clearly, unless the authorities are also prepared to move in the area of monopoly control, any other state efforts to develop small business will be meaningless in the long run. There is little if any use in fostering the development of a small business only to see it either eliminated or absorbed by big business (1986, p. 105).

In other words, if free enterprise is to be encouraged and bolstered through the promotion of small black enterprises, the process has to be guided and protected by state intervention (in areas such as subsidized credit) and state regulation (for instance in the area of monopoly control).

Notes

1 See for example the policy proposals on small enterprises drawn up by the 'Work for the Future Conference', 1980, pp. 73–4.

2 Hesketh maintains that small informal enterprises often have very high rates of return on capital and that as a result 'small borrowers are able to pay relatively high rates of interest on working capital which is turned over quickly' (1989, p. 33). However in citing evidence of high rates of return, Hesketh misrepresents the research findings of Nattrass & Glass (1986). Hesketh cites rates of return which had not yet been adjusted for depreciation of fixed capital or entrepreneurial labour costs. Indications are that once such adjustments are made, the rates of return are very much lower (see Nattrass & Glass 1986, p. 51; Nattrass & Nattrass, 1988, p. 19).

References

Beavon, K., & Rogerson, C., 'The Informal Sector of the Apartheid City: The Pavement People of Johannesburg', in Smith, D.M. (ed.), *Living Under Apartheid: Aspects of Urbanisation and Social Change in South Africa*, Allen and Unwin: London, 1982.

Bienefeld, M., 'The Informal Sector and Peripheral Capitalism: The Case of Tanzania', *Bulletin of Development Studies*, vol. 6, no. 31, 1975.

Bromley, R., 'The Urban Informal Sector. Why is it worth Discussing', *World Development*, vol. 6, nos. 9/10, 1978.

Chuta, E., 'Upgrading the Management Process of Small Entrepreneurs in West Africa', *Public Administration and Development*, vol. 3, 1983.

Chuta, E. & Liedholm, C., 'Employment Growth and Change in Sierra Leone Small Scale Industry, 1974–1980', *International Labour Review*, vol. 121, no. 1, 1982

Davies, R., 'Informal Sector or Subordinate Mode of Production: A Model', Bromley, R. & Gerry, C. (eds.), *Casual Work in Third World Cities*, Macmillan: London, 1979.

De Kok, R., 'Garbage Picking as a Strategy of Survival', *Development Studies Unit Working Paper no. 16*, University of Natal, 1986.

Dewar, D. & Watson, V., *Unemployment and the Urban Informal Sector: Some Proposals*, Urban Problems Research Unit, University of Cape Town, 1981.

Fields, G.S., 'Rural-Urban Migration , Urban Unemployment and Underemployment and Job-Search Activity in L.D.C.s', *The Journal of Development Economics*, June, 1975.

Harris, J. & Sabot, R., 'Towards a More General Search Model', in Sabot, R. (ed.), *Migration and the Labour Market in Developing Countries*, Westview Press: Colorado, 1982.

Hart, K., 'Informal Income Opportunities and Urban Employment in Ghana', *Journal of Modern African Studies*, vol. 11, no. 1, 1973.

Hesketh, M., 'Financing Small Enterprise — A Review of Regulatory Factors', *Indicator*, vol. 6, no. 3, Winter 1989.

ILO (International Labour Organization), *Employment, Incomes and Equality*, ILO Mission to Kenya, Geneva, 1972.

ILO (International Labour Organization), *Employment, Incomes, Social Protection, New Information and Technology*, ILO, Geneva, 1984.

Krige, D., *The Urban Informal Sector in South Africa: What Options for Development? A Case Study of KwaMashu, Natal*, Unpublished Masters Thesis, University of Natal: Durban, 1985.

Le Brun, O. & Gerry, C., 'Petty Producers and Capitalism', *Review of African Political Economy*, no. 7, 1975.

Leiman, A., 'The Informal Sector — A Brief Literature Survey', *Economics Learning Resources* no.13, School of Economics University of Cape Town, 1988

May, J. & Stavrou, S., 'The Informal Sector: Socio-Economic Dynamics and Growth in the Greater Durban Metropolitan Region' *Rural Urban Studies Working Paper No.18*, Rural Urban Studies Unit University of Natal Durban, 1989.

Mazumdar, D., 'The Urban Informal Sector', *World Development*, vol. 4, no. 8, 1976.

Mbona, D., 'Car Washers Revisited', Paper presented at the *Association for Sociology in South Africa Congress*, University of the Witwatersrand, 1989.

McCarthy, C., 'Aspects of Small Enterprise Promotion in Developing Countries: The South African Case', *Development Studies Southern Africa*, vol. 5, no. 1, 1982.

Moser, C., 'Informal Sector or Petty Commodity Production: Dualism or Dependence in Urban Development', *World Development*, vol. 6, no. 9/10, 1978.

National Manpower Commission, *Report on an Investigation into Small Business in the Republic of South Africa with Special Reference to the Factors that may Retard the Growth and Development Thereof*, Council for the Promotion of Small Business, 1984.

Nattrass, J. & Glass, H., *Socio-Economic Structures of Katlehong, Vosloorus and Tokoza*, Development Studies Report, University of Natal: Durban, 1984.

Nattrass, J. & Glass, H., *Informal Black Business in Durban*, Natal Town and Regional Planning Commission Supplementary Report, vol. 18, 1986.

Nattrass, J., Nattrass, N. & Krige, D., *The Development of Small and Very Small Business*, Development Studies Unit Report, University of Natal, 1986.

Nattrass, N., *Like Chalk and Cheese: An Evaluation of Two KwaZulu Development Corporation Projects in Natal*, Unpublished Masters Thesis, University of Natal: Durban, 1984.

Nattrass, N., 'Street Trading in Transkei — A Struggle against Poverty, Persecution and Prosecution', *World Development*, vol. 15, no. 7, 1987.

Nattrass, N. & Nattrass, J., *Small Formal Business in Durban*, Natal Town and Regional Planning Commission Supplementary Report, vol. 31, 1988.

Obregon, Q., 'The Marginal Pole of the Economy and the Marginalized Labour Force', *Economy and Society*, no. 3, 1974.

Peattie, L., 'An Idea in Good Currency and How it Grew: The Informal Sector', *World Development*, vol. 15, no. 7, 1987.

Reynders, H., 'Black Industrial Entrepreneurship', *South African Journal of Economics*, vol. 45, no. 3, 1977.

Roberts, B., *Cities of Peasants: The Political Economy of Urbanization in the Third World*, Edward Arnold: London, 1978.

Rogerson, C. & Hart, D., 'The Struggle for the Streets: Deregulation and Hawking in South Africa's Major Urban Areas', *Social Dynamics*, vol. 15, no. 1, 1989.

Sandbrook, R., *The Politics of Basic Needs: Urban Aspects of the Poverty Problem in Africa*, Heineman: London, 1982.

Sethuraman, S., 'The Urban Informal Sector in Developing Countries', *International Labour Review*, vol. 116, no. 3, 1977.

Sethuraman, S. (ed.) *The Urban Informal Sector in Developing Countries: Employment, Poverty and Environment*, ILO, Geneva, 1981.

RSA, White Paper on *Privatization and Deregulation in the Republic of South Africa*, WPG87, Government Printer: Pretoria, 1987.

RSA, White Paper on *a Strategy for the Creation of Employment in the Republic of South Africa*, WPC–1984, Government Printer: Pretoria, 1984.

Stiglitz, J. & Weiss, A., 'Credit Rationing in Markets with Imperfect Information', *American Economic Review*, 1981.

Tokman, V., 'An Exploration into the Nature of Informal-Formal Sector Relationships', *World Development*, vol. 6, no. 9/10, 1978.

Weeks, J., 'Uneven Sectoral Development and the Role of the State', *Institute of Development Studies Bulletin*, vol. 5, no. 2/3, 1973.

Wellings, P. & Sutcliffe, M., 'Developing the Urban Informal Sector in South Africa: The Reformist Paradigm and its Fallacies', *Development and Change*, vol. 15, no. 4, 1984.

Wilkinson, P. & Webster, D., 'Living in the Interstices of Capital: Towards a Reformulation of the Informal Sector Concept', *Social Dynamics*, vol. 8, no. 2, 1982.

Work for the Future Conference, *Conference Summary and Policy Proposals*, University of Natal: Durban, 1980.

World Bank, *Employment and Development of Small Enterprise*, World Bank, Washington D.C., 1978.

Poverty, the state and redistribution: some reflections

15

Francis Wilson

Introduction

It is being widely argued in South Africa, indeed it is part of the new conventional wisdom, that wherever possible activities currently being run by the state should be privatized. Following not only the rhetoric of the Reagan-Thatcher years but also the realities of lessons learnt around the world, from Nigeria to Poland, 'the state' is castigated as being inefficient. In South Africa the state, it is said, has grown 'too big': it misallocates resources in a most wasteful way, it encourages corruption and its employees do very little work in return for the substantial salaries they earn. Furthermore, taxes are too high and discourage productive economic activity. The primary function of the South African state, says one widely-read wit, is to transfer funds from Johannesburg (where real entrepreneurs create the wealth) to Pretoria (where inefficient bureaucrats misspend it). The only reason why countries fail to grow fast, says another South African commentator, is excessive government participation in the economy. 'Without exception', he writes, 'the misery in third world countries is caused by big government' (Leon Louw, 1989, pp. 27 & 32).

It is against the background of these arguments that some reviewers of the overview report for the *Second Carnegie Inquiry into Poverty and Development in Southern Africa* have strongly criticized the book, particularly its recommendations regarding strategies for action. The editor of *Business Day*, for example, found it:

> deeply depressing that the Carnegie study should so assiduously avoid looking at models of success in eliminating poverty in order to sustain the discredited argument used by such creatures as Mussolini and Verwoerd as well as by the socialists – for massive state intervention to redistribute wealth – at the cost of creating it (Ken Owen, *Cape Times*, 30 January 1989).

In the *Financial Mail* the anonymous reviewer found it unfortunate that despite warning against a bureaucratic jungle, abusive state power, and low growth, the authors of the Carnegie report went on to:

> propose plans that would make the jungle denser, lead to more abusive State power and, through high taxes and big government, sabotage the ability to grow (*Financial Mail*, 3 February 1989).

In a similar vein Rudolf Gouws, group economist at Rand Acceptances Bank, criticizes the report for proposing strategies which would effectively increase the relative size of the state in the South African economy, in turn having a negative impact on the capacity of that economy to grow and to generate the wealth needed for eliminating poverty (*Die Suid-Afrikaan*, April 1989). In *Finansies en Tegniek*, Christo Volschenk expresses concern that the report does not really consider how much the state can increase its involvement in the economy, nor how far the process of redistribution of wealth can go before the goose that lays the golden egg simply dies (*Finansies en Tegniek*, 3 February 1989).

In response to these criticisms, it should be said immediately — if only in passing — that the Carnegie report is by no means blind to the dangers of state interference. Indeed the report contains trenchant criticism of much state policy in South Africa, together with warnings about the probable consequences of excessive state intervention in many aspects of a future economy. At the same time, it points to some of the dangers and drawbacks of recommending free markets for **all** spheres of economic activity.

It does not, of course, rely only on state action to deal with the problem of poverty. Recommendations are wide-ranging and include: the crucial role of non-governmental organizations (including, specifically, business/free-enterprise organization), the need for deregulation of large areas of the economy, particularly in the informal sector, and the necessity for the state to create appropriate frameworks within which markets can operate efficiently and equitably (for example by means of land reform); as well as frameworks for investing in basic infrastructure (by various means, including public works programmes based on employment guarantee schemes).

Nevertheless the issue raised by these reviewers is an extremely important one. It takes us, as Savage has pointed out (Savage, 1989, p. 94), to the heart of the debate about the critical issue of the role of the state in dealing with poverty.

The state and its economy: some empirical evidence

In attempting to examine the argument that rigorous analysis leads inevitably to the conclusion that the most effective policy for eliminating poverty in any society (including South Africa) would always be to decrease (by means of privatization) rather than to increase the role of the state, let us start with some of the facts.

In the United States, total central government expenditure (expressed as a percentage of GNP) rose from 19 per cent to 25 per cent between 1972 and 1986. In the United Kingdom, over the same period, this proportion rose from 32 per cent to 41 per cent. Reagan and Thatcher notwithstanding, the state, particularly in Britain, is playing a large and increasing role in those two economies.

What about other countries? Is there, perhaps, some correlation between the relative importance of the state in any economy and such factors as the standard of living, the rate of growth, or even the quality of life? And how does South Africa compare with other countries? Table 15.1 provides some basic information but it is important to note that the data relate only to expenditure by the central government and do not take account of the different proportions, in various countries, of expenditure by decentralized parts of the state through such bodies as provincial or city councils. Nevertheless the information is instructive.

Table 15.1:
CENTRAL GOVERNMENT EXPENDITURE AND QUALITY OF LIFE INDICATORS
FOR NINETEEN COUNTRIES (1986)

Country	Percent of GNP	GNP/capita		
		$(1986)	Average annual growth (1965–86)	Life Expectancy at birth (1986)
India	16	290	1,8	57
Japan	17	12 840	4,3	78
South Korea	18	2 370	6,7	69
Switzerland	19	17 680	1,4	77
U.S.A.	25	17 480	1,6	75
Brazil	26	1 810	4,3	65
Singapore	27	7 410	7,6	73
South Africa	27	1 850	0,4	61
Australia	28	11 920	1,7	78
W.Germany	30	12 080	2,5	75
Sri Lanka	31	400	2,9	70
Zimbabwe	35	620	1,2	58
United Kingdom	41	8 870	1,7	75
France	44	10 720	2,8	77
Sweden	44	13 160	1,6	77
Botswana	49	840	8,8	59
Netherlands	57	10 020	1,9	77
Hungary	63	2 020	3,9	71
Israel	72	6 210	2,6	75

NOTE:
In some cases (particularly that of South Africa) the World Bank figures, used here, for life expectancy are higher than those provided in Unicef's *The State of the World's Children 1988.*
SOURCE:
World Development Report, 1988

Table 15.1 indicates that there appears to be no correlation whatever between the size of the state, measured by central government expenditure as a proportion of GNP, and the performance of that economy, measured either by wealth (GNP) per capita or by the average annual growth rate over the past 20 years. Similarly there does not appear to be any correlation between any of the indicators mentioned above and the quality of life, measured by life expectancy (in years) at birth.

Table 15.1 shows that the relative size of the state in the South African economy is not that large, compared with other countries, whilst the rate of growth of this economy has been abysmal.

By contrast, Louw cites evidence in an unidentified World Bank study of 1983 which suggests, he says, that low government participation rates (as measured by tax revenues) have coincided not only with more rapid economic growth but also with a more rapidly rising share of national income going to the poorest 40 per cent (Louw, 1989, p. 27).

Clearly more empirical work needs to be done; nevertheless, on the basis of the evidence contained in Table 15.1, if the ratio of central government expenditure to a country's gross national product is a reasonable measure of the relative size of the state in a national economy, it cannot be argued that a large state sector is **necessarily** bad for economic growth or for the quality of life. Which leads us to the major point that I wish to argue in this paper — namely that the optimum size (proportion) of the state can be different in different circumstances, and that it depends critically on a number of factors including the pattern of expenditure of the state, the efficiency of the bureaucrats who run it and also, to a lesser extent, on fiscal policy and the sources of state revenue.

As far as the actual funding of state expenditure is concerned, there can clearly be a marginal rate of taxation which is so high that all further economic activity is discouraged. We need however to examine with some care the various sources of government revenue before asserting that further revenue-raising is inevitably going to be economically harmful. Table 15.2, which is far from comprehensive, has been drawn up simply to illustrate this point.

From the three parts (a,b and c) of this table we can deduce that the level (which is measured as a proportion) of the sort of taxation on which economists tend to focus most attention, namely that of income, profit and capital gains, will itself depend not so much on the proportion that government revenue forms of GNP as on the way in which that revenue has been collected. Thus we find that although the state in Sweden spends a high proportion of its GNP; the level of taxation on income, profit and capital gains is relatively low. South Africa's taxation on these sources of income is double that of Sweden's (despite the fact that South Africa does not tax capital gains), but significantly less than that of Australia.

We note also that in South Africa domestic taxes on goods and services (such

Table 15.2a:

SOURCES OF CENTRAL GOVERNMENT CURRENT REVENUE 1986
EXPRESSED AS A PERCENTAGE OF
TOTAL CURRENT GOVERNMENT REVENUE.

Country	Taxes on income, profit & capital gains	Social security contributions	Domestic taxes on goods & services	Taxes on international trade and transactions	Other taxes	Non-tax revenue
	(1)					
Sweden	16	30	30	1	8	16
Brazil	18	21	16	2	4	39
S.Korea	25	2	43	15	4	13
South Africa	52	1	33	3	3	9
Australia	60	0	24	5	1	11
Japan	67	0	19	2	8	5

Table 15.2b:

TOTAL GOVERNMENT CURRENT REVENUE
AS PERCENTAGE OF GNP

Country	(2)
Sweden	41
Brazil	27
S.Korea	19
South Africa	23
Australia	26
Japan	13

Table 15.2c:

TAXES ON INCOME, PROFIT AND CAPITAL GAINS
AS A PERCENTAGE OF GNP

Country	Percentage
	$(1) \times (2)$
Sweden	6,6
Brazil	4,9
S.Korea	4,6
South Africa	12,0
Australia	15,6
Japan	8,7

SOURCE:
World Development Report 1988

as sales tax) are relatively high as a source of government revenue. On the other hand, social security contributions in South Africa constitute 0,23 per cent of GNP compared with 12,3 per cent of GNP in Sweden. Of course some of these differences are more in the nature of book entries (with some countries, for example, paying social security benefits out of central taxes rather than from specially earmarked contributions); nevertheless they do point to important factors which must be taken into account in any analysis of the economics of public finance.

Gelb, Knight & Sabot, in a recent study for the World Bank, challenge the views of Adam Smith, who views most government employees as unproductive. They adopt what they describe as the 'now-conventional' approach to development which 'views government as imperfect but well-meaning and educable, as definitely part of the solution rather than as part of the problem'. **Both** approaches, they assert, are simplistic. What is required is a more sophisticated theory of policy-making (1988, p. 23). That is surely correct. Whilst government certainly has to be part of the solution, parts of it are by no means necessarily always and everywhere well-meaning or even educable. A significant proportion of the huge bureaucracy in the Soviet Union today, for example, is clearly very much part of Gorbachev's problem.

This is not the place to pursue that more sophisticated theory. Our goal here is more modest: it is simply to make the point, emphasized elsewhere in this volume by le Roux, that whilst some of the arguments in favour of privatization of nationalized industries have come to be more widely accepted in recent years, it surely remains true that there are other aspects of economic life that can be handled more efficiently and effectively by government than by private enterprise. **What** these aspects may be will vary according to the particular historical circumstances of the government and the economy in question.

The South African challenge

In South Africa today, the particular circumstances challenging policy-makers relate to the pattern of poverty and wealth created by a century of industrial revolution, powered primarily by the development of the gold mines. That pattern is traced out in the Carnegie report. The proportion of the total population (including those in the TBVC [1] areas) living below subsistence (measured as the urban minimum living level) in 1980 was estimated to be 50 per cent. For blacks throughout the country, the proportion was estimated to be nearly two-thirds (60–65 per cent), whilst for those living in the reserves no less than 81 per cent of the households were in dire poverty.

This poverty is linked to deep inequality (see McGrath's chapter in this volume). Using the Gini coefficient (which is one technical measure of inequality), South Africa has been found to have the greatest degree of inequality of the 57 countries of the world for which statistics are available. This data is for 1978, since when it is possible that the degree of inequality in South Africa may have fallen somewhat and/or the Gini coefficient in other countries may have risen. South Africa may no longer be at the top of the world table, although it certainly remains high up. This degree of inequality is important because, as Raymond Aron has argued, in any society with such a chasm between rich and poor, human community is impossible. The consequences of this divide are exacerbated in South Africa because it tends to follow the colour line. Whilst poverty is not confined to any one colour-caste it is concentrated mostly amongst blacks. Whilst almost one-third of all black households, for example, earned less than R500 per year in 1975, only 2 per cent (one in fifty) of whites were this poor. Similarly, whilst 95 per cent of black households had an annual income of less than R3 000, only 11 per cent of whites were in the same position. The racial divide is reinforced geographically as may be seen from the fact that in 1983 the annual disposable income per capita for blacks in the metropolitan areas was R1 366 whilst in the 'non-growth areas' (primarily the reserves) it was R388. For whites throughout the country, the per capita figure averaged R6 242.

The widespread poverty indicated by these figures is manifested in a number of different forms throughout the country. There is not space to deal with them in any detail here. Suffice it to note a few facts pertaining to two or three of the many faces of poverty. South Africa is one of the few countries in the world which normally exports food in considerable quantitites. Yet it is also a country in which there is widespread hunger and malnutrition; and where disease associated with poor nutrition takes a heavy toll in deaths, particularly amongst children. For blacks in the country as a whole, the infant mortality rate over the period 1981–85 averaged somewhere between 94 and 124 per 1 000 live births, which was eight to ten times greater than the rate for white South Africans (12) and also worse than the national average in a number of other countries in Africa including Algeria (81), Botswana (72) and Zimbabwe (76).

One of the most striking features of poverty in South Africa is the cost, to the poor, of water (which is by no means always clean) in terms of time, effort, and money. People have been found to spend more than three hours a day fetching and carrying water, expending energy equivalent to that used by miners wielding a pick. In some areas where water is located too far to fetch, poor people end up paying up to 67 times as much (in an extreme case) as middle-class householders in Cape Town do for fresh water flowing out of their kitchen taps (Wilson & Ramphele, 1989, pp. 49–50).

A clear image of poverty in South Africa is provided by the sight of a group of elderly black women, each carrying home on her head a load of firewood weighing up to 50 kg, walking underneath an Escom power line on the way. South Africa produces 60 per cent of the electricity in the entire continent and currently, because of excess capacity, has power stations wrapped up in mothballs, yet almost two-thirds of the total population (and approximately 80 per cent of all blacks) within the country do not have access to that energy for their household requirements (*op. cit.* p. 44).

Grossly overcrowded housing, high rates of murder, rape and other forms of assault, widespread illiteracy, and high levels of unemployment are other manifestations (and further causes) of poverty in South Africa today. It is this pattern, traced through the rural and urban areas of the country, that poses such a formidable challenge to all those thinking through appropriate economic policies to be pursued in a democratic, non-racial society.

Redistribution with growth

In arguing, as the Carnegie report did, that any new government must aim both for growth and for a redistribution of wealth and income, it was saying no more than seemed perfectly obvious. However use of the word 'redistribution' seems to have touched off a reaction by some critics which suggests that they feared some sort of Stalinist liquidation of kulaks was being recommended. So perhaps it would be sensible to spell out a little more fully the sorts of policies that might be part of the redistribution process.

The essence of the argument is that the extreme inequality that exists in the South African political economy flows in large measure from the way in which the state, controlled for over 300 years by whites, has been systematically used to appropriate assets (such as land) or to invest resources (for example in education or in loans to farmers) primarily for the benefit of whites. The process of redistribution then requires ways to be found to reshape this historical bias in such a way as to reduce inequality (as measured by a high Gini coefficient) and to deracialize the pattern of income distribution. At the same time, as was argued in the Carnegie report, it is essential that all such policies are compatible with, indeed supportive of, a process of rapid economic growth.

Table 15.3:

SOCIAL SECURITY AS A PROPORTION OF GNP

Date	Per capital SA income in 1966 US dollars	Actual social security expenditure as a percentage of personal income	Predicted values from international cross-section
1949	362	7,2	3,9
1959	441	6,9	4,6
1969	602	5,1	6,4
1975	658	4,5	7,0

SOURCE:
Simkins, 1984, p. 30

One important part of any policy of redistribution with growth is the pattern of state expenditure. In South Africa, Charles Simkins has drawn attention to the fact that in the 30 years after the Second World War, expenditure on social security, which had been well above that expected for a country with its per capita income, fell to well below the value predicted from comparison with the international data (see Table 15.3).

Commenting on these figures which show that in South Africa the proportion of GNP devoted to social security expenditure has moved from being well above that expected in 1949 (given the level of average per capita income) to a proportion in 1975 which was well below that expected, Simkins argues that this perverse movement may in part be explained by changes in the definition of welfare expenditure in a world of greatly changing entitlements but that it 'must also be a testimony to a period of rigid political repression' (1984, p. 30). Great damage was done, for example, to black education in the second half of the 1950s and most of the 1960s by Verwoerd's policy with regard to its financing. Are there, asks Simkins:

> any indications from the post 1975/6 period to indicate that this percentage decline has been halted or reversed? One is the rapid expansion of education; another is the rise in old age pensions. No clear indication in respect of agricultural subsidies and health are apparent. Housing policy, on the other hand, is steadily deteriorating under the influence of misguided principles, a circumstance we shall come to regret as surely as we now regret black education policy (op. cit., p. 30).

In other words, the decisions made by the state regarding its pattern of expenditure on such items as housing, education or social welfare, (including pensions and unemployment benefits) will have a profound effect on the distribution of resources within a society. In a Carnegie Post Conference paper, the working group on the Public Allocation of Resources examined the possible impact of a policy of redistribution with growth. It focused on the possibility of increasing social investment expenditure on education, health, social welfare, and housing under different possible growth rates for the economy over the period 1983–90. The difference in the possibilities, depending on the growth rates assumed, were startling. They range from a pessimistic scenario with little movement towards justice and development in the context of declining per capita after-tax incomes; through a median scenario with a more than 100 per cent increase in black per capita educational expenditure, plus 15 per cent improvements in health expenditure, more than 50 per cent increase in social welfare payments to blacks, and the state financing 40 per cent of the serviced housing sites required by the growing urban population. An even more optimistic scenario, based on more rapid economic growth, held out the possibility of a considerably more rapid progress towards equal per capita spending on South Africans of all races by the state (Simkins et al., 1985, p. 18). This exercise, whilst speculative, is useful in focusing attention on two crucial factors: firstly the importance of the role of the state in shaping the pattern of its expenditure so as to ensure

better housing, health, and social security for the very poor in society; and secondly the fundamental necessity for growth if these goals are to be achieved. In
reality, growth rates were even slower than the most pessimistic forecast whilst
the demands of the state in other areas, notably defence, have escalated such
that by the end of the 1980s the state seems more likely to be reducing social
investment expenditure rather than increasing it.[2]

In summarizing the findings of a workshop convened specially to examine
the interaction between macro-economic policy and the problem of poverty,
Moll concluded that:

> A variety of income redistribution measures can be imagined for an economy like
> that of South Africa.... Based on Latin American experience, (it is suggested that)
> redistribution measures are difficult to implement but are more effective and long-
> lasting where they are supply-side directed (e.g. school feeding, land reform) and
> have a relatively low long-term fiscal commitment rather than undifferentiated
> demand-side measures (e.g. large nominal wage-rises) (Moll, 1989, p. 36).

Land reform is critical not least because the process should help compensate
for historical injustices. But such a demand, as Moll points out, implies tough
political issues such as whether to expropriate or part-expropriate land owned
by white farmers for redistribution and, if so, on what basis. 'There is evidence
from other countries, however, that land reform with popular participation
can be productively efficient and lead to far more labour intensive production
than large capitalist farming — it could hopefully make a dent in the numbers
of unemployed people' (ibid., p. 37; see also Jeffrey Sachs cited in Wilson &
Ramphele, 1989, p. 315).

Important though it may be, land reform is not the only issue — for, as a
number of studies in the Carnegie Inquiry showed, absolute poverty in South
Africa is above all a rural or peri-urban problem, affecting particularly the
unemployed, aged, women, female-headed households, children, and the sick.

'Income distribution efforts to reach these groups', argues Moll, 'would be difficult to implement effectively since they lack economic and political power and
their economic involvement is marginal. In other countries, organised urban
workers have often ended up with the lion's shares of redistributional benefits. Clearly, imaginative redistributive efforts would be needed; ideas might
include food stamp-type programmes, school feeding, preventative health care,
rural housing, land reform combined with large-scale agricultural training and
marketing schemes, and effective pensions and social security systems. Redistribution efforts aimed at children from poor families (school feeding, education,
clothing, child-care, sports facilities) are particularly interesting in this respect.
They tend to be relatively straightforward and cheap to carry out, they encourage economic growth, are egalitarian, selective and irreversible' (Moll, ibid.
p. 38).

Conclusion

The debate about the proper role of the state in alleviating poverty in South Africa is only just beginning and is likely to become even more heated. Clearly there is room for fundamental differences of opinion. But in our view the argument should revolve not so much around some theoretical question about the optimum proportion of GNP that should be spent by the state, as around the practical question concerning how the state actually spends the resources at its disposal in particular circumstances. Virtually all the criticism of the economic track record of the present government made by the most ardent 'free marketeers' are beyond dispute. Indeed the degree of waste, of corruption, and of misallocation of scarce resources is a legacy which will haunt South Africa for years to come. But whilst there are areas of the economy that clearly require the bracing medicine of privatization and removal of government restrictions, it is just as apparent that the government has a central role to play (not least by means of allocating public funds) in reshaping the pattern of growth in such a way that resources are channelled to the poor. There is a real danger that a policy of privatization which might make for greater efficiency in one situation could be applied in different circumstances in such a way that its major impact, far from creating greater efficiency or benefiting the poor, is to redistribute resources **to the rich.** In an important public statement, the head of the Department of Medicine at the University of Cape Town, reacting to a press report about the crisis facing the country's most famous hospital, Groote Schuur, made the point:

> In addition to the adverse effects of fragmentation (along ethnic lines), encouragement of privatization in the field of health care has stimulated the growth of many private hospitals which syphon off nursing, technological and medical staff, cream off the lucrative aspects of medical care and promote the impoverishment of academic centres. ...The economics of health expenditure are such that fragmentation and privatization waste resources, and prevent the development of an efficient, equitable and socially desirable health care system with appropriate mixes of primary, secondary and tertiary services (S.R. Benater, Letter to *Cape Times,* 20 September 1989; brackets added).

Without a process of redistribution which narrows the very wide gap between rich and poor in South Africa, the political stability necessary for investor confidence to sustain economic growth is simply not possible. In this process of growing towards equality, the state has a central role to play. One major task from now on must surely be to deepen the debate as to how best it can do so.

Notes
1 Transkei, Bophuthatswana, Venda and Ciskei.
2 Much of this section has been drawn directly from Wilson & Ramphele, 1989, p. 316.

References

Anon., 'The Poverty of Economics', *Financial Mail*, 3 February 1989.

Gelb, A., Knight, J.B. & Sabot, R.H., 'Lewis through a Looking Glass: Public Sector Employment, Rent Seeking, and Economic Growth', *World Bank PPR Working Paper Series*, WPS 133, 1988.

Gouws, R., 'Armoede nie so Ontwortel', *Die Suid Afrikaan*, April, 1989.

Louw, L., 'Demystifying Poverty in South Africa', *Southern African Freedom Review* vol. 2, no. 4, Autumn, 1989.

Moll, T.C.,'Macro-economic Policy and Poverty', *Carnegie Post-Conference Series* no. 20, Cape Town, 1989.

Savage, M., Review of Uprooting Poverty, *S.A.Sociological Review* vol. 1, no. 2, April 1989.

Simkins, C., 'Public Expenditure and the Poor: Political and Economic Constraints on Policy Choices up to the Year 2000', *Carnegie Conference Paper* no. 253, Cape Town, 1984.

Simkins, C., Abedian, I., Hendrie, D. & le Roux, P., 'Justice, Development and the National Budget' *Carnegie Post-Conference Series* no. 6, Cape Town, 1985.

Unicef, *The State of the World's Children 1989*, New York, 1989.

Wilson, F. & Ramphele, M., *Uprooting Poverty: The South African Challenge*, David Philip: Cape Town & New York, 1989.

World Bank, *World Development Report 1988*, Washington, 1988.

Education and the economy   **16**

George Trotter

Introduction

The relationship between education and economic development is highly complex. It depends on the relations between education and political development, as well as those between schooling and population growth. Unlike economic growth (which usually refers simply to the rise in real gross national product per capita), the concept of economic development carries with it the additional connotations of institutional and technological transformation. The literature on education and development tends to be concerned with the potential which education holds for economic and political transformation.[1] This contribution has a more modest objective: to examine the current educational system in South Africa, and to consider its possible role in the future of our economy.

This chapter is divided into four sections. The first briefly examines the theoretical role traditionally ascribed to education, insofar as economic growth, development, and the distribution of income are concerned. The second section describes the educational infrastructure of South Africa, and makes special reference to the allocation of resources to education. Section three briefly examines some of the empirical evidence linking education in South Africa to economic growth and to the changing pattern of income distribution. The final section deals with the question of how educational resources should most appropriately be allocated to ensure continuing orderly socio-economic development in post-apartheid South Africa.

A theoretical overview of the economic role of education

For many decades, economists have been interested in education for a number of reasons. Economics is concerned with the way we use scarce resources to satisfy our many and diverse needs or 'wants'; and education uses resources. Recognizing this, many studies on the economic role of education have taken the form of production function analyses, which have attempted to identify the contribution of education to total factor productivity. But the output of the 'educational industry' has elements of both consumption and investment, so education may be viewed as both an input and an output.

To the extent that education is an investment, it carries a cost in terms of resource use, and it must yield a return. On a theoretical level it is important to distinguish between private and social rates of return. Individual benefits and costs are used to calculate private rates of return, which are relevant to the individual's decisions about his or her own education. When the calculation is concerned with benefits accruing to society as a whole, and costs which include public as well as private educational expenditure, the result is a social rate of return. This is the rate which should be considered when formulating public educational expenditure policy.

The calculation of rates of return is fraught with difficulties on both the cost and the benefit sides. Apart from the distinction between private and social costs, there are other dichotomies, each of which necessitates a choice: marginal and average cost; direct and indirect cost; accounting and opportunity cost; *ex post* and *ex ante* cost; and fixed versus variable cost. For pragmatic reasons, it is customary, when calculating social costs, to include four main components: the total expenditure of the educational authorities; the actual money outlays of the institutions that are not covered by subsidies from these authorities; the private education-related out-of-pocket expenses of pupils or students and their families; and the opportunity costs of attending educational institutions.[2]

There is certainly evidence to suggest that education leads to higher earnings; this is obviously a significant private benefit. As Blaug put it, 'The amount of education that an individual possesses is, in all modern economies of which we have knowledge, positively correlated with earnings' (1976, p. 23). The difference between the post-tax lifetime earnings of those with and those without a certain level of education provides a convenient, if somewhat oversimplified, measure of the private benefit derived from that education.

The social benefits of education include returns which accrue to members of society other than the person being educated. These will include 'such imponderables as socially and politically responsible behaviour, (and) the direct financial advantages which accrue to employers and fellow workers, and to the state in the form of increased tax revenue from higher incomes'.[3] These external benefits of education — while probably significant — cannot be measured, and the researcher generally uses the pre-tax lifetime earnings differentials of all those who received the education as a proxy for social benefits.[4] The 'true' social benefit is thus higher than the measured social benefit, and it could be argued that the amount of education provided by the state falls short of the ideal.[5]

Although social costs, then, are greater than private benefits, the difference between social and private costs is usually even greater. Government subsidization is never fully recouped by progressive taxation of the higher earnings of those with more education. Thus private rates of return are almost always higher than the corresponding social rates.

Viewed as human capital, education plays an important part in the productive processes in, and thus the growth of, the economy. Indeed, in an early study, Denison found that 23 per cent of the growth of total real national income in the United States during the 1950s might well have been the result of the increased education of the labour force (1962). It is tempting to postulate an unambiguous causal relationship between more education and a higher growth rate. However, the direction of the causality is unclear. It is just as possible that higher growth leads to more education. Moreover, it is difficult to pinpoint the contribution of education on its own. Many would argue today that greater expenditure on the wrong kinds of education simply raises aspirations in a way which could frustrate the labour force and reduce the growth rate; or that it might do little more than redistribute incomes to those fortunate enough to have access to the education.

The link between education and the distribution of income is also rather tenuous. The effect of increased years of schooling on income inequality depends upon a host of factors, and some studies have actually queried the significance of schooling as a determinant of income distribution.[6] Marin & Psacharopoulos have, however, successfully tested the hypothesis that, in developing countries, increasing investment in education does not normally aggravate income inequalities, and may even reduce them (1976, p. 332).

What will happen if inequalities in the provision of education are reduced? According to traditional (neo-classical) economic theory, this should both reduce the inequality of earnings and raise average incomes. Once again, this is not inevitable, for there are many forces outside of the economic system such as trade union power, monopolies, social class and so on, which explain the distribution of income.

Central to the link between education and economic activity is the concept of equal opportunity in education. More equal access to schooling is usually considered to be desirable as a social end in itself, but its economic effects have not been unambiguously established. Samuel Bowles, for one, cautioned against claiming significant income redistribution effects for educational reforms (1973, pp. 346–56). He suggested that the most important implication of increased educational access might be the inculcation of an awareness of inequality, and the consequent undermining of its legitimacy. In a similar vein, Martin Carnoy et al. (1982) pointed out that, whatever the economic effects of educational expansion, the demand for it is a fact of political life, and a crucial element of political legitimacy for any government.

Educational resource allocation

Educational statistics and trends

South Africans (in the sense of those living within the geographical boundaries of the original Union of South Africa) come under the educational jurisdiction of one of 14 different authorities.[7]

For someone researching the financial aspects of educational control over time, the matter is complicated by the fact that the various authorities assumed financial control in different years, when the homelands or national states gained independence. Thus, for example, problems of comparability arise, since separate accounts are not available for KaNgwane and KwaNdebele in 1975. In that year, the education for those two areas was still provided by what was then the Department of Bantu Education.

Some idea of the quantitative changes in South African education in recent years may be gained from the data presented in Tables 16.1 to 16.3. Table 16.1 shows the pupil:teacher ratios in the years 1975, 1985 and 1987; Table 16.2 gives the average annual growth rates for pupil and teacher numbers and for average school size between these years. Table 16.3 shows the average annual rates of increase in the numbers of students at all tertiary institutions for the same periods.

Table 16.1:

PUPIL : TEACHER RATIOS, 1975, 1985 & 1987

	1975	1985	1987 (Preliminary)
Blacks	54,5	41,1	40,8
Coloureds	30,6	25,4	23,5
Indians	27,3	22,6	20,4
Whites	20,4	19,3	16,8

NOTES:
Bophuthatswana, Ciskei, Transkei and Venda are included in 1975, but excluded in the other two years. The figures include pre-primary and special schools, as well as private schools; but exclude correspondence colleges.
SOURCE:
South African Statistics 1988, Pretoria, Central Statistical Service, 1988, Section 5. This is also the source for Tables 16.2 and 16.3.

Although the discontinuity in the data for black education makes it difficult to draw comparisons over the entire period, it is remarkable that black pupil numbers increased by an annual average rate of 1,4 per cent over the ten year period 1975–85, despite the fact that the TBVC countries disappear from the statistics during that time.[8] The decline in the pupil:teacher ratio over the

Table 16.2:

AVERAGE ANNUAL RATES OF INCREASE IN PUPIL
AND TEACHER NUMBERS AND SCHOOL SIZE
1975–85 AND 1985–87 (PERCENTAGES).

	Pupil numbers	Teacher numbers	School size
1975–85			
Blacks	1,4	4,3	1,3
Coloureds	2,6	4,5	1,9
Indians	2,4	4,3	0,1
Whites	1,7	2,3	1,8
1985–87			
Blacks	1,1	1,1	0,7
Coloureds	0,1	0,9	0,3
Indians	0,0	1,0	–0,4
Whites	–0,8	0,6	–4,3

decade is distressingly high in the TBVC countries. Black pupil and teacher numbers have increased at almost the same rate over the two year period 1985–1987, leaving the ratio very close to 41 pupils per teacher. The average size of black schools has increased over the 12 years, indicating that pressure was experienced by capital facilities in this sector.

Pupil:teacher ratios fell steadily over the entire period for the other three population groups. Indeed, for Indians and whites, the numbers of teachers continued to increase over the later two year period, while the number of Indian pupils fell fractionally, and the number of white pupils decreased by 0,8 per cent per annum. The disparity between black facilities on the one hand, and Indian and white on the other, is highlighted by the fact that while black schools became more crowded over the period 1985–87, the average size of both Indian and white schools fell by 0,4 per cent and 4,3 per cent respectively.

Table 16.3:

AVERAGE ANNUAL RATES OF INCREASE OF STUDENT NUMBERS,
ALL TERTIARY INSTITUTIONS, 1975–85, 1985–87, & 1975–87.

	1975–85	1985–87	1975–87
Blacks	8,76	16,10	9,95
Coloureds	9,19	0,80	7,74
Indians	NA	NA	6,12
Whites	4,81	–4,80	3,15

NOTE:
No figures were available for Indian student numbers in 1985.

Table 16.3 reveals an interesting pattern of growth in the number of tertiary students at universities, technical and vocational institutions and teacher training colleges. Over the entire 12 year period, the number of black students increased at a rate of almost 10 per cent per annum and whites at only 3 per cent, while the coloured and Indian growth rates fell between these two extremes. However, the first two columns show that there were some significant differences in the rates within the period. Over the first decade, the annual increase in numbers in coloured tertiary education was actually greater than that of blacks (just over and just under 9 per cent respectively), and both of these were somewhat higher than the white rate of just below 5 per cent. However, over the period 1985–87, the annual rate of increase in black students in tertiary education nearly doubled to 16 per cent; the coloured student population hardly grew at all (less than 1 per cent); and the number of white students fell at an annual average rate of nearly 5 per cent.

In addition to the recent extremely rapid increase in the number of black tertiary students at all institutions, it is important to realize that several universities, including those traditionally regarded as 'black', are fast becoming non-racial. The following facts provide some indication of the changes occurring in the student population of our universities:

* The proportion of black students at all universities (including UNISA) increased from less than one-twelfth in 1975 to one-quarter in 1987.
* The percentage of black students at all the so-called 'white' residential universities increased from 0,4 per cent in 1975 to 3,9 per cent in 1987.
* Of all the black students at the universities (excluding UNISA) in 1987, 18,2 per cent were not at the so-called 'black' universities.
* In 1987, less than 56 per cent of Indian university students attended the University of Durban-Westville.
* The racial composition of UNISA students changed dramatically over the period 1975–87. The proportion of blacks rose from 13 per cent to 28 per cent, and there were also slight increases in the percentages of coloureds and Indians (from 4 to 5 per cent, and from 8 to 11 per cent, respectively). The proportion of whites dropped correspondingly from 75 per cent to 56 per cent.[9]

A more detailed examination of the composition of tertiary students in South Africa indicates that in 1987, 43 per cent of the tertiary students were at universities, 41 per cent were training to be teachers, and only 16 per cent were at all the technical and vocational training institutions. Given the need for skilled and technically trained personnel in our country, this would seem to be a singularly inappropriate distribution of tertiary students. In the United Kingdom, by way of comparison, 48 per cent of the tertiary students were at Polytechnics in 1984.[10]

Educational forecasts involve complex estimations, and should be based on cohort analysis and appropriate survival ratios, so no attempt has been made to forecast directly from the data used in Tables 16.1 to 16.3. These tables do, however, give a good idea of the recent trends, and it is clear that, as far as school enrolments are concerned, 'the future growth in the number of pupils will come from blacks, while coloured, Asian (*sic*) and white pupil numbers show a declining tendency over the long term' (Dostal, 1988, p. 18). Dostal's forecasts of pupil numbers for the year 2020 bear out this statement. They are shown in Table 16.4, together with the totals for 1987.

Table 16.4:
SCHOOL PUPIL NUMBERS IN THOUSANDS, 1987, AND FORECASTS FOR 2020, INCLUDING THE TBVC COUNTRIES

	1987	2020
Blacks	6 645	12 401
Coloureds	837	778
Indians	237	228
Whites	1 062	899

SOURCE:
Dostal, *Notebook on Educational Trends and Perspectives*, Stellenbosch, Institute for Futures Research, 1988, p. 18.

Educational expenditure

How much is it costing to meet the needs of South Africa's burgeoning educational system? This question will be answered in two parts. First, the extent of government expenditure will be examined; and then this will be related to the concept of social cost, which will give a more comprehensive indication of the use of resources for education.

Between 1975 and 1985 (the most recent year for which detailed expenditure estimates are available), expenditure by all government authorities on all levels of education increased in current terms from R1 045 million to R6 563 million, or by a multiple of 6,3. The amounts spent on black education rose from R165 million to R2 178 million, or by a multiple of 13,2. The white institutions, however, still received just over half of the funds in 1985. Fifty-eight per cent of all the expenditure went to the primary schools, and 41 per cent to the secondary schools.[11]

All these figures must, of course, be viewed in relation to inflation and the changes in pupil and student numbers. Taking both these factors into account, expenditure per pupil increased over the decade in real terms[12] for all groups, with the annual increase being the highest for blacks at 9 per cent, and the lowest for whites at 2 per cent; while increases for coloureds and Indians were 6 per cent and 5 per cent respectively. This resulted in the average expenditure per school pupil increasing over the decade by a multiple of almost eight for blacks, while the multiples for coloureds, Indians and whites were six, five and four respectively.

Since 1985, the gap has apparently closed even further, with blacks experiencing positive real rates of increase in expenditure per pupil in 1986 (5 per cent) and 1987 (6 per cent). There was an extremely high real rate of increase of 18 per cent for Indian pupils in 1987, after a decline in 1986; but the other two groups experienced real declines over both years, with a real rate of decrease of 22 per cent for whites in 1987.

A comparison of rates of growth between the population groups indicates a closing of the gap between white and black per capita expenditures, but an examination of the relative position of these groups shows that there is still a vast discrepancy. In 1975, the ratio of white to black per capita expenditure was almost 15; by 1985 it had virtually halved, having fallen to 7,6. By 1987, the average ratio had dropped even further, to 5,4.[13]

All these facts indicate that the authorities are recognizing and beginning to address the problem of inequity in schooling expenditure, but there is still a long way to go.

When examining expenditure at the tertiary educational level, the concept of 'per student expenditure' for the different groups must be treated with caution, for neither the universities nor the technikons are amenable to the clearcut racial classification which may be applied to schools and teacher training colleges. Bearing in mind this limitation, it nevertheless appears that, while average expenditure increased over the decade 1975 to 1985 by a multiple of about 3,5 for all students, the increase for black students at all tertiary institutions — a multiple in excess of six — was well above this. In real terms, there was a fractional increase of 0,2 per cent per annum for each tertiary-level student. Comparing the groups, only blacks experienced an annual increase in expenditure per student (6,4 per cent), while the annual decreases for the other groups were 0,1 per cent for coloureds, 0,2 per cent for whites, and 4 per cent for the average Indian student.[14]

The most recent available statistics on educational expenditure are those provided by the Institute of Race Relations. According to this source, the total expenditure budgeted for all the education departments in South Africa for the year ending March 1988 was R8 133 million, distributed as indicated in Table 16.5.

When quantifying the 'costs of education' in South Africa, it is common practice to cite the totals of the departmental votes of the many educational authorities. However, of the total public sector educational expenditure of R6,5 billion incurred in 1985, current expenditure from education department votes totalled R5 715 million, and capital expenditure on education R573 million.[15] Together, these constituted 96 per cent of public sector expenditure.

Table 16.5:
TOTAL BUDGETED EDUCATIONAL EXPENDITURE IN S. A., 1987–88

	R'000
Black education in 'white' areas	1 487 840
Self-governing states	1 116 427
Independent states (TBVC)	795 983
Coloured education	1 007 569
Indian education	404 647
White education	3 320 700
Total	8 133 166

SOURCE:
Race Relations Survey, 1987/88, p. 150.

If one assumes that the same proportion applied in 1987, the departmental expenditure of R8 133 million would have constituted 96 per cent of an overall total expenditure on education of R8 472 million. This, incidentally, represents 17,7 per cent of total government expenditure, compared to a proportion of just over 19 per cent in the year ending March 1986. This percentage will rise to 18,6 per cent by March 1990, according to the 1989 budget speech.[16]

The proportion of the gross national product devoted to education has recently fluctuated around 6 per cent. Notwithstanding the numerous features of the South African economy which lead many to consider it to be predominantly third world in character (Moulder, pp.1–5), this percentage is closer to Psacharopoulos's 'developed countries' average of 5,7 per cent for 1974, than to the 'developing countries' figure of 3,9 per cent (1980, p. 6).

Total social costs

The expenditure by the authorities is only a part of the total resource cost of education in the country. Indeed, public sector educational expenditure accounted for only 61 per cent of the total social costs of nearly R11 billion in 1985. The two further significant components of social cost were private direct costs and opportunity costs, which constituted about 12 per cent and 18 per cent, respectively.

The remaining 10 per cent of the social cost is made up of private sector contributions to formal and non-formal education. This means that the state contributes about six times as much to education as does the private business sector. If the proportion of contributions from this sector could be increased over time, the system would eventually become less reliant on state guidance and support, and there would probably be an increase in allocative efficiency. But such an increase in the amount of private support via direct contributions would not automatically result in a substantial increase in resources. There is a limit to the private sector's capacity for providing financial support, either through direct donations or via the fiscus.

Table 16.6:
PERCENTAGE DISTRIBUTION OF TOTAL SOCIAL COSTS
BY POPULATION GROUP, AND BY LEVEL OF EDUCATION, 1985

	Social costs	Population percentage	Government educational institution enrolment percentage
Blacks	35,7	68,1	73,2
Coloureds	10,2	10,5	9,8
Indians	5,1	3,2	3,1
Whites	49,0	18,2	13,9
Total	100,0	100,0	100,0
Level 1	34,5		
Level 2	34,9		
Level 3	30,6		
Total	100,0		

SOURCES:
Trotter, 1988, Tables 6.1, 6.2 and 6.3, pp. 84, 86 and 87; and Bureau of Market Research, 1986, pp. 25 and 53, for expenditure on Training Schemes.

Table 16.6 allocates the total costs among the four population groups, and shows the equivalent percentages for the population composition and for enrolments at government educational institutions. The percentage of total costs relating to coloureds does not differ significantly from the proportion of the population they comprise, or percentage they form of the total enrolments: these are all around 10 per cent. About 5 per cent of the total costs is attributable to Indians, which is slightly higher than their 3 per cent representation in the population and in total enrolments. Glaring disparities occur for blacks and whites. About 36 per cent of the social costs are incurred in respect of blacks, who constitute over two-thirds of the population, and account for almost three-quarters of enrolments. However, nearly one-half of the costs are incurred on behalf of whites, who constitute less than one-fifth of the population and one-seventh of enrolments.

Table 16.6 also shows the division of social cost between Levels 1, 2 and 3 — primary and pre-primary schooling, secondary schooling, and all other types of education respectively. Slightly more than one-third of the social cost was incurred in respect of each of the first two levels of schooling. It is interesting to note that the proportion of costs allocated to pre-tertiary schooling (69,4 per cent) is very close to the average of 70,7 per cent for six countries calculated by the World Bank in 1980 and cited by Psacharopoulos (1980, p. 6).[17]

Empirical evidence for South Africa

What conclusions can be drawn from the data presented in the previous section? There can be no doubt about the gross imbalance between expenditure on whites and that on the other groups. Although the inequity has been reduced over the 12 years considered — for example, the white:black per capita real expenditure ratio fell from 12 to 5,4 — it is still at an unacceptable level, particularly when coupled with the perceived inequalities in the standards of education of the black and white systems. It was also suggested that there may be an over-emphasis on university education, and a relative neglect of technological and vocational training institutions.

While the statistics on the structure and finances of our systems provide an essential background to an understanding of the problem facing South African education, they do not provide evidence of any link between education and economic growth or development; nor do they do more than suggest directions for future educational development. However, there have over the years been frequent references in the economic and educational literature to the significance of education for economic growth and development in South Africa.[18] For example, Joubert found that formal education contributed 14,5 per cent to the growth rate of the gross national product between 1960 and 1970 (1976, p. 258).[19]

The author undertook a study of social rates of return to education in the Durban Metropolitan Region in 1984. The weighted average social rates of return were found to be nearly 16 per cent for coloureds, about 14 per cent for blacks and Indians, and just over 13 per cent for whites. All these exceeded the inflation-adjusted return to physical capital in South Africa, which stood at 12,5 per cent at the time (1984, p. 42), suggesting that continued investment in the education of all groups would be of net social benefit to the community. The highest marginal rates of return were recorded for the senior primary level for coloureds, technical secondary education for Indians, and junior primary education for blacks, in that order.[20]

While by no means claiming complete generality for the results of the Durban study, it is felt that some of the conclusions reached for that region may well be applicable to this country as a whole. For example it is suggested that society will benefit from continuing to apply resources to education for all population groups but that the greatest emphasis should be on the provision of primary education for the black and coloured communities and of technical training for the Indian community (Trotter, 1984, pp. 88–9).

What of the evidence linking education and the distribution of incomes in South Africa? Over ten years ago, the author conducted a study using time-series as well as cross-sectional South African data (1977). An hypothesis that higher levels of education led to higher median annual incomes was strongly supported. The effects of a change in the educational level on the distribution of incomes were not so clearly established, although the analysis was consistent with the suggestion that more education could tend to improve this distribution, which was in line with the Marin & Psacharopoulos (1976) hypothesis referred to near the beginning of this chapter. Finally, there was tentative support for the hypothesis that greater equality in the distribution of educational attainments was associated with more equality in the distribution of incomes over the period 1960–70. The implication was that the continued expansion of educational facilities in this country would not adversely affect the very inequitable income distribution, and might indeed improve it.

However, results for one period need not necessarily be generally applicable at all times. A set of data which contradict the conclusion suggested above was pointed out by Malherbe: the share of educational expenditure received by blacks in South Africa rose from 11 per cent in 1930 to over 25 per cent in 1970, while their share of incomes remained constant over that period at about 27 per cent (1977, pp. 653–4). The matter is thus far from resolved, and it would be unwise to claim that, in post-apartheid South Africa, the provision of additional education — or even steps to increase the equity of its provision — would guarantee greater equality in income distribution.

What of the future?

There is little doubt that expenditure on education in this country will have to be given continued high priority in the future. Quite apart from its significance for economic growth, there is no doubt that increasing the educational level of the people, and in particular attaining parity in expenditure in as short a time as possible, are pressing political imperatives. There is simply no point in debating the finer points about the rates of return to different levels, or the relative contributions of human and physical capital to economic growth, while the average black pupil is still receiving one-fifth as much of the resources allocated to the average white; or while 58 per cent of the teachers in the black educational system and 38 per cent in coloured schools do not have a post-secondary qualification.[21]

The Freedom Charter implies the need for one educational system which provides equal education for all who desire it:

> All apartheid laws and practices shall be set aside ... There shall be equal status ...
> in the schools for all national groups and races ... Education ... shall be equal for
> all children.

The de Lange Committee Report also propounded basic principles which are fundamental to educational reform, and it referred to the necessity for 'equal opportunity for education... for every inhabitant, irrespective of race, colour, creed or sex...' (1981, p.14) The Buthelezi Commission's report of the education specialist working group called for a 'common high standard of educational provision to be achieved as soon as possible', and also stated that 'There is a need for a unified system of education under the direction of one Minister, with non-discriminatory provision of educational services for all' (1982, p. 272). The broad principle of equality of educational provision has apparently also been accepted by the present South African government, although the organizational means whereby it is to be implemented remain in dispute.

If these principles are to become more than grandiose pronouncements, there will have to be a massive injection of funds. The formidable financial implication of attaining parity within a reasonable period of time was a problem stressed by the de Lange Committee, and they pointed out in their Main Report that the attainment of equality within ten years at the national level would necessitate an increase in current expenditure of between 75 per cent and 160 per cent in real terms, which is clearly an almost impossible task.

Now parity could be achieved either by finding additional resources in vast quantities for black, coloured and Indian education, thus raising these groups to the level of white per capita expenditure; or by redistributing available resources, so all groups enjoy the same average expenditure. The first alternative is economically unrealistic, except perhaps over an unacceptably long period of time, given the wide range of social demands made upon the fiscus. The second alternative, while theoretically capable of far more rapid implementation, will be politically unpopular with the present electorate, for it means a rapid lowering of the resources devoted to the average white pupil. A mild form of redistribution has been evident for some time. Although the increases in national expenditure in the 1989/90 budget for black education and for all education were the same (19 per cent), the budgeted increase in black educational expenditure in the previous year was 40 per cent.

An obvious problem is the precise manner in which significant redistribution can take place. Although funds can be fairly easily switched from white to black schools in respect of equipment, it will not be possible to divert salary expenditures without a lengthy period of training — even assuming that the present teacher-training facilities are to be used far more efficiently, and on an integrated basis. A further avenue for redistribution is presumably the area of capital construction, particularly given the vast backlog of classrooms in black education, and their comparative aggregate oversupply in white education.

The only way to hasten the timetable for the achievement of parity is to find more funds for education. It should be noted that privatization, while it has important allocative effects on the quantities of different types and levels of education, would not ensure a greater quantity of resources. It could, however, reduce the burden on the fiscus, as would a scheme to charge university students fees equivalent to the full cost of their tuition.[22] The only way to secure more of the national product for education would be to sacrifice its use for other purposes; just as the only way for the state to find more public money for education would be to drastically re-order its priorities.

The problem is compounded by the probable cost of the wasteful duplication which takes place in this country's educational system. A recent Urban Foundation study attempted 'to determine the extent of, and, if possible, to estimate the cost of under-utilized facilities; duplication of administration, and organizational deficiencies; and to comment on potential economies which might arise from privatization, rationalization and integration' (see Trotter, 1988, p. 90). This turned out to be an extremely difficult task, since officials of the various educational authorities were understandably reluctant to suggest which amounts of expenditure could become redundant if authorities were merged, or if control were centralized.

The only known printed estimate of the cost of duplication is that suggested by du Pisanie & Meintjes (1986). They assumed that the elimination of duplication would result in an entirely arbitrary reduction of 25 per cent in the expenditure on legislative and general executive functions. However, a different view was put forward by Corbett (1988, p. 14), who argued that this may be rather optimistic, particularly if there is an increase in the provision of services following a unified administration: more, not less, bureaucrats may be necessary.

Referring to all the functions of government, Savage has stated that, 'The economic costs of running 151 Departments, each having separate managerial and administrative staff, separate budgets, separate accounting procedures and often providing duplicated facilities and services (are) difficult to probe' (1986, p. 9). He then cited an estimate by David Dalling, MP, who claimed that the cost of duplicated services in the field of education was R100 million annually. If this was the figure in 1985, it would have constituted only about 1 per cent of the total social cost of education; or 1,5 per cent of the total government expenditure on education.

Quite apart from the possible savings which might result from the elimination of a multiplicity of departments administering education, there is the very real waste implicit in the under-utilization of facilities. Savage pointed out that there were 'over 1 035 spare places in eight "white" schools in central Cape Town' in 1986 (ibid., p. 16). Ardington drew attention to the contraction in numbers of pupils at white primary schools in the suburbs of Durban in 1988, while black pupils living nearby had to attend schools in distant areas (1987, pp. 53–6). The figures in Tables 16.1 and 16.2 are indeed consistent with these facts: between 1985 and 1987, white pupil numbers declined by almost 1 per cent per annum, and the pupil:teacher ratio fell from over 19 to below 17.

Gaydon cited the Minister of Education and Culture in the House of Assembly as stating that the number of vacant places at 'white' teacher training colleges increased by 5 per cent between 1986 and 1987 (1987, p. 15).[23] Two of these colleges closed down over that period. During 1986, more than one-fifth of the places at all 'white' colleges were vacant, and they could have been used to increase the number of trained black teachers by some 10 per cent. The demand for white teachers will continue to decline in future, while the inevitable trends in black education make it imperative to increase the number of teachers for that system at a rate which is simply not possible within the present facilities set aside for them.

The financial implications of rationalizing the use of these facilities are substantial: if 'white' vacancies were used for the training of black teachers, capital expenditure totalling about R40 million could be saved. The Department of Education and Training is planning to spend more than R73 million on segregated training facilities which would be available at the earliest by 1990. The waste implicit in this is obvious, when compared with the situation which could prevail if there was integration of the teacher-training facilities.

Of course, the additional colleges planned for blacks might not even guarantee parity. For declining white pupil growth rates will make it progressively more difficult to bring black pupil:teacher ratios into line with those in the white educational sector. In its determination to pursue the apartheid option, the government is actually shooting at a moving target.

During October and November, 1988, five 'Education Futures' seminars were held under the auspices of Education Board of the Mobil Foundation of South Africa. According to Professor Mark Delancey, who prepared a draft summary of the proceedings:

> The most widely held view that found expression in all of the seminars was a sense that something is seriously wrong with the current education system in South Africa... One point did emerge, and with almost universal approval: education in the future of this country must be non-racial education... There was (also) wide agreement that education was inadequately funded (1988, pp. 1, 5 & 31).

This epitomizes the crisis in education today: the political dimension is considered as important as the economic. There are other aspects which also need urgent attention: for example, the structural and the organizational, the cultural and linguistic, the technological, and above all the pedagogical. Matters such as the purpose of education, the motivation of the teachers and the students and pupils, and the appropriateness of the curriculum, are beyond the scope of this chapter, but are fundamental to the effectiveness of education in a post-apartheid South Africa. Thus, while it is often argued that there should be a greater emphasis on general education, literacy and numeracy have always proved to be significant in the development process, and it is common knowledge that basic and primary education are an essential component of the educational system of any less developed country (Foster, 1987, p. 96). This is certainly consistent with one of the research findings cited earlier: 'The greatest emphasis should be on the provision of primary education for the black and coloured communities...' (Trotter, 1984, pp. 88–9).

What is the role to be played by non-formal education in the future of the system? Recent research has shown that this sector commanded only a minute fraction (0,2 per cent) of the total resources in 1985. It seems likely that this fraction is growing almost exponentially. Contributions from the business sector to non-formal activities appeared to have doubled in real terms during each of the two years 1984 and 1985 (Trotter, 1988, p. 54). However, it seems unlikely that non-formal education could ever make any serious inroads into the formal structures, given the numbers of pupils involved. In any event, there is no evidence to indicate that non-formal education is more cost-effective than formal.

From the economist's perspective then, it is inevitable that the one problem which seems to loom like a spectre above all others, is the lack of resources for educating the rapidly-growing population. Is it too much to hope that the planners and politicians will listen to all those interested in the future of our educational systems, and heed the signals provided by the research? What is needed for political stability and healthy economic growth in a post-apartheid South Africa is a unified non-racial educational system, which moves swiftly and resolutely towards redressing the various imbalances of the past. Resources must be found for the continued expansion of primary education, for literacy programmes, for teacher training and upliftment, and for technical and vocational training. Above all, an inequitable racial distribution of resources, apart from being wasteful, will not be tolerated in a new dispensation, and must be eliminated as rapidly as possible if all are to play a productive role in a thriving future South Africa.

Notes

1 See, for example, Foster, 1987 and Holsinger, 1987.
2 For a more detailed discussion, see Trotter, 1988, pp. 70–4.
3 Report of the Work Committee: Education Financing, Pretoria, Human Sciences Research Council, July 1981, p. 1.
4 The objections against this practice are legion, but there are also defenders of the methodology (see Blaug, 1976, pp. 200–5). Psacharopoulos (1980, pp. 40–4) considers the case against the use of earnings as an indication of productivity enhancement in some detail, and concludes that, while many of the arguments are interesting and, indeed, valid in their own right, they do not constitute a damaging attack on this approach.
5 For a more detailed discussion of this and other related aspects, see Blaug, ibid., chs. 2, 6 and 7.
6 See for example Smith & Morgan, 1970; Hoerr, 1973; and Oulton, 1974.
7 Prior to 1985, this figure was 17, since regular white schooling and teacher training was administered, controlled and financed by the four autonomous Provincial

administrations. Since 1985, this educational sector has been financially administered by the House of Assembly through its Department of Education and Culture.
The Department of National Education is responsible for the so-called 'white' universities, the Technikons, and certain special schools for whites. All aspects of the
education of the Indian and the coloured communities fall respectively under the
House of Delegates and the House of Representatives. Black education in so-called
'white areas' of the country, including schools, special schools, the so-called 'black
universities' and Technikons for blacks, is the concern of the Department of Education and Training. To complete the picture, education in what are now the six
self-governing states and the four independent countries is controlled by their own
individual Departments of Education (the six self governing states are Gazankulu,
Kangwane, KwaNdebele, KwaZulu, Lebowa and QwaQwa; the four independent
countries are Bophuthatswana, Ciskei, Transkei and Venda).

8 If the TBVC countries are included, the average annual rate of growth of black pupil
numbers was almost 5 per cent (Trotter, 1988, p. 23.)

9 *South African Statistics 1988*, pp. 5.39–5.42.

10 Central Statistical Office, *Annual Abstract of Statistics*, 1987 Edition, London, Her
Majesty's Stationery Office, Table 5.6, p. 94.

11 Trotter, 1988, Table 2.5, p. 18.

12 That is, correcting for increases in the consumer price index.

13 In the white community, about four-fifths as much is spent on primary and pre-
primary as on secondary schooling. The ratio is just under two-thirds for coloureds
and Indians, and less than half in the case of black schools. The data in this section
are derived from Trotter, 1988, p.23; *Race Relations Survey, 1987/88*, Johannesburg,
South African Institute of Race Relations, 1988, p. 151 (for 1986 and 1987 figures);
and *South African Statistics 1988*, p. 8.21 (for the consumer price index).

14 Trotter, 1988, Table 2.5, p. 18; and *South African Statistics 1988*, Section 8.

15 Trotter, 1988, p. 85.

16 *South African Statistics 1988*, Section 21; Table 9, p.13; and *Statistical/Economic Review
in Connection with the Budget Speech, 1989/90*, W.P.B.–'89, p. 31.

17 The countries are Colombia (66 per cent), Ethiopia (75 per cent), Mexico (77 per
cent), Senegal (80 per cent), Syria (64 per cent) and Tanzania (62 per cent).

18 For example, see Terreblanche, 1970; Sadie, 1971; and Malherbe, 1977.

19 Joubert used an earnings function approach.

20 The rates obtained in this study were obviously lower than the private rates calculated by Joubert. Furthermore, black education was excluded from his analysis. It is
comforting to note that the rates of return obtained in South African studies are not
grossly out of line with rates calculated by Psacharopoulos for a sample of other countries. See Psacharopoulos, 1973, p. 24. For a detailed discussion of the comparison,
see Trotter, 1988, pp. 79–81.

21 *Race Relations Survey, 1987/88*, p. 166.

22 This step is logically implied by a comparison of the private and social benefits
of tertiary and basic school education. The political sensitivity of such a measure,
however, would almost certainly necessitate a government-sponsored bursary scheme,
which would tend to reduce the impact of the scheme. See the Report of the Work
Committee of the CUP Investigation, Committee of University Principals, 1987.

23 This is also the source of the statistics in the rest of this paragraph.

References

Ardington, A., 'Shoes for Cinderella', *Leadership SA*, Indaba Issue, 1987.

Blaug, M., *An Introduction to the Economics of Education*, Penguin: Harmondsworth, 1976.

Bowles, S.,'Understanding Unequal Economic Opportunity',*The American Economic Review*, May 1973.

Bureau of Market Research, Report no. 133, Pretoria, 1986.

Buthelezi Commission, *The Requirements for Stability and Development in KwaZulu and Natal*, vol. 2, H & H Publications: Durban, 1982.

Carnoy, M., *et al.*, 'The Political Economy of Financing Education in Developing Countries', Paper presented to the Annual Meeting of the Bellagio Group, Ottawa, Canada, May 1982.

Central Statistical Service,*South African Statistics 1988*, Government Printer: Pretoria, 1988.

Committee of University Principals, *The Responsibility and Influence of Various Sectors such as the State and the Public and Private Sectors in Respect of the Financing of Universities*, Report of the Work Committee of the CUP Investigation, Committee of University Principals: Pretoria, 1987.

Corbett, P., 'The Limits to Economic Policy Differences between Members of a Federation: with Special Reference to the KwaZulu/Natal Region', Unpublished paper given at the Workshop of Regionalism and Restructuring in Natal, University of Natal: Durban, 28–31 January, 1988.

Delancey, M., *The Education Futures Seminars: A Summary of Discussion*, Unpublished paper: Cape Town, 1988.

de Lange Committee Report, Human Sciences Research, *Provision of Education in the RSA*. Council: Pretoria, July 1981.

Denison, E.F., *The Sources of Economic Growth in the United States and the Alternatives Before Us*, Committee for Economic Development: New York, 1962.

Dostal, E.,*Notebook on Educational Trends and Perspectives*, Institute for Futures Research: Stellenbosch, 1988.

du Pisanie J.A. & Meintjes G.J., *Implications of Fiscal Parity in KwaZulu/Natal by 1995 and 2000 Respectively*. A Report Commissioned by the Durban Metropolitan Chamber of Commerce, October 1986.

Foster, P., 'The Contribution of Education to Development', in Psacharopoulos, G. (ed.), *Economics of Education: Research and Studies*, Pergamon Press: Oxford, 1987.

Gaydon, V., *Race against the Ratios*, South African Institute of Race Relations: Johannesburg, 1987.

Hoerr, O.D., 'Education and Equity in Malaysia', *Economic Development and Cultural Change*, January 1973.

Holsinger, D.B., 'Modernisation and Education', in Psacharopoulos, G. (ed.), *Economics of Education: Research and Studies*, Pergamon Press: Oxford, 1987.

Joubert, R.J.O., *Enkele Ekonomiese Aspekte van Suid-Afrikaanse Onderwysinvestering: 'n Verdienstefunksiebenadering*, Unpublished Dissertation: Johannesburg, 1976.

Malherbe, E.G., *Education in South Africa — vol. 2: 1923–77*, Juta: Cape Town, 1977.

Marin, A. & Psacaharopoulos, G., 'Schooling and Income Distribution', *The Review of Economics and Statistics*, August 1976.

Moulder, J., *Academic Support Programmes: Some Neglected Factors in a Complex Environment*, Unpublished paper: Pietermaritzburg, undated.

Oulton, N., 'The Distribution of Education and the Distribution of Income', *Economica*, November 1974.

Psacharopoulos, G., *Returns to Education*, Elsevier: London, 1973.

Psacharopoulos, G., *Higher Education in Developing Countries: A Cost-Benefit Analysis*, The World Bank: Washington, 1980.

RSA, *Statistical/Economic Review in Connection with the Budget Speech, 1989/90*, W.P.B.–'89.

Sadie, J.L., 'Population and Economic Development in South Africa', *The South African Journal of Economics*, September, 1971.

Savage, M., 'The Cost of Apartheid', Inaugural Lecture, University of Cape Town, 27 August 1986.

Smith, J.D. & Morgan, J.N., 'Variability of Economic Well-being and its Determinants', *The American Economic Review*, Papers and Proceedings, May 1970.

Terreblanche, S.J., 'The Relative Contribution of Tangible and Human Capital Formation to Economic Growth', *The South African Journal of Economics*, March, 1970.

Trotter, G.J., 'Education and Income Distribution', *The South African Journal of Economics*, December, 1977.

Trotter, G.J., *A Survey of Educational Facilities and Social Rates of Return to Education in the Durban Metropolitan Region*, Economic Research Unit: Durban, 1984.

Trotter, G.J., *The Social Costs of South African Education*, Economic Research Unit: Durban, 1988.

The choice of trade strategy: past reflections and future prospects

17

Merle Holden

Introduction

In developed economies any analysis of trade policy works on the assumption that there isn't a particular bias towards import-competing or exportable industries. In developing countries on the other hand, and particularly among development economists, there has been the perception that the economy requires a firm hand in allocating resources according to a policy of either import substitution or export promotion.

During the 1950s and 1960s the predominant trade strategy adopted by developing countries was import substitution. This choice was based on the post-war arguments supporting export pessimism and the expected future benefits of protecting infant industry. Prebisch (1952) argued that the declining terms of trade for primary products would prejudice any developing country adopting an outward looking policy. Even if a country fostered manufacturing industry, Nurkse (1959) pessimistically estimated that exports from developing countries would not be absorbed into foreign markets. In Latin America in particular these views were taken as justification for encouraging industrialization for the domestic market through comprehensive protective measures.

During this period, world output grew at 5 per cent per annum while world trade grew at 7 per cent per annum. This growth confounded the export pessimists and benefited those countries which either actively promoted exports or did not heavily bias their economies towards import substitution. The Far East economies of Hong Kong, South Korea, Taiwan and Singapore — the Gang of Four — are examples of the pursuit of this strategy. In the main, academic opinion has swung firmly behind the adoption of similar policies for other developing economies. However, the oil crises of the 1970s, the debt crisis of the 1980s and the over-valued dollar in the early 1980s have resulted in declining world output and trade. These lower growth rates have resulted in pressure for protection in the developed world, and have raised the spectre of export pessimism once again.

In South Africa the experience with trade strategy was similar to that in many other developing countries. In the post-war period import substitution was vigorously encouraged. This was followed by a reassessment in the 1970s, with attempts to encourage production for export. Since 1986 South Africa has had to face economic sanctions against agricultural goods, coal, clothing and textiles in the USA and parts of the European Community.

The questions which will be addressed in this paper relate to the effectiveness of past trade strategy in South Africa. In particular, the role of exports in promoting industrialization will be examined. Finally, consideration will be given to the appropriate trade strategy for South Africa in the face of these economic sanctions.

Definitions of trade strategies

Trade strategies have been classified according to the degree of incentive given to produce either for the export market or the domestic market. The strategy of import substitution has been defined as the adoption of an effective exchange rate for imports which exceeds that for exports. An export promoting regime occurs when the effective exchange rate for exports and imports is equal (Bhagwati, 1978). Where the effective exchange rate for exports exceeds that for imports the strategy has been classified as ultra export promoting (Bhagwati, 1988).

Figure 17.1:

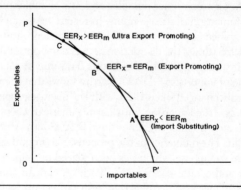

The effective exchange rate for exports (EER_x) is the number of units of domestic currency received for a one dollar international transaction, plus the value of export encouragement schemes and subsidies to exporters. The effective exchange rate for imports (EER_m) is the number of units of domestic currency paid for a one dollar international transaction, plus tariffs, import premiums and surcharges.

The definitions of the different trade strategies relate to the average level of incentives given. This means that even if on average greater incentives are being given to exporting firms than to import substituting firms, it is possible that some import substituting firms could enjoy a higher level of incentive than the average given to exporters.

Figure 17.1 shows the production patterns of an economy, given the different definitions of trade strategy. PP' represents the production possibility curve between exportables and importables. At point A, EER_x is less than EER_m, and production is biased towards production for the domestic market. At point B where EER_x is equal to EER_m, the regime is export promoting; and at point C where the EER_x is greater than the EER_m the economy is biased towards the production of exportables, and is classified as ultra export promoting.

Import substitution in South Africa

Since the Second World War, import substitution has been encouraged in South Africa through a system of import tariffs and quantitative restrictions. The import quotas have been applied with varying severity to deal with recurring balance of payments problems. The Viljoen Commission pointed out in 1958 that the system of quantitative controls also provided domestic industry with adequate protection. Lachman (1974) suggests that during the 1960s the system of import permits, which favoured imports of capital goods and excluded a wide range of foreign consumer durables and non-durables, contributed to a structural transformation of the economy. In recent years, import quotas have been gradually phased out to be replaced with equivalent tariffs.

McCarthy (1988) draws the distinction between import substitution defined as the change in the composition of imports, and import substitution which reduces the ratio of imports to GDP. McCarthy shows that the ratio of imports to GDP has hardly changed since 1920, with the average propensity to import remaining at 0,24. In comparison with Latin American economies which in general have an average import:GDP ratio of 0,10, South Africa's import tendency is still high. The difference in the propensity to import can be explained both by the heavy emphasis which has been placed on import substitution in both consumer and capital goods by the Latin American countries, and the maintenance of higher levels of effective tariff protection on consumer goods and low levels of protection on capital equipment by South Africa.

An early study of effective tariff protection in South Africa (Holden, 1974) shows an average level of 15 per cent on goods for domestic consumption, 6 per cent on intermediate goods and 2 per cent on capital goods in 1963/64. The disaggregated levels of effective protection over the period 1956/57 to 1963/64 were used in a later study (Holden & Holden, 1978) to test for an association between effective rates of tariff protection and resource changes in the economy.

This study showed that those industries where substantial import substitution had taken place were industries which had enjoyed high levels of effective protection. In addition resources had been attracted into these industries from the rest of the economy.

For the period 1967–73, Zarenda (1977) shows that import replacement occurred largely in coal and other mining, other foodstuffs, textiles, printing and publishing, basic chemicals, metal products, and other manufacturing industries. Furthermore, Zarenda finds that those sectors which experienced negative import substitution over this period were grain, sugar and animal feeds, wool scouring, cotton ginning and dyeing, clothing, footwear, synthetic resins, plastic materials and manmade fibres, paints, plastics, machinery and motor vehicle parts.

Further estimates were made of the degree of import substitution for the period 1971–78. The methodology took into account the different input coefficients for 1971 and 1978 (Morley & Smith, 1970), ensuring that both the direct and indirect imports were included in the estimates of import substitution.[1]

Table 17.1 shows the results of these calculations. Motor vehicle parts experienced the greatest degree of import substitution followed by other manufacturing, wool scouring and cotton ginning, other basic chemicals, textiles, other machinery, wood and wood products and non-ferrous metals. Those sectors where significant import penetration or negative import substitution took place were other transport equipment, agricultural machinery, railway equipment and printing. The calculations show that the bulk of import substitution was occurring in those sectors producing intermediate goods.

It is not possible to establish whether the level of tariff protection has influenced the degree of import substitution, as there are no recently published studies of effective protection for the South African economy. However, McCarthy (1988, p. 9) reports that 'the modal effective rates of protection for non-primary goods have been estimated to fall between 20 and 30 per cent.' When determining whether or not protection has influenced the pattern of import substitution, access to disaggregated effective protective rates is necessary, and even then the ranking of these rates and their effects on resource allocation would have to be treated with care (Holden & Holden, 1978).

Table 17.2 shows that import substitution is all but complete in the consumer goods industries. The import penetration ratio for clothing has declined from 10,8 per cent in 1965 to 7,2 per cent in 1985. The ratio for footwear has risen from 3,4 per cent to 10,4 per cent despite protection, while textiles have declined from 37,8 per cent to 15,8 per cent.

The intermediate goods such as wood, paper and paper products, and chemicals and metals have also experienced substantial declines in import penetration ratios, whereas machinery, rubber, motor vehicles and transport equipment still have high import penetration ratios.

Table 17.1:

IMPORT SUBSTITUTION IN SOUTH AFRICA
FROM 1971 TO 1978 (R MILLION)

Agriculture, forestry and fishing	0,0131
Gold and uranium ore mining	0,0043
Coal mining	0,0822
Other mining	-0,0782
Meat, dairy products and fish processing	0,0416
Grain, sugar and animal feeds	0,0130
Other food processing	0,0197
Beverage industries	-0,0048
Tobacco products	0,1109
Wool scouring, cotton ginning and dyeing	0,2825
Spinning, weaving, knitting of textiles	0,1999
Clothing	0,0555
Leather, leather products	0,1405
Footwear	0,0081
Wood and wood products	0,1721
Furniture	0,0125
Pulp, paper and paper board	-0,0336
Paper containers	0,0268
Other pulp, paper and paper board	0,0686
Printing and publishing	-0,0918
Fertilizers and pesticides	0,0448
Synthetic resins, plastics and man-made fibres	0,0586
Other basic chemicals and petroleum and coal products	0,2756
Medicine and pharmacy preparations	-0,0056
Soaps and toiletries	-0,0472
Paint and other chemical products	0,0039
Rubber products	0,0217
Other plastic products	0,0311
Glass and glass products	0,1182
Other non-metallic mineral products	-0,0052
Iron and steel basic industries	0,1425
Non-ferrous metal basic industries	0,1621
Structural metal products	-0,0158
Other fabricated metal products	0,0920
Agricultural machinery and equipment	-0,2314
Other machinery, except electrical	0,1754
Electrical machinery and apparatus	0,1242
Radio and television equipment	0,1167
Motor vehicles	0,0642
Motor vehicle parts	0,5094
Railway equipment	-0,1692
Other transport equipment	-0,6798
Other manufacturing industries	0,3621

Table 17.2:
IMPORT PENETRATION RATIOS FOR SELECTED STANDARD INDUSTRIAL
CLASSIFICATION (SIC) CATEGORIES (PERCENTAGE)

	1965	1970	1975	1980	1985
Food	9,7	11,3	12,7	6,0	7,7
Beverages and Tobacco	4,5	5,3	4,0	2,4	4,9
Textiles	37,8	30,2	20,8	15,8	15,8
Clothing	10,8	14,6	10,1	6,7	7,2
Footwear	3,4	8,4	10,5	8,6	10,4
Wood & wood products	25,0	19,7	18,7	12,0	9,3
Paper & paper products	23,4	24,3	17,9	16,4	13,6
Chemicals	25,0	25,2	16,5	15,1	15,1
Metals & metal products	21,1	17,1	16,5	7,0	11,1
Non-metallic products	22,8	17,7	12,6	6,3	20,0
Rubber products	21,4	20,2	19,3	22,8	20,6
Machinery	50,3	57,0	52,3	50,1	52,1
Motor vehicles & transport equipment	37,1	39,2	34,5	31,4	30,0

NOTES:
Import penetration is defined as the proportion of imports in the domestic consumption,
where domestic consumption contains both domestic production and imported goods.
SOURCE
Kahn, 1987.

Should South Africa at the present time encourage further import substitution? Du Plessis (1973) and Bell (1975) were of the opinion that further growth
could be stimulated through import substitution. We have seen that the scope
for further import substitution lies largely in intermediate and capital goods,
where in most cases economies of scale are necessary for low-cost production. In
conclusion, further import substitution is possible for South Africa, given the
high average propensity to import. However if sales are confined to the limited
domestic market, costs will remain high. Alternatively, if import-substituting
firms were required to export part of their output as a prerequisite to obtain-
ing protection in the domestic market, economies of scale could eventually be
achieved.

Export promotion in South Africa

In the early 1970s doubt arose as to the ability of import substitution to provide
further employment and growth in the economy. The Reynders Commission of
Enquiry was appointed to investigate the possibilities for growth in the export
sector of the economy. The Commission reported in 1972 and was followed
by the Van Huyssteen Committee's proposals which culminated in 1978 with
adoption of the system of Categories A–D of assistance to exporters and the
principle of uniformity of incentives to exporters.

The assistance given to exporters during the 1970s is not necessarily a switch by policy-makers to a trade strategy of export promotion as defined by Bhagwati (1988). The export incentives are an attempt to redress some of the bias which existed against exports in the fifties and 1960s. Effective exchange rates for exports and imports have not been calculated for South Africa as the necessary data is unavailable. However, aside from a few notable exceptions, given the performance of exports since the reduction in the bias against them, it would be fair to say that the effective exchange rate for imports is probably still greater than that for exports.

Table 17.3:
EXPORT SHARES IN TOTAL EXPORTS (PERCENTAGE)

	1957	1964	1971	1978	1983	1985
Agriculture, fish & forest	18,9	15,6	9,6	7,4	3,8	4,8
Mining	53,1	58,5	56,6	59,6	50,4	62,3
Food	7,6	10,2	12,2	7,4	2,8	3,5
Beverages and tobacco	0	0,7	0,5	0,4	0,1	0,1
Textiles	2,2	1,8	3,7	1,7	1,2	1,6
Clothing and footwear	1,3	0,8	0,9	1,0	0,2	0,2
Wood and wood products	0	0,1	0,1	0,4	0,2	0,2
Furniture	0	0,1	0	0	0	0
Paper and paper products	0,7	0,9	1,2	0,8	1,0	1,9
Printing and publishing	0	0,3	0,2	0,1	0	0
Leather & leather products	0	0,2	0,4	0,1	0,1	0,2
Rubber products	0,6	0,2	0,2	0,1	0	0,1
Basic chemicals & petrol	4,2	3,1	7,6	6,4	2,2	3,4
Non-metallic products	0,4	0,4	0,8	0,7	0,2	0,2
Basic metals	4,0	5,4	4,5	8,5	12,1	17,5
Metal products	0,9	0,9	1,5	0,8	0,3	0,4
Machinery excl. electrical	1,7	1,1	2,1	0,8	0,7	1,3
Electrical machinery	0,5	0,3	0,8	0,3	0,2	0,3
Motor vehicles & transport	0,9	0,7	1,0	0,8	0,7	1,0
Miscellaneous	2,0	1,5	3,0	2,9	0,9	1,5

Tables 17.3, 17.4 and 17.5 show the shares of exports by selected Standard Industrial Classification (SIC) classifications in total exports, in manufactured exports and exports in each category as a proportion of total output in each sector from 1957 to 1985.

Table 17.3 shows that the role of mining exports, in particular gold, has not diminished over the last 30 years, with mining exports accounting for 62,3 per cent of total exports in 1985. What is notable is the declining importance of agricultural, fishing and forestry exports, while manufacturing exports rose from 28 per cent of total exports in 1957 to 32,9 per cent in 1985. During

Table 17.4:
EXPORT SHARES IN MANUFACTURED EXPORTS (PERCENTAGE)

	1957	1964	1971	1978	1983	1985
Food processed	27,0	39,7	36,2	22,3	12,1	10,2
Beverages and tobacco	1,1	2,7	1,5	1,1	0,6	0,4
Textiles	7,9	7,0	10,9	5,1	5,2	4,9
Clothing and footwear	4,6	2,9	2,7	3,0	0,7	0,9
Wood and wood products	1,0	0,5	0,3	1,1	0,7	0,7
Furniture	0,5	0,4	0,1	0,2	0,2	0,2
Paper and paper products	2,7	3,3	3,4	2,4	4,3	5,5
Printing and publishing	0,4	1,2	0,6	0,3	0,1	0,1
Leather & leather products	0,2	0,7	1,2	0,4	0,4	0,6
Rubber products	2,4	0,9	0,6	0,3	0,2	0,2
Basic chemicals & petrol	15,0	12,3	22,2	19,4	9,7	10,0
Non-metallic products	1,5	1,4	2,3	2,2	0,7	0,8
Basic metals	14,3	21,1	13,2	25,6	52,8	51,9
Metal products	3,3	3,5	4,4	2,3	1,1	1,2
Machinery excl. electrical	6,1	4,4	6,2	2,3	3,2	3,7
Electrical machinery	1,8	1,3	2,5	1,0	0,9	0,9
Motor vehicles & transport	3,1	2,7	3,0	2,3	3,0	3,0
Miscellaneous	7,1	5,9	9,0	8,6	4,0	4,5

the period of reduced bias against exports from 1971 to 1985, manufactured exports did not increase their share of total exports. Table 17.4 shows that within manufactured exports, basic metals increased their share dramatically from 14,3 per cent in 1957 to 51,9 per cent in 1985. In 1985 basic metals accounted for 17,5 per cent of total exports (Table 17.3).

The export performance of a sector is also demonstrated by the share of exports in domestic production. Basic metals exports as a proportion of output increased from 26,5 per cent in 1957 to 77,7 per cent in 1985 (Table 17.5). Miscellaneous industries, textiles, paper and paper products, and leather and leather products also improved their performance over this period. The clothing and footwear industries have remained firmly wedded to the domestic market, exporting a mere 4,3 per cent of domestic production. The share of exports in domestic production increased for many of the sectors between 1983 and 1985, reflecting the effects of the depreciated rand. There is no empirical evidence to suggest that basic metals may have received greater incentives to export than did other sectors, yet aside from basic metals the export performance of other sectors in economy failed to respond to the improved system of incentives.

Table 17.5:
EXPORTS AS A PROPORTION OF TOTAL PRODUCTION (PERCENTAGE)

	1957	1964	1971	1978	1983	1985
Agriculture	25,0	24,0	13,0	17,4	26,4	23,7
Mining	93,0	87,0	80,0	80,0	97,0	66,0
Food processed	11,8	17,4	16,0	15,3	7,7	10,3
Beverages and tobacco	2,9	6,0	2,8	3,5	1,2	1,1
Textiles	16,4	10,9	14,2	11,4	13,2	20,4
Clothing and footwear	5,4	4,8	5,3	10,3	1,9	4,3
Wood and wood products	5,6	2,7	1,6	9,5	4,7	7,4
Furniture	2,3	2,5	1,0	2,8	2,1	3,3
Paper and paper products	10,5	9,1	8,6	9,0	11,0	22,3
Printing and publishing	0,2	4,8	1,7	1,6	0,3	0,6
Leather & leather products	3,0	15,0	21,3	10,8	10,7	17,3
Rubber products	11,2	4,5	3,8	2,7	1,9	2,9
Basic chemical & petrol	6,5	10,5	14,7	13,1	5,2	6,6
Non-metallic products	10,4	3,4	4,4	7,3	1,9	3,7
Basic metals	26,5	29,7	10,8	25,4	57,6	77,7
Metal products	4,9	3,8	4,6	3,4	1,3	2,7
Machinery excl. electrical	12,0	9,1	9,8	4,6	4,9	11,6
Electrical machinery	4,2	3,4	4,4	2,4	1,9	3,4
Motor vehicles & transport	2,2	3,1	2,8	3,2	3,4	6,7
Miscellaneous	27,9	22,4	24,4	45,9	31,0	63,2

SOURCES:
The sources for Tables 17.3, 17.4 and 17.5 were Central Statistical Services *Quarterly Bulletin of Statistics* (various issues).

The role of exports in developing the manufacturing sector

There has been increased interest in recent years in the relationship between the expansion of exports and economic growth. This interest was stimulated by the economic success of the newly industrialized countries (NICs) which had emphasized export promotion strategies. Most of the research concludes that export growth has made a substantial contribution to these economies (Michaely, 1977; Balassa, 1978, 1981). A recent study by Chow (1988) suggests that not only have exports stimulated growth in the NICs, but that growth of exports has developed manufacturing industry which in turn has expanded exports themselves. Exports have promoted the growth of the national income while structurally transforming these economies, and the development of manufacturing industries has not been a prerequisite for the exports.

A recent study of the relationship between growth in exports and manufacturing in South Africa (Holden, 1989) shows that over the period 1947–87, total exports and manufacturing output had bi-directional causality in the sense that exports influenced manufacturing growth and in turn manufacturing growth influenced export growth. In the period 1947–70, total exports and manufacturing output were not related in either direction, whereas from 1968 to 1987 there was once again a strong bi-directional causality between the two variables.

When mining exports were excluded from exports, merchandise exports and manufactured output experienced bi-directional causality over the entire period. However it was significant that from 1947 to 1970, although manufactured exports did not stimulate manufacturing growth, the growth of manufactured output did promote the growth of exports. It has been hypothesized, and there is empirical support for the view (Holden, 1985) that exporters in South Africa tend to export when the domestic economy is in recession. The results support this view as manufacturing output growth would have preceded export growth. These results also show that from 1968 to 1987 manufactured exports were strongly influencing the growth of manufacturing output, and in turn manufacturing output was enhancing export growth. This means that exports and the development of manufacturing industries accompanied and reinforced each other. The reasons for these relationships will be a potentially fruitful area of further research.

In conclusion, it was found that during the period when import substitution was almost complete in consumer goods, exports had become important for further growth and industrial development. South Africa through its exports of basic metals, basic chemicals, textiles and paper products was able to expand the domestic market by having access to international markets. In addition, the growth of these exports and industrial development were inextricably linked. The tragedy of economic sanctions deepens in the face of evidence such as this.

The real exchange rate and the trade regime

The stance of trade policy cannot be established without reference to the role of the real exchange rate. The competitiveness or profitability of manufactured exports can be ascertained by examining movements in the real exchange rate. Defining the real exchange rate as the price of manufactured exportables relative to other goods and services in the economy,[2] Figure 17.2a shows monthly movements in the real exchange rate from 1973 to 1987.

These calculations indicate that the incentive to produce for the export market was gradually discouraged from 1975 to 1984, supporting Bell's (1987) contention that South African manufacturing had suffered a decline in competitiveness. It was only with the severe nominal depreciation of the rand in 1984 and 1985 that the index for the real exchange rate rose and reversed this trend. This improvement in the real exchange was reflected in an increase in the

Figure 17.2a & b:

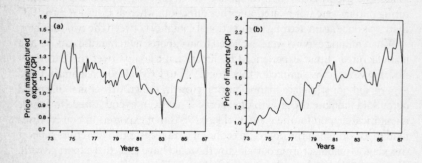

proportion of output exported by most of manufacturing industry in 1985.

The competitiveness of importables can also be shown by movements in the real exchange rate. For this purpose the real exchange rate is defined as the price of importables relative to the general price level. Figure 17.2b shows the monthly movements in this real exchange rate for the period 1973–87. In the early 1970s the incentive to produce importables for the domestic market improved. At this time the increase in index was a reflection of the rise in the world oil price and this provided the stimulus to expand the production process of oil from coal in South Africa. However, from 1975 to 1984 the index changed minimally, only improving with the depreciation of the rand in 1984.

Future prospects

Any discussion of the choice of trade strategy for South Africa would have to take cognizance of the existence and future extension of sanctions against South African exports. The effect of sanctions on the economy can be demonstrated with a general equilibrium model. The production possibilities and consumption preferences in this model are shown graphically in Figure 17.3. Sanctions will result in a deterioration in the terms of trade, moving the economy from point A to point B and decreasing the level of economic welfare from point C to point D.[3] This decrease in welfare has been estimated to range between 2 and 0,4 per cent of GDP, depending on the relevant elasticities of supply and demand for exports (Holden & McGrath, 1986).

The general equilibrium model shows that in the absence of intervention the imposition of sanctions will reallocate resources in the direction of import substituting activities. Should policy-makers intervene further and embrace import substitution as did the Latin American countries in the 1960s? In view of the role played by manufactured exports in developing the manufacturing

Figure 17.3:

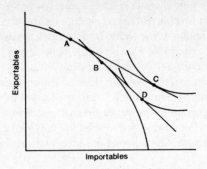

sector, and the costs of inefficient import substituting production, such an inward-looking policy would be a costly alternative.

Many countries which have promoted exports have been successfully able to penetrate the markets of the industrialized countries. However, this success has given rise to demands for protection, thus threatening these exports. Despite this protection, the exports of these countries have continued to grow. Bhagwati (1988, p. 42) suggests that 'protection is far less effective than one thinks, simply because there are many ways in which exporting countries can get around it while continuing to increase their export earnings.' Bhagwati also admits that this has only been achieved at some cost to the exporters. In a similar fashion, exporters in South Africa have found other markets and employed middlemen as sanctions have been imposed. It would seem that both protection and sanctions are porous and South African exporters have not been deterred by either. To give further encouragement to import-substituting activities at this time would place exporters at a greater disadvantage in the market place for scarce resources such as skilled labour and capital.

Those South African goods which enjoy free access to the industrialized markets are usually of strategic value to these countries. South Africa is either the sole supplier or can exert a measure of control over these markets. To reap the benefits of this bargaining power, consideration should be given to the imposition of export tariffs. This would improve the terms at which they are traded, and partially offset the welfare losses incurred on other exports.

A major difference between the development of the NICs and South Africa lies in their natural resource endowments. Paradoxically, the abundance of natural resources in South Africa has presented a problem for development in terms of the phenomenon of deindustrialization. When the price of natural resources — gold in particular — has increased, real wages have risen throughout the economy (McGrath, 1983) as labour has been reallocated to the booming sector. At the same time the increase in exports has tended to appreciate the currency in real terms. This real appreciation, plus the increase in real wages, has squeezed the manufacturing sector. Its development has been retarded, and the economy has been unable to achieve the same degree of specialization in its manufactured exports as have the East Asian NICs.

The manufacturing sector could be shielded from the effects of a resource boom through appropriate tax policy. Taxation of wages in the resource sector would reduce the pressure on wages in the manufacturing sector, while taxes on the profits of the booming sector to subsidize imported capital goods to the manufacturing sector would ameliorate the effect of the real appreciation of the rand.

Conclusion

South African trade policy has changed from being strongly import-substituting, to providing limited incentives to exporters. The bias inherent in import substitution as against exports has been reduced but not eliminated. This policy has encouraged some growth in exports while import substitution has continued in specific sectors of the economy. It was found that once the easy stage of import substitution was achieved, the beneficial effects of growth in exports were felt in manufacturing. Therefore, the benefits of export-led growth to the South African economy cannot be overemphasized.

The implementation of any trade strategy should take cognizance of the role of the real exchange rate in fostering growth in the manufacturing sector. It was found that the real appreciation of the currency in the 1970s and early 1980s would have discouraged manufactured exports. Furthermore, movements in the real exchange rate failed to significantly encourage import-substituting activities.

It is likely that economic sanctions will form a significant part of the economic landscape for the foreseeable future in South Africa. In view of the role played by exports in developing the manufacturing sector, policy-makers will have to decide whether to offset the effects of sanctions by providing additional subsidization to affected export firms. The benefits from this strategy of further industrialization and employment would provide a more secure, longer-term basis for growth.

Notes

1 The identity used to measure import substitution was:

$$x_i + m_i = f_i + a_{ij}x_j \quad i = 1...n$$

where
m_i = imports
x_i = gross production
f_i = final demand, both domestic and foreign
a_{ij} = input – output coefficient

Then in matrix notation

$(I - A)x + m = f$
$x + (I - A)^{-1} = (I - A)^{-1}f$
$m^* = (I - A)^{-1}m$
$z^* = x + m^*$

and

$$IS_i^* = \left(\frac{m_{io}^*}{m_{it}^*} - \frac{m_{io}^*}{z_{it}^*} \right) \cdot z_{it}^*$$

m_o^* and m_t^* were calculated using the input coefficients from the input-output tables for 1971 and 1978 respectively.

2 A discussion of the appropriate definition of the real exchange rate and calculations of the real rate are given in Holden (1988a).

3 Unemployment can be generated in this model if it is assumed that the factors of production are specific to each sector and that wages are inflexible in a downward direction (Holden, 1988b).

References

Balassa, B., 'Exports and Economic Growth: Further Evidence', *Journal of Development Economics*, 1978.

Balassa, B., *The Newly Industrializing Countries*, Pergamon Press: New York, 1981.

Bell, R.T., 'Production and Foreign Trade in South African Development Strategy', *South African Journal of Economics*, vol. 43, no. 4, 1975.

Bell, T., 'International Competition and Industrial Decentralization in South Africa', *World Development*, vol. 15, no. 10/11, 1987.

Bhagwati, J., *The Anatomy and Consequences of Exchange Control Regimes*, National Bureau of Economic Research: Cambridge, 1978.

Bhagwati, J., 'Export Promoting Trade Strategy Issues and Evidence', *Research Observer*, vol. 3, no. 1, 1988.

Chow, P., 'Causality between Export Growth and Industrial Development : Empirical Evidence from the NICs', *Journal of Development Economics*, vol. 26, no. 1, 1988.

Du Plessis, T.A., 'Nywerheidsontwikkeling-Vraagfaktore', *South African Journal of Economics*, vol. 41, no. 4, 1973.

Holden, M., Effective Tariff Protection and Resource Allocation in South Africa from 1956/57 to 1963/64, Unpublished Ph.D Dissertation, Duke University: Durham NC, 1974.

Holden, M., 'Exchange Rate Policy for a Small Open Economy in a World of Floating Rates: The Case of South Africa', *Economic Research Unit*, Occasional Paper no. 17, University of Natal: Durban, 1985.

Holden, M., 'Definitions and Calculations of Real Exchange Rates: An Application to South Africa', *Economic Research Unit*, Occasional Paper no. 20, University of Natal: Durban, 1988a.

Holden, M., 'Unemployment in a Sector Specific Trade Model in the Presence of Economic Sanctions', Unpublished working paper, Department of Economics, University of Natal: Durban, 1988b.

Holden, M., ' The Role of Exports in Developing the Manufacturing Sector in South Africa from 1947 to 1987', Unpublished manuscript, 1989.

Holden, M. & Holden, P., 'Effective Tariff Protection and Resource Allocation: A Non-Parametric Approach', *Review of Economics and Statistics*, vol. LX, no. 2, 1978.

Holden, M. & McGrath, M., 'Economic Outlook', *Indicator South Africa*, vol. 4, no. 2, 1986.

Kahn, S., 'Import Penetration and Import Demand in the South African Economy', *South African Journal of Economics*, vol. 55, no. 3, 1987.

Lachman, D., 'Import Restrictions and Exchange Rates', *South African Journal of Economics*, vol. 42, no. 1, 1974.

McCarthy, C.L., 'Structural Development of South African Manufacturing', *South African Journal of Economics*, vol. 56, no. 1, 1988.

McGrath, M., *Distribution of Personal Income in South Africa in Selected Years over the Period 1945 to 1980*, Unpublished Ph.D Dissertation, University of Natal: Durban, 1983.

Michaely, M., 'Exports and Growth: An Empirical Investigation', *Journal of Development Economics*, no. 4, 1977.

Morley, S. & Smith, G., 'On the Measurement of Import Substitution', *American Economic Review*, vol. LX, no. 4, 1970.

Nurkse, R., *Patterns of Trade and Development*, Wicksell Lectures, Almguist and Wicksell: Stockholm, 1959.

Prebisch, R., 'Problemas Teoricos y Practicos del Crecimiento Economico', United Nations, Economic Commission for Latin America, 1952.

Zarenda, H., *The Policy of State Intervention in the Establishment and Development of Manufacturing Industry in South Africa*, Unpublished MA Dissertation, University of the Witwatersrand: Johannesburg, 1977.

Sanctions, economic growth and change

18

Carolyn Jenkins

Introduction

Most of the nations of the world are pressurizing South Africa in various ways with a view to changing the system of apartheid which still dominates the country's political, economic and social structures. Some measures adopted, such as the sports or cultural boycotts, have as their goal a change in certain aspects of apartheid; others, like economic sanctions, aim to precipitate a change in the entire South African system.

For some countries, the imposition of sanctions is merely an expression of disapproval of the country's internal policies or the provision of moral support for the system's opponents. There are, however, many who advocate the promotion of political and social change in South Africa by the forcing of economic (and political) crisis through the isolation of the country. The effectiveness of international sanctions in achieving either the interim or the ultimate goal has been, and will continue to be, a matter of debate. There is much uncertainty with regard to the effects of sanctions on the economy and on the pace and direction of change, a factor which has not prevented a serious commitment to the goals and philosophy of the campaign.

In the following section, the sanctions already imposed will be outlined in tabular form and a brief history of the campaign given. The major portion of the chapter will be devoted to an assessment of the effects of the 1980–89 measures on the pattern and flows of capital and trade, on movements of people, and on economic growth during this period. The effects of future developments in the sanctions campaign on growth, employment and income are projected through to the turn of the century. The chapter will conclude with a comment on the usefulness or otherwise of sanctions as a tool for promoting socio-political change in South Africa.

A brief history of the sanctions campaign

Demands for the severance of economic links between the rest of the world and South Africa were first made after the Sharpeville incident in March 1960 by Albert Luthuli, then President of the African National Congress and Nobel

Peace Prize winner. Economic sanctions have remained a key pressure strategy of many groups seeking an end to the country's policy of racial discrimination.

The first move against this country by a major foreign power was undertaken in 1962, when the Kennedy Administration banned the supply to South Africa of arms that could be used in 'enforcing apartheid'. The following year the United Nations Security Council called on member states to impose, voluntarily, an arms embargo against South Africa (United Nations, 1987).

Repeated United Nations resolutions calling for the voluntary cutting of trade, transport and financial links with the Republic have been approved. To date, however, the only mandatory action which has been undertaken by the Security Council is the arms embargo (1977), which includes a ban on the transfer of nuclear technology. This is because the USA, the UK and (until 1988) France and West Germany vetoed further mandatory measures.

Actions taken up to 1989 by organizations of states and national governments are summarized in Table 18.1. The most far-reaching measures adopted by any government of a country with significant South African links were those passed by the US Congress in 1986. Until then, despite considerable pressure from the anti-apartheid lobby, the US had done little more than support the arms embargo and restrict loans from the export-import bank, especially to the South African government and parastatals. In October 1985 the Reagan Administration banned the importation of Kruger Rands and limited the export of computers and nuclear technology. These measures were felt to be inadequate, and in September 1986 the Comprehensive Anti-Apartheid Act (CAAA) was passed (in spite of the President's attempted veto), imposing a wide range of trade and investment sanctions. At the end of the 1980s, there was still considerable pressure in the Democrat-controlled Congress to approve legislation providing for an almost complete severing of links between the US and South Africa, as well as extra-territorial penalties for non-US companies taking advantage of the American withdrawal. However, having abandoned the policy of 'constructive engagement', the White House continued to favour the route of communication and contact, expanded assistance to the victims of apartheid, and southern African regional diplomacy and negotiation.

In Europe, the 12 members of European Economic Community (EEC) endorsed their support of the arms embargo. In 1985, they banned oil exports to South Africa, prohibited the sale of computers to the South African police and military, and withdrew their military attachés from the country. Additional EEC restrictions imposed in July 1987 included bans on new investment and on the importing of certain iron and steel products and gold coins. A voluntary ban on the promotion of tourism in South Africa was also instituted. Further independent action was taken by other European countries, notably the Scandinavian states, which progressively introduced comprehensive trade and investment embargoes (with the exception of some strategic minerals) against

Table 18.1: SANCTIONS ADOPTED AGAINST SOUTH AFRICA

	ARMS/MILITARY CO-OPERATION	OIL	NUCLEAR TECHNOLOGY	COMPUTER HARDWARE/SOFTWARE	OTHER TECHNOLOGY TRANSFERS	ALL GOVERNMENT PROCUREMENT	TERMINATION OF EXPORT SUPPORT	FRUIT AND VEGETABLES	SUGAR	WINE	IRON AND STEEL	COAL	URANIUM	KRUGERRANDS	OTHER MANUFACTURED GOODS	PRODUCTS OF PARASTATALS	NEW DIRECT INVESTMENT	PRIVATE LOANS	GOVERNMENT LOANS	TERMINATION DOUBLE TAX AGREEMENTS	LANDING RIGHTS	NATIONAL CARRIERS TO S.A.	TOURIST PROMOTION	PENALTIES FOR BREAKING EMBARGOES
U.N. SECURITY COUNCIL	●		●	○										○			○							
COMMONWEALTH (excl. U.K.)	●	●	●	●		●		●	●	●	●	●	●	●				●	●	●	●	○	●	
EUROPEAN COMMUNITY	●	●	●	●							●						●							
NORDIK STATES	●		●	●	○	●	●										●	●	●			●		
ORG. EAST CARIBBEAN	●	●		●			●	●	●	●	●	●	●	●			●	●	●	●	●	●	●	
OAU (except SDCC)	●	●	●	●	●	●	●	●	●	●	●	●	●	●	●	●	●	●	●	●	●	●	●	
SOCIALIST BLOC	●	●	●	●	●	●	●	●	●	●	●	●	●	●	●	●	●	●	●	●	●	●	●	
AUSTRALIA	●	●	●	●		●	●		●	●	●	●	●			○		○	○	○			●	
AUSTRIA	●	●	●								●						●		●	○	○			○
BELGIUM	●	●	●								●						●	○						
BRAZIL	●	●																						
CANADA	●	○		●		●	●	●	●	●	○	●	○	●			○	○	○	○	●	●	●	○
DENMARK	●	●	●	●	●	●	●	●	●	●	●	●	●	●	●	●	●	●	●		●	●		○
FINLAND	●	●	●	●		●	●	●	●	●	●	●	●	●			●	●	●		●	●		
FRANCE	●	●	●	○	○						●		●				●							
GREECE	●	●									●						●							
HONG KONG											○		○				○	○	●					
ICELAND	●	●	●	●	○	●											●	●	●					
INDIA	●	●	●	●	●	●	●	●	●	●	●	●	●	●	●	●	●	●	●	●	●	●	●	
IRELAND	●			○		●	●	●	○	○	●	○					●			○	○			○
ISRAEL	●	●									○						●	●	●					
ITALY	●	●	●	●							●		●	●			●	○						
JAPAN	●		●	●	●		●				●	○		○			●		○	○		●	●	
LUXEMBOURG											●						●	○						
NETHERLANDS	●	●	●			○	●				●	○	●				●	○	●	●				●
NEW ZEALAND	●		●	●		●	●	●	●	●	●	●	●					○	○				●	
NORWAY	●	●	●	●	●	●	●	●	●	●	●	●	●	●	●	●	●	●	●		●	●		●
PORTUGAL	●	●	●	●							●		●	●			●							
SEYCHELLES	●																					●		
SINGAPORE	●		●	●				●	●	●	●	●	●	●	●	●			●					
SOUTH KOREA																	●	●	●					
SPAIN	●	●	●	●							●		●	●			●					●		
SWEDEN	●	●	●	●	●	●	●	●	●	●	●	●	●	●	●	●	●	●	●			●	●	●
SWITZERLAND			●	●													●							
TURKEY			●										●				●					●		
UNITED KINGDOM	●	●	○	●		○					○	○	●	●			○	○	●				○	●
U.S.A.	○	●	●	○			●	●	●	●	●	●	●	●	●	●	●	●	●	●	●	●	●	●
WEST GERMANY	●	●	●	○							○		○				○		○	○				○

SOURCES:
Lipton, 1988; *Leadership SA*, 1988/9, p. 39; Van Wyk, 1988 pp. 66, 67.

the Republic from 1979 onwards.

The Commonwealth countries, with the exception of the UK, imposed a wide range of bans on commodity and capital flows to and from South Africa in 1985, tightening restrictions on the sale of arms, oil and computers and on financial flows to South Africa. The long-standing ban imposed on the sale of oil by the Organization of Petroleum Exporting Countries (OPEC) in 1973 has been supported by numerous other nations, although towards the end of the 1980s crude oil and petroleum products were still entering South Africa. One of the reasons for this is that while oil-exporting countries had committed themselves to the oil embargo, very few major shipping states had done so, thus creating a substantial loophole.

In Africa, the effective severing of trade and investment links has been rare, despite the continual call for economic sanctions on the part of the Organization of African Unity, members of the Non-Aligned Movement and individual African states. Particularly for members of the Southern African Development Co-ordination Conference (SADCC), economic sanctions could cause severe internal problems, because, with the exceptions of Angola and Tanzania, they are integrally economically linked with South Africa. Their dependence on this country as a regional superpower has to some extent been responsible for the reluctance of some nations to impose even more severe sanctions, because of the potentially damaging consequences for the SADCC countries.

In contrast to the selective embargoes and restrictions of the 1970s, stringent economic sanctions have been imposed only since 1985/86. The move to sanctions is somewhat surprising, given what appears to be a consensus of academic opinion that sanctions do not 'work' in the sense of achieving their stated goals. In addition, although surveys of black attitudes towards sanctions have come up with diametrically opposed findings, the Washington-based Investor Responsibility Research Centre has concluded (in its assessment of these surveys) that the majority of South African blacks do not support comprehensive sanctions (*South African REPORTER*, June and September, 1988; South Africa Review Service, 1988).

Ultimately, however, the inevitability of further sanctions is not directly related to whether or not they 'work' or to whether or not the majority of South Africa's black population wants them. Nor, contrary to what is often claimed by South Africans, is the issue that other countries see themselves as morally superior with no histories of discrimination and no current problems of racism, or, for that matter, that they believe that South Africa is the only country where human rights are violated on a large scale.

The issue is four-fold. Firstly, the South African question touches a raw wound in the Western world, and has become the focus of the powerful twin emotions of white guilt and black anger. The evils of the apartheid system are real and not imaginary, and they are inflicted by a white group eager to take its place among the civilized, industrialized Western nations. The system must therefore be opposed by those nations if Western integrity in the area of human rights is to be maintained.

Secondly, an international forum has been developed by respected black liberation leaders calling for sanctions, and wide media coverage has periodically been given to developments in South Africa, to the point where other nations have felt compelled to enter the struggle. Short of war, economic and cultural isolation are seen as appropriate instruments for encouraging change. As a result, sanctions are imposed by countries wishing to be seen to be doing something, even if these measures do not 'work' (although it is hoped that they do).

Thirdly, the truculence of the South African government in the face of international pressure, and what appears to be zero movement towards real change, is causing foreign exasperation. This is certainly making more unacceptable the position of those who have hitherto maintained that South Africa's solution is rather to be achieved through economic growth and international negotiation.

Finally, the sanctions campaign has developed its own momentum, and nations and interest groups will pressurize one another into the further isolation of South Africa.

Effects of sanctions in the 1980s

Capital flows
Historically, the economy has been crucially dependent on inflows of foreign capital for the financing of both domestic investment and current account deficits (that is, the excess of imports over exports). While direct investment, particularly the financing by multinational corporations of foreign subsidiaries, made up more than half of total foreign liabilities during the 1960s, it declined in relative importance during the 1970s, evidencing a greater dependence on indirect investment, especially foreign loans, by the Republic.

The retreat of foreign companies, especially those based in the US, has accelerated during the 1980s. In 1984 seven US companies disinvested; 40 left during 1985, 49 during 1986 (out of the total of 65 foreign companies which withdrew that year), 58 during 1987 and almost 80 during 1988. British firms also had to count the cost of operating in South Africa, and of those firms with interests in this country, 20 per cent had departed by the end of 1987. The withdrawal of foreign companies has, to date, not had as significant an impact as might have been expected. Investment by multinationals in subsidiaries does not necessarily lead to regular, large inflows of long-term direct investment. Expansion occurs by reinvestment of profits earned in South Africa, with foreign companies together retaining between 30 and 76 per cent of profits over the years from 1960. In most cases disinvestment has occurred by selling assets to (usually) South African investors, and the existing plant has continued to operate, generally with the same staff and normally with technological, licensing, franchising and trademark links intact. The shock withdrawal of Barclays Bank in November 1986, for example, was accompanied by almost euphoric pleasure on the part of some of its senior staff that the 40 per cent stake, valued at about R200 million, was passing into South African hands (Anglo American Corporation and others) for R166 million, a discount of about 17 per cent. None of the approximately 25 000 employees were to lose their jobs, and certain international advantages such as 'visa' cards would remain.

While the direct implications of disinvestment are likely to be minimal for employment, reduced access to foreign capital could have serious consequences for the rate at which job creation occurs. This is exacerbated by the sale of foreign assets to local entrepreneurs, which absorbs South African capital into non employment-creating ventures. A further cost is the increased industrial concentration which has occurred, with many of the buy-outs being undertaken by existing industrial giants, notably Anglo American Corporation and Sanlam. Furthermore, the negative psychological impacts of company withdrawals on both domestic and international business cannot be underestimated.

Of even more immediate concern for the economy is the success achieved by the disinvestment campaign in halting bank loans to South Africa. The vulnerability of the economy to this measure arises from its increased dependence, particularly on the part of the public sector, on foreign loans to finance overspending on investment and consumption. During the 1970s and early 1980s, political instability and the consequent falling profitability of direct investment resulted in an increased reliance on short-term borrowing, which placed an increased debt-servicing burden on the economy. In 1985, the sharp depreciation of the rand (caused by large-scale sales of the currency and the refusal of some creditor banks to roll over short-term debt) placed the country in a position where it was unable to meet its repayment obligations. A four month moratorium on the $14 billion short-term debt was declared in August 1985, and this was later extended to 31 March 1986. The agreement reached in February 1986 between South Africa and its 30 major international creditor banks allowed for repayment of no more than 5 per cent of the debt before February 1987, albeit at an increased interest rate. Since that date, the country has consistently been able to meet its rescheduled commitments.

This should however not obscure the precarious position of an economy which is facing large deficits on the capital account of the balance of payments as shown in Table 18.2. The virtual cessation of inflows of direct investment, and the outflow of capital used for stock exchange transactions as well as non-direct investment, together with the obligation to regularly repay outstanding short-term debt has necessitated a reduction in domestic expenditure and the further depreciation of the domestic currency in order to encourage surpluses on

Table 18.2:

BALANCE OF PAYMENTS IN CURRENT PRICES (R MILLIONS)

Year	Current account balance	Long-term capital movements	Short-term capital movements	Changes in liabilities relative to reserves*
1980	2 818	–478	–1 804	–2
1981	–4 089	542	419	2 123
1982	–3 345	2 423	797	36
1983	–78	–238	290	1 107
1984	–2 220	2 563	–1 772	542
1985	5 925	–445	–8 786	2 071
1986	7 196	–3 060	–3 037	–2 283
1987	6 152	–1 698	–1 371	–1 167
1988	2 939	–1 052	–5 611	1 925

* Liabilities related to foreign reserves include all foreign short-term liabilities of the Reserve Bank and other Banking institutions, and short-term foreign loans to the Central Government by foreign banks and authorities
SOURCE:
South African Reserve Bank *Quarterly Bulletin*, June 1988, p. S–64.

the current account. While the disruptive effect of capital outflows on current transactions was lessened with the reintroduction of the dual exchange-rate system in 1985, any upswing in the domestic economy with its consequent increase in demand, or any loss of export markets places an immediate strain on the balance of payments.

One further complicating factor, sometimes cited as a greater problem than disinvestment, is the growing investment in foreign assets by private South African companies. Although the strict measures currently controlling the outflow of domestic funds make this difficult, total direct investment abroad increased in real terms by 105,2 per cent between 1980 and 1985. It declined in real terms by some 22 per cent in 1986 however, mainly due to a fall in share premium, reserves and undistributed profit, and long-term loans abroad. Increasingly, South African capital, reluctant to invest at home, has been finding more profitable and less risky opportunities abroad. This places further strain not only on the balance of payments, but also on the ability of the economy to expand its productive capacity.

Trade flows
Bans on South Africa's imports had, by the end of the 1980s, been restricted to petroleum, arms and nuclear trade and computer equipment, the last-mentioned usually applying to government, military and police bodies. The CAAA, however, banned US sales of computers to the government and parastatals completely, a measure which was also applied by Australia, Austria, Japan and

Scandinavia. The Americans have been particularly careful in recent years about the destinations of their computer exports, usually reserving the right to inspect equipment at any time in order to check that it is being used for the purpose for which it was sold. A round of checks made early in 1988 provoked a storm of protest amongst South African businessmen who felt that American interference with domestic business was going too far.

Data on volumes, values and sources of imports of these strategic items are unobtainable. In the statistics that were published up until January 1986 (when official publication ceased in the interests of 'secrecy'), they were included under 'other unclassified goods and balance of payments adjustments', an item which between 1980 and 1986 amounted to between 15 and 28 per cent of total imports. Very little can therefore be said about the direct consequences of these sanctions on the availability of strategic commodities. One very obvious result is the need that has been created for South Africa to become self-sufficient in the production of these items — a driving force behind the development of the oil-from-coal and armaments industries.

Given the dependence of the South African economy on technology which is developed abroad and transferred to this country (embodied in imported capital equipment), bans on the sale of sophisticated equipment and technology transfers have the potential, with time, to reduce the rate at which development can occur. The longer these sanctions are in effect, the greater the technological gap that can result. Benefits might accrue to the economy if this encourages the introduction of techniques of production and product development more appropriate to the needs of the domestic economy. By 1989, however, restrictions on imports (imposed, for different reasons, by both the domestic and foreign governments) and the rise in the cost of imports as a result of the depreciation of the rand, had simply resulted in a burgeoning second hand market for foreign-made capital equipment in those subsectors unable to finance research and development or import-substitution projects.

The closure of markets for certain South African exports has begun to make itself felt in the affected industries, although the depreciation of the rand means that locally produced goods are competitive in world markets. In real (rand) terms, merchandise exports, excluding gold, have risen through the mid-1980s. As can be seen from Table 18.3, the volume of exports in the 1980s fell between 1980 and 1983, but regained ground in 1985, rising to a peak from the latter half of 1986 through to 1988. The value of merchandise exports, excluding gold, rose substantially from 1984 to 1986, earning the country much-needed foreign exchange to finance both imports and outflows of foreign capital. The value of net gold exports also rose consistently, although volumes were declining. It has been of vital importance to the economy to maintain a high level of exports while attempting to cut back on imports, so as to run surpluses on the current account of the balance of payments in the face of large

Table 18.3:
PERCENTAGE CHANGES IN SELECTED CURRENT ACCOUNT ITEMS

Year	Merchandise Volume*	Exports Value	Net gold exports Volume*	Value
1980	1,3	10,8	–3,2	68,9
1981	–10,6	–1,9	–2,9	–17,8
1982	–0,6	5,9	0,7	3,4
1983	–10,2	0,6	0,0	15,1
1984	10,2	26,5	6,5	17,7
1985	23,1	58,6	–1,9	32,3
1986	7,0	22,4	–9,2	8,1
1987	0,2	0,4	–3,4	6,4
1988	7,3	25,2	2,9	10,3

* At constant 1985 prices.
SOURCE:
South African Reserve Bank *Quarterly Bulletin* December 1988, p. S–114

capital-account deficits.

The implementation of sanctions measures resulted, however, in a shift in the relative importance of the country's major trading partners. After the passage of the CAAA in 1986, South African exports to the US fell dramatically by 40 per cent in 1987. Exports of goods specifically banned under the CAAA, such as uranium products, iron, steel and coal, fell to almost zero. Some exports not listed also ceased, such as gold and silver (bullion and ore), industrial diamonds, motor fuel and shellfish. In the first nine months of 1987, the two-way trade between the US and the Republic fell from R5 368 million (in the same period in 1986) to R3 844 million. Once the country's largest trading partner, the US was overtaken in significance by Japan. In 1987, Japan's two-way trade with South Africa rose nearly 20 per cent to R8 540 million, prompting both American ire that it was filling the gap left by the US withdrawal, and Japanese embarrassment at its evident willingness to do business with Pretoria.

Trade with the UK and West Germany, fourth and third in importance in trading relations, also declined. In 1986 British trade with South Africa fell by 15 per cent, although it rose again somewhat in the following year. In 1987 South African exports to Germany dropped by 25 per cent in deutschemark terms (about 20 per cent in rand terms, from R3,1 billion to R2,5 billion). This fall was primarily due to a decline in German purchases of gold and Kruger Rands, the latter falling by almost 90 per cent as a result of the EEC ban. Gold exports fell by 53 per cent, which was the same percentage as the decline in coal sales to Germany. In 1986, as relationships with France deteriorated, exports to that country fell by 40 per cent.

The cessation of publication of trade statistics in January 1986 means that the precise effects of the 1985–86 round of sanctions on specific exports cannot

Table 18.4:
SPECIFIC EXPORT ITEMS IN CURRENT PRICES (R MILLIONS)

Year	Edible fruit and nuts	Sugar and confectionery	Mineral fuels (most coal)	Iron and steel products	Coin	Other unclassified
1980	288,5	404,3	753,0	1 024,2	1 489,0	10 417,8
1981	309,5	265,1	1 109,9	1 029,5	1 287,2	8 908,6
1982	403,6	213,5	1 253,3	1 133,0	924,5	9 576,6
1983	356,8	163,4	1 259,3	1 114,5	1 524,8	10 484,4
1984	533,3	213,9	1 800,1	1 544,7	943,6	13 429,2
1985	428,7	354,4	3 226,1	2 694,1	343,2	18 322,5

SOURCE:
Central Statistical Services Monthly Abstract of Trade Statistics, January — December, 1980–85.

be traced. Table 18.4 lists the values of exports of some restricted items, but the success of a ban on a commodity vulnerable to sanctions can only really be seen in the column headed 'coin', since restrictions on the purchase of Kruger Rands have been in effect for longer than those on other goods.

Since 1986, certain export industries, notably coal mining, sugar and deciduous fruit, have complained of falling export revenues and reduced profitability, necessitating the laying off of workers. However, markets for these and other restricted exports were still being found, either by circumventing regulations or by successfully locating alternative buyers. Export industries affected by sanctions were also investigating alternative local uses for their output.

At the turn of the decade, the foreign exchange constraint on economic growth was a consequence not of trade sanctions, but of large net capital outflows. These necessitated a reduction in domestic absorption and the depreciation of the currency in order to encourage surpluses on the current account. The disruptive effect of capital outflows on current transactions was lessened to some extent by the dual exchange rate system. The government's policy of export promotion had the potential advantages of maintaining employment levels and developing linkages with the economy, although its success needs to be evaluated over a longer period of time.

Tourism and migration

One other aspect of the country's external relations which is interesting to consider is the movement of people across its national borders. This is interesting both in the light of the refusal of many countries to allow the promotion of tourism in South Africa and because of the attention given to one of the more alarming results of political and economic instability, the 'brain drain'.

After a decline in the number of visitors to the country in 1985 and 1986, numbers of people arriving on a non-permanent basis rallied again in 1987,

Table 18.5:

TOURISM AND MIGRATION

Year	Visitors	Immigrants	Emigrants	Net gain/loss
1981	708 710	41 542	8 791	+ 32 751
1982	659 913	45 784	6 832	+ 38 952
1983	704 444	30 483	8 247	+ 22 236
1984	792 387	28 793	8 550	+ 20 243
1985	727 552	17 264	11 401	+ 5 883
1986	644 502	6 994	13 711	−6 717
1987	703 351	7 953	11 174	−3 221
1988	804 985	10 400	7 767	+ 2 633

SOURCES:
Central Statistical Service Report no. 19–01–14 and Monthly News Releases, January 1981–April 1989.

reaching a record high in 1988. As the figures in Table 18.5 show, total numbers arriving in 1987 were 3,3 per cent down on 1985 figures and 11,2 per cent down on 1984 figures, but 9,1 per cent up on the numbers arriving in 1986. In 1988, 14,4 per cent more people arrived than in the previous year. While the 1987–88 increase arose in the numbers arriving for both holiday and business reasons, the main growth was in tourism, which increased by 11,1 per cent in 1987 and by over 15 per cent in 1988. Typically about 75 per cent of foreign visitors come for holiday purposes (about half of them from Africa). The growth in tourism can to some extent be attributed to the favourable rate of exchange for foreigners, particularly those from Europe and America. Despite the possibility that a weak exchange rate means that tourism could be earning less foreign exchange for the country, these figures are interesting as an indication of foreign perceptions regarding South Africa and of the success or otherwise of the anti-apartheid lobby at discouraging tourism to South Africa.

Migration figures reproduced in Table 18.5 reveal a steady decline in the number of immigrants through the 1980s, with a sharp fall in 1986 and increases in 1987 and 1988. In 1986, which is the latest year for which detailed statistics are available, close on one-third of the immigrants came from the UK, while nearly 27 per cent arrived from Zimbabwe. Of those who were economically active, 36 per cent were classified as professional, technical and related workers. Numbers of people emigrating rose noticeably in 1985–87, although these figures were not as high as those for 1977 and 1978 following the Soweto uprising: 26 000 in 1977 and 20 686 in 1978. The number of emigrants dropped sharply in 1988, resulting in a net gain of permanent residents. Of the 5 578 economically active people who left in 1986, over 40 per cent were classified as professional, technical and related workers, about 20 per cent of those being engineers. The single most popular destination was the UK (40 per cent), followed by Australia (29 per cent).

Even allowing for inaccuracies in the data, it is evident that the 1980s have seen increasingly negative perceptions as to the longer-term prospects for South Africa, although a turnabout was experienced towards the end of the decade. Critical shortages in skilled manpower have caused concern, particularly among the ranks of engineers, accountants, actuaries and computer operators. Emigration of highly educated personnel, particularly as a result of loss of confidence in the country's future, has exacerbated the problem.

Prospects for the 1990s

The most likely scenario, dependent of course in a large measure upon internal developments, is that South Africa will enter the 1990s a long way from comprehensive embargoes. The country will never face complete isolation, because of the dependence of the Western world on its strategic mineral exports, and because alternative sources of imports and markets for exports will be found. It would be very difficult to internationalize sanctions under American or United Nations leadership and, even if that were to occur, the enforcing of a comprehensive boycott of this country is probably impossible.

In any event, South Africa has the resources and the hard-headed resolve to resist economic siege, and has, at any rate, been preparing for such action for many years. Although heavily dependent on trade, the country has domestic deposits of almost every key raw material input needed for an industrial economy, except for bauxite and crude oil. The latter may yet be discovered in exploitable quantities near Mossel Bay, and great efforts have been made to eliminate dependency on oil by converting domestic coal to oil (SASOL), extracting oil from oil shale and producing ethanol from sugar cane. In addition, strategic imports (including computer and aircraft parts) have been stockpiled, providing a cushion for the economy during the search for alternative sources of these commodities or the completion of import substitution projects.

In both of these last-mentioned courses of action, South Africa has historically had some success. The country clearly has the capacity to circumvent trade restrictions, even if supplies are obtained at a higher cost, and, following the oil and arms embargoes, has developed extremely sophisticated weaponry and oil-from-coal technology. Despite this, the country's dependence on foreign technology remains one of its most significant areas of vulnerability. Inability to either obtain or manufacture, for example, fighter aircraft, has lost South Africa supremacy of the air in its military conflicts. Crucial dependence on high-technology imports, particularly computers and capital goods, will not foreseeably be overcome. At any rate, the process of import substitution industrialization itself initially requires technology and capital equipment from abroad, a factor which could constrain development if foreign supplies were curtailed.

With regard to South African exports, about 65 per cent of export earnings are from gold, diamonds and strategic minerals on which the Western world is to a large extent dependent. America, for example, obtains from South Africa 61 per cent of its chromium imports, 53 per cent of imported vanadium and industrial diamonds, 42 per cent of imported platinum group metals, and high percentages of manganese, ferromanganese and antimony imports. South Africa ranks among the top three producers of all these minerals and also produces 44 per cent of the West's gold output. A boycott on any of these commodities would be virtually unenforceable. The remaining 35 per cent of export earnings, which are mainly from steel, coal and agricultural goods, as well as some manufactured commodities, are more vulnerable to embargoes.

Given however the efforts at sanctions-busting, co-ordinated by the Secretariat for Unconventional Trade and the Private Sector Export Advisory Committee, it has been estimated that even reasonably well-enforced, comprehensive UN sanctions would cut total export receipts by less than 25 per cent. The current piecemeal measures would probably reduce export earnings by far less, especially since the weak rand makes exports more competitive on world markets.

One area in which sanctions will continue to have a more significant effect on the economy is in the restrictions that have been placed on South Africa's acquisition of sufficient foreign capital to meet its debt-repayment obligations and to finance economic growth. Financial sanctions aimed at reducing both foreign direct investment and loans, together with waning business confidence, have made the country dependent on trade surpluses if foreign exchange is to be accumulated. Since the authorities regard international debt commitments as a top priority and are attempting to honour them meticulously, any upswing in the economy, with its corresponding increase in import spending, needs immediately to be contained because of the balance-of-payments constraint. No further growth in import volumes can be afforded, and new imports are being controlled by increasing the cost of consumer credit and imposing import surcharges. Disinvestment measures have therefore been effective in applying pressure on the South African economy, exacerbating internal obstacles to growth and ruling out any hope of raising the economic growth rate above 2,5 or 3 per cent given current economic structures.

The net result of the trade and investment embargoes would be continuing recession over the medium term, which would deepen as constraints on growth and development made themselves felt in the longer term. Preparation for sanctions would add to the problems already engendered by difficulties in the procurement of foreign resources; contributing to an under-utilization of capital, adding to inflation and costing further growth.

The economy requires an annual growth rate of at least 5 per cent in order to create work for the estimated 350 000 new job-seekers each year, and in excess of this rate if it is to begin to reduce the large and growing problem of unemployment. The official rate of registered unemployment for whites, coloureds and Indians is between 2 and 3 per cent of the economically active population. An estimate of unemployment among blacks, including rural agriculture and the informal sector, places it close to 40 per cent of the economically active population. Although at present about 45 per cent of the black population is still confined to the rural areas, urbanization is occurring rapidly, because black rural agriculture is unable to sustain the local population which is growing at about 2,5 per cent annually. The rate of increase among urban blacks is greater than 7,5 per cent a year, adding to the pressure for a rapid increase in modern sector employment opportunities and fuelling the sense of urgency about solving the current crisis in housing shortages. Government policy is hopelessly inadequate in dealing with these problems. Part of the rationale for deregulation is to create a climate for self-employment, a goal which is inevitably to be thwarted by the need to keep the lid on domestic spending, both public and private. Rising unemployment in the 1990s must therefore be anticipated.

Despite the upswing of the last two years which reversed the negative growth of the early 1980s (with the exception of 1984's mini-boom), per capita real disposable income midway through 1988 is about 10 per cent lower than in 1984 and 14 per cent lower than in 1980. Growth rates of the economy which fall below the growth rates of the population cause a drop in the real incomes of both white and black workers. A reduction in average real disposable income to below 1970 levels can be expected by the turn of the decade, increasing the numbers of those living in absolute poverty. While this factor alone may not affect the racial shares of income, when coupled with increasing unemployment, particularly among unskilled workers, income inequality will worsen over time. This trend may be reinforced by a redistribution of wealth towards big business. The increase in share prices relative to the prices of fixed income securities and fixed property since June 1986 has redistributed wealth to the more privileged, and the acquisition of formerly foreign-owned assets at below market prices has consolidated the strong position of white capital. The premium on skills, caused by the brain drain and the additional demands of import substitution and local development of technology, will further redistribute income in favour of the better educated and better paid. This will not only worsen the distribution of income between blacks and whites as groups, but also that between urban and rural blacks, as educated and skilled blacks are drawn into technical and professional occupations.

There is every possibility that the problems will work to reinforce themselves. Increasing unemployment, falling real disposable income, inflation pressures and low or negative rates of growth will cause the domestic market to shrink even if the number of consumers is rising. Coupled with continuance of tight monetary policy and a tightening of fiscal policy in future budgets, this will further discourage domestic investment. Counter to this, efforts at import substitution will stimulate certain sectors of the economy, providing some opportunities for economic growth and development. Growth, however, is unlikely to exceed 3 per cent per annum in the foreseeable future, unless the gold price does something unexpected.

The economic hardship experienced in South Africa during the 1980s cannot be said to be a consequence solely of sanctions. Domestic factors, like internal instability, macroeconomic policy errors on the part of government, and adverse external market factors, have played a far more significant role in creating the problems. Sanctions may, however, work to exacerbate the situation and to make economic recovery more difficult. It could be argued that this would be worth the pain if the outcome is a more equitable political and social order. The chances of this are remote. Targeted sanctions, such as the sports and movies boycotts, have had success in peeling away some of the aspects of petty apartheid. On the other hand, sanctions targeted at the government — or broad measures aimed at South Africa generally — have not encouraged significant change, nor have they made the toppling of the system more possible. They may have had some success with respect to certain issues such as the achievement of agreement over the future of Namibia, the changes which have been made to some racially discriminatory legislation, and a more conciliatory approach to black leaders. However, generally speaking, they appear to have hardened conservative white attitudes, engendering a siege psychosis and prompting expression of a fundamental unwillingness to relinquish privilege or priority. Furthermore, the government will continue to devote resources to the implementation of compensatory policies to reduce the impacts of sanctions. Market forces too will allow for adjustments to be made. This somewhat reduces the ability of the outside world to influence developments within South Africa too significantly. Ultimately, the country's problems will need to be resolved by its own people, including those in exile or in prison.

The implications of economic isolation for post-apartheid South Africa also need to be considered. If sanctions do result in a severe shortage of financial and physical capital and technical know-how, as well as a loss of export markets, this will cause economic stagnation and serious problems on the balance of payments. Any government that then comes to power will inherit this situation, and will find it as difficult as the present government to correct the problems. The future prosperity of the country will also be threatened by the almost certain reluctance of private foreign investors to reinvest capital in a country from which it has previously been withdrawn, particularly if that country is suffering structural economic damage and political instability.

Conclusion

The 1980s have seen a broad range of sanctions applied to South Africa with varying degrees of effectiveness in terms of their power to cause damage to the economy. The cessation of foreign capital inflows has caused disruptions — the difficulty of acquiring foreign loans causing more problems than the withdrawal of multinational companies. With time, however, the deprivation of new long-term direct investment will hamper growth. Of concern is the lack of confidence of local businessmen, and their consequent search for more profitable, less risky opportunities abroad, creating what has been termed 'internal disinvestment'. With respect to trade restrictions, it appears that alternative sources of prohibited imports are being found, and domestic production of these items has been initiated. Banned exports include only those goods of little or no strategic importance to the countries imposing the restrictions. Nevertheless, the impact on South African trade has illustrated the harm that can be caused if sanctions become more comprehensive and more widely applied. To date the availability of alternative markets has buffered the export industries affected by the prohibitions. Tourism for both holiday and business purposes has so far been little damaged in terms of numbers of foreigners arriving each year, although the net (permanent) loss of people through migration is a reflection of negative perceptions as to the country's prospects. The 1985/86 level of sanctions impositions is clearly being survived with a positive growth rate, but the costs to the economy grow with each additional embargo.

Continued incremental sanctions in the 1990s would gradually squeeze the economy, initially affecting sectors dependent on high technology imports and sectors exporting agricultural and manufactured products, steel and coal. The long-term detrimental effect on most activities through slow growth, the drain of skills, diminished access to foreign resources and increasing social unrest, would possibly not have the desired political effects. Although its dominance in the southern African region is unlikely to be eroded significantly, increasing isolation will reduce South Africa's ability to fulfil its potential as a middle-ranking power. Sanctions will be costly, given the country's dependence on foreign exchange and foreign investment, and any short-term gains will be outweighed by the long-term damage to the economy.

References

Central Statistical Services, Monthly *Abstract of Trade Statistics*, Government Printer, Pretoria, January 1980–December 1985.

Central Statistical Services, Monthly *News Releases*, Government Printer, Pretoria, January 1981– April 1989.

Central Statistical Services, *Report. no. 19-01-14*. Government Printer, Pretoria.

Lipton, M., *Sanctions and South Africa: The Dynamics of Economic Isolation*, Special Report no. 1119, Economist Intelligence Unit, January 1988.

South Africa Review Service, 'Leaving South Africa: The Impact of US Corporate Disinvestment', July 1988.

United Nations Centre Against Apartheid, *Report no. 87–10569*; *Report no. 87–10593*, 1987.

Van Wyk, K., 'State Elites and South Africa's International Isolation: A Longitudinal Comparison of Perception', *Politikon*, vol. 15, no. 1, 1988.

Capital goods, 'dependence' and appropriate technology[1]

19

Charles Meth

Introduction

This chapter has its origins in a difference of opinion I had with Jill Nattrass in 1977 on the importance of the 'capital goods' industry in South Africa. Her position is summed up in the following statement:

> ...measures should be taken to encourage the development of a broadly based machine tools section (*sic*) in South Africa, as it is argued that one of the major 'spin offs' from the development of such a sector is the development of techniques of production that are specifically designed to suit local conditions (Nattrass & Brown, 1977, p. 44).[2]

The second spur to the writing of this chapter is a (friendly) disagreement I have with Dave Kaplan who has put forward a broadly similar view (1987 & 1988). Neither Kaplan nor Nattrass have examined the South African 'capital goods' sector to find out what it can and does produce, and why. Both are content to focus their attention on the most highly visible capital good, 'machine tools',[3] and to construct their plea for a strengthened capital goods industry on the basis of the weakness of the local machine tools industry.

I shall debate the above position on three levels. Firstly I take issue with their advocacy of a more 'appropriate technology' for South Africa. Appropriate technology, as usually understood in the context of a labour surplus economy, means labour-intensive technology which generates jobs and reduces 'dependence' on foreign technology. However, once questions of political economy, productivity and international competitiveness are included in the equation, the issue of what technology is appropriate becomes more complex. In order to re-examine some of the ideas behind dependency and appropriate technology, I draw a distinction in the first section of the chapter between 'core' and 'peripheral' capital goods.

Secondly, I argue that South Africa has as much of a capital goods industry as might reasonably be expected. This industry has a significant capacity both to produce capital goods, and to provide the 'back-up' services for 'absorbing' imported capital goods.

Thirdly, I disagree with the idea that promoting the machine tools industry will lead to more 'appropriate' technology. Part of the difficulty concerns what is meant by 'appropriate'. If appropriate means a greater reliance on labour in a labour surplus economy so as to make better use of an assumed 'comparative advantage', then I argue that competitive and technological forces are often such that more sophisticated capital-intensive technology is often the appropriate option in the interests of capitalist development. If on the other hand, appropriate means a socially desirable level of employment and distribution of income, then I argue that a substantial redistribution of wealth and a restructuring of demand patterns (and hence of industry itself) is needed rather than the promotion of an already healthy machine tools industry.

This argument rests in turn on the proposition that it is the form of accumulation — import-substituting industrialization (ISI) in South Africa's case — and the concomitant wealth and income distribution, that determines the type of capital goods required. It will be shown that ISI in South Africa resulted in a large and varied manufacturing sector, heavily over-populated by sheltered firms all demanding different machines in small numbers.

The chapter begins with a discussion of the distinction between core and peripheral processes and capital goods. This is followed by a critique of 'appropriate technology' arguments and an analysis of the political-economic roots of South Africa's manufacturing structure. In the final section, some indication of the relative size of the capital goods industry in South Africa is given. An analysis of imports of 'machinery' is then undertaken, in an attempt both to reveal the extent of dependency on imported machinery (and technology) and also to provide some measure of the contribution of the South African capital goods industry to capital formation. The chapter focuses on the manufacturing industry (which uses about half of the machines in the country) mainly because this is where data on capital formation is best.

'Core' and 'peripheral' processes and capital goods

When economists speak of 'capital goods' in the abstract they usually mean commodities used to produce other commodities. Most empirical studies define as 'capital goods' the output (or parts of the output) of the industries involved in the production of metal products, machinery, electrical machinery, as well as some of the output of the industries that produce transport equipment. Some confusion results because of the absence of an agreed definition.

In the process of production one may distinguish two types of capital good — those which 'transform' the object(s) being 'worked', and those which facilitate the transformations. The former are described as 'core' goods and the latter as 'peripherals'.

'Core' transformations are those processes which alter the physical and/or chemical properties of determinate inputs to produce determinate outputs. These outputs may themselves be inputs into other production processes. 'Core' capital goods range in size and complexity from simple hand-tools to special-purpose machines which fill whole buildings. At one end of the spectrum lie the general-purpose machines, usually operated by skilled workers, and at the other the special-purpose machines, limited to a small range of transformations. As one moves away from these special-purpose machines, it becomes possible, by replacing certain key components of the machine, (for example the die-set in an eccentric press), to achieve increasing degrees of job flexibility. A wide variety of machines are capable of being 'converted' in this way.

Comprehensive control by the operator over a given repertoire of cutting or other actions, especially in the field of metal-working,[4] is the characteristic of a special class of general-purpose machines for performing 'core' transformations. These are normally referred to as 'machine tools'. This group of capital goods can perform a wide range of transformations. In the past, such machines were operated only by skilled craftsmen. They were the standard machines used for one-offs or small batches. Some of the most dramatic changes in production processes, made possible by advances in electronics and computer technology, have occurred in this field.

A second group of 'core' devices is used to assemble commodities. These range from micro-electronic components to marine diesel engines standing six storeys high. In general, this class of productive activities has proved much harder to mechanize and to automate.[5] A wide range of specialized jigs, fittings and fixtures are available to facilitate assembly, but nevertheless, much (sometimes highly skilled artisan) labour is required. Automation of assembly tasks formerly carried out by humans — of which electronic goods and automobile assembly are probably the most prominent examples — is proceeding apace. In these types of transformation, robots represent one of the more important technological developments. Robots are capable of such a wide variety of tasks, ranging from spot welding or spray painting (both 'core' processes) to so-called 'pick and place' operations, that in their case, the core/peripheral distinction breaks down (Hunt, 1983).

'Peripheral' capital goods are used in production to solve the problems of housing the core processing units, of providing a plant services such as electricity or steam, and of containing, handling and transporting the materials being transformed. This involves the application of fairly standardized and widely-diffused techniques and devices.

With the rapid penetration of computers into what was previously the pre-serve of engineers, designers, draughtsmen, managers and clerical personnel (working in a manner that has changed little for many decades), the 'peripheral' functions of conceptualization and co-ordination are becoming increasingly capital-intensive. Even at the present low levels of integration, very substantial amounts of electronic data-processing equipment are now in use, most of it imported. The office of the future is likely to be fully integrated into production, in what Kaplinsky (1985) describes as 'systemofacture', thus blurring the distinction between 'core' and 'peripheral' processes.

Despite the increasing importance of robots and computers which overlap the conceptual boundaries of core and peripheral processes, it is still important to draw the distinction. A country which imports more peripheral capital goods is less 'dependent' on foreign technology than one which imports more core capital goods — even though the ratio of total capital imports to GDP might be the same in both countries. In the final section of this chapter it is argued that for this reason, South African manufacturing 'dependence' on foreign technology is a lot less severe than commonly believed.

Appropriate technology arguments

The concept of appropriate technology in economics usually boils down to the prescription that the organization of production should be in harmony with the endowments of the economy in question. Devotees of free enterprise attempt to equate this with the unfettered workings of the market, arguing that this leads to 'efficient' allocation. The history of capitalist rapacity,[6] and the fact that analysts of this ilk normally take the existing income distribution as given (and not to be altered except through the workings of the market) should be sufficient to alert most people to the severely limited nature of such analyses.

More welfare-oriented economists argue for labour-intensive technology as a means of generating employment and facilitating income redistribution. Criticism of 'appropriate technology' in this paper must be understood not to be a surrender to the most advanced technologies, but rather a call for a more comprehensive and nuanced analysis of technology in general. This concerns both the nature of appropriate technology and the means of generating it.

To understand why particular technologies are used, it is as necessary to look in detail at the commodities being produced as it is to raise questions about whether or not there exists a local 'capital goods' manufacturing capacity capable of generating appropriate technology. Those who would counter the depredations of the imposers of 'inappropriate technology' (engineers ignorant of 'better' alternatives? greedy multi-national corporations?) with policies geared towards promoting 'appropriate technology' may well be able to bring about marginal improvements in the allocation of resources, but given existing patterns of demand in South Africa, it is almost certain that they overstate the scope for this. A range of production techniques may well exist for certain products, but in many instances this probably consists of choices between various sophisticated techniques. Once the decision has been taken to produce a commodity, 'appropriate technology' may, at the end of the day, simply consist in leaving off the most recent bits of automated control apparatus, so that some of the work can be carried out by human agents. 'Appropriate technology' for a given commodity basket is more likely to be concerned with 'peripheral' than with 'core' processes.

Soete (1985) argues that much technological advance saves on both capital and labour, and that the pressures of competition increasingly force the adoption of the 'best practice' techniques of those at the frontiers of technology on to all producers. Since direct labour costs in most branches of manufacturing are low and falling,[7] the only significant labour-using production transformations are the 'assembly' operations. As has been noted above, low-cost robots are now starting to make significant inroads into this area as well. The 'new' international division of labour, which permitted third world countries to grow rapidly on the basis of (cheap) labour-intensive production, stands in danger of being reversed by technological advances in the advanced capitalist economies (Jones & Womack, 1985; Hoffman, 1985). Thus the competitive dictates of best-practice capital-intensive technology are such that even though a country may have an abundant supply of labour, capital-intensive techniques are the more rational and appropriate choice.

There is evidence that under certain conditions, particular technological or investment decisions, guided by the principle of choosing 'appropriate' technologies, have had beneficial consequences for development (Dahlman *et al.*, 1987, pp. 766ff). In the 1970s, the proponents of 'appropriate technology' devoted some effort to attacking the naïve proposition that firms in developing countries could choose (relatively costlessly) from the wide variety of technologies available internationally, the combination most suited to their needs (Soete, 1985). They offered a convincing set of explanations why 'inappropriate technologies' were applied (Stewart, 1977), but unfortunately they also put forward a somewhat less than convincing set of policy prescriptions for overcoming the problem.

Frances Stewart, doyen of the 'appropriate technology' school, and of whom Jill Nattrass was a great admirer, insists that a political economy approach ('built into the analysis from the start and not tacked on as an afterthought') is essential to an understanding of the question of choice of technique (1983, p. 291). This is true. However her proposed macro-policies for undoing the harm caused by 'inappropriate technology' are decidedly utopian and uninformed by adequate political-economic analysis. While she is aware that 'current options may be severely limited by past decisions ... on account of self-reinforcing tendencies — political, economic and technical' (1983, p. 291), her major policy prescription, tinkering with what she calls the 'composition of units', is pure pie-in-the-sky. She argues that:

...the government may modify the balance of choice in the economy as a whole by altering the proportion of resources controlled by various units, or what we shall call the composition of units in the economy. For example, small-scale units generally use more labour-intensive technologies than large-scale ones, whether they are public or private. By shifting control of total resources, the government may stimulate the use of more appropriate technology in the economy as a whole, even though it has not altered the decisions of any unit (1983, p. 282).

It always comes as something of a surprise to discover otherwise competent analysts resorting to the use of euphemisms which undermine their own arguments. 'Units' do not 'control resources'. Wealthy capitalists and powerful bureaucrats (with whom the capitalists and their hangers-on are usually in league) do. 'Small-scale units' are usually (but not always) poor people struggling for a 'modification of the balance' by calling, if not for socialism, then at least for a redistribution of income and wealth in their favour. 'Large-scale units', who hold the balance of political and economic power, are virulently opposed to such measures.

Those who maintain that developing a capital goods industry will foster more appropriate (labour-intensive) technologies, beg all sorts of questions about what technology is actually appropriate (for both growth and economy-wide job creation) and how political-economic forces structure choice of technique. The following section discusses how the roots of South Africa's technological structure lie in her political-economic history.

South Africa's political economy of accumulation

South Africa's economic history provides an excellent illustration of Marx's proposition that the process of capital accumulation is always contradictory and structured by class conflict. State policy, itself often reflecting the interests of the politically powerful classes, has at times acted as a vehicle for rapid accumulation and at other times been a fetter on economic growth.

Class struggles in South Africa (and elsewhere) are complex affairs. The relationship between capital, black and white workers and the state in South Africa suggests that each of the contending groups has sufficient power to impose on the others conditions that act as major impediments to the accumulation process.

The extreme repression that accompanied the creation of a 'bounded' labour market, enforced through institutions created to 'canalize' black labour, has meant that the state has had its hands more or less full in 'dealing' with that labor, and with the struggles of the oppressed masses. The cost of white working class and petit bourgeois quiescence (that is, high and rising standards of material prosperity), is the stuff of every liberal analysis of 'apartheid', but the price which capital forced the state to pay is frequently overlooked. Capital in South Africa, with multinational capital importantly represented, has enjoyed relative freedom of action in the restricted domestic market, notwithstanding control boards, the 1968 Physical Planning Act, and all the other regulatory paraphernalia conventionally portrayed as fetters on capital.[8]

This is not to suggest that the restrictions on labour mobility have not been irksome to certain fractions of capital, but rather that the combination of restrictions ('excessive' control of the labour market) and relative absences of restraint (ease of entry into most areas of production, fostered to increase 'competition') have interacted to give a particular character to the process and form of capital accumulation. This has resulted in large numbers of capitalists flocking to offer an exceptionally wide range of locally-produced commodities to a small but affluent market. The process, facilitated by the natural resource endowment of the economy, has had a crucial structuring effect on the pattern of output and technological choice in the manufacturing sector. This is discussed in the following section.

'Lotus eating' and economic development

Manufacturing concerns in South Africa, many of which are part of the giant mining corporations, have always relied on the export earnings of the mining or agricultural sectors to pay for imported capital goods. In other words, the manufacturing sector, the major user of imported capital goods in South Africa, is 'parasitic', in that it 'cannot' generate the foreign exchange required to pay for these goods. Relatively easily-available foreign currency or loans have been used to buy capital goods to start enterprises which, after their 'infancy', have had little or no hope of meeting the 'competitive' criterion necessary for their continued existence in a capitalist world.

The problem is by no means unique. Although it is well known that development paths are importantly constrained by resource endowments, it is not always recognized that an abundant set of endowments does not guarantee 'development'. Paradoxically, 'excessive' generosity on the part of nature can impede development. This proposition is encapsulated in 'Ranis's Law', which Arndt (1987) expresses as follows: 'Lucky is the country that has no mining sector and few farmers' or 'a country's development prospects are inversely proportional to its natural resources endowment' (p. 14).

Attempts to unravel this paradox can however, obscure the complexities of development. According to Arndt, for example:

The cultural case for Ranis's Law is simply the temptation of 'lotus-eating'. Countries with an ample endowment of natural resources do not have to work so hard at doing well economically, or they may think so. Countries which lack natural resources must make the most of their human resources — capacity for hard work, discipline, thrift, skills, enterprise (1987, p. 15).[9]

Arguments based on alleged cultural traits (divorced from an understanding of the laws specific to capitalist production) are somewhat dubious. One can however reduce the weakness of the above claim by identifying the agency or agencies responsible for investment activity, and substituting these for the word 'country', on the grounds that 'countries' do not generally 'work' or 'invest' or 'make the most of resources'. In capitalist economies, capitalists invest for the purpose of making profits. The state invests as well, often for reasons that have little direct connection with 'profits'. To understand the 'failure' of South African manufacturing, one must examine the motivations of these agencies.

A non-exporting manufacturing sector

It is common cause that many South African manufacturers are reluctant, even now, to enter the export market. The development of the manufacturing sector has, by and large, taken the form of a vigorous programme of import-substituting industrialization (ISI), some significant proportion of this being the creation or expansion of parastatals. Much investment has been for strategic rather than for 'purely economic' reasons, many enterprises being either unprofitable or having their 'profits' underwritten by the state. Private sector investment in manufacturing has been cushioned by the state against some of the harsh realities of capitalist competition on an international scale. This 'cushion' has taken the form of (contradictory) efforts to secure a cheap labour force, as well as the provision of comprehensive tariff barriers.

Sheltered from external competition,[10] the highly concentrated manufacturing sector, whose ability to maintain profit levels through 'price over-recovery' has been noted by several commentators (du Plooy, 1988; BTI Report no. 2663, p. 4), shows signs of severe structural rigidity. The continued existence of 'inefficient' firms has probably served to exacerbate the seriousness of successive business cycles, and has hindered the perpetual restructuring necessary for the maintenance of a competitive position.

Accumulation based on import substitution soon proved unsustainable, and it was argued many years ago by the Reynders Commission that: '...import replacement cannot be relied upon to maintain or regain its dominant position as the prime mover of a high rate of economic development', and that '...in future exports would have to play a more important role as generator of growth in the South African economy' (1972, pp. 7–8; cited in McCarthy, 1988, p. 18).

The ISI strategy permitted rapid accumulation and high profitability for some capitalists in the period before about 1974, but did not reduce, on aggregate, the propensity to import manufactured goods (McCarthy, 1988, pp. 13–14). Imports *per se* are not the problem however. Kubo (1985, Tables 2 and 3) showed that the import content of both exports and domestic final demand rose sharply in Korea and Taiwan during periods of rapid growth, as did imports as a percentage of GDP. In Taiwan, rapid development of a local machinery industry was accompanied by ever-increasing demands for imports of machine tools (Amsden, 1985, p. 277). The problem lies in the failure to expand exports, rather than in the high levels of imports.

Many economists have commented on the relationship between the 'distorted' patterns of production in South Africa and the highly skewed income distribution. The usual prescription for overcoming this is simply 'more growth' (with trickle-down). Few people are prepared to face the full irrationality of the production structure and to ask hard questions about what must be done. Some representatives of the capitalist class recognize however that the rule of the market can, under certain conditions, be truly malevolent. A joint study by an influential capitalist grouping, published in the depths of the post Soweto depression, noted that:

> ...the premium ...placed in the past on product variety as an important part of consumer freedom has led both to a high propensity to import, and to a considerable degree of uneconomic diversification being forced upon local producers...

> Freedom of choice is only likely to bring about the desirable results if that freedom is used responsibly...

> The small size of the South African market, the predilection for highly differentiated products and the consequent vulnerability of the domestic market to imports at the cost of manufacturing volume viability is greatly aggravated by the often large number of competing producers for any particular market or market segment. This has resulted in a high degree of market fragmentation which in many cases leaves each with a market share too small to enable it to exploit economies of scale to any significant extent...

This is traced to three root causes:

> ...the policy followed by the South African government over a number of years, namely of allowing and pursuing an unrestricted freedom of entry into most markets as a cornerstone of promoting competitive market conditions...[11]

> ...the lack of a defined overall industrial development strategy...

> ...the incorrectly assessed expectations for the growth of black purchasing power... (AHI/SAFCI/SEIFSA, 1977, pp. 117–118)

Apart from the corners into which the 'apartheid state' has backed the economy (for example, the SASOLs, ARMSCORs and other trappings of autarchy), the 'problem' in South Africa is the entirely rational (at least in the short-term) 'lotus eating' habits of the capitalist class. Capitalists are in business not for the joy of competition, but to make profits. Facing them are two formidable antagonists, namely other capitalists (both within and outside the national economy) and workers. If they can persuade the state to shield them from either or both, they will do so with alacrity. Since the demand for capital goods is a function of the expected profits that will flow from investment, and since significant state intervention can influence the climate in which those profits are generated, it is clear that the types of capital goods demanded depend importantly on this 'climate'. From the argument above, it should be obvious that conditions in South Africa make 'appropriate technology' a non-starter.

Size and diversity in South African manufacturing

One of the most striking characteristics of the South African manufacturing sector, especially when viewed in the context of the continent of which it is part, is its sheer size and diversity.

If we describe as 'industries' the sets of establishments aggregated together at the 5-digit (sub-group) Standard Industrial Classification (SIC) classification level in the Manufacturing Census, then in South Africa in 1979 there were 159 manufacturing 'industries' spread over 27 'major groups' (3-digit classification).[12] The 1979 Manufacturing Census in South Africa covered 17 126 establishments, representing an employment total of 1 339 000 workers. Some of the 'industries' comprise as few as five establishments (crayons, chalk, pens and pencils — employing 885 workers) or employ as few as 152 workers (orthopaedic appliances and supplies — 18 establishments). At the other extreme the 'printing and publishing industry' (34 015 workers) consisted of 940 establishments.

'Sub-groups' take as their names the descriptions of the commodities they produce or occasionally the type of production process used, and it is obvious from these descriptions that each 'industry' will require different special purpose machines in production. For example, of one of the 'industries' cited above, common sense tells us that 'crayons', 'chalk' 'pencils' and 'pens' will be produced using processes that differ very significantly, one from the other. In other words, a simple examination of the 5-digit data in the Manufacturing Census reveals that small numbers of an extremely wide range of machines are going to be required by the various 'industries' that make up the manufacturing sector, to say nothing of other sectors of the economy where similar diversity might obtain. Further insight into this diversity may be gleaned from an examination of the output of the South African capital goods industry and of the import statistics. This examination forms part of the next section.

Imports and local output of capital goods

South Africa's capital goods industry

The 'industry' (sub-group) responsible for the production of most of the 'core' and 'peripheral' machines produced in this country, 'Special Industrial Machinery and Equipment, except Metal and Woodworking Machinery', was for a long time the fourth largest (in terms of employment) of the 159 industries identified earlier. In 1979 this industry employed 44 249 workers. There were 654 establishments in the sub-group, and although it contained giants like Dorbyl[13] most of the firms were quite small.[14] Following the collapse of investment in manufacturing after 1982, the industry has fallen upon hard times, but that is precisely the impact on the investment goods sector one would expect the business cycle to have.

To understand why the industry is not larger still, one has merely to turn to the AHI/SAFCI/SEIFSA report referred to earlier. This document discusses in detail the difficulties faced by both the 'jobbing' and the 'proprietary and production line equipment' manufacturers in the industry. Once again the overriding factor is the: '...comparatively small size of the South African market'. This is complicated by factors such as the: '...high technology requirements of the South African market', and the '...lack of standardization among buyers who have become used to an infinite variety of selection between similar products from diverse sources of supply' (1977, pp. 86ff).

One way to demonstrate the capacity of the South African capital goods industry is to first of all show what types of machines are imported, and then to estimate the ratio of imports in the total value of investment in plant, equipment and machinery in the manufacturing sector. The resulting pattern of imports may then be compared with anecdotal evidence of some of the achievements of the capital goods industry.

Imports of machinery

The term 'broad-based machine tool industry' is bandied about with little apparent reflection on precisely how many categories of 'machines' are involved. In the 1978 presentation of the Foreign Trade Statistics, 'boilers, machinery and mechanical appliances, parts thereof' is divided into 65 groupings with 550 separate sub-groupings. One of these, 'machine tools for working metal or metallic carbides' (the group of commodities known as machine tools) breaks down into 60 further sub-groupings in which one can distinguish individual machines such a 'single spindle bench-mounted drill press'.

The descriptions of imports are sufficiently comprehensive to permit them to be sorted with confidence into the categories 'core' and 'peripheral' machines or devices. It is also a relatively simple matter to identify the destinations or end-uses of some significant proportion of the imported 'machines'. The results of such an exercise are given in Tables 19.1 and 19.2.

Table 19.1:
IMPORTS OF 'CORE' MACHINERY AS PERCENTAGE OF
TOTAL IMPORTS OF MACHINERY, BY SIC MAJOR DIVISION AND
MAJOR GROUPS IN MANUFACTURING.

	1968 %	1970 %	1975 %	1980 %	1985 %
Agriculture (84.24,25,26,27 & 28)	3,2	2,8	4,2	2,3	2,2
Mining and quarrying (84.56)	1,3	1,7	1,8	0,7	0,9
Manufacturing					
Food (84.29 & 30)	1,6	1,3	1,7	0,8	1,1
Paper & printing (84.31,32,33,34 & 35)	3,1	4,6	3,6	3,9	3,1
Textiles (84.36,37,38,39 & 40)	5,9	6,5	5,2	5,1	3,7
Clothing (84.41)	1,4	1,1	1,0	0,8	0,9
Leather (84.42)	0,4	0,4	0,2	0,3	0,2
Basic metals (84.43 & 44)	2,7	1,0	2,9	1,0	0,4
Non-metallic minerals (84.46 & 57)	0,3	0,2	0,2	0,1	0,4
Wood and furniture (84.47)	0,7	1,0	0,6	0,6	0,4
Machines NEC (84.59)	5,9	5,4	6,0	5,1	7,1
Sub-total: Core machinery in manufacturing (excl 84.45)	22,0	21,5	21,5	17,8	17,3
Machine tools & hand-held tools (84.45,48,49 & 50)	9,1	7,9	8,0	8,6	4,0

NOTE:
Values in this table are percentages of total imports of 'Boilers, machinery and mechanical appliances, parts thereof', (Chapter 84 — CCC (BTN) Nomenclature at 4-digit code level)
SOURCES:
Foreign Trade Statistics, various years.

'Core' machinery and devices for the manufacturing sector account for about one-fifth of South Africa's 'machinery' imports. The ratio shows a tendency to fall over time, although one would not want to attach too much importance to this because of the relative crudeness of the data. It is possible that some portion of the goods listed as 'peripheral' in Table 19.2 are actually 'core' goods, especially in the catch-all category 'miscellaneous process equipment' — this would however make but a 2 or 3 per cent difference to the end result. The figures in Table 19.1 are given a conservative bias by the inclusion of the category 'machines NEC' (not elsewhere classified). This contains such delights as non-domestic vacuum cleaners, nuclear reactors and machinery for road building, as well as a large residual 'other'. Assuming that the 'core' goods required in 'metal products', 'machinery', 'electrical machinery' and 'motor vehicles' are included

Table 19.2:
IMPORTS OF 'PERIPHERAL' AND 'OTHER' MACHINERY AND EQUIPMENT AS PERCENTAGE OF TOTAL IMPORTS OF MACHINERY.

	1968 %	1970 %	1975 %	1980 %	1985 %
Peripheral machinery and equipment					
Steam equipment (84.01,02,03 and 05) plus 84.04 in early reports)	4,1	2,3	1,7	5,3	5,9
Pumps, valves etc. (84.10,11 & 61)	9,0	9,5	8,6	9,5	10,2
Furnaces (84.13 & 14)	0,8	0,4	1,0	0,3	0,5
Refrigeration equipment (84.15)	2,6	2,7	1,2	1,4	2,1
Miscellaneous process equipment (84.16,18,19,20 & 21)	4,5	4,7	4,8	4,2	5,8
Mechanical handling (84.22)	4,0	4,7	5,7	2,0	3,2
Machine components (84.62 & 63)	5,7	4,3	6,7	6,4	7,2
Heaters (84.17)	3,1	2,4	3,1	14,5	2,8
Air conditioners (84.12)	1,0	1,3	0,2	0,3	0,6
Miscellaneous (84.58,59,60,64 & 65)	1,4	1,3	1,4	1,3	1,9
Sub-total: Peripherals	36,2	33,6	34,4	45,2	40,1
Other machinery and equipment					
Prime movers (84.06,07 & 08)	13,9	14,2	9,6	6,6	6,6
Earthmoving equipment (84.09 & 23)	7,1	9,5	12,3	8,3	6,3
Office machines (84.51,52,53,54 & 55)	7,1	8,8	8,1	10,4	22,7

NOTES and SOURCES:
as for Table 19.1.

in the categories 'machines NEC' and 'machinery and hand-held tools', then Table 19.1 covers industries which employ more than 75 per cent of the total manufacturing sector workforce.

'Machine tools and hand-held tools' have been treated separately, in part because they are used in almost every sector of the economy. Large numbers of machine tools find their way into maintenance workshops in agriculture, mining, electricity, gas and water, construction and transport. If we include machine tools with the other 'core' goods, then 'core' goods account for between 25 and 30 per cent of the imports of 'machinery' or about 5 or 6 per cent of total imports. This means that they are about twice as important in monetary terms as the imports of 'textiles', or about half as important as 'transport equipment'.

'Peripheral' machines and devices account for about 40 per cent of total imports of 'machinery'. From Table 19.2 it is obvious that this group contains a large variety of items.

Imports of 'prime movers' (mainly engines for motor vehicles) declined in relative importance over the period, although this may well be partly a cyclical phenomenon. Nonetheless they account for almost the same percentage of machinery imports as machine tools, which underscores the important role of the motor industry in the development of manufacturing. In recent years, imports of 'core' goods have been eclipsed by the rapid growth in the importation of 'office machines', mainly computers.

In the unlikely event that South Africa produced 'appropriate core machines', the need to import vast quantities of peripherals would not diminish, indeed it would probably increase, for this is the very stuff of which 'capital goods' are made. Thousands upon thousands of different 'things' are required — in ones or twos sometimes, or sometimes in hundreds, but almost always in such quantities as to make local manufacture uneconomical. Only the very largest economies can afford the diversity of industry that self-sufficiency entails. The fact that an economy imports large quantities of 'peripheral' goods is no index of 'dependence' — the 'appropriateness' of peripheral capital goods depends on the way in which the different elements are combined — whether or not the elements are imported is largely irrelevant.

Industry-specific dependency ratios

By expressing the value of imports of 'core' goods identified above in any of the manufacturing industries as a percentage of the expenditure on 'additions' to the stock of 'plant, machinery and equipment' (new plant only), we obtain a measure of import dependence of much greater precision than the highly aggregated estimates currently available.[15] Table 19.3 gives the dependency ratios for 'core' capital goods in manufacturing for the period 1970–85.

Table 19.3:
RATIO OF IMPORTS OF 'CORE' MACHINES TO NEW 'PLANT, MACHINERY AND EQUIPMENT' INSTALLED IN MANUFACTURING

	1970	1972	1976	1979	1982	1985
Food	27,7	36,4	25,9	13,7	23,2	19,0
Paper and printing	138,1	53,6	116,6	67,2	120,6	42,3
Textiles	132,9	105,8	155,3	182,2	148,2	117,6
Clothing	92,5	140,1	145,2	169,9	113,6	118,6
Leather	516,7	101,4	55,9	54,6	59,1	42,5
Basic metals	7,7	13,3	16,6	11,9	9,8	8,5
Non-metallic minerals	8,2	2,2	8,0	6,2	9,6	11,7
Wood and furniture	86,2	36,6	41,3	73,3	45,5	28,1
Total manufacturing	31,9	29,1	26,8	18,2	32,2	37,7

SOURCES:
Foreign Trade Statistics, various years, and Manufacturing Census. Statistics according to major groups and sub-groups: South Africa, various years.

Turning to individual industries, we confirm what we would have expected from the Table 19.3, namely that the largest importers of 'core' goods,[16] paper and printing, textiles, and clothing, are the most 'dependent'. Dependency ratios in excess of 100 per cent result either from discrepancies between the data sets[17] or possibly from the fact that machinery merchants purchase more units of particular machines than do the end users. Such a situation obviously cannot prevail for too long, so one is forced to the conclusion that the data can provide little more than rough orders of magnitude.[18] Nevertheless, the results are roughly in line with what casual empiricism might lead one to expect. It is difficult to estimate the impact of changing relative prices on the import dependency ratio. Rising relative prices of imported capital goods, caused by adverse movements in the exchange rate (which have been a characteristic of the past several years) would cause the degree of dependence to be overstated. High local inflation rates on the other hand would have the effect of counteracting this. Given the crudity of the data with which we are working, there is little virtue in attempting to correct for these changes.

Clothing factories are essentially sheds containing large numbers of (imported) sewing machines and a cutting machine or table. Local content is therefore likely to be minimal. Printing works are similar, being unlikely to contain any locally-produced machinery. Textile mills are more complex and the number of 'peripherals' is appreciably greater, but nonetheless, they contain a preponderance of imported 'core' machines. Paper producers are similar, but their huge size generally permits the incorporation of a far greater proportion of South African produced capital goods.[19]

Factories in the food industry, on the other hand, show much lower levels of dependence. More than one-third of the capital goods in this industry are devoted to sugar production. Sugar mills typically contain very high proportions of locally-manufactured 'core' machines. Dependency ratios are even lower in the basic metals industry where imported 'core' machines are supplemented by large numbers of locally-manufactured machines and devices.

In terms of sheer size, the 'capital goods' industry in South Africa is large. Anyone with the slightest knowledge of the engineering prowess of the industry will know that it is capable, either alone or in collaboration with overseas contractors, of tackling massive projects.

At the time of its construction, SASOL II for example, was the largest process plant ever built at one time. Of R2,3 billion total cost, R640 million was spent on foreign contracts and R620 million on contracts placed with South African producers. Because such large amounts of labour were required on site, more than 60 per cent of the total cost of the project was spent in this country (supplement to *Financial Mail*, 16 November 1979, pp. 50–7). The list of such undertakings is long — the giant Escom power stations planned in the late 1970s, some of which were commissioned during the 1980s, each cost well in excess of R2 billion, and in each case more than 70 per cent of the money was spent in

South Africa. Apart from the expenditure on labour on site, the main reason for this was the high local content of the steam generating equipment and ancillaries (supplement to *Financial Mail*, 24 September 1982, p. 17). Similarly, when Tongaat/Hulett built their R150 million sugar mill at Felixton on the Natal north coast in the early 1980s, the design was 'in-house' and much of the fabrication was carried out in South Africa by their own engineering subsidiary company (supplement to *Financial Mail*, 24 September 1982, pp. 68–70).

In the early 1970s (in anticipation of a boom which did not materialize), Anglo-Alpha expanded their Dudfield works into one of the largest in the southern hemisphere. Of R52 million total contract cost, R18 million was used to buy equipment overseas and the remainder was spent on civil, mechanical and electrical contracts in South Africa. One the of the largest 'core' components, a rotary kiln 90 metres long and 5 metres in diameter, was built to exacting tolerances by Vecor Engineering in Vanderbijlpark (*Power and Plant in Southern Africa*, March 1978, pp. 30–43).

Smaller projects abound, each of them demonstrating a capability to produce and maintain equipment of the highest degree of sophistication — 4 megawatt gearless mill drives (ring motors), for example, of which there are only about 30 in the world, built locally by Siemens with 50 per cent local content (*Engineering Now*, September/October 1988, p. 1); the largest bedding and blending plant in South Africa for the Sishen/Saldanha project, German design, 85 per cent local content (supplement to *Financial Mail*, 1 October 1976, p. 31) and so on (almost) *ad infinitum*.

Amidst all the hand-wringing about the absence of a 'capital goods' industry capable of producing 'appropriate' technology, the existence of an excellent example of precisely that, namely a large local producer of in-field loaders for sugar cane and timber, and more recently of industrial tractors, rough-terrain forklifts, front-end loaders and dump trucks, seems to have been somewhat overlooked.[20] Growth has been based on the development of ingenious solutions to local problems like the extremely hilly nature of Natal's sugar farms, or the need to protect ecologically-sensitive ground cover during logging operations, and its products have proved to be highly attractive to users elsewhere, including the discerning US market. The firm uses highly customized machine tools (Computer Numerically Controlled (CNC) for flexibility), and imports certain critical items such as power transmissions and hydraulic components, but local content averages 80 per cent or more on every machine. It is significant that in its drive for improved quality, the firm relies not on labour-intensive methods, but on CNC technology.

The cane loaders developed by the firm improved in-field loading productivity by several hundred per cent, but since the acreage under cane remained roughly constant, the negative impact on employment is likely to have been substantial.

This brings us back to the issue outlined in the beginning — what technology is appropriate. A knee-jerk reaction saying that because of the negative employment consequences, it is not, is unsatisfactory. Improved productivity, international competitiveness and increased foreign exchange earnings have a dynamic impact which may well result in increased job opportunities elsewhere. The belief that more labour-intensive technologies are necessarily welfare-improving flies in the face of the harsh dictates of capitalist accumulation. Policies which hope to redistribute income and generate substantially more jobs have to address the form and nature of capitalist development itself.

Conclusion

South Africa has a competent engineering (capital goods) industry which is as large as one could reasonably expect. Given the size and diversity of the manufacturing sector, it is unrealistic to believe that a local capital goods industry could produce anything more than a narrow selection of the core machines required. A major restructuring of the pattern of demand (which is distorted by gross income inequality and South Africa's natural resource endowments) is required before the potential for a larger more 'appropriate' capital goods sector can be realized.

However, given the competence and capacity of South Africa's machine tools sector, albeit small, it is incorrect to argue that the existence of 'inappropriate technology' is the result of an inadequate domestic capital goods sector. If economic opportunities for the development of 'appropriate technology' existed, the capital goods industry would respond accordingly. The fact that it has not suggests that under the existing conditions, such opportunities are the exception rather than the rule. Despite South Africa's abundance of unemployed labour, the dynamics of technological change and capitalist accumulation seem to suggest that it is economically irrational to adopt the 'appropriate' labour-intensive technology so often advocated by the well-meaning. Radical economic transformation is required before such 'appropriate technology' becomes a realistic option.

Notes

1 This paper is a considerably shortened version of much longer work (Meth, 1989) on the same topic — as most people will know, it is much easier to sprawl one's ideas over 50 pages than to present them concisely in 20! The longer paper does however cover very much more ground, especially with regard to the diffusion of technology and the specific problems of machine tool development. I would like to thank Nicoli Nattrass for her kind assistance with the task of shortening this work, and her useful criticisms of many of the ideas presented here. The coherence the paper presently has is in large measure due to her valuable suggestions. Naturally, the usual disclaimer about the responsibility for errors applies.

2 At this point in the paper Jill Nattrass cited Stewart, 1977.

3 Kaplan also treats the telecommunications industry as a significant part of the capital goods industry.

4 Machinery for working wood and other such raw materials, is, in some ways, similar to metal-working machinery.

5 There is some disagreement over the precise meaning of the terms 'mechanization' and 'automation'. Kaplinsky (1985, p. 424) cites a common definition of automation as: '...a technological method that tends to reduce current production costs in terms of man hours per unit of output ... Its loose use practically as a synonym for advanced mechanization may shock the technologist, but serves the purposes of economists.' He also gives a more subtle definition which serves to emphasize the control characteristics of automation technology (cybernetics), namely that: '..."automation" is a technology quite distinct from mechanization and it is concerned with replacing or aiding human mental effort as distinct from aiding man's physical effort'.

6 The Soviets have also not distinguished themselves in this matter.

7 Direct labour costs in the South African manufacturing sector are about 10–11 per cent of total costs (Meth, 1988). In the motor industry the figure is a mere 6,3 per cent (BTI Report no. 2627, p. 41).

8 This hypothesis was put forward informally by Dave Kaplan at a seminar organized by the Labour and Economic Research Centre (LERC) held at the University of Durban-Westville in September 1987. He has not yet, to the best of my knowledge, developed it formally. It is an adaptation of work done on the East Asian NICs by researchers at the Institute of Development Studies at the University of Sussex. See Hamilton, 1984; Wade, 1984; and Foster-Carter, 1987.

9 Similar claims are readily found in the literature. See, for example *Economic Bulletin for Europe*, vol. 39, no. 4, 1987, p. 970.

10 See for example the discussion in AHI/SAFCI/SEIFSA, 1977, p. 124. South African manufacturers are said to have '...become too accustomed to being protected from price-cutting from abroad in times of international stringency.'

11 There would appear at first sight to be some contradiction between the finding that many industries are over-populated by firms in furious competition, and the well-known fact that most of the industries making up the South African manufacturing sector are heavily concentrated. This contradiction is readily resolved when market size is compared with the minimum efficient scale of production. In the motor industry, for example, seven producers (in 1979 there were eleven!) vie for a small (shrinking at present) market. Demand for some commodities is so small that even one local producer is one too many.

12 Some of the major groups contain only one sub-group.

13 Dorbyl's six divisions — heavy engineering; railway products; structural engineering; projects and construction; auto motive products and marine engineering, employed 24 000 workers in 1982 (supplement to *Financial Mail*, 24 September 1982, p. XXXVI).

14 There are several difficulties involved in the aggregation or disaggregation of 'industries' to obtain a ranking by size. If, for example, it could be established that capital goods and the labour processes used in the chemical industry were all roughly the same, then that industry would be much larger than the sub-group 'Special Industrial

Machinery'. For the purposes of identifying capital goods usage patterns in motor vehicle manufacture, on the other hand, it may be more sensible to divide it into two separate industries, namely vehicle assembly and component manufacturers. This could be justified in terms of the very different machinery and labour processes used respectively in each. As a matter of interest, the former employed 34 841 workers in 1979, and the latter 21 743 (S A Statistics, p. 12.28), making them them both much smaller than 'Special Industrial Machinery'.

15 See for example Kahn, 1987.

16 Relative that is, to the proportion of the total capital stock employed in that industry.

17 Kaplan (1988, p. 6) refers to the fact that the valuing of imports 'fob' (free on board) rather than 'cif' (carriage, insurance and freight) or at market value, understates the extent of import dependence. The ratios given in the Table 19.3 would obviously be affected by changes in the proportion of total final cost represented by the various charges, especially import duties or surcharges. As long as these variations are not too great, however, the ratios given, whilst understating 'dependence', will pick up trends reasonably well.

18 Some of these high values have simple explanations, for example, I have not bothered to separate out imports of industrial and domestic sewing machines.

19 Paper mills rank amongst the largest of the capital investments in South Africa. Sappi's Ngodwana mill cost R800 million (supplement to *Financial Mail*, 24 September 1982, pp. 56–58). Expansion and capital replacement at Anglo American's Mondi Paper Mill in Durban will cost R400 million (*Engineering News*, 10 February 1989, vol. 9, no. 5, pp. 1–2).

20 Information on this company's activities was given in a Corporate Report which appeared as a supplement to the *Financial Mail*, 11 October 1985.

References

AHI/SAFCI/SEIFSA (Afrikaanse Handelsinstituut; South African Federated Chamber of Industries, and Steel and Engineering Industries Federation of South Africa), *Survey into Gross Import Substitution Potential for South African Manufacturing Industry 1975–80*, Johannesburg, 1977.

Amsden, A.H., 'The Division of Labour is Limited by the Rate of Growth of the Market: The Taiwan Machine Tool Industry in the 1970s', *Cambridge Journal of Economics*, vol. 9, September 1985.

Arndt, H.W., 'Industrial Policy in East Asia', *Industry and Development*, vol. 22, 1987.

Board of Trade and Industry, *Annual Report 1987*, Report no. 2663, (RP 63/1988), Government Printer: Pretoria, 1988.

Board of Trade and Industry, *Investigation into the Industry Manufacturing Passenger Cars and Light Commercial Vehicles*, Report no. 2627, Government Printer: Pretoria, 1988.

Central Statistical Services, *Input-Output Tables 1978*, Report 09–16–05, Government Printer: Pretoria, 1978.

Central Statistical Services, *Census of Manufacturing: Statistics According to Major Groups and Subgroups: South Africa*, Government Printer: Pretoria, Various years.

Central Statistical Services, *South African Statistics 1986*, Government Printer: Pretoria, 1986.

Dahlman, C.J., Ross-Larson, B. & Westphal, L.E., 'Managing Technological Development: Lessons from the Newly Industrializing Countries', *World Development*, vol. 15,
no. 6, June 1987.

Department of Customs and Excise, *Foreign Trade Statistics*, Government Printer: Pretoria, various years.

du Plooy, R.M. 'Productivity in South African Industry', *South African Journal of Economics*, vol. 56, no. 1, March 1988.

Foster-Carter, A., 'Korea: from Dependency to Democracy?' *Capital and Class*, vol. 33,
Winter 1987.

Hamilton, C., 'Class, State and Industrialisation in South Korea', *IDS Bulletin*, vol. 15,
no. 2, Institute of Development Studies: Sussex, 1984.

Hoffman, K., 'Clothing, Chips and Comparative Advantage: The Impact of Micro-
electronics on Trade and Production in the Clothing Industry', *World Development*,
vol. 13, no. 3, March 1985.

Hunt, V.D., *Industrial Robotics Handbook*, Industrial Press Inc: New York, 1983.

Jones, D.T. & Womack, J.P., 'Developing Countries and the Future of the Automobile
Industry', *World Development*, vol. 13, no. 3, March 1985.

Kahn, S.B., 'Import Penetration and Import Demands in the South African Economy',
South African Journal of Economics, vol. 55, no. 3, September 1987.

Kaplan, D., 'The Limited Development of the South African Capital Machine Tool
Industry: Causes and Consequences', *Social Dynamics*, vol. 13, no. 1, June 1987.

Kaplan, D., 'The South African Capital Goods Sector and the Economic Crisis: Impli-
cations for Economic Development', in Gelb, S. (ed.), *The Economic Crisis: Recent
Economic Trends in South Africa*, LERC (Labour & Economic Research Centre):
Johannesburg, Draft edition, November 1988.

Kaplinsky, R., 'Electronics-based Automation Techniques and the Onset of Systemofacture: Implications for Third World Industrialization', *World Development*, vol. 13,
no. 3, March 1985.

Kubo, Y., 'A Cross-country Comparison of Interindustry Linkages and the Role of
Imported Intermediate Goods', *World Development*, vol. 13, no. 2, December 1985.

McCarthy, C.L., 'Structural Development of South African Manufacturing Industry —
A Policy Perspective', *South African Journal of Economics*, vol. 56, no. 1, March 1988.

Meth, C.E., 'Maldistributed Income, Excessive Consumer Freedom and Inappropriate Technology', Occasional Paper, Economic Research Unit, University of Natal:
Durban, 1989, (forthcoming).

Meth, C.E., 'Productivity and the Crisis', in Gelb, S. (ed.), *The Economic Crisis: Recent
Economic Trends in South Africa*, LERC (Labour & Economic Research Centre):
Johannesburg, Draft edition, November 1988.

Nattrass, J. & Brown, R.P.C., 'Capital Intensity in South African Manufacturing',
Black/White Income Gap Project, Interim Research Report No.4, Department of
Economics, University of Natal: Durban, 1977.

Reynders Commission, 'Report of the Commission of Inquiry into the Export Trade of
the Republic of South Africa', Government Printer: Pretoria, RP 69/72, 1972.

Soete, L., 'International Diffusion of Technology: Industrial Development and Technological Leapfrogging', *World Development*, vol. 13, no. 3, March 1985.

Stewart, F., *Technology and Underdevelopment*, Macmillan: London, 1977.

Stewart, F., 'Macro-policies for Appropriate Technology: An Introductory Classification, *International Labour Review*, vol. 122, no. 3, 1983.

Wade, R., 'Dirigisme Taiwan-Style', *IDS Bulletin*, vol. 15, no. 2, Institute of Development Studies: Sussex, 1984.

INDEX

NB: All entries refer to South Africa unless otherwise indicated. Cited authors are only indexed when there is discussion of their ideas.